CLARENDON LAW SERIES

CLARENDON LAW SERIES

EQUITY

2nd edition

SARAH WORTHINGTON

Deputy Director and Professor of Law

London School of Economics and Political Science

OXFORD

UNIVERSITY PRESS

OXFORD

UNIVERSITY PRESS

Great Clarendon Street, Oxford OX2 6DP

Oxford University Press is a department of the University of Oxford.
It furthers the University's objective of excellence in research, scholarship,
and education by publishing worldwide in

Oxford New York

Auckland   Cape Town Dar es Salaam   Hong Kong   Karachi
Kuala Lumpur Madrid Melbourne Mexico City   Nairobi
New Delhi Shanghai Taipei Toronto

With offices in

Argentina Austria Brazil Chile Czech Republic France Greece
Guatemala Hungary Italy Japan South Korea Poland Portugal
Singapore Switzerland Thailand Turkey Ukraine Vietnam

Oxford is a registered trade mark of Oxford University Press
in the UK and in certain other countries

Published in the United States
by Oxford University Press Inc., New York

ISBN 978-0-19-929050-5

Printed in the United Kingdom by
Lightning Source UK Ltd., Milton Keynes

Contents

PART II Property

PART IV Contract

Foreword to the First Edition

This is an important and unusual book. It is not a textbook, for it cites no cases and mentions no academic literature, though the bibliography which lies behind it is immense. It is not a monograph, for the breadth of its subject-matter is enormous, covering the entire landscape of Equity in the modern world. It claims to be an elementary exploration of Equity's place in our legal system, but it addresses with penetrating intelligence the most demanding and controversial questions which our dual system of law and Equity continues to raise.

The unifying theme is Dr Worthington's belief that, with the aid of rigorous analysis, which she supplies in abundance, Equity can be successfully integrated into a unified system. She is certainly right in saying that integration is unlikely to be as difficult as is often supposed, and that there has already been a significant measure of practical integration and cross-fertilization between the two jurisdictions. This process is set to continue. Doctrinal integration will take longer, but we are even now beginning to see the faint outlines of the future shape of a unified system.

The great virtue of the work is that it puts principle (not doctrine, which is not at all the same thing) first. Many of the disjunctions between the different remedial responses of law and Equity are justified by principle. But some undoubtedly are not. In exploring the possibilities for future integration, Dr Worthington identifies the issues on which the disjunction lacks principle, and indicates the responses which a unified and coherent system, based on considerations of policy, might make. Here she confronts some of the most intractable questions which remain outstanding today, and courageously supplies tentative answers. Not everyone will agree with them, of course; but it would be unwise to disagree without giving them serious consideration. At the heart, of course, is the dividing line between proprietary and personal rights, which she rightly describes as one of the most troubling theoretical and practical distinctions currently facing the law.

Dr Worthington has produced a monumental work but she wears her erudition lightly. Her book is eminently readable, which is more than one can usually say of works on legal subjects. No one who is interested in the future development of the law will want to be without it; and no one who has any part to play in that process can afford to be.

The Rt Hon The Lord Millett

Preface to the Second Edition

The most dramatic difference between this second edition of *Equity* and the first is the inclusion, this time, of selected references to key cases and academic commentary. I predicted that their omission in the first edition would please some readers and annoy others—as indeed it did, and greatly so. Now I predict that my particular choices will please some and annoy others. So be it.

The aim of this second edition remains the same as for the first. Indeed, the text is largely unaltered, apart from the additional cluttering of footnotes. As in the first edition, the first objective is to expose the range and detail of equity's impact on the modern legal landscape. This book does not provide a comprehensive account of equity, but it does describe the key principles and concepts in order to enable the reader to see how equity works. It adopts a functional approach to equity: it describes what equity does, not what equity is; it is elementary in the sense that it deals in basic concepts. The second objective of this edition, as with the first, is to argue that the time has come to integrate equity and the common law, combining the learning from both to deliver a more rational and coherent legal regime fit for the twenty-first century.

Equity jurisprudence has influenced every area of the common law. It has altered our notions of property, contract, tort (civil wrongs) and restitution. The result is a sophisticated, discriminating and subtle set of legal rules. This book is not an argument against such discrimination or subtlety. It is an argument against dualism. A discriminating approach may look at a legal problem and determine to resolve it in one way rather than another because the problem is perceived to be of one type rather than another. Dualism, in the sense in which it is criticized here, allows one body of principles to classify a legal problem in one way, and another body of principles to classify it in another way, and each to propose different solutions. This is not a desirable state of play. Thankfully, even with our common law/equity divide, it is not a common state of play. It is, however, a pervasive risk.

With the second and more provocative agenda, the goal is not to re-shape the common law completely, but nor is it simply to advocate further rationalization and cross-fertilization across the existing common law/ equity divide. A legal system ought to be designed to contribute to the proper functioning of society. It is not the only mechanism, nor, probably, the most important. But it is important, and it is important that it delivers consistent results to similar problems. As times change, so will perceptions of desirable responses to particular problems. But it is unlikely that any society will be content that the same problem should admit of different solutions on different occasions without attracting criticism for being unjust or unfair or irrational. This book is about protecting the rationality of the law. The institution requires that if it is to command respect.

Finally, who is this book for? What is a 'Clarendon introduction'? Different people will give different answers. I regard the book as an extended essay on the current state of equity and an exposition of its future prospects. It is not a reference book. Its aim is to persuade, or at least to inspire reflection and debate; it is not simply to inform. I have selected my references to cases and commentary accordingly. I have tried to set out accurately, but succinctly, the current state of play, including the various disagreements in those explanations (and there are plenty). I have then argued for a rational and coherent way forward, a way that is based on principles and contemporary needs, rather than on an exposition of the rules of the law as presently conceived and the narrow logical inferences that lawyers draw from the statutes and cases. Of course, readers will not necessarily agree with my conclusions. But the book will have succeeded, at least on one level, if it sparks a renewed awareness of this fascinating and disparate area of the law.

The debts acknowledged in the first edition are carried forward, and multiplied, in this edition. Family, friends, colleagues, students, and the production team at OUP all merit special thanks. Thank you to all.

Sarah Worthington
LSE
February 2006

Preface to the First Edition

The study of Equity holds deep fascination for some and fear for others. With a little luck, this book will swell the numbers in the former camp. Equity was born as a jurisdiction to deal with difficult cases. When the common law's general rules appeared not quite apt in the circumstances, equity might intervene with different, more discriminating resolutions—resolutions that left the common law's general rules intact, but qualified them by providing for a different approach in defined circumstances. Think of equity's rules on specific performance, injunctions, estoppel, and even its rules on trusts and fiduciary obligations. Other legal systems might well adopt similar strategies when faced with similar problems, but their new rules soon become seamlessly integrated within the general fabric of the law. A distinctive equity jurisdiction keeps its resolutions isolated, segregated in a box labelled 'solutions to hard cases'. No wonder equity earned a reputation as 'hard law'.

In dealing with equity's 'hard law', this book has two objectives (see pp. 17–19). The first is to expose the range and detail of equity's impact on the modern legal landscape. This is no small task, since equity has left little of the law of property or obligations untouched. The second is more provocative. It is to persuade readers that the time has come to unpack this box of 'hard law' and redistribute it to its appropriate home, properly integrating the learning into a coherent and integrated common law regime. All of this is undoubtedly strong meat for an introductory text.

This book cites no cases and names no commentators. This will annoy some and please others, although the intention was neither. The book is about legal ideas and their rigorous and principled analysis. The genesis of the thinking behind most chapters is not easily summarized. Moreover, the reading that might be recommended to those who are new to the area is not necessarily appropriate for hardened fans. At both extremes, and everywhere in between, judges and academics are equally inspirational. The task of selecting appropriate high points in cases and commentary is simply impossible in the space allowed.

Nevertheless, a preface permits some singling out of names. Jim O'Donovan, now at the University of Western Australia, taught with passion and sparked my fascination with the jurisdiction. Later, at the University of Melbourne, Michael Bryan and Tony Duggan (now relocated to the University of Toronto) proved inspirational colleagues as I tried my own hand at teaching the subject. In the UK, I owe my greatest debts to Roy Goode and Len Sealy. These last four colleagues each read the manuscript in its entirety. I remain overwhelmed by their generosity, and thankful for their intellectual insights. Peter Birks and Peter Millett also read the manuscript, Peter Birks with his editorial hat on, and Peter Millett because he had most generously agreed to write the Foreword. As with much else I have written, my heaviest intellectual debts are owed to this small group of people: they will undoubtedly recognize their footprints in the text. More generally, Hugh Collins, Charles Mitchell, and James Penner all read parts of the text and provided challenging intellectual debate; I have learnt much from them. Finally, four more people and two books: no equity lawyer, and certainly no equity lawyer educated in Australia, could fail to acknowledge the enormous debt owed to Meagher, Gummow and Lehane (Meagher, Gummow and Lehane, *Equity: Doctrines and Remedies* (Butterworths: Sydney, 1992)); as well, I still have a heavily annotated copy of Paul Finn's *Fiduciary Obligations* (Law Book Co.: Sydney, 1977), the only monograph I purchased as an undergraduate. For everyone else, a general thank you must suffice: all my family, and too many friends, colleagues and students have, in various guises, found their way into this book. Many read chapters and provided perceptive comment: they will know who they are. Thank you to all.

On the production front, Jane Stapleton and Peter Cane first invited me to take on this project. Peter Birks, when he took over as General Editor of the series, encouraged me to be direct and 'Clarendon-ish'. The staff at OUP have handled the production process with smooth and friendly efficiency. I thank them all.

Sarah Worthington
LSE
April 2003

Table of Cases

Part I

Introduction

I

Dual Legal Systems: Common Law and Equity

This is a book about law, and in particular about the body of law known as 'Equity'. However, even the most experienced of lawyers finds it difficult to give a short, intelligible answer to the question, 'What is Equity?' For those coming to the subject for the first time, it is simpler to begin the explanation from very much more familiar territory. Picture a dozen kindergarten children playing a game. They will invariably make up the rules as they go along. The initial rules will be short and to the point. Perhaps they will simply be that the team with the most goals wins and to score a goal you must kick the ball between two markers. As the game progresses, the rules will inevitably become more elaborate: the ball can only be kicked; it must not be thrown or carried. Rules will be added to deal with unexpected situations or unfair practices: the game must stop while an injured player is out of action; players cannot unfairly crowd the goal. Purely accidental or irrelevant infringements might be ignored. Umpires might be appointed to adjudicate on doubtful goals and police infringements. Different incidents will doubtless attract different consequences: certain infringements might result in players being sent off, others in a free kick. All of this is seen as inevitable evolution, even by five-year-olds.

RULES AND THEIR NATURAL EVOLUTION

This simple story offers some surprisingly perceptive insights. Every group activity instinctively adopts rules. No children's game can operate without them, nor can any society. Yet it is also universally recognized that any general rule will inevitably operate unfairly in certain circumstances. This is not a new idea, but the result is a constant tension between the desire for universal, generalized rules and the need for individualized, context-specific, fact-sensitive justice. The tension is played out by developing more sophisticated, discriminating, sensitized rules, but rules that are nevertheless general. In this way society's initial basic rules inevitably evolve into more advanced, refined, and discriminating forms.

Effective rule evolution is commonly based on repeated practical experience. This is how kindergarten games evolve. The first decisions are based on particular individual circumstances. In subsequent cases, however, fairness demands that like situations be treated alike or that new factors be identified as permitting further discrimination. In the end the pattern evident in these particularized, individualized decisions can be restated as a generalized, universal rule. (A system of *legal* rules developed according to this practice is a legal system based on *precedent*.) This 'slow-build' evolutionary strategy recognizes that it is difficult to articulate practical, comprehensive, and sophisticated rules at the outset. Attempting to do so is risky. Costly mistakes are likely. Indeed, a 'fast-build' strategy where all the rules are articulated at the outset will only work if it is based on extensive past experience and if flexibility is deliberately built into the system so that unexpected circumstances can be accommodated. This is usually achieved by formulating the rules in very general terms so that they can bear different interpretations in different circumstances. Context-specific conventions can then be built up to underpin the application of the general rules. (A system of legal rules operating according to this strategy is a system based on a legal *code*.)

The kindergarten game illustrates this inevitable evolution of rules. It also illustrates how the 'slow-build' mechanism attempts to balance the competing drives for generalized rules and individualized justice. But the game highlights a further crucial feature of rules. The evolving rules must remain coherent and rational. Like situations must be treated alike; different situations must be treated differently, and, crucially, in rationally different ways. In the kindergarten game, great skills should be greatly rewarded; lesser ones, less so. Serious infringements should be severely penalized; less serious ones, less so. Every effort must be made to ensure that each of these judgements is based on a proper assessment of all the appropriate facts. Experience may throw up instances of lack of coherence, and the rules will then need to adapt to reassert coherence.

This idea of coherence is critical. Different games may have different rules, but each set of rules must be designed to be internally coherent. Imagine what would happen if our five-year-olds were to have two sets of umpires monitoring their game, one applying red rules and red practices and delivering red responses to the events, the other applying green rules and green practices and delivering green responses to the events. The game would descend into chaos. The red umpire might recognize goals that the green umpire does not. Each team's score would then depend upon which umpire was in control at the appropriate time. The same would be true of the assessment of infringements and the awarding of penalties: the red umpire would make her assessment on the basis of red practices and deliver decisions based on red rules; the green umpire would make his decisions on the basis of green practices and deliver decisions based on green rules.

Of course, the best way to bring order to such a bizarre game is simply to agree that only 'purple rules' are to apply. Whatever the red and green rules may have contributed to devising the purple rules, the truth is that a new game will have been created. Any other solution is more difficult. It requires careful regulation of the interaction between red and green rules and red and green umpires. One possibility is to give the red and green umpires different, independent, spheres of operation. This seems simple, but it is likely to raise intractable demarcation disputes, not to mention the practical difficulties of futile appeals by players to the 'wrong' umpire. Another possibility is to agree that the decisions of the red umpire must always prevail, but that the green umpire is to carry out most of the work unless there are good grounds for interference. The problem, then, is that the red umpire has enormous, probably unacceptable, discretion. Indeed, countless strategies exist but every one of them presents its own difficulties. This is simply not the rational way to set up the rules of any game.

More importantly, the difficulties will escalate over time. No strategy for regulating the relationship between the red and green umpires can guarantee that the rules of the game will remain internally coherent. If the red and green rules continue to evolve, as they inevitably will, then the boundaries between the two bodies of rules will become blurred. Both umpires may eventually come to regulate very similar situations using very different strategies. The red umpire may order a defaulting player off the field for deliberately impeding another player in a particular fashion; the green umpire may allow the other side a free kick in circumstances that appear very similar. The result is that like situations will not seem to be treated alike. This will not be due to errors by the umpires; it will be the result of the internally rational but different developments of the two bodies of red and green rules. This is not the only problem. Without any formal mechanism for comparison of red and green practices, the red umpires may deal with serious and minor infringements in one way, the green umpires in another. The necessary relativities between skills and their rewards (or infringements and their penalties) will become lost. Without internal coherence, the game will fall into disrepute. The clear lesson from this outlandish mind game is that the best systems of rules usually evolve within an integrated hierarchy, not a dualist structure.

CIVIL LAW AND COMMON LAW SYSTEMS

What does all this discussion of children's games, and red and green umpires, have to do with the law? A great deal, so it seems. The teams playing children's games are a microcosm of society. As with children's games, societies too need to be governed by coherent, rational bodies of rules. Like the rules in children's games, society's rules will also inevitably evolve: primitive societies have primitive rules; more sophisticated societies necessarily develop more sophisticated rules. Furthermore, as with different games, different societies can quite reasonably operate under different rules with no untoward consequences. French legal rules do not have to be the same as German legal rules. But, within the French or German legal system, as within children's games, like situations must be treated alike, and different situations must be treated in defensibly different ways. The analogy with children's games suggests that this is only possible if the rules evolve in a manner that pays conscious attention to maintaining comprehensive and appropriate relativities between rules and their rewards or rules and their sanctions.

This coherent development is most likely to happen within an integrated unitary legal system, and, predictably, this is how the legal rules of most modern societies have evolved. Most societies start out with some sort of primitive general statement of the basic rules necessary to achieve order in a civilized society. They then develop these rules, borrowing from other practices, learning from the successes and failings of others—just as children do. The unremitting goal is to keep evolving an increasingly sophisticated legal regime designed to best fit the society's ever-evolving needs. These societies may start out with some sort of precedent-based regime, but many eventually adopt a legal code. This process of legal development is exemplified by the *civil law* systems of most of Europe (excluding England, Ireland, Northern Ireland, and Wales), southern and central American countries, Japan, and Turkey. These legal regimes are now all typified by written codes that aim to provide clear and comprehensive (although evolving) statements of the entire body of State law. These various national codes owe much to early Roman law traditions, although each nation state has adapted the template, fashioning its own rules and tailoring them to its own local customs.

Given these civilian models, it seems quite remarkable that England should choose a completely different and distinctive strategy. Unlike its civilian counterparts, its legal regime is precedent-based and dualist. The choice of a precedent-based system does have attractions. Indeed, the strategy reflects the normal practices of individuals in developing their own internal moral principles and views on life. Even the early invaders, who might have been expected to import their own regime, perhaps saw compelling political advantages in preserving the appearance of legal stability, and working for change from within the system. This is possible with a precedent-based system. What is much harder to defend is the English adherence to a dualist model. This consciously reflects the bizarre vision of the children's game with red and green umpires and distinctive red and green rules and practices. This strategy is likely to create havoc in children's games, and the potential problems for a whole society are correspondingly greater. Imagine the possibilities. The 'red' judges may say that X is not bound by a contract, but the 'green' judges say she is; or the 'red' judges may say that X owns an asset, but the 'green' judges insist that Y owns it. The next section describes how this extraordinary situation came about, although no description seems able to explain why this evolutionary path, not another, seemed so compelling.

Not only did this remarkable situation survive, but it was replicated in the many countries that inherited the English legal model. The legal framework in these countries is now described as *common law*, to distinguish it from the civil law jurisdictions described earlier. The common law model operates in England, the United States, Canada, Australia, New Zealand, India, and many other countries that were once part of the British 'Empire'. In each of these countries the original English laws have inevitably evolved over time to reflect quite distinctive national circumstances and national political and social imperatives. Like civil law, the common law is not a monolithic enterprise. Indeed, the degree of divergence that now exists between different common law countries, despite these common origins, is testament to the inherent flexibility of a precedent-based evolutionary system. If judges are so minded, new ideas can be readily integrated into the regime. This is most evident in the United States. Its political history made it likely that it would quickly borrow from elsewhere, especially from civil law learning, sometimes also shunning common law practices if only to underline its dissatisfaction with English politics. Equally, of course, if judges are so minded they can use a precedent-based system to stultify progress, simply urging that there is no legal precedent to justify a decision for change.

THE ORIGINS OF COMMON LAW DUALISM

To describe the emergence of this seemingly bizarre dualist common law model, it is necessary to look back to the medieval period in England. At that time, the universal law of the realm (the 'common' law of England) was administered by the King's Judges. Adopting the language of our children's game, this was the 'green law' of the realm, and the Judges were the 'green umpires'. The law administered by these Judges evolved, predictably, in response to various social, political, and economic pressures for change. However, if changes were not rapid enough, or if the particular circumstances suggested that the Judges' decision was 'unfair', litigants could appeal directly to the King. The King was seen as the fount of justice, personally responsible for ensuring that his subjects were treated fairly and justly. The King eventually delegated this important function to his Chancellor, the chief administrator of the realm. The King's Chancellor was given wide powers to prevent injustices or supply deficiencies where the common law was seen to operate unfairly. The Chancellor's jurisdiction was not confined to specific issues: he was free to deal with injustices relating to substantive issues of law, to procedure or to remedies. This mitigating jurisdiction of the Chancellors eventually evolved into a recognizable body of principles, rules and practices. Again adopting the language of our children's game, this was the 'red law' of the realm, and the Chancellors were the 'red umpires'.

The parallels with our imaginary children's game are clear. The law of the realm—the common law of England—could not be described simply as the law administered by the Judges (green law), or as the law administered by the Chancellors (red law). It was a combination of both. There was a clear-cut institutional separation between the green law and its practices and judges, and the red law and its practices and judges. Each operated out of separate courts. Litigants had to ensure that they approached the 'right' judges to deal with their particular dispute. If they made a mistake, they would be forced to start the whole process again in the appropriate court. The King's Judges operated principally from the court of King's Bench, the Court of Common Pleas and the Court of the Exchequer. These Judges administered the rules of the 'Common Law' according to 'Common Law' practices and procedures. The Chancellors operated from the Court of Chancery, administering the rules and principles of 'Equity' according to 'Equitable' practices and procedures. The modern position has built on this heritage. The common law now comprises the evolutionary successors to these two bodies of law, supplemented by extensive statutory rules enacted in legislation passed by Parliament. Described like this, 'Equity' is simply the body of rules, principles, and remedies that derive from those initially developed and administered in the English High Court of Chancery. Although accurate, such a definition is hardly satisfying: is reveals almost nothing of what Equity *is*.[1]

The early practices adopted by the English Kings and their Chancellors were not unusual. Most early legal systems adopt similar strategies, vesting the King or religious men with the power to deal with injustices that might arise from the rigid application of rudimentary generalized rules. A King's 'bounty' or a priest's 'mercy' could save litigants from unpalatable injustices. But such bounty is not law, and most legal systems eventually develop rule-based, legal solutions to the problems. The English legal system did not immediately react like this. At the crucial time the courts of the King's Judges seemed unable or unwilling to develop new legal rules to address the complaints. Three factors were particularly significant—politics, the writ system, and the jury system. Every legal action was commenced by writ (written order) and determined by jury. A writ was a royal prerogative granted by the King permitting a litigant to pursue a claim. These writs provided the only procedural routes to bring a case to court, and the writs indicated the relief to which an aggrieved party might be entitled in different circumstances. If there was no permitted form of writ, then there was no Common Law remedy. The role of the judge was simply to determine whether the writ was of a form which gave the court jurisdiction; the facts—and hence the outcome of the case—were determined by jury.

[1] Notice the terminology. The difficulty arises because 'common law' is a term that has different meanings in different contexts. The different meanings have all been used already, but without explanation. The term can be used, in its narrowest sense, to distinguish between 'Common Law' and 'Equity', and the different jurisdictional histories of the two judge-made bodies of law. The term can also be used in a wider sense to distinguish between *all* judge-made laws ('common law') and the laws enacted by Parliament ('statutes'). This distinction contrasts the different rule-making bodies, and uses 'common law' to encompass both 'Common Law' and 'Equity', as previously described. Finally, the term can be used in a still wider sense to distinguish between 'common law' jurisdictions and 'civil law' jurisdictions. In this context, 'common law' encompasses *all* the laws of the relevant common law jurisdiction, be they judge-made (including both 'Common Law' and 'Equity') or enacted by parliamentary statutes. In this book, 'Common Law' and 'Equity' are capitalized only when they are used in the first sense. This is not the general practice in other writings, however. Readers must usually determine the particular meaning from the context. Here, 'common law' in its second two senses is safely left to context.

The problem with this approach was that the substantive law lay in the writs. So long as the judges were prepared to exercise significant discretionary powers in dealing with different writ forms and in presuming certain factual issues, the Common Law could evolve. If judges chose to interpret the writs rigidly, however, then the Common Law could easily be stultified. Despite earlier liberal practices, by the late fourteenth century the rigid approach prevailed. Writs had to conform to a limited range of available forms and the forms were interpreted restrictively. The reasons for this were political. This was a period of intense power struggles between the King, Parliament, and the judges. The formalization of the writ system was intended to curb the power of the Chancellor (at least in his less famous role as the writ-issuing agency) and, through him, the King. However, the real (if unintended) result was to limit the types of claim available at Common Law.

Indeed, even with claims that were clearly permitted, the jury system reduced the scope for ready evolution of formal legal rules into more discriminating forms. When judges explained the law to juries, they tended to express the rules in the simplest form possible so that the jury would understand; they resisted adding layers of sophistication that might eventually have changed public understanding of the law. Of course, juries themselves might inject commonly agreed, evolving social norms into their determinations, but this practice did not deliver legal rules. Juries did not need to give reasons or ensure coherence with earlier cases. It followed that even though the results might have been acceptable, the legal regime remained stagnant.

In short, the Common Law found itself unable to absorb into its own framework the ideas underpinning the Chancellor's 'bounty'. The problem was not the Common Law's adherence to a system of precedent. Modern legal developments demonstrate the vibrant potential of such a system to generate law reform. The problem was the political context that led to an overly rigid interpretation of these precedents.

Given this state of play in the King's courts, the evolutionary pressure to convert 'bounty' to 'law' sought another outlet. The earlier discussion of children's kindergarten games reinforces the idea that societies are predisposed to operate by rules rather than by royal gift. As a result, the Chancellor's jurisdiction itself began to develop its own distinctive system of legal rules. Because the early Chancellors were often catholic clerics or nobles, trained in Latin and French languages as well as Roman civil and canon law, they borrowed from what was familiar to them. They investigated complaints in a civilian, Roman manner (using written pleadings and no jury) and made decisions on the basis of general, substantive principles of law infused with notions of morality, in the civilian mode. As calls for Chancery intervention grew, and consistency became increasingly important, Chancellors also attempted to provide rational justifications for particular applications of principle. These reasoned decisions, especially those from the late seventeenth century onwards, made it even easier to systematize Equity, and a body of Equitable principles—a body of 'red rules'—developed.

The impetus to convert Equity from bounty to law was itself partly political. The power struggles between the Chancellors and the King's Judges put Equity under inevitable pressure to become more law-like; its decisions would never be entirely politically acceptable unless they could be characterized as rational, predictable, and objective.[2] The political upheavals in seventeenth-century England added to these general pressures. The democratic revolutionary forces threatened to destroy Equity if it maintained its close associations with the monarch and with royal prerogative justice. Equity could either conform to these demands, or remain outside the legal realm. As law, it would inevitably speak the language of rights and duties; as an arm of royal discretion, it would not—it would simply operate by way of royal gift.

Equity reacted positively to these pressures. It did become law. This progression necessitated some sort of rule to regulate the relationship between the Common Law and Equity, between the green umpires and the red umpires. Initially the rule was very simple. The Chancellors—the red umpires—played a very understated role; they would only intervene when it was absolutely necessary to avoid injustice. Of course this did not last. The pressure was on Equity to expand, and in the early seventeenth century there was a notorious and spirited political battle for power between the Chancellor and the Lord Chief Justice.[3] The Chancellor won. The new rule governing the relationship between the green and red umpires was that, in the event of a conflict, the rules and practices of the red umpires—the Chancellors—prevailed over the rules and practices of

---

[2] The degree to which Equity's concept of 'conscience' was transformed during this period is signalled in the judgment of Lord Nottingham in *Cook v Fountain* (1676) 3 Swanst 585, 600 (36 ER 984): 'With such a conscience as is only *naturalis et interna* this court has nothing to do: the conscience by which I am to proceed is merely *civilis et politica* and it is infinitely better for the public that a trust, security or agreement should miscarry than that men should lose their estates by the mere fancy and imagination of a Chancellor.'

[3] *Earl of Oxford's Case* (1615) 1 Ch Rep 1, 21 ER 485.

the green umpires—the King's Judges. In effect, the rules of Equity trumped the rules of the Common Law.

All of this history represents the orthodox description of Equity's emergence. The story may be part reality and part Equity mythology.[4] Nevertheless, the account remains disturbingly unsatisfying. Dualism is such a counter-intuitive approach that no amount of history or politics quite satisfies as vindication of the choice. Whatever the alleged reasons, it remains odd that early English practices of law and bounty were not simply merged into more sophisticated legal rules. It is perhaps more odd still that hundreds of years later, when the Equitable rules were held to trump inconsistent Common Law rules, integration did not then occur. The two bodies of rules could have been readily merged, and any inconsistencies dealt with by applying the straightforward rule that 'Equity governs'. Instead, it seems that the personal attractions of judicial power and the rigid rules of precedent conspired to ensure that this was neither politically nor legally possible.

Dualism continued. However, the successful systematization of Equity had a profound impact upon the Common Law. As Equity's practices became more formalized and, as a result, more constrained, Equity no longer provided such an amenable outlet for legal change. The evolutionary pressures on the Common Law therefore increased. These pressures reached a head in the nineteenth century, and the inevitable response was, finally, to relax the Common Law's own severe procedural constraints. Several important changes were made. Litigants were given a right of action without appeal to the Chancellor. More importantly, the writs that had prescribed the permitted forms of action were abolished in favour of fact pleading. This meant that matters once treated as issues of fact to be decided by juries became the concern of judge-controlled law, and judges had to state the principles underlying their decisions. The construction of these principles often required real creative imagination. Moreover, the strategy liberated the development of the Common Law: principles were refined and new rules appeared as judges honed legal rules by distinguishing the circumstances before them from those which had been material to an earlier application of principle. The parallels with the earlier practices of Equity's Chancellors are telling.

---

[4] The model that emerges from this history puts the Common Law and Equity in sharp opposition. The reality suggests greater accommodation. Nevertheless, contemporary perceptions of the future of the two jurisdictions—which is the focus of this book—have been shaped by the myth as much as, if not more than, by the reality.

Despite this convergence of Common Law and Equitable practices, dualism persisted. The fundamental shortcomings of the strategy were largely ignored, and any emerging integrationist moves were firmly confined to the administrative front. Recall that litigants could be caught out because they had commenced their action in the 'wrong' court, one that was powerless to give them a remedy under its own distinctive rules. This practical difficulty was eventually solved in the nineteenth century, when the Judicature Acts 1873 and 1875 finally fused the administration of the King's Bench and Chancery Courts. This meant that judges hearing cases could use either Common Law or Equitable rules as appropriate, regardless of the formal designation of the court. Intellectually, however, there was a prevailing commitment to dualism, to green and red rules and practices, and to a rigid separation of the two. Despite the practical changes, judges effectively continued to operate as green or red umpires as the circumstances dictated, but without wearing green or red badges or appearing in green or red courts. The conduct of legal advocacy maintained its segregation into Common Law and Equity (or Chancery) practices or 'bars'. Legal education itself often perpetuated this ongoing dualistic approach by focusing on the differences and incompatibilities between the two systems rather than on their evolving overall coherence. And so it is that the two separate and independent jurisdictions—the Common Law and Equity—have continued up to the present day notwithstanding the logical appeal of the integrated unitary alternative.

DUALISM IN ACTION—THE EARLY DISTINGUISHING CHARACTERISTICS OF COMMON LAW AND EQUITY

From the outset, the rules of the Common Law and Equity—the 'green' and 'red' rules of the common law legal system—differed from each other in several important ways. The story of Equity's evolution makes it plain that Equity's *substantive rules*, at least at the outset, differed from those of the Common Law. Equity was originally only called upon to intervene when the Common Law rules were seen to be inadequate. It follows that if Equity reacted at all to the situation, it necessarily reacted differently from the Common Law. Sometimes Equity would deny rights where the Common Law accorded them. For example, Equity might declare a contract not binding even though it was binding at Common Law. Equally, sometimes Equity would grant rights where the Common Law denied them, as where it declared that a party owed Equitable obligations of confidentiality, or secrecy, which were not recognized by the Common Law. When and why Equity deigned to react like this is a matter for later chapters; for now it is enough to note that the substantive rules of the two bodies of law were inevitably different.

Such substantive differences can be problematic. As each distinctive body of law evolves, each might eventually assert that it has the right to intervene in circumstances that appear to bystanders to be identical. For example, the Common Law reacts in one way to third party recipients of legal property; Equity reacts in a different way to third party recipients of Equitable property.[5] This same problem was recognized in the children's kindergarten game. There it was predicted that the green and red umpires might eventually come to regulate the same forms of conduct, but to do so differently. This creates a serious problem: a legal system with rules that regulate the same behaviour in different ways has lost coherence. One of the important tasks for the modern common law is to work out ways to restore this lost coherence, either by re-aligning inconsistent remedies or rationalizing their distinctions.

The likelihood that the Common Law and Equity will deliver different responses to the same facts is exacerbated because, from the outset, the Common Law and Equity adopted quite different *remedial strategies*. This is the second important difference between the Common Law and Equity. The Common Law usually gives money remedies. These awards are quantified in different ways depending upon the type of breach. The different quantification rules reflect the three substantive subdivisions of the common law of obligations into contract, civil wrongs and unjust enrichment. Broadly speaking, awards for breaches of *contract* aim to put the claimant in as good a financial position as if the contract had been properly performed. For example, a vendor will have to pay *expectation damages* to a purchaser to compensate her for the unacceptably poor quality of goods delivered: the courts will assess the market value of the goods that should have been delivered and the market value of the goods in fact delivered, and award the claimant the difference. Awards for *civil wrongs* (or 'torts'), such as negligence or nuisance, aim to put the claimant in as good a position as if the wrong had not been committed. For example, a negligent driver will be obliged to pay *compensatory damages* to cover the cost of repairs to any property he has damaged because of his negligent driving. Finally, awards for *unjust enrichment* aim to remove from the defendant any enrichment that it would be unjust for him to retain. For

[5] See Chapter 6, 179–89.

example, a person whose bank account is accidentally credited with a windfall will generally have to make *restitution* of the overpaid sum.

Equity usually reacts differently. It typically orders the defendant to *do* something, perhaps to hand over an item of property, to specifically perform a contract, to cease creating a nuisance, to correct a document (or sign it, or deliver it up for cancellation), and so forth. Even when its orders do concern money, they are usually orders to pay over some defined and identifiable fund. Very rarely does Equity simply order the payment of money, and when it does it adopts techniques that are different from those employed by the Common Law.[6]

These different remedial strategies can exacerbate problems at the jurisdictional boundary, where the Common Law and Equity purport to deal with the same issues but do so in different ways. For example, both the Common Law and Equity now claim some jurisdiction over defendants who behave negligently and cause damage to those they should be treating carefully. The problem is that each jurisdiction then responds differently; like situations are not treated alike.[7] This suggests incoherence in the legal regime. But the problems go deeper than this. As the Common Law and Equity evolve down their separate jurisdictional paths, each delivering structurally different remedies, there is no formal mechanism for comparing the relative impact of Common Law and Equitable intervention: there is no mechanism for ensuring that the infringement of highly prized rights attracts highly valued remedies, and lesser infringements attract lesser remedies when viewed across the jurisdictional boundary. For example, the remedies for interference with Common Law property rights are quite different from the remedies for interference with Equitable property rights.[8] If the common law system is to remain coherent, then this intra-jurisdictional perspective is crucial.

The third difference between the Common Law and Equity is in the different *enforcement techniques* each has for insisting upon compliance with its remedies. At Common Law a money remedy is a debt owed to the claimant, and defaulting debtors can be compulsorily stripped of their assets to the extent necessary to pay the debt. In Equity, defaulting defendants are considered to be in contempt of court if they refuse to comply with the relevant court orders. Originally defendants could be

---

[6] It uses different rules for quantification, and effects the payment by ordering the taking of an account, not by the more direct route of ordering the payment of a sum of money: see Chapter 6, 165–7.

[7] See Chapter 6, 161–8.

[8] See Chapter 4, 93–7, and Chapter 6, 168–74.

thrown into prison for such contempt: in a very real sense Equity acted
'on the person' to ensure that its orders were carried out; the Latin tag is
that Equity acts *in personam*. This type of physical enforcement is one of
the earliest mechanisms adopted by primitive societies to ensure compliance with the law. However, Equity took this idea of specific enforcement
very much further than this. If Equity thought the claimant was entitled
to certain property, then of course it would order the defendant to deliver
the asset to the claimant on pain of imprisonment for failure to do so.
However, because these orders *had* to be carried out—the claimant *had*
to be given the property—these orders eventually came to be regarded as
giving the claimant ownership of the asset *in Equity* even before any
physical delivery by the defendant, and, eventually, even before the court
had even made its order for delivery. This technique effectively converted
personal remedial obligations into property, with all the attendant protections the common law reserves for property interests.[9] The Common Law
had nothing to match this, and this stark difference marks yet another
feature that militates against coherence in the common law regime.

Finally, Equity's *procedures* for deciding cases were originally quite
different from those of the Common Law. Recall that early Common Law
courts required all actions to be commenced by writ, and writs to be
worded in one of a limited number of technical formats. Parties had to
present formal pleadings (including a statement of the claim by the
claimant and a statement of defence from the defendant); witnesses
presented their evidence orally to a judge and jury; the judge decided
questions of law, the jury questions of fact. Some of the injustices that
Equity was asked to rectify related to these procedures. The formalities
could be counter-productive; witnesses could be intimidated and juries
influenced. Equity adopted quite different procedures. It allowed
actions to be commenced by more informal petitions; it relied heavily
on affidavit evidence (i.e. sworn, written statements); it co-opted further evidence so as to better determine the issues, and it did this by
inventing new processes of discovery (requiring parties to provide a list
of all the relevant documents in their possession, and to make those
documents available for inspection on request) and interrogatories
(allowing parties to submit written questions to each other before the
trial, and requiring written answers to be provided); and it avoided
juries, preferring instead to allow judges to decide issues of both law
and fact. Justice cannot be dispensed if procedural rules impede the

---

[9] See Chapter 3, 63–73.

proper resolution of the case, and in this area at least, intellectual dualism soon gave way to the demands of fairness and justice. Common law court procedure is now determined by statute, but many of the old practices of Chancery have been adopted and refined for general use.

Modern common law continues to reflect many of these early jurisdictional differences between the Common Law and Equity. The strain on the system is becoming increasingly obvious. In particular, the substantive and remedial differences, untrammelled by any formal mechanism for ensuring coherence, are becoming increasingly risky. An integrated system might well display the same range of distinct and distinctive practices, but, crucially, their introduction would be carefully and comprehensively assessed to ensure that the legal landscape retained a rational and coherent profile.

EXPLORING EQUITY AND ADDRESSING ITS DEMANDING QUESTIONS—THE FUNCTION OF THIS BOOK

This brief exposition of the emergence of Equity is sufficient to reveal the principal reasons why those coming to study the subject for the first time face such a daunting task. First, there is clearly no 'general theory of Equity'. Equity is not like the law of contract, or even like the law of civil wrongs, directed at dealing with some particular aspect of legal regulation in modern society. It cannot be described, analysed, and evaluated on the basis of its achievements in meeting such a tightly defined goal. It does not even have a distinctive role in delivering a broad reform agenda based on fairness and justice; the Common Law and statute clearly share that platform. This means that Equity lacks a distinctive theoretical 'peg'; those that might serve the purpose are shared with the rest of the common law. And yet it also seems clear that the grip of intellectual dualism can only be satisfactorily explained and justified by discovering some sort of unique and distinctive commitment to the philosophy and practice of the law.

Secondly, there is the sheer breadth of Equity's subject matter. Equity's interventions have ranged across the entire common law legal landscape. Sometimes its intrusions have supplemented the Common Law rules when the circumstances seem to justify interference. For example, contracts are sometimes specifically enforced, apparently binding agreements are sometimes overridden, and property is sometimes specifically restored. Understanding this supplementary role seems impossible without some degree of engagement with the Common Law rules themselves. At other times Equity's intrusions have produced new rules where the Common Law has none. Equity imposes obligations of loyalty or confidence, for example, and creates new interests in property. The industrious student is left with the sense that studying Equity requires a sophisticated command of the entire body of the common law.

As if this were not enough, the Equity student soon realizes that it is not simply the big picture that is difficult. Much of the detail of Equity is also controversial. Judicial and academic disputes touch almost every area of Equity's intervention. These debates make the subject lively and engaging, but they can be intimidating to the novice. They make it difficult to give unqualified descriptions of many of Equity's practices.

Given all of this, a book aimed at providing an advanced introduction to the Equitable jurisdiction faces a formidable task. It is simply impossible to cover all the interesting debates, or even all the important issues. This book confines itself to two related objectives. The first is to expose Equity's impact on the modern legal landscape. Equity has had a profound influence on the Common Law of property, contract, tort, and unjust enrichment. In successive Parts, this book examines Equity's principal incursions into each of these areas. It is clear that Equity has left no arena untouched. The goal is to describe Equity's various strategies. It is not to explain why the Common Law chose not to intervene, nor is it to consider whether Equity's stance was politically or socially justified. The focus is on the modern landscape, not on the history of Equity's development. Moreover, the aim is to expose the bare bones of the general principles, not to descend into the detail of the rules and their peculiar nuances and varied exceptions (although the reader should remain constantly aware that there are many of these—the law can be infuriatingly tricky at times). The focus is on English Equity; it is simply impossible to cover all the other jurisdictional distinctions in a book this size, although the expectation is that the analysis is general enough to be relevant to readers from all jurisdictions. In striving to be elementary, this book cites very few cases and confines commentators to the end-of-chapter and general bibliographies.[10] Nevertheless, the intellectual debt owed to the enormous numbers of judges and academics whose ideas have enlivened this subject will be evident without the impossible task of naming each and every one of them.

---

[10] The first edition named no cases and cited no commentators at all.

The second objective is far more challenging. It is to expose the possibilities for coherent substantive integration of Common Law and Equity. Integration of administration has already occurred. Integration of doctrine is pressingly urgent. The mind games played earlier in this chapter make this plain. Nevertheless, the prevailing commitment of most judges, practitioners, and academics is to intellectual or doctrinal dualism. Indeed, continuing dualism in the common law is said to be inevitable. The two jurisdictions, Common Law and Equity, are supposed to be so unique that they cannot be integrated. The arguments invariably come down to two core concerns. First, Equity's rationale for intervention is said to be conceptually different from the Common Law's: Equity is said to be conscience-based and moral in a way that the Common Law is not. Secondly, Equity's intervention is said to be irredeemably discretionary in a way that the Common Law's is not. These arguments are addressed in more detail in Chapter 10. Each assertion seems overstated, although each merits careful consideration. Part of the agenda in exposing Equity's principal strategies for intervention is to question this perception of Equity. In the chapters which follow, the description of Equity's main principles and their modern application is combined with an articulation and assessment of Equity's actual, and evolving, interface with the Common Law. The picture that emerges is one of significant practical integration and cross-fertilization between the two jurisdictions. This picture tests the claim of inevitable dualism and at the same time advances a strategy for analysing and applying Common Law and Equity as a unitary system of common law.

REVIEW

In one way or another this entire chapter has been devoted to different aspects of the bizarre common law dualist legal system, with its separate bodies of Common Law and Equitable rules. As the early parts of this chapter show, even children understand that integrated rule systems operate better—more rationally and more coherently—than dualist systems. Integration facilitates the aim of treating like cases alike. It also facilitates the aim of treating different cases in appropriately different ways. A dualist system runs the risk of losing its rational coherence. Judges in dualist systems are inevitably constrained in their ability to identify similarities and draw distinctions; their analysis is limited by accidental jurisdictional divides, when coherence across the legal landscape demands a comprehensive frame of reference.

Given these indisputable propositions, the common law regime appears extraordinary. The history of this odd dualist system can be described, but a convincing vindication of its emergence or justification for its continuation seems elusive. It remains deeply unsatisfying that the best definition of the Equitable jurisdiction must resort to historical accident rather than philosophical or doctrinal ideals: Equity can really only be described as the body of rules, principles, and remedies which evolved from those that were initially developed and administered in the English High Court of Chancery before 1873. The remainder of this book seeks not only to describe this jurisdiction, but also to challenge the merits of continuing with this vision of Equity.

SELECTED BIBLIOGRAPHY

Adams, G. B., 'The Origin of English Equity' (1916) 16 Columbia Law Review 87.

——, 'The Continuity of English Equity' (1917) 26 Yale Law Journal 550.

Baker, J. H., 'The Court of Chancery and Equity' in J. H. Baker, *An Introduction to English Legal History* (4th edn, London: Butterworths, 2002).

Getzler, J., 'Patterns of Fusion' in P. Birks (ed.), *The Classification of Obligations* (Oxford: Clarendon Press, 1997).

Haskett, T., 'The Medieval English Court of Chancery' (1996) 14 Law and History Review 245.

Holdsworth, W. S., 'The Relation of the Equity Administered by the Common Law Judges to the Equity Administered by the Chancellor' (1916) 26 Yale Law Journal 1.

——, 'Equity' (1935) 51 LQR 142.

Maitland, F. W., *Equity: A Course of Lectures*, ed. A. H. Chaytor and W. J. Whittaker, rev. J. Brunyate (2nd edn, Cambridge: Cambridge University Press, 1969), Lectures 1 and 2.

Mason, A., 'The Place of Equity and Equitable Remedies in the Contemporary Common Law World' (1994) 110 LQR 238.

——, 'Equity's Role in the Twentieth Century' (1997/98) 8 King's College Law Journal 1.

Meagher, R. P., Heydon, J. D., and Leeming, M. J., *Meagher, Gummow and Lehane's Equity: Doctrines and Remedies* (4th edn, Australia: Butterworths, 2002).

Pound, R., 'The Decadence of Equity' (1905) 5 Columbia Law Review 20.

Shiner, R., 'Aristotle's Theory of Equity' (1994) 27 Loyola of Los Angeles Law Review 1245.

Vinogradoff, P., 'Reason and Conscience in Sixteenth-Century Jurisprudence' (1908) 24 LQR 373.

2

Legal Systems and Legal Rights

Every society needs a legal system to define its operating practices in political, commercial, and social spheres of activity. This system does not simply provide a set of rules; it also determines who has the authority to make new rules and resolve disputes, and how this is to be done. In western democracies, the legislature, the executive, and the judiciary all play crucial roles. In common law systems, however, the judiciary's role is unusually significant. The judiciary does not simply resolve disputes according to settled rules; it also has the capacity to invent new rules. Its strategies can be as blatant as recognizing legal rights and obligations where none existed before. The most obvious modern example is the Common Law's recognition of a general tort of negligence,[1] but over time this same process has produced the entire framework of the common law of obligations. Equity played its part, inventing new legal rights by recognizing new interests in property[2] and subjecting individuals to new forms of obligations.[3] Usually judicial invention is more subtle, however. Legal rights are valued because of the protection they are accorded by the legal system. Over time, a hierarchy is established. It follows that legal rights can be restructured, judicially, simply by according different degrees of protection to different rights. This chapter surveys the techniques introduced by Equity to vary remedies, defences, and procedural practices so as to deliver a more attuned hierarchy of legal rights and, as a result, a more sophisticated legal system.

This evolving discrimination is Equity's most pervasive, and least well acknowledged, contribution to the modern common law landscape. Orthodox descriptions of Equity usually focus on its individual context-specific interventions. The detail then disguises the broader objective. Worse still, the impression created is one of fundamental differences,[4]

---

[1] *Donoghue v Stevenson* [1932] AC 562. See Chapter 6, 161–2.
[2] See Chapter 3, 63–7.   [3] See Chapter 5, 131–4, 145–7, 148–52.
[4] Recall the distinguishing characteristics of the Common Law and Equity: Chapter 1, 13–17. These differences are undoubtedly real, but the ends to which they were directed suggest coherence, not division, within the common law.

not of coherent integration. In this chapter the goal is to understand how Equity's strategies play into the broader objective, and to demonstrate that there is nothing irredeemably 'Equitable' in the strategies themselves. With the benefit of hindsight, these strategies are simply the most obvious options for discriminating between rights; flexibility in any part of the legal system might have permitted their adoption. The fact that Equity first took up the role, rather than the Common Law, now seems no more than an accident of history.

LINKING LEGAL RIGHTS AND LEGAL REMEDIES

Think about what we mean by legal rights. Legal rights are often contrasted with moral rights and mere expectations. For example, you may hope to be paid by your employer, loved by your mother, or given a present on your birthday. These hopes, and many like them, are routinely met, yet very few are legal rights. You do have a legal right to be paid by your employer: if you are not paid, you can call on formal institutions within society to help enforce your rights. By contrast, no formal institution will compel mothers to meet their moral imperatives. As for birthday presents, these are matters of mere expectation, not of moral or legal rights. Yet this is not the only way the world could work: the law could insist on present-giving; it could lock up unloving mothers.

The important point to note is that legal rights are a matter of society's choice. A legal rule creates legal rights and imposes legal duties or obligations *because* the rule is supported by legal sanctions and protected by society's legal institutions. In primitive societies, the requisite rules are primarily concerned with regulating basic social interactions and allocating essential resources; as societies develop, the rules necessarily become more sensitive to social and moral concerns. Maslow's hierarchy of needs predicts this changing focus. In civil law jurisdictions, legal rights are written into codes. In common law jurisdictions, by contrast, many legal rights are identifiable only because the courts sanction their infringement. *If* the court imposes sanctions, then we know that legal rights and legal duties must be in issue. If new circumstances begin to attract legal sanctions, then new legal rights are being created.

The idea of legal rights goes further than their initial recognition, however. Rights are measured by the remedies they attract. A legal right means one thing if the infringer is forced to pay money, and another if he is imprisoned or forced to perform certain acts of restoration or rectification. How the law responds is crucial. If different sanctions are provided for the infringement of different rights, then it is possible to rank rights, ensuring that society's most highly valued rights attract the most highly valued remedies.

Equity plays a significant role in ranking legal rights. Recall that the Common Law usually responds to the infringement of legal rights by ordering money remedies.[5] In quantifying these remedies, the Common Law distinguishes between different classes of obligations. However, all contract rights are then treated alike; so too are all civil wrongs and all unjust enrichment claims. Equity affords a mechanism for discriminating *within* these classes. It sometimes replaces money remedies by orders that the defendant *do* something. Equity's best-known remedies are orders for *specific performance* of contracts (orders insisting that the defendant perform the contract as agreed) and *injunctions* (general orders that the defendant perform or desist from some act). These merit further attention. But Equity's lesser-known remedies are also valuable: Equity sometimes orders specific restitution of assets;[6] or rectification, delivery up, or cancellation of documents; or the appointment of a 'receiver' charged with the protection of the claimant's property if it seems to be at risk in the defendant's hands. These various orders can all be used to discriminate between superficially similar rights. *Some* contracts must be specifically performed; *some* civil wrongs and unjust enrichments must be remedied by action, not merely by money. In this way some rights are effectively privileged over others. The result is a more sophisticated and discriminating legal regime.

SPECIFIC PERFORMANCE

The Common Law responds to contract breaches by ordering money damages calculated to put the injured party in the same financial position she could reasonably have expected to be in had the contract been properly performed.[7] If a seller breaches his sales contract, for example, the buyer can recover damages calculated to compensate her for non-delivery, or defective delivery, or late delivery. This strategy encourages the seller

---

[5] See Chapter 1, 14–15.   [6] See Chapter 6, 169–74.

[7] Sometimes the Common Law alters the way in which damages are assessed, adopting a 'reliance' measure rather than an 'expectation' measure, but nevertheless the remedy remains money. Indeed, the switch seems designed to simplify proof of the quantum, not to allow greater recovery: the 'expectation' measure marks a theoretical cap on compensatory damages. However, see also the discussion of disgorgement damages in Chapter 5, 154–5. If the injured party can *terminate* the contract for breach, she may sometimes be able to obtain restitution of the defendant's unjust enrichment as an alternative to contract damages: see Chapter 9, 279–83.

to perform his promises properly. If he fails, he will have to pay, rather than perform, to put the buyer in an equivalent position. However, the buyer cannot simply insist that the seller perform properly. She cannot force the seller to deliver the promised goods on time and in perfect condition; she can only recover money damages for his failure to do so.[8] A contract to sell an ordinary car to a consumer is regarded in the same way as a contract to sell a Matisse painting to a collector or to supply life-saving drugs to a hospital. One contract is not seen as more deserving of special treatment than another.

Over time, this monolithic approach came to be seen as inappropriate. It ignored the relativities that society attached to different contractual rights. Because the Common Law was hidebound by its writ system, Equity stepped in. It ordered specific performance of certain contracts under threat of imprisonment for contempt of court if the infringer failed to comply with the order. Equity especially favoured those contracts where money remedies patently did not meet the market objectives of the parties' engagement.

Market-based distinctions

The easiest and best-known category of specifically enforceable contracts comprises contracts of sale where there is no available market for the subject-matter. Without a market, buyers simply cannot use their Common Law damages to purchase an equivalent substitute: the Common Law response then seems inadequate. Equity intervened, and ordered specific performance. The test suggests that specific performance is generally available for the sale of unique items such as Ming vases, Matisse paintings, or shares in private companies (since these are not available on the open market), but not for contracts for the sale of ordinary goods or shares traded on stock exchanges. Indeed, if the purchaser is entitled to specific performance because she cannot readily obtain a substitute (a Ming vase, say) in the market, then the vendor, too, can insist on performance should the purchaser decide to renege on the deal. It is immaterial that the vendor is only after money. Equity's strategy recognizes that these contracts are important not simply because the underlying asset is rare, but also because interested buyers and willing sellers are equally rare. The market is made more attractive if both vendor and purchaser can insist on specific disposal or specific delivery.

---

[8] And neither the Common Law nor Equity will allow the parties themselves to introduce terms designed to ensure specific performance of their contract: see Chapter 7, 219–20.

Perhaps surprisingly, the paradigm case for specific performance in this category is a contract for the sale of land. Because of the enormous historical significance of land as a source of personal wealth in early England, courts of Equity adopted the view that each plot of land was unique: no amount of money would enable a claimant to find an equivalent substitute on the market. This historical view is now so entrenched that courts will grant specific performance of a contract for the sale of land even when the purchase is solely for investment purposes, so that a money remedy might seem perfectly adequate to meet the needs of the particular claimant.

The irrelevance of the parties' individual circumstances reinforces the notion that Equity is favouring *types of contracts*, not parties who appear hard done by. Indeed, take a contract for the sale of an ordinary car. This contract is not specifically enforceable. If the vendor refuses to perform, the purchaser is only entitled to money damages. Moreover, the court will not revise its approach if it turns out that the vendor is insolvent and cannot pay these damages. Even if the purchaser has paid for the car, the vendor will not be forced to deliver, only to pay whatever (inadequate) damages his insolvency allows.[9]

Functional distinctions

Equity also privileges contracts where the particular benefits intended by the contract simply cannot be replicated in damages.[10] Two contrasting examples are illustrative. The first is where the contract is designed to give security (such as a mortgage) for the repayment of a loan.[11] A bank may agree to advance a loan for the purchase of a house, taking a mortgage to secure repayment. This gives the bank the right to sell the house and recover its unpaid loan out of the proceeds. Equity will not specifically enforce the loan itself, but if the bank has already advanced the funds and the borrower defaults on his repayments, then Equity will specifically

---

[9] Various protective strategies exist, although they are difficult to appreciate at this stage. If *title* to the car has already passed to the purchaser, even though the car has not yet been delivered, then the purchaser is better protected: see Chapter 3, 52–5. Title transfer is determined by the contract between the parties, or by default rules in the Sale of Goods Act 1979, ss 17, 18, 20A. If this does not afford protection, and the purchaser has already paid the price, then her *restitutionary* remedy entitling her to recover the price may be protected against the vendor's insolvency by a purchaser's lien secured against the car: see Chapter 9, 304.

[10] E.g., *Adderley v Dixon* (1824) 1 Sim & St 607, ordering specific performance of an agreement to assign the debts of a bankrupt, since damages could not be assessed, and therefore could not afford a complete remedy.

[11] See Chapter 3, 77–82.

enforce the security; it will not confine the bank to money damages. The insolvency protection intended by the security arrangement would be rendered a nullity were the response otherwise. Indeed, without such specific enforcement, legal security would lack all its modern power and effect. We will revisit security interests in the next chapter.[12]

The other example within this category is quite different, and perhaps a little suspect. It concerns contracts for the benefit of strangers (i.e. those who are not parties to the contract). For example, A may want to sell his property in a way that benefits his wife, or child, or favourite charity, rather than himself. He may therefore agree to transfer his property to B on the understanding that B will pay £50,000 to C (being A's wife, or child, or favourite charity). If B refuses to perform and A sues for breach of contract, the Common Law rules will only allow A to recover nominal damages. The reasoning is simple: even if B had performed properly, A would have received nothing, so A is no worse off because of the breach. It is C who has lost out, but the Common Law insists that C cannot sue for damages because she is not a party to the contract. If, instead, Equity allows A to sue B for specific performance, then the intended contractual benefit will be delivered to C. This is clearly better than leaving C without a remedy, yet these cases often do not fit the model of 'important' contracts deserving to be privileged. The underlying deal can be of the most pedestrian kind, and it is clear that Equity's real objective is simply reform of the Common Law's much-criticized rules.[13] The problem is that Equity lacks the tools to deliver coherent reform. It cannot simply insist that damages are paid to C: it has no general jurisdiction to order damages; it can only order the defendant to perform. The result is that reform is implemented in a way that delivers indefensible disjunctions in the common law. Three party deals concerning ordinary goods, for example, are privileged over two-party deals relating to the same asset. The common law, via statute, has only recently acknowledged that more rational and coherent reform is necessary, and the new rules now often permit C to sue B directly for remedies for breach of the contract.[14]

---

[12] See Chapter 3, 77–82. The obligations that arise under a trust (Chapter 3, 63–7) are also specifically enforced, although here the justifications are often more difficult: see especially Chapters 4, 5, and 6, at 102–10, 134–8, 168–72 respectively.

[13] *Beswick v Beswick* [1968] AC 58 (HL) (where it is perhaps arguable that the contract was sufficiently 'important'); *Coulls v Bagot's Executor and Trustee Co Ltd* (1967) 119 CLR 460 (Aust HCt). See Chapter 8, 264–9.

[14] Contracts (Rights of Third Parties) Act 1999.

Resisting orders for specific performance

Equity's privileged enforcement of important contracts has some inherent limitations. Even if the contract *is* important, Equity will not insist that the defendant perform his side of the bargain if he was duped into signing the deal,[15] or if performance is simply impossible, or if the claimant is not also ready, willing, and able to perform,[16] or if the defendant can advance any one of Equity's usual defences to persuade the court that the remedy is not warranted.[17] For example, if the defendant has promised to sell his Ming vase to the claimant, the courts will not order specific performance if the agreement was induced by the claimant's misrepresentation, or if the vase has been smashed or stolen, or if the claimant is clearly unable to pay, or has somehow waived her rights under the deal.

In addition, Equity will not order specific performance if this would cause the defendant unwarranted hardship which is out of all proportion to the claimant's real losses. This final discretionary element in orders for specific performance is often said to mark a stark disjunction between the Equitable jurisdiction and the Common Law's jurisdiction to order damages. The inference is that specific performance is a discretionary remedy, while Common Law damages are as of right. This alleged divergence plays into the argument that integration of the two jurisdictions is impossible.[18] In fact the two jurisdictions appear to approach matters in a remarkably similar fashion. Take an example from each. Equity might refuse to order a mining company to specifically perform its promise to restore mined land to its former state because, to Equity, the cost appears exorbitant and wasteful given that the claimants no longer occupy the land. The claimants will, instead, be confined to Common Law damages (although precisely how these ought to be assessed so as to deliver something more than nominal damages remains controversial).[19] But the Common Law retains the same discretion. It might, similarly, refuse to order full cost of cure damages to pay for the cost of proper performance of the defendant's promise to build a swimming pool six inches deeper than the one provided. The cost of digging out the shallow pool and replacing it with a deeper one can appear, to the Common Law, exorbitant

---

[15] See Chapter 7, 204–14.

[16] This limitation is termed the requirement of 'mutuality': the court will not order specific performance unless it can secure the performance due to *both* parties.

[17] See below, 34–40.   [18] See Chapter 1, 14–15, and Chapter 10, 331–5.

[19] *Tito v Waddell (No 2)* [1977] Ch 106 (Megarry V-C). Also see *Cooperative Insurance Society Ltd v Argyll Stores (Holdings) Ltd* [1998] AC 1 (HL), declining to order specific performance of the lease of a failing business.

and wasteful given the claimant's real losses from the breach. The claimant will then be confined to Common Law damages for loss of amenity, not cost of cure.[20] All of this makes sense. The common law, in both its Equitable and Common Law guises, retains a discretion to refuse orders that are pointless or wholly disproportionate to the resulting benefit.

Policy considerations

Predictably, the process of discriminating between contracts is heavily influenced by policy. This is easily highlighted by two examples. The first concerns Equity's treatment of contracts for personal service. Suppose the claimant has engaged the best author (or painter or architect) for a particular job, so that no amount of money can buy an equivalent service on the market. Specific performance would privilege the contractual engagement, but it can contradict the even more important social value of individual autonomy. In balancing the competing policy imperatives of market efficiency and individual autonomy, Equity refuses to order specific performance where there are connotations of enforced subservience and pseudo-slavery. However, where these connotations are not raised, the arguments in favour of specific performance are allowed to run their natural course. On this basis, courts commonly refuse specific performance of cultural and artistic engagements, but not of more routine service contracts.[21]

The second example concerns Equity's treatment of gifts. The common law's general rule is that promised gifts are not binding, no matter how seriously the promise is intended: the courts will not force the donor to deliver the promised benefit or pay damages if he fails to do so. The Common Law modifies its approach if the donor makes his promise by way of formal deed.[22] The special formalities associated with deeds are considered adequate to make the promise binding. For example, if the donor promises, by deed, to give the donee his Picasso painting, then the donee can sue for money damages if the agreement is breached. Equity, however, refuses to favour the engagement by ordering specific performance. Equity would certainly intervene if the donee had promised some form of

---

[20] *Ruxley Electronics & Construction Ltd v Forsyth* [1996] AC 344 (HL).

[21] Although see *Lumley v Wagner* (1852) 1 De GM & G 604, 42 ER 687.

[22] A document bearing the word 'deed' or some other indication that the document is intended to take effect as a deed must be signed by the individual making the deed and by a witness, and it must be 'delivered', meaning that there must be some conduct on the part of the person executing the deed to show that he intends to be bound by it: Law of Property (Miscellaneous Provisions) Act 1989, s. 1(2), (3). Deeds no longer need to be sealed, so the old adage that the document needed to be 'signed, sealed and delivered' is no longer apt.

counter-performance, but Equity does not see agreed gifts as warranting special, privileged treatment.[23] Again, the policy concerns are apparent.

This process of policy-based differentiation between contracts will inevitably continue. Return to our earlier examples of contracts for the sale of an ordinary car to a consumer, a Matisse painting to a collector, and life-saving drugs to a hospital. At Common Law the only remedy for the vendor's breach is damages regardless of the nature of the contract. It is now clear that Equity would specifically enforce the second contract (for the Matisse painting) but not the first (for the car). Whether Equity would specifically enforce the contract for the sale of the life-saving drugs is more difficult. If there is a world shortage of the drug and a medical crisis on hand, then these 'ordinary' drugs become 'special and unique' goods, and Equity will order specific performance. Unless there is such a dire emergency, however, Equity is currently likely to refuse specific performance and leave it to Common Law damages to offset the hospital's additional costs in getting alternative supplies at short notice.[24] In many cases this is perfectly acceptable; it will entail no risk to patients. On the other hand, modern sentiment may suggest that this contract is intrinsically 'important' whatever the circumstances. If this is the case, then additional rules for discrimination must be adopted, although the vehicle for evolutionary change is now likely to be statute rather than either Equity or the Common Law.

None of this evolutionary differentiation is inherently problematic. The law is simply responding to society's need for greater legal sophistication. Contracts are recognized as more or less 'important'; the Common Law monolith is being divided. More important contracts are specifically enforced; less important ones are remedied by damages alone. The disjunctions arise when these initial ideas are developed further, with little regard for the coherence of the broad reach of the common law landscape. As we will see in Chapter 3, some specifically enforceable contracts give the claimant an Equitable property interest in the underlying asset (the Ming vase or the life-saving drugs). As between claimant and defendant, this probably matters little. It reinforces the idea that the claimant is entitled to the asset that the defendant has refused to transfer. But *property* interests can detrimentally affect third parties. Whether

---

[23] *Jefferys v Jefferys* (1841) Cr & Ph 138, 41 ER 443.
[24] *Howard E Perry & Co Ltd v British Railways Board* [1980] 2 All ER 579, 586 (Megarry V-C); *Dougan v Ley* (1946) 71 CLR 142; although contrast the injunction—not specific performance—ordered in *Sky Petroleum Ltd v VIP Petroleum Ltd* [1974] 1 WLR 576.

these additional consequences are either justifiable or desirable is something that needs to be considered very carefully.[25]

INJUNCTIONS

Equity's second and more general strategy for differentiating between rights is by granting or withholding injunctions. Injunctions are orders issued by the court compelling the defendant to act, or refrain from acting, in some way. For example, a builder about to construct a building that breaches restrictive covenants can be ordered by the court not to proceed with the building works. The claimant is not simply entitled to recover damages after the event for the wrongful interference with her rights; she can obtain an injunction before the event to ensure that no damage is ever done. This means that her right to the benefit of the restrictive covenant is better protected than some of her other general rights, which sound in damages only.

Types of injunctions

Injunctions are enormously flexible remedies. Recall that specific performance compels the performance of a contract according to its terms, leaving the court with no discretion to settle its own conditions for performance. Injunctions are not so limited. They can prevent or compel an enormous range of activities, all on terms determined by the court. They can restrain defendants from acting (*prohibitory* injunctions), as in our earlier example, or they can compel activity (*mandatory* injunctions). They can be ordered before the claimant's rights are infringed (*quia timet* injunctions), again as in our example.[26] They can be issued on a permanent or a temporary basis, and they can be *interlocutory* (granted pending trial)[27] or *final* (granted after full determination of the legal issues). All of this makes injunctions powerful legal tools. As with orders for specific performance, a failure to comply with their conditions is a contempt of court. This vast array of potential orders means that Equity can discriminate between rights in a wide variety of ways.

Resisting injunctive orders

Many of the constraints governing injunctions are analogous to those limiting orders for specific performance. Predictably, final prohibitory injunctions are the easiest for claimants to obtain. If the claimant can

---

[25] See Chapter 3, 63–7, Chapter 6, 168–89, and Chapter 8, 264–9.
[26] *Redland Bricks Ltd v Morris* [1970] AC 652 (HL).   [27] See below, 40–4.

prove to the court that her legal rights are being (or will be) violated by the defendant's conduct, then she is *prima facie* entitled to a final injunction restraining the defendant from persisting with (or instigating) the infringement. The builder proposing to breach a restrictive covenant is readily restrained in this way. Because the claimant has fully proved her case and the court order does no more than *prevent* the defendant from acting in a certain way, there are rarely any countervailing interests that suggest the injunction should be denied and the claimant confined to a damages award. Should this happen, however, there is now a statute that permits the damages award to include damages for future harm, something that Common Law damages awards cannot do.[28]

Claimants find it harder to persuade the court that a mandatory injunction is warranted. The courts are then concerned to see that the mandatory activity does not cause undue hardship to the defendant; again, the parallels with orders for specific performance are evident. Finally, interlocutory injunctions raise still further difficulties, which are considered in more detail later in this chapter. Added to all this, there is yet again the idea that Equity will not act in vain, so an injunction will not be ordered where it would achieve no useful purpose. Typically, the courts will refuse an injunction to restrain a breach of confidence once the information is in the public domain.[29] Nor will Equity act contrary to the public interest, even when the claimant has satisfactorily proved all the other elements of her case.[30] And, finally, a defendant can advance all the usual defences to persuade the court that an injunction is not warranted.[31] All of these limitations are similar to those encountered with orders for specific performance.

Further limits to this Equitable jurisdiction are harder to pin down. Predictably, injunctions are only ordered to protect recognized legal rights; they are not made simply to put a stop to unjust or unfair or dishonourable conduct that does not amount to a recognized legal wrong. For example, injunctions will not be ordered to prevent aggressively competitive marketing strategies,[32] nor to restrain pregnant women from having abortions.[33] The orthodox view is also that Equity will not order an injunction unless the right infringed is some sort of property right, as

---

[28] See Chapter 6, 159–61.

[29] *AG v Observer Ltd (Spycatcher case)* [1990] 1 AC 109 (HL).

[30] And this now includes interests protected by the Human Rights Act 1999: *Cream Holdings Ltd v Banerjee* [2005] 1 AC 253 (HL).

[31] See below, 34–40.   [32] *White v Mellin* [1895] AC 154 (HL).

[33] *Paton v Trustees of British Pregnancy Advisory Service* [1979] QB 276.

in our earlier example of a restrictive building covenant. This may well have been the case initially, but the assertion is now quite controversial. Clearly it does not apply to injunctions to protect Equitable rights: a confidence is not a property right, and yet Equity will order an injunction to restrain the breach of a confidence.[34] Nor does it seem to apply to injunctions to restrain breaches of statutory rights, or breaches of negative stipulations in contracts. And yet it appears to be the reason—or one of the reasons—why Equity does not issue injunctions to prevent 'mere' defamation (as opposed to publication of a libel), or trespass to the person. Finally, injunctions were initially ordered only where money damages were regarded as inadequate. This means that injunctions were, and still are, rarely ordered to restrain wrongful dealings with most items of personal property; money is seen as adequate recompense. Outside that arena, however, the requirement that Common Law damages must be inadequate appears to have lost much of its force; indeed, some think that the requirement no longer exists. All of this suggests that the Equitable jurisdiction is becoming increasingly liberal over time.

Common Law and Equity

This liberalization was repeated in later Common Law developments in the area. At the outset the Common Law courts had no inherent jurisdiction to order injunctions. The power was granted to them by statute in the mid-nineteenth century, but not in the same terms as the Equitable jurisdiction. It did not incorporate all the discretionary bars favoured by Equity, but nor did it apply to Equitable rights or permit the court to order *quia timet* injunctions to deal with legal wrongs which were merely threatened. This meant that for a time the Common Law and Equity courts applied different rules to determine whether an injunction was appropriate. This dualism persisted even when the Judicature Act 1873 gave all courts the power to issue injunctions whenever it should appear 'just and convenient' to do so (words repeated in the current statute[35]). A wider jurisdiction is hard to imagine, and reason suggests that the distinctive Equitable jurisdiction should have been comprehensively superseded by this statutory counterpart well over a hundred years ago.[36] There is nothing to be gained by duplication or division. Courts need to make relevant comparisons across the broad sweep of the common law

---

[34] See Chapter 5, 152–4.   [35] Supreme Court Act 1981.
[36] But see the reliance on the terms of the statute in *Gouriet v Union of Post Office Workers* [1978] AC 435 (HL).

landscape to ensure that similar rights attract these privileges in similar ways. The more difficult task is to determine *which* rights merit this special treatment. Because injunctions are so flexible, and the rights that they might impinge upon are so varied, the options for discrimination and differentiation are more complicated than with orders for specific performance.

THE SIGNIFICANCE OF DEFENCES

The evaluation of legal rights and the process of differentiation between them do not stop at the linkage between rights and remedies. The law can profoundly alter the value of rights by its liberal or restrictive recognition of defences (or excuses), that wholly or partly negate the defendant's liability. Some defences are specific to a particular cause of action; some operate quite generally. For example, a defendant accused of negligence may argue that the claimant, too, was negligent, and that the resulting damage was therefore caused by both parties, not by the defendant alone. This is an argument based on the statutory defence of 'contributory negligence', and the defendant hopes, in advancing it, to reduce his damages liability to his share of the damage caused. This defence is clearly only applicable to claims in negligence. Similarly, claims in unjust enrichment are subject to the specific defence of change of position.[37] Equity has introduced four important general defences that may reduce the defendant's liability and, correspondingly, the claimant's entitlement to relief. These are *delay* (especially *laches*), *waiver* (and release), *set-off* and *'clean hands'*. Each merits comment.

DELAY AND THE EQUITABLE DOCTRINE OF *LACHES*

Delay is probably the most commonly advanced Equitable defence. The gist of the defence is that a defendant should not have the threat of litigation hanging over him indefinitely: legal claims should have a natural lifespan, and rights that are not enforced should eventually lapse. One way of ensuring this is to allow the defendant a defence based on the fact that the claimant has delayed for too long in pursuing her claim. This defence tries to balance the public interest in seeing justice done against the public interest in avoiding protracted litigation.[38] The problem with protracted litigation is not just uncertainty for the defendant. The delay

---

[37] See Chapter 9, 275, 309–10.
[38] *Lindsay Petroleum Co v Hurd* (1874) LR 5 PC 221 (PC), 239–41.

adds to the risk of an unwarranted decision by the court because the relevant evidence may be imperfectly reconstructed or completely lost.

Although the Common Law did not develop a judge-made defence based on delay, modern common law jurisdictions now invariably enshrine the idea in Statutes of Limitation. In the UK, such statutes have existed since the early seventeenth century.[39] These statutes provide fixed time limits for the prosecution of many Common Law and Equitable causes of action. Typically the time limit is six years from the date the cause of action accrues, which is usually the date of the defendant's breach. With some more serious causes of action, the limitation period is longer. For example, the limitation period for contracts created by deed, or for secured debts, is generally twelve years; and for actions against trustees or actions for fraudulent breach of trust involving trustees, no time limit at all is imposed—the beneficiary can sue at will. These statutes also recognize that fixed periods of limitation can sometimes work an injustice. If the action concerns fraud or mistake, or if the defendant has deliberately concealed the relevant facts from the claimant, for example, then the claimant may not even be aware that she has a claim until the limitation period has expired. In these cases, the statutes generally provide that the limitation period is only to run from the date on which the claimant actually discovered, or could with reasonable diligence have discovered, the fraud, mistake, or concealment.

In cases where the statute prescribes a limitation period, Equity has no role to play. It cannot shorten or extend the prescribed period simply because the circumstances appear to warrant it. However, the statute is not comprehensive. It does not cover many claims for Equitable relief, including those for specific performance, rescission, rectification, or injunction. Where the statute does not impose a time limit (including actions against trustees, where the Act sets no time limit), then Equity can intervene. It has two mechanisms. First, it can apply the statute by analogy, thus adhering to the maxim that 'Equity follows the law'.[40] It often adopts this strategy. Indeed, it goes to great lengths to ensure that like situations are treated alike, whether the claim is at Common Law or in Equity. For example, if a contract between the parties also had the effect of constituting one of the parties a fiduciary of the other,[41] the fiduciary breaches will be time-barred after six years by analogy with contract

---

[39] Now see the Limitation Act 1980.
[40] E.g. *Knox v Gye* (1872) LR 5 HL 656 (HL), 674 (Lord Westbury).
[41] See Chapter 5, 140–2.

claims.[42] Alternatively, Equity's second mechanism is to impose a *de facto* time limit (not nominated in a fixed number of years) by simply allowing the defendant a defence based on the claimant's delay. This is the Equitable doctrine of *laches*. This is necessarily the strategy where there is no possible analogy with the Common Law,[43] or where the Act expressly states that it is not to apply.

Equity's special rules on delay—or *laches*—are not quite like the statutory limitation of action rules. Mere delay, however long, is not enough by itself to provide a defence. The defendant can rely on the delay only if the claimant is aware of her rights, and her failure to institute proceedings suggests that she has either acquiesced in the defendant's conduct, or has caused the defendant to alter his position in reasonable reliance on the claimant's acceptance of the status quo or otherwise permitted a situation to arise which it would be unjust to disturb.[44]

Acquiescence, under the first limb of this two-pronged test, is inferred if the claimant knows of her rights (or has the means of knowing of them), and does nothing to enforce them; without knowledge there can be no acquiescence. Under this limb there is no need for the defendant to be prejudiced by the delay. Typically, the claimant may have made gifts to the defendant as a result of the defendant's undue pressure on her.[45] If the claimant knows that these gifts can be recalled but nevertheless delays for a long time in instituting her claim, then she will be held to have acquiesced in the gifts: her claim will be defeated by *laches* and acquiescence.

The second kind of *laches*, consisting of delay with prejudice to others, is much more common. Many different forms of prejudice are regarded as unacceptable.[46] For example, a claimant who is aware of her rights to either impugn or affirm a hazardous or speculative transaction will not be allowed to let time run so that she has actual knowledge of the profitability of the venture before making her choice. Claimants seeking to set aside speculative mining transactions in these circumstances have often

---

[42] *Paragon Finance plc v Thakerar & Co* [1999] 1 All ER 400; *Coulthard v Disco Mix Club Ltd* [2000] 1 WLR 707; contrast *Nelson v Rye* [1996] 1 WLR 1378, which has been either distinguished or simply not followed in many later cases.

[43] See, e.g., *Cohen v Cohen* (1929) 42 CLR 91 (Aust HCt).

[44] *Lindsay Petroleum Co v Hurd* (1874) LR 5 PC 221 (PC), 239; *Orr v Ford* (1989) 167 CLR 316 (Aust HCt). The idea is well discussed in *Erlanger v New Sombrero Phosphate Co* (1878) 3 App Cas 1218, 1279 (Lord Blackburn) and *Rochefoucauld v Boustead* [1897] 1 Ch 196 (CA), 209–12 (Lindley LJ), both citing *Lindsay Petroleum*.

[45] See Chapter 7, 209–14.

[46] The classic statement of the rule is that of Sir Barnes Peacock in *Lindsay Petroleum Co v Hurd* (1874) LR 5 PC 221, 239–40 (although the words are apparently those of Lord Selbourne LC: see *Orr v Ford* (1989) 167 CLR 316, 341).

been denied relief. So, too, with claimants who are seeking recovery of arrears of profits: they will not be allowed to stand by while the defendant makes profitable but unauthorized use of their property, and then claim all the profits.

For the most part these statutory and Equitable forms of the defence of delay seem deliberately concerned to ensure that like cases are treated alike, and that unacceptable disjunctions do not arise regardless of whether claims are generated at Common Law or in Equity. Interestingly, the only obvious problem is a recent one. It concerns actions for recovery of profits. Where the Equitable rules apply, recovery is not allowed if there is either acquiescence or prejudice, even if the delay itself does not appear to be excessive. Until recently, all profits claims arose in Equity. Now, however, profits claims are also available for certain breaches of contract.[47] This development is problematic in several respects, but one is that the limitation periods for these profits claims will be decided under the common law statutory regime. The statutory six-year limitation period pays no regard to the factors accommodated by the Equitable rule. Claimants seeking profits disgorgement will be treated differently depending upon whether their claims arise at Common Law or in Equity. This type of disjunction is not based on any rational concern, and only serves to bring the law into disrepute.

WAIVER (OR RELEASE)

The second important Equitable defence is waiver or release. Legal rights do not have to be exercised; indeed, often they are not. For example, a company may decide not to sue its directors for losses caused by a negligent management decision; a purchaser may ignore his supplier's late delivery of goods. In these circumstances the legal right does not simply disappear. Usually the claimant remains free to change her mind and sue the defaulting director or the tardy supplier. In some cases, however, she will be regarded as having waived her rights against the defendant or released him from his obligations. She is then barred from suing because the defendant has a defence of waiver or release.

The cases on Equitable waiver are in a state of confusion, so it is difficult to be definitive. This is especially so where the right being waived is a Common Law right. The prevailing view is that a waiver will not be effective unless it is supported by consideration (and so is then

---

[47] *AG v Blake* [2001] 1 AC 268 (HL). See Chapter 5, 154–5.

more properly called a release).[48] This mirrors the Common Law rules on waiver of Common Law rights, which require the release to be given by binding contract (and at Common Law, this also includes a waiver contained in a formal deed). Where the right being waived is an Equitable right, the Equitable rules are different, and less controversial. Then it seems true that the waiver can be gratuitous, and can be delivered without formalities (perhaps orally, or even by conduct), so long as there is proof that the claimant knows of her rights but has expressed a fixed and certain intention to immediately release those rights.[49] This intention can be proved by lapse of time, or by other circumstances. Thus it seems that *laches*, acquiescence and waiver (and estoppel, too[50]) are all intimately linked (or perhaps all rather confused).

The need for this type of defence is clear, but there seems to be no good reason for its different rules at Common Law and in Equity. Indeed, the distinctions mirror current confusions about which promises should be regarded as legally binding. The Common Law insists on consideration (or the formalities of a deed). Equity, too, insists that 'Equity will not assist a volunteer' (which appears to replicate the Common Law's concern for consideration), but it then undermines this idea with its notions of estoppel. Once a coherent approach to legally binding promises has been worked out,[51] it ought to be possible to say, quite simply, that the claimant has waived (or released) her legal rights against the defendant if (and only if) she has made a legally binding promise to do so. It should be irrelevant whether the rights being waived are legal or Equitable.

SET-OFF

The idea behind the defence of set-off is simple, although the practical rules governing its application are not. Consider an example. Suppose C has a claim against D for £1,000, and D has a claim against C for £900. On the face of it, both of these claims will be fully satisfied if D simply pays C £100. Looked at another way, D can reduce his liability to C by setting-off his own claim against C. This netting of claims appears so sensible that it usually comes as a surprise to learn that the law does *not* usually allow set-off where the claimant and defendant have claims and counter-claims against each other. This takes some explaining.

[48] *Reeves v Brymer* (1801) 6 Ves 516, 31 ER 1172; *Commissioner of Stamp Duties (NSW) v Bone* [1977] AC 511 (PC). But contrast *Wekett v Raby* (1724) 2 Bro PC 386, 1 ER 1014.
[49] *Wright v Vanderplank* (1856) 8 De GM & G 133, 147; 44 ER 340, 346 (Turner LJ). Also see *De Bussche v Alt* (1878) 8 Ch D 286, 314.
[50] See Chapter 8, 241–8.   [51] See Chapter 8, 248–54.

Set-off is clearly valuable. In our example, it means that C is not liable to pay £900 to D: she is not in breach of contract, even if she refuses to make the payment. In the long run, however, the defence does not radically alter the financial position of either party assuming both are solvent. The defence only becomes crucial if one of the parties is insolvent. Suppose C is insolvent and her creditors will only be paid 50 pence in the pound. If set-off is allowed, then the claims will be netted: C will not be required to pay anything, and D will have to pay C £100, as before. But if set-off is not allowed, then each claim must be treated independently. This means that D must pay C £1,000, and must pay the full amount because he is solvent. C, on the other hand, is liable to pay D £900, but she will in fact only pay £450 because of her insolvency. The net effect, without set-off, is that D will be £550 out of pocket. If the claimant is insolvent, the defence provides D with vital insolvency protection. Moreover, it does this at the expense of C's other unsecured creditors: if D is allowed notional full recovery of his claim, then the other creditors are penalized by having access to a correspondingly smaller insolvency pool.

Given the serious insolvency consequences associated with set-off, the law must decide when the defence should be available. Insolvency set-off is allowed only if the claim and counter-claim are mutual;[52] this means they must arise between the same parties and concern the same subject matter. If the claim is for the price of goods, for example, and the counter-claim is for damages for their poor quality, then set-off is allowed; if the counter-claim is coincidentally for overdue rent payments, however, then set-off is not allowed. These insolvency rules displace the wider non-insolvency contractual (i.e. agreed between the parties), statutory and Equitable versions of set-off. Although there are clear differences of detail between all these rules, all are directed at the same ends. All impose some sort of limitation on the types of claims that can be set off against each other. The Equitable idea may have been adopted and refined, but there seems to be no philosophical disjunction in direction or method, whatever the divergence in detail.

'CLEAN HANDS'

The fourth and final defence for this section is Equity's defence of 'clean hands'. The expression is derived from one of Equity's maxims: 'He who comes to Equity must come with clean hands.' Once again, the defence has Common Law parallels. The common law regime hesitates to allow

---

[52] Insolvency Rules 1986, r. 4.90.

claimants to benefit from enforcing their legal rights when their own conduct has been questionable. The Common Law draws the line by (generally) refusing to assist claimants whose conduct is illegal.[53] Equity draws the line differently, by (generally) withholding Equitable relief (but not Common Law relief) where the claimant's conduct is somehow 'improper', even if it does not amount to a legal wrong. The impropriety must be necessarily and immediately related in some way to the relief the claimant is seeking.[54] For example, a claimant seeking an order for specific performance may be refused Equity's assistance if it turns out that she procured the defendant's agreement by misrepresenting the facts to him, even if she did so quite innocently. In these circumstances, the claimant will be denied specific performance, although she will retain her Common Law rights.

The Equitable defence may well reflect the fact that Chancery began as a court of conscience, but it is also perfectly consistent with the broader common law sentiment that claimants should not be allowed to abuse the judicial process. The effect of the defence is to ensure that the special privileges afforded by Equitable remedies are only available to claimants who have acquired their underlying rights with all the necessary propriety.

Very rarely, an Equitable remedy is ordered despite the claimant's impropriety. This is only done when granting Equitable relief is more advantageous than refusing it. For example, the primary action may be for an injunction that will prevent a multiplicity of suits, or for delivery up and cancellation of a document where its continued circulation would lead to the further deception of the public.

THE IMPACT OF PROCEDURAL PRACTICES

The final factor in differentiating between legal rights is regulation of the manner in which the parties bring an action to court. Rights are worth more if they are easily enforced, and if enforcement is predictable and consistent. From the outset, Equity adopted quite different procedures from those used in Common Law courts. Equity recognized that justice cannot be dispensed if procedural rules impede the proper resolution of the case. Modern statutory procedure has now adopted and refined many of Equity's old practices for general use. Actions can be commenced by

---

[53] See Chapter 8, 259–61.

[54] And unrelated impropriety, however obvious, is not a bar: *Grobelaar v News Group Newspapers Ltd* [2002] 1 WLR 3024 (HL).

relatively informal pleadings; defendants are allowed (and can occasionally be compelled) to give evidence; additional interested parties can be joined in the proceedings; and disclosure of documents can be ordered. These statutory rules ensure that there are no longer serious disjunctions between Common Law and Equitable practices.

Notwithstanding these statutory rules, Equity continues to have a significant impact on modern procedural practices. This section looks at three controversial practices: interlocutory injunctions; search orders (*Anton Piller* orders); and freezing orders (*Mareva* injunctions). Each illustrates the enormous power of procedural rules.

INTERLOCUTORY INJUNCTIONS

Suppose a claimant wants the benefit of a restrictive covenant, or certain information to be kept secret, or the defendant to deliver particular goods. She cannot be left without any protection until the dispute is finally resolved, perhaps on appeal. This process may take months or years, and the claimant's alleged rights may then be worthless. The defendant may have built his offending buildings, disclosed the secret information, or sold the goods to third parties.

An *interlocutory injunction* may assist. This is a short-term injunction designed to maintain the status quo pending trial. The injunction could prevent buildings being built, secrets being revealed, or assets being disposed of, pending final resolution of the legal dispute in court. The difficulty is that the court has to decide whether or not to grant the injunction before the parties have fully argued their case. If the wrong preliminary decision is made, then one party's interests may be damaged without good cause. To reduce the risks, courts look to the 'balance of convenience' between the parties. This involves assessing the harm each side is likely to incur if the injunction is granted and if it is not, and whether that harm could be compensated for in money when the issues are finally determined at trial. Any injunction is then usually supported by cross-undertakings in damages, whereby the claimant promises to compensate the defendant for any consequential losses should the injunction turn out not to have been warranted.[55]

Even this test misses the real difficulty, however, which is that the court's initial stance often signals the practical end to the dispute without the benefit of a full trial. For example, a defendant prohibited by interlocutory injunction from manufacturing and selling a product that

---

[55] *American Cyanamid Co v Ethicon Ltd* [1975] AC 396 (HL).

allegedly breaches the claimant's patent may well be forced out of the competing business even though the underlying issues have not been fully tried. But if the courts do nothing, the *claimant* may be equally wrongly forced out of business by the unfair competition provided by the defendant. The real difficulty is the time it takes to come to a final resolution of the issues before the courts.

SEARCH ORDERS (*ANTON PILLER* ORDERS)

Equity's search order is a specific and aggressive form of interlocutory injunction. Evidence plays a vital role in prosecuting a case. Without the necessary evidence, justice cannot be done and legal rights are of little value. Very early in its history, Equity found it unacceptable that the Common Law courts could not compel disclosure of documents. Equity reacted, and disclosure is now part of the ordinary process of litigation. However, disclosure is unlikely to prove effective against defendants who are minded to destroy vital evidence as soon as they are alerted to the threat of litigation. Last century, this problem plagued the prosecution of cases involving pirated copies of musical records and tapes: as soon as litigation loomed, potential defendants would remove or destroy the necessary evidence and so escape the legal consequences of their activities.

To overcome the problem, Equity developed its own search order (previously known as an *Anton Piller* order, named after one of the earliest cases in which such an order was made[56]). This order compels the defendant to allow the claimant to enter his premises to inspect, remove, or make copies of documents and property belonging to the defendant. Naturally, the application for the order is made without the defendant's knowledge, and without him having a chance to make his case, since the whole purpose is to take the defendant by surprise and so prevent the destruction of necessary evidence. Given these features, a search order looks very much like a police search warrant issued to a private individual. The theoretical difference is that the claimant does not have a *right* to enter the defendant's premises; instead, the defendant is under a duty to permit entry. However, the defendant's failure to comply will put him in contempt of court, so the difference is largely academic. Indeed, the parallels with search warrants are now reinforced by statutory rules that prevent the defendant resisting the order on the ground of privilege

---

[56] After *Anton Piller KG v Manufacturing Processes Ltd* [1976] Ch 55 (CA).

against self-incrimination, at least in relation to allegations of passing-off and breach of intellectual property rights.[57]

Courts themselves now recognize that a search order has the potential to enable claimants to go on 'fishing expeditions', looking for evidence of wrongful acts not previously suspected. In order to minimize speculative and oppressive use of the order, they have formulated several procedural safeguards to protect defendants, and have imposed on claimants seeking such orders a duty to make full and frank disclosure of all relevant matters to the court and to give undertakings to pay damages should the order prove unwarranted. Nevertheless, the potential for abuse remains. Not only are the defendant's civil liberties at risk, so too is the defendant's business. Claimants may remove the defendant's goods and hold them pending trial, which is then delayed as long as possible. This effectively forces the defendant's business to close down, thus achieving the claimant's aims without any formal trial. Once again, the difficult balancing exercise facing the courts reflects the dramatic power of procedural practices.

FREEZING ORDERS (*MAREVA* INJUNCTIONS)

Difficulties in obtaining evidence or maintaining the status quo are not the only problems faced by claimants. Justice can also be subverted if orders for damages are deliberately evaded. Determined defendants can spirit their assets away when litigation looms, thus making it impossible for claimants to execute any damages claim that might be ordered in their favour against the now apparently impoverished defendant. Injunctions ordered prior to trial have again proved useful. This time the particular form of order is termed a freezing order (previously known as a *Mareva* injunction, again named after one of the earliest cases in which such an order was made[58]). It is an order restraining the defendant from disposing of his assets. It can be directed at specific assets, or worded more generally. The order does not give the claimant any privileged proprietary interest in the defendant's assets; it simply freezes them, preventing the defendant from dealing with them except according to the terms of the order. The order is personal against the defendant, so it cannot be

[57] Supreme Court Act 1981, s. 72, responding to the contrary finding in *Rank Film Distributors Ltd v Video Information Centre* [1982] AC 380 (HL).

[58] After *Mareva Compania Naviera SA of Panama v International Bulkcarriers SA* [1975] 2 Lloyd's Rep 509, [1980] 1 All ER 213 (CA), and now given statutory force in the Supreme Court Act 1981, s. 37(3).

made unless the defendant is amenable to the jurisdiction of the court. However, provided this is the case, the order can relate to the defendant's world-wide assets, including any future acquisitions. Breach of the order is a contempt of court for both the defendant and any third party (such as a bank) who is aware of the order.

Given that an individual can usually do what he likes with his own assets (subject to any special rules relating to insolvency), these freezing orders are quite unusual. They have been subjected to considerable criticism, with some commentators insisting that courts have no jurisdiction, statutory or otherwise, to grant such orders without usurping the functions of Parliament. Only Parliament, it is suggested, can tamper with property rights in this way. On the other hand, these orders are justified as necessary to enable a claimant to obtain satisfaction at law, and to preserve the credibility of the legal system. As with the injunctions considered earlier, the courts face a difficult task in attempting to balance the claimant's and defendant's interests. An order will not be granted unless there is a real threat that the defendant will attempt to evade a potential damages award, and if an order is granted the claimant must give an undertaking as to damages. Nevertheless, these orders still retain the potential to work gross injustices on defendants. The defendant's assets are frozen before the issue has even been tried. This may be enough to put the defendant out of business, even though the courts avowedly presume innocence until guilt is proven.

DECLARATIONS

One further strategy deserves brief mention. The early Common Law courts would not give answers to hypothetical ('moot') questions: claimants could not simply ask the court to spell out their legal rights; they had to bring a specific dispute before the courts. Whether Equity was equally constrained is a matter of dispute. From the mid-nineteenth century, however, various statutes attempted to modify this rule, culminating in the Judicature Act 1873 which granted the court plenary power to make 'declaratory orders' (subject, of course, to the usual rights of appeal). Courts will still not answer completely hypothetical questions, of course, but they can now define the rights of the parties even when there is no underlying dispute to resolve.

Declarations can be made that a person is a member of a club; that her purported expulsion is invalid; that she is the owner of land; that the terms in a will or a trust have a particular meaning; that a contract exists or has been breached or terminated; that an agreement is binding or illegal; or that a form of notice is reasonable. The list is endless. Indeed, a declaration may prove appropriate in virtually any situation imaginable.

This added power may seem inconsequential, but it attaches significant advantages to parties' legal rights. It is faster and therefore cheaper than the usual alternative of protracted litigation or arbitration. It enables courts to give negative relief—for example, that no contract exists, or that no breach has occurred, or that the claimant is not a beneficiary. Finally, it can be made in circumstances where no other relief is available, either because the parties have not allowed the dispute to get to that stage, or because there is no other legal remedy in existence. In short, it serves as an efficient procedural mechanism for bolstering legal rights.

REVIEW

This chapter has focused on Equity's role in constructing a rational hierarchy of legal rights. The common law landscape has changed profoundly over the years. This evolutionary process has been unremittingly directed at delivering a more discriminating, sophisticated legal system. This system recognizes that different legal rights have different values, and should therefore be accorded different degrees of protection. More highly valued rights are associated with more highly valued remedies, more limited defences, and more helpful procedural practices. The strongest hierarchical alignment is between rights and remedies; the weakest is between rights and the procedures for enforcing them. This is as it should be. All rights, even the least valuable, deserve to be judged by procedural strategies that ensure accurate, predictable, and fruitful resolution of the underlying disputes.

From a modern perspective, there is obvious coherence in the Common Law and Equitable rules on procedure and defences. The objectives are the same in both jurisdictions, although the assessment of when these objectives have been reached is subtly different. The Equitable rules are generally more expansive. If disclosure is essential in the pursuit of fair trials, for example, then Equity is prepared to extend the rules to ensure effective disclosure in the face of a defendant's attempts to evade it. If rights can be waived provided the claimant truly intends this consequence, then Equity is prepared to extend the rules to include various informal arrangements that meet this test. In any event, these areas are now severely circumscribed by statutes, which have themselves been devised with an eye to both the Common Law and Equitable rules. As a result, much of the rational mapping of the common law in these areas has already been done, and the picture is agreeably coherent even though some of the detail may still need developing.

The issue of remedies is less simple. Remedies define the value of rights; they do not merely assist in their enforcement. Clearly not every legal right warrants the same sort of remedy. In any legal system, a hierarchy of rights will inevitably evolve. Equally clearly, a hierarchy of remedies must evolve; a legal 'system' demands generalized and coherent rules, not unconstrained judicial discretion.

This chapter described Equity's effective differentiation of Common Law rights. Equity employed a simple strategy. It supplemented the Common Law's uniform awards of money remedies with its own characteristic performance remedies, but it did so only in certain restricted privileged cases. The result is a coherent, differentiated legal landscape, delivered by dint of Equity and the Common Law working in tandem, paying regard to the desirable relativities in legal rights. What this chapter did not explore, however, is the difficulty of achieving a coherent hierarchy of legal rights *across* the jurisdictional divide. Common Law rights may present a coherent pattern; so too may Equitable rights. However, there is no formal mechanism for checking that, between the two jurisdictions, the Common Law and Equity are not dealing with similar issues in quite different ways. The risk that they are is the risk of incoherence in a dualist legal system. Some of the resulting difficulties are highlighted in succeeding chapters. For now, however, what matters is simply the various strategies that Equity has made available for differentiating between legal rights and developing a more sophisticated legal landscape.

SELECTED BIBLIOGRAPHY

Burrows, A., *Fusing Common Law and Equity: Remedies, Restitution and Reform* (Hochelaga Lecture, University of Hong Kong and Sweet & Maxwell, 2002).

Devonshire, P., 'Freezing Orders, Disappearing Assets and the Problem of Enjoining Non-Parties' (2002) 118 LQR 124.

Handley, K. R., 'Exploring Election' (2006) 122 LQR 82–97.

Mason, A., 'The Place of Equity and Equitable Remedies in the Contemporary Common Law World' (1994) 110 LQR 238.

Schwartz, A., 'The Case for Specific Performance' (1979) 89 Yale Law Journal 271.

Waddams, S., 'Johanna Wagner and the Rival Opera Houses' (2001) 117 LQR 431.

SELECTED CASES

AG v Observer Ltd (Spycatcher case) [1990] 1 AC 109 (HL)

American Cyanamid Co v Ethicon Ltd [1975] AC 396 (HL)

Anton Piller KG v Manufacturing Processes Ltd [1976] Ch 55 (CA)

Beswick v Beswick [1968] AC 58 (HL)

Cooperative Insurance Society Ltd v Argyll Stores (Holdings) Ltd [1998] AC 1 (HL)

Coulls v Bagot's Executor and Trustee Co Ltd (1967) 119 CLR 460 (Aust HCt)

Cream Holdings Ltd v Banerjee [2005] 1 AC 253 (HL)

Gouriet v Union of Post Office Workers [1978] AC 435 (HL)

Grobelaar v News Group Newspapers Ltd [2002] 1 WLR 3024 (HL)

Lindsay Petroleum Co v Hurd (1874) LR 5 PC 221 (PC)

Lumley v Wagner (1852) 1 De GM & G 604, 42 ER 687

Mareva Compania Naviera SA of Panama v International Bulkcarriers SA [1975] 2 Lloyd's Rep 509, [1980] 1 All ER 213 (CA)

Norwich Pharmacal Co v Commissioners of Customs and Excise [1974] AC 133 (HL)

Ruxley Electronics & Construction Ltd v Forsyth [1996] AC 344 (HL)

Sky Petroleum Ltd v VIP Petroleum Ltd [1974] 1 WLR 576 (Goulding J)

Part II

Property

3

Creating Property

To many minds, Equity's greatest contribution to the law has been its manipulation of traditionally accepted concepts of property. This chapter deals with two strategies that Equity adapted to achieve its radical ends. The next chapter deals with two more. The underlying ideas seem simple, but their impact has been unparalleled. Equity's first strategy is straightforward. Equity would sometimes regard certain assets as property even when the Common Law did not. This meant that these assets could be traded; they became usable wealth, at least in Equity's eyes. For example, Equity treated debts as property long before the Common Law did. The Common Law used to insist that debts were simply personal contracts that entitled the creditor to receive payment from the debtor. Equity differed; it allowed creditors to transfer their debts to third parties. Creditors could trade in debts and obtain immediate cash returns. This dramatically increased the flow of capital in the market place; indeed, debts are now commodities in their own right. Equity's second strategy for manipulating concepts of property is more complicated. Equity will sometimes say that A 'owns' a car (or a company share, or an insurance pay-out) even though the Common Law says that B does. If the law is to make sense, then Equity and the Common Law cannot be using 'own' in quite the same sense. This chapter considers what it means when Equity says that A 'owns' property, and why the assertion is so ingenious.

SIMPLE IDEAS ABOUT PROPERTY

Most non-lawyers think of property as a 'thing'. A car or a horse is tangible property; a share in a company or copyright in a literary work is intangible property. However, the idea of property is more complicated than this. The first hint of this complication comes from the realization that not all 'things'—even things of value—are necessarily property. Human beings are not property (although slaves and married women once were); nor are jobs or reputations. The key to 'property' is something more subtle.

In the nineteenth century, the philosopher, Jeremy Bentham, suggested that property is not a 'thing' but a 'relationship'. The word *property* is simply shorthand for a special relationship between an individual and a thing. A horse is property—and a human being is not—because of the nature of the rights an individual has over the thing, not because of the nature of the thing itself. With a horse, some individual (the owner) has the right to control who rides the horse and who does not, who obtains the prize money when the horse wins the Derby and who does not, who can purchase the horse and who cannot. If the relationship gives the individual certain special rights, then we call the thing 'property' and the relationship and its associated rights are 'proprietary'. Without these special rights, the thing is not called property and the relationship and rights in respect of it are not proprietary; they are merely *personal*.

But even this does not quite get to the nub of the issue. We need to know what essential difference distinguishes 'proprietary' rights from 'personal' rights. It turns out that the crucial difference is not the right to enjoy particular benefits. Both types of right will deliver enjoyment. A job, which is not property, can be enjoyed just as much as a car, which is. Strange as it seems, the essential difference is the right to *exclude* strangers from access to the underlying thing. The owner of a car can stop strangers from climbing in; a shareholder can prevent strangers from exercising his vote at the company's annual general meeting. An employee, by contrast, cannot insist that others are excluded from undertaking allotted tasks or from making claims on the wages pool. This can be generalized by saying that proprietary rights (such as ownership of goods) give the right-holders legal rights against strangers. Personal rights (such as jobs) do not; personal rights usually only entitle the right-holder to make demands of the right-giver (such as the employer).

There is another side to this. If owners of property can exclude others, then equally they can permit others to have access—they can give, share, or sell their property rights to third parties. This transferability gives property its commercial value: property can be traded. The twin benefits of transferability and excludability are the important markers of property. They indicate that an individual's relationship with the thing is 'proprietary'.

THE IMPORTANCE OF PROPERTY

Although these twin attributes of transferability and excludability are clearly valuable, they need some unravelling to see why the idea of property sometimes generates heated debate. From Aristotle to modern-day law and economics scholars, the starting point in justifying the need for property is usually economic. The core idea is that a society that safeguards property is wealthier than one that does not. Resources will only increase in value if people work to develop them, and this will only happen if people own the resources and reap the rewards (and bear the losses) of their efforts. On this basis, perhaps all 'cashable' resources should be classed as property. But ownership brings with it the right to control allocation and access. This has political, social, and moral dimensions. Some rights are so valuable, it seems, that they should not be subject to distribution at the whim of individual 'owners'. Rights to human beings (and, perhaps more questionably these days, to human body parts or genetic materials), rights to the air we breathe, the right to vote, the right to read or work or play—none of these is 'property', although it is salutary to realize that this need not be so.

The law's changing perception (and it is a constantly changing perception) of what is property and what is not reflects the contemporary balance between commercial and economic demands and social and moral constraints that society is prepared to condone. There is no legal charter listing the things that are property and the things that are not. Things (or, more accurately, 'rights') are 'property' if, and only if, the law accords them the special forms of protection associated with property (i.e. the right to exclude others) and permits special powers of control (i.e. the right to permit access). If a 'thing' (or a right) is accorded these special privileges, then it is property. As society evolves, the boundaries move: things that were not regarded as property can be accorded the attributes of property, and things that were once regarded as property can lose that status.

If all of this seems like high theory, then the significance of the underlying ideas can be thrown into sharp relief by a simple example. If a commercial trader becomes insolvent, owing his creditors £100,000, then the trader's assets will be sold and the proceeds distributed *pro rata* amongst his personal creditors.[1] Insolvency involves a shortfall, and the philosophy guiding the law is that the trader's creditors should all bear the loss equally. If the trader has few assets, these innocent creditors may all recover as little as 5 per cent of what is owing to them. Often the shortfall is even worse. This is the risk associated with any personal claim

---

[1] This is the general rule, although certain debts are given preferential treatment by statute: Insolvency Act 1986.

against a debtor: the claim is only as valuable as the debtor's credit standing. But the crucial point is that it is only the *debtor's* assets that are collected into the pool to be sold to repay any creditors. If a particular creditor can show that assets in the debtor's possession are not the debtor's, but belong to him, then he can withdraw these assets from the pool: he can exclude the debtor and the debtor's creditors from having access to *his* property. A creditor's *property* rights are protected on the debtor's insolvency in a way that his *personal* rights are not.

This means that different creditors may find themselves in quite different predicaments depending upon their relationship with the debtor. Suppose a supplier has sold the trader a computer for £2,000, but has not yet received payment for it. The supplier is likely to see the computer swept into the pool of assets and sold off to fund the debts owing to all creditors. If the pool of assets is worth £10,000 (a tenth of the total debt owed), then the supplier will only recover £200 of his £2,000 debt. He will undoubtedly be aggrieved that he cannot simply take back 'his' computer given that the trader has not yet paid for it. The reason he cannot has everything to do with property rights. When goods are sold, the purchaser usually becomes the owner when the goods are delivered, if not before.[2] If this is the case, then the trader will own the computer even though he has not yet paid for it. He will have all the proprietary rights associated with the computer; the supplier will only have a personal right to be paid £2,000. All the trader's property, including the computer, is used to fund all the debts owing to creditors, including the supplier. The inevitable shortfall means that the supplier's personal claim for £2,000 is likely to abate dramatically in the insolvency.

But a small change in the facts can radically alter the outcome. Suppose the supplier had leased the computer to the trader, rather than selling it to him. Under this arrangement, the supplier retains ownership of the computer, and the trader's rights of possession are conditional on paying the leasing charges. On insolvency, the computer would not be swept into the pool of assets and sold off to fund the debts owed to creditors. Instead, the supplier would be entitled to retake possession. *He* would have the proprietary rights in the computer, including the right to exclude the trader and his creditors from access to it.

---

[2] Sale of Goods Act 1979, ss. 17 and 18. Prior to delivery, a purchaser can only become the owner if the proposed sale property is specifically identified and appropriated to the contract; if this is not the case, the purchaser merely has the benefit of the contractual (non-proprietary) promise to sell: *Re Goldcorp Exchange Ltd (in rec)* [1995] 1 AC 74 (PC).

The lesson from this is that creditors who have proprietary rights are far better protected than creditors with personal rights should their debtor become insolvent. Because of the stark difference in the treatment of personal and proprietary claims in insolvency, creditors scramble to have their rights classified as proprietary rather than personal. Creditors whose claims are merely personal are *unsecured creditors*; creditors whose claims are backed by proprietary rights are *secured creditors*. In many insolvencies, the secured creditors (perhaps especially banks) are often in a position to lay claim to virtually all of the debtor's assets, leaving the unsecured creditors to shoulder the entire loss. The type of protection accorded to secured creditors depends upon the nature of their proprietary rights. These proprietary rights can arise because the parties have deliberately arranged their affairs to deliver this protection, as in our leasing example; this is also what banks do when they take mortgages to secure home loans. However, proprietary interests can also arise by judicial intervention (by operation of law), when the courts decide that the circumstances warrant this degree of protection even though the parties themselves have not contemplated it. Both strategies are controversial. The modern mood favours a return to forcing creditors to share losses equally. Nevertheless, later chapters make it clear that much of Equity's intervention has traditionally been seen as delivered through strategies that create privileged proprietary rights.[3] The criticism—or one of the criticisms—is that these Equitable strategies further erode the position of unsecured creditors. The other side of the coin, however, is that property is important and should be protected, and that agreed security arrangements and privileged proprietary remedies are essential in protecting and promoting social and commercial activity.

LIMITATIONS ON TRANSFERABILITY AND EXCLUDABILITY—TESTING THE BOUNDARIES OF PROPRIETARY RIGHTS

From what has been said, it might be thought that property ownership is inevitably associated with the right to full enjoyment of all that the property has to offer, the right to transfer the property at will, and the right to exclude anyone who seems about to interfere. This is not true. Ownership is rarely associated with absolute rights to enjoy, to transfer, or to exclude strangers.

---

[3] But see Chapter 9, 290–4, 303–7, for the modern debates.

A little reflection confirms this. Ownership of a car does not entitle the owner to drive at any speed on any side of the road (no matter how enjoyable the prospect). The right to enjoy property is restricted by rules designed to protect the interests of others. Equally, the right to transfer property to others can be restricted. Shares in privates companies can often be sold to existing shareholders only: the aim is to keep the business in known hands, so ownership of the share comes with restricted rights of transfer. Nevertheless, the share is still 'property'. Finally, the right to exclude strangers from interfering with property may also be limited. The law commonly insists that property rights are not good against the whole world, but only against those people who know about the right and are therefore said to have 'notice' of it. This explains why we have public registers of so many property rights, such as rights in land, shares, patents, and so forth. Sometimes—especially where there are registers, but in other circumstances too—a property right affects not only those who actually know about it, but also those who could and should know about it (and so are said to have *constructive notice* of the right). Importantly, despite these various restrictions on enjoyment, transferability or rights against third parties, the rights retain their designation as proprietary rights (or 'real' rights, or rights *in rem*).

This creates a difficulty. If these characteristics can be restricted, especially the peculiarly 'proprietary' characteristics of transferability and excludability, then where do we draw the line between proprietary and personal rights? How extensive can the restrictions be before the essential attributes of property are lost? The theoretical response is more difficult than the practical one. Some element of transferability is essential if a right is to be regarded as property, but clearly this attribute can be heavily circumscribed without loss of the proprietary tag. The restricted transfer rights commonly associated with shares in private companies illustrate this. Reduced transferability affects the commercial value of the property; it indicates that the property cannot be freely traded. Nevertheless, commercial parties can readily factor this into their price calculations. (In any event, the restriction is an agreed restriction relating to rights that would otherwise be freely transferable if the restriction were waived.) Restricted rights to exclude strangers create more of a problem. A large part of the value of property lies in the protection it delivers against others. This protection is only possible if the relevant rights of exclusion can be asserted against those who might potentially interfere. In commercial contexts, the right to exclude other creditors if the debtor is insolvent is regarded as especially valuable. Although some restrictions on excludability are acceptable, a right is usually only regarded as proprietary if this insolvency priority remains relatively intact.[4] For this reason, excludability is commonly regarded as the crucial feature of proprietary rights.

MORE COMPLICATED IDEAS ABOUT PROPERTY—PROPERTY AS A 'BUNDLE OF RIGHTS'

The conceptual shift to thinking about property as a relationship rather than a thing, and realizing that transferability and excludability are the core features of a proprietary right, still leaves many of the subtleties of property undiscovered. Consider what it means to 'own' an asset. Honoré famously described the standard incidents of ownership as including the right to possess (although intangible property cannot be possessed), the right to use, the right to manage, the right to the income from the thing, the right to the capital, and the right to transfer. Even if we could agree that all these rights are essential to ownership, it is clear that they need not all be absolute. For example, a homeowner is entitled to live in her house and use it largely as she wishes. Importantly, however, she does not cease to be the owner when she leases the house to tenants, mortgages it to the bank, or grants her neighbour a right of way through the back garden. The various rights which go to make up ownership—and define the owner's special relationship with the property—can be parcelled out amongst a host of competing users without destroying the core rights which determine who owns the property. The 'owner' does not necessarily have *all* the rights over the thing. This realization adds a gloss to the idea of property. Ownership is not simply 'a' right; it is a 'bundle of rights'. Moreover, the bundle of rights that describes ownership does not define it precisely. An owner can transfer some of the rights in her ownership 'bundle' without ceasing to be the owner.

This 'bundle of rights' idea can be developed in still more sophisticated ways. When the owner of a house parcels out rights to various third parties, she gives some of them 'bundles of rights' which can themselves be described as proprietary, even though they do not amount to ownership. The tenant has a right to possess the property (on specific terms); the bank has the right to repossess the property and sell it (again, on

---

[4] Of course, the law could deny excludability in insolvency contexts, but law and economics scholars make the point that interfering with pre-insolvency property rights simply because the debtor is insolvent will inevitably give creditors unwarranted incentives to push the debtor into early insolvency.

specific terms); the neighbour had the right to use part of the property (once again, on specific terms). We distinguish these various bundles of rights by different labels. We say that the owner has an ownership interest in the property; the tenant a lease (a possessory interest); the bank a security interest; and the neighbour an easement. All these proprietary interests can exist concurrently. Moreover, the labels provide only a rough guide to the underlying bundles of rights. In all these examples, the rights themselves are determined by agreement between the parties. Not all tenants have the same rights, nor do all security holders, yet all have *some* sort of proprietary interest in the owner's house.

This conceptual shift from thinking about property as a 'thing', to thinking about it as a relationship, and now thinking about it as a 'bundle of rights' is crucial. It allows for a much more sophisticated interplay of relationships dealing with the use of things. 'Ownership' is only one of many possible proprietary interests in a particular thing. Other people besides the owner can also have different proprietary interests in the thing.

Notice, however, that not every right that an owner might allocate to others is necessarily a proprietary right. Owners commonly invite guests to their homes for dinner, or allow tradesmen to enter to perform work. These people certainly have rights, but they do not have proprietary rights. The test is transferability and excludability. Neither the guest nor the tradesman can exclude strangers from the house or transfer rights in the house to strangers.

Now that we have explored some of the core ideas about property, we are in a position to see how Equity manipulated these ideas to expand still further the boundaries of property.

EQUITY'S RECOGNITION OF NEW FORMS OF PROPERTY

Recall that social, political, moral, and economic values play an important part in determining whether certain things, or certain bundles of rights, will be regarded as property or not. Moreover, perceptions change. Once the law regarded slaves as property; now it does not. From what has already been said, we can see how these transitions might be achieved. One of the important attributes of property is that it is transferable: it is not just wealth; it is *usable* wealth. Without this attribute, however tightly circumscribed, a right is unlikely to be classed as property. For example, a contract of employment is clearly valuable; it generates wealth. But an employee cannot deal with his job; he cannot sell it to a third party for cash. However, if a right that is not transferable is somehow made transferable, the ultimate effect may be to create a new form of property.[5] Equity did this. It created new forms of property by permitting the transfer of rights that were not transferable at Common Law. Equity regarded these rights as proprietary (and transferable); the Common Law regarded them as personal (and not transferable).

To understand how Equity did this, and its economic significance, requires a short detour into terminology. The common law has a system of classifying rights (or wealth) that is quite different from the simple divisions we have dealt with so far. We have divided rights into property rights (where the bundle of rights includes transferability and excludability) and personal rights (where these attributes are lacking). The common law's older classification system thought of *all* rights as 'property' regardless of any special attributes of transferability or excludability. It then subdivided these rights according to the nature of the underlying 'thing', rather than the relationship of any person to that thing.

According to this classification system, property (or 'rights' or 'wealth') is first sub-divided into *real property* if it is an interest in land and *personal property* if it is any other interest.[6] Personal property is then further subdivided into *choses in possession* (or 'things in possession', to translate the French) and *choses in action* (or 'things in action'). Choses in possession are rights that can be claimed or enforced by possession. Examples include ownership of tangible assets such as cars, computers, or oil, all things that are capable of being physically held in possession. Choses in action are rights that can only be claimed or enforced by taking action against the right-giver, not by taking physical possession. Examples are debts, shares, or financial derivatives, where there is no thing that is capable of being physically held in possession. With debts, for example, the right-holder needs to sue the debtor to enforce the right. Although the detail cannot properly be understood yet, it is possible to have both Common Law and Equitable choses in action. Common Law (or 'legal') choses in action are those which, historically, could be enforced by action in a Common Law court. Debts, bills of exchange, insurance policies, and company shares are all examples. Equitable choses in action, such as the

---

[5] The need for excludability is discussed below, 62.

[6] Note that this involves a completely different use of the words 'real' (as in 'proprietary') and 'personal', although there is some sense of common lineage: 'real' rights reflected the fact that the Common Law would allow recovery of the asset itself (the asset being land); 'personal' rights sounded in damages only.

beneficiaries' rights to a share in the trust estate, are those which, historically, could only be enforced by action in the Court of Chancery.

Historically the Common Law considered it impossible to transfer *any* choses in action to third parties. Only interests in land and interests in tangible property were transferable. If we try to marry the two classification systems, then the Common Law regarded interests in real property and tangible property as *proprietary* interests; interests in intangible property were merely *personal* interests. This is unsurprising. It is consistent with most early views of property. When children or members of primitive societies think of property, they think of tangible assets such as land and goods; they do not think of choses in action such as promises of goods or services from friends or neighbours.

Equity changed this. It adopted a more expansive view of which forms of wealth should be treated as transferable property, or tradeable assets. It ignored the Common Law distinction between choses in action and choses in possession and allowed many (although not all) legal and Equitable choses in action to be freely transferable in Equity. The requirements for an effective transfer in Equity were very simple. The particular property had to be clearly identified, and the transferor had to communicate to the recipient his clear intention to transfer his property rights (either absolutely or some part of them).[7] There was no need for any formalities, and the transfer could be by gift or contract. Even today, the rules remain relatively simple, although modern statutes have now introduced compulsory writing requirements for the transfer of Equitable choses in action.[8] The significance of this different approach cannot be overestimated. Equity regarded some of these intangible rights as property; early Common Law, on the other hand, regarded them all as purely personal, enforceable only between the parties concerned, not transferable and not meriting protection against the world (or even a section of it).

Equity's different response no doubt reflected changing social and economic perceptions of usable wealth, and if Equity had not delivered legal change then the pressures would undoubtedly have been felt elsewhere. As it is, the Common Law perception of property has now changed too, although the change has been achieved by statute rather than by judicial intervention.[9] A general statutory provision now permits

[7] Before communication, the purported assignment is revocable.
[8] Law of Property Act 1925, s. 53(1)(c).
[9] Although it is true that by the nineteenth century the Common Law rule had its own exceptions and what was left of the rule was commonly evaded by various mechanisms: *Norman v Federal Commissioner of Taxation* (1963) 109 CLR 9 (Windeyer J).

the legal transfer of choses in action,[10] and specific statutes make special arrangements for particular sub-classes of choses in action (such as copy-rights, company shares, and policies of life assurance). This means that it is now possible to assign (or formally transfer) many choses in action at law, not just in Equity. All of this is designed to meet the commercial needs of modern society, where much wealth is held ultimately in the form of intangible assets (such as shares, bank deposits, and loans), rather than tangible assets. In short, both the Common Law and Equity now concede that, in general, these forms of intangible wealth ought to be transferable.

The changing Common Law rules have not consigned Equitable transfers to history. The Equitable route (even with its compulsory writing requirement for Equitable choses in action) is still much used. Sometimes this is because the assignment is only possible in Equity. For example, the statute makes it impossible to assign *part* of a debt at law; this can, however, be done in Equity. Sometimes it is to alleviate the adverse consequences of compliance with the strict requirements of Common Law. For example, compliance with the necessary statutory writing requirements may have unwanted consequences, such as liability to stamp duty. Finally, there are accidents. An assignment initially intended to take effect at Common Law may simply fail to satisfy some aspect of the statutory scheme. In these cases, assuming that the Equitable requirements are met, the assignment simply operates in Equity.[11]

This evolutionary change in the rights that the law regards as propri-etary seems, to modern eyes, unexceptional. Indeed, as both the Common Law and Equity now regard many choses in action as assignable, there does not even seem to be any risk of incoherence in the legal system. But in our discussions so far one important feature has undoubtedly been overlooked, and one complicating factor needs to be highlighted.

First, consider the feature that has been overlooked. We have talked blithely of assignments at Common Law and in Equity without ever stopping to think that these different mechanisms may have different consequences. Suppose A is owed £100 by B. If A assigns the debt to C at Common Law, following the statutory procedure, then A loses any rights to the debt and C becomes the Common Law owner of the legal chose in action. This is simple. It mirrors the transfer of a tangible asset such as a

---

[10] Law of Property Act 1925, s. 136.
[11] *William Brandt's Sons & Co v Dunlop Rubber Co Ltd* [1905] AC 454, 461 *per* Lord Macnaghten.

car. A was the legal owner; now C is. But now suppose that A effects the transfer in Equity. The Common Law does not recognize the transfer: at Common Law, A is still the Common Law owner of the debt. Equity, by contrast, does recognize the transfer: in Equity, C is the Equitable owner of the debt. This means that after the debt is transferred using the Equitable procedure, the Common Law says that A is the owner and Equity says that C is the owner. This result appears to be a nonsense. It is not, although it will take some working out in the next section to establish exactly what it means.

Secondly, consider the complicating factor. The focus here has been on transferability, and how Equity expanded the notion of property by conceding that certain rights could be transferred. We have ignored excludability, and its associated insolvency protection. Again suppose that A is owed £100 by B. This means that A is the owner of a chose in action (a debt). Think carefully about the attributes of this right. We know that A can transfer this right to C, either by the statutory procedure or by the older Equitable procedure. But if B becomes insolvent, then A's (or C's) claim to £100 will abate along with the claims of all of B's general creditors. The debt does not afford A (or C) any protection on B's insolvency—there is nothing from which B, or B's creditors, can be excluded. The chose in action has the attribute of transferability, but not the attribute of excludability and its associated insolvency protection. This is why debts are commonly described as 'personal' rights, not proprietary rights.[12] But in another sense debts *are* property, and more complicated transfer options can deliver a degree of insolvency protection to third parties, as we will see when we look at the use of debts as security.[13] The key is to realize that the property under discussion is not a right to £100; it is the intangible claim against B (with its value depending upon B's credit standing).

These complications aside, the crucial point is this: Equity 'created' new forms of property by changing the boundaries between personal rights and proprietary rights. It did this by contradicting the Common

---

[12] See above, 55–7. Note that modern Common Law has added to the armoury of protection available to choses in action by introducing the tort of 'inducing a breach of contract'. The tort makes it a legal wrong for strangers to interfere with A's chose in action by attempting to induce B not to perform according to his agreement with A. The result is that 'personal' rights embodied in choses in action are accorded a measure of protection against interference from strangers. This parallels the protection accorded to 'proprietary' rights, and we might conclude that the dividing line between contract and property (i.e. between personal rights and proprietary rights) is becoming increasingly blurred.

[13] See below, 77–81.

Law and permitting certain 'personal' rights to be transferred to third parties. These limited personal rights were thereby converted into transferable, usable wealth. The legal regime—and the social and economic regime—immediately became more sophisticated. Of course, these new forms of property needed legal protection, and so there was pressure on the legal system to evolve still further to deliver this protection, as we shall see in later chapters.

EQUITY'S RECOGNITION OF NEW CATEGORIES OF INTERESTS IN PROPERTY

Equity's second strategy for 'creating' property was quite different. This strategy took hundreds of years to emerge, although we can now describe it relatively simply. Put starkly, Equity took a 'bundle of rights' already regarded by the Common Law as 'proprietary' and divided the bundle between two or more people so that the interests of each were still significant enough to be regarded as proprietary. Explained like this, the strategy is not at all remarkable. The Common Law did precisely the same thing: recall our homeowner, who could divide her 'bundle of rights' with her tenant so that both had different proprietary interests in the house. What was truly remarkable, and unique, was *how* Equity divided the bundle, and the social and economic advantages that this additional sophistication then delivered.

Understanding the 'how' is best done through history. In Equity mythology, the story begins with the Crusaders.[14] Before the Crusaders went off to war, they would often transfer their lands to a trusted friend to manage for the benefit of their families. The arrangement was intended to evade certain compulsory tax and succession rules that would have come into play should the Crusader be killed in battle. Of course, the Common Law offered no support for these arrangements. If the Crusader returned from battle to reclaim his land, the Common Law held that he no longer had an estate: he had transferred all his rights to his trusted friend, who was now the owner. And if the Crusader was killed, then his family had no legal rights either: the trusted friend might feel morally bound to comply with the arrangement, but he was not legally bound; according to the Common Law, he had no contract with individual family members and the estate was his, not theirs.

---

[14] In truth, the Crusaders may have formed only a small percentage of the parties using this route to avoid unwelcome succession rules.

Predictably, disappointed family members petitioned the Chancellor to remedy this state of affairs. We might now wonder what could have persuaded the Chancellor to intervene in an arrangement so clearly intended to evade the Common Law. Nevertheless, by the thirteenth century, if not earlier, the Chancellor began to enforce the obligations undertaken by the trusted friend (now called the *trustee*). The Chancellor conceded that the trusted friend was the legal owner of the estate, but insisted that he was bound to manage the estate for the benefit of the family (now known as the *beneficiaries*) according to the agreement with the Crusader.

Put another way, the Chancellor recognized the beneficiaries as having personal rights against the trustee that entitled them to demand that the estate (the *trust property*) was managed according to the agreement. This was a dramatic contradiction of the Common Law position, which even today still usually insists that such rights can only arise if the beneficiaries themselves have a legally binding contract with the trustee.[15] The Chancellor constructed Equitable rights for the beneficiaries from the private arrangement between the Crusader (now described as the *settlor*) and his friend. This was the dramatic but essential first step in the evolution of new Equitable proprietary interests, although at this stage the beneficiaries' rights were clearly only personal rights against the trustee concerning his management responsibilities. Adopting the terminology introduced earlier, the beneficiaries had an Equitable chose in action. This chose entitled them to the enjoyment of the property managed by the trustee.

Equity's next step is now familiar. Equity reclassified these personal rights as proprietary rights. The process is not one of simply 'renaming' the rights, but of affording them special protection. This did not happen immediately, but by the nineteenth century it was certainly true that beneficiaries could transfer their bundles of rights to third parties (using the Equitable mechanism for the assignment of choses in action). More importantly, beneficiaries were protected on the trustee's insolvency: the beneficiaries could remove 'their' estate—their trust property—from the pool of trustee's assets which was to be sold and distributed to the trustee's general creditors. In short, they could exclude the trustee and the trustee's general creditors from interfering with their rights. The strength of this insolvency protection, and its parallels with the position the beneficiaries would have been in had they been the legal owners of the

---

[15] Although now see Contracts (Rights of Third Parties) Act 1999.

trust property, led to the beneficiaries being described as the *Equitable owners* of the trust property.

Indeed, the parallels with legal property did not stop there. The beneficiaries were also protected in non-insolvency situations. Just as legal owners of property can exclude interference by third parties, so too can beneficiaries. These rights to exclude third parties need a little thought. The legal owner of land can exclude trespassers, for example. The trustee, as legal owner of the land, can do the same. The beneficiaries do not need this sort of protection. The risk to them is that trustees who are so minded can sell off the trust property to third parties, take the money and run. The risk is high because trustees, as Common Law owners, can readily present themselves as having the right to sell the property. The beneficiaries could then be left with nothing. Equity adopted two strategies to deal with this problem. The first gave the beneficiaries rights of excludability. Equity insisted that any third parties who knew or ought to have known (i.e. had *constructive notice*) of the beneficiaries' rights had to recognize them. Some Common Law and statutory property rights, especially intellectual property rights, are also recognized only on this basis. The rule was worked out in this way. If the trust estate was *given* to a third party, he had to acknowledge the beneficiaries' interests once they were revealed to him. Although the third party became the Common Law owner of the property by virtue of the gift from the trustee, the beneficiaries could insist that the third party recognize their concurrent interest in the property (their Equitable ownership). On the other hand, if the trust property was *sold*, wrongfully, to a third party, then the beneficiaries could only insist that the third party recognize the beneficiaries' concurrent interests in the property if the third party had constructive notice that these interests existed at the time of his purchase. These rules meant that the only third parties who were unaffected by the beneficiaries' Equitable property rights were those who were innocent, honest, third-party purchasers without the necessary notice of the beneficiaries' rights. (These rare people—'bona fide purchasers for value without notice of the Equitable interests'—are sometimes known as 'Equity's darlings.'[16]) Equity's second strategy for protecting the beneficiaries' Equitable interests against the risks of defaulting trustees belongs in the next chapter. Equity allowed the beneficiaries to insist that if their lands had been wrongfully sold, then the proceeds of sale received by the trustee should become the new, substituted, trust property.[17]

---

[16] See Chapter 4, 95–7.   [17] See Chapter 4, 98–100.

Although the process took hundreds of years, once all these rules were in place it was clear that the rights of beneficiaries had become proprietary in almost the strongest sense imaginable. From a modern perspective, the beneficiaries' rights are transferable; they afford protection on the trustee's insolvency; and they entitle the holder to exclude interference by all third parties who have constructive notice of their existence. These rights could only be more proprietary if they allowed *all* third party infringements to be remedied. Moreover, as with all property, the rights were proprietary as soon as they were created. There was no need to wait until the courts actually enforced a particular protective rule; the knowledge that protection would be forthcoming was enough. The entire process was ingenious because Equity had not simply converted a personal right into a proprietary right. It had first *created* the novel personal right, and only then did it effect the conversion to proprietary status.

So what exactly is this novel right? What *is* Equitable ownership? The answer is that 'it depends'. Common Law ownership is the same. Think back to our homeowner and her tenant. Their different proprietary interests depend upon the precise terms of their arrangement. 'Ownership' and 'leasehold tenancy' might give a flavour of the interests involved, but the precise compass is a matter for agreement. It is the same with Equitable ownership. The term gives a flavour of the rights involved. The beneficiary is entitled to the benefits of the property being managed by the trustee. These benefits might include the right to reside in the property or to receive the income it generates. However, the possibilities are endlessly variable. They can be defined at will by the particular terms of the arrangement between the settlor (historically, our Crusader) and the trustee. Indeed, although the discussion so far has centred on a trustee's management of land, the trust property need not be land; it can be any item of tangible or intangible property, whether legal or Equitable.

This flexible arrangement between the settlor and the trustee under which the trustee holds trust property for the benefit of beneficiaries is called a *trust*. Our focus has been on the proprietary aspects of trusts, but Equity also made dramatic contributions on the personal front, developing the peculiar and distinctive notion of 'fiduciary' obligations. These obligations were initially devised to regulate trustees engaged in the management of trust property, although their compass is now much broader.[18] For now, however, what is important is Equity's ingenious strategy for

---

[18] See Chapter 5, 129, 140–2.

creating new categories of proprietary interests. Equity took the bundle of rights representing Common Law ownership and hived off from it a separate bundle of rights which entitled their holder to enjoy specified benefits from the property. The trustee (like our homeowner) retained Common Law ownership and management powers over the property; the beneficiary had 'Equitable ownership'.[19] Later in this chapter we will see Equity employ exactly the same strategy in constructing Equitable charges (which deliver yet another form of Equitable proprietary interests in an underlying asset). Equitable ownership rights are regarded as proprietary, not personal, simply because they now include rights to transfer to third parties and rights to exclude strangers. The legal evolution that delivered the trust took place over hundreds of years, but the trust is now commonly regarded as one of Equity's greatest contributions to the common law. Indeed, civil law jurisdictions—which do not have a concept of Equitable ownership—are increasingly looking at the enormous social and commercial advantages offered by the trust vehicle. These advantages are outlined later in this chapter, but first we need to understand better the various ways in which trusts are created.

CREATING TRUSTS—EXPRESS, CONSTRUCTIVE, AND RESULTING TRUSTS

Clearly trusts can be created by consensual arrangements between the settlor and the trustee. This is what the Crusaders attempted to do even before the law allowed it. Now such trusts are used in a wide range of circumstances, from multi-million pound pension trusts to relatively small family settlements. These trusts are *express trusts*, expressly created by the parties to achieve their own desired ends. The settlor transfers the trust property to the trustee on trust for the beneficiaries, specifying the terms of the trust in as much or as little detail as necessary. Indeed, the settlor can even declare himself to be the trustee, thereby cutting out the middle man.

The initial transfer of trust property from settlor to trustee sometimes requires special formalities; for example, land transfers and share

[19] Students would then like to say that the legal owner's 'bundle of rights' consists of a 'legal ownership' bundle and an 'Equitable ownership' bundle, so that the legal owner *is* also the Equitable owner. This is wrong, although the point always seems counter-intuitive to students. An analogy helps persuade. Students rarely apply the same logic to suggest that a homeowner is also a tenant, even though the homeowner *could* divide her ownership rights into ownership and tenancy rights.

transfers must be appropriately registered. This aside, express trusts can often be created quite informally.[20] All that is necessary is that the '*three certainties*' are met. First, the settlor's *intention* to create a trust must be certain. It is not necessary to use the word 'trust', and intention can even be inferred from the circumstances, but it must be an intention to benefit the beneficiaries *by way of trust*, not by gift or loan or contract or any other way. Secondly, the identity of the *trust property* must be certain: the trustee must know exactly what property must be managed.[21] Finally, the identity of the *beneficiaries* must be certain.[22] A complete list is unnecessary, but the settlor must define the class of beneficiaries sufficiently clearly so that the trustees know who is entitled to the benefit of the trust.[23] For example, a settlor may set up a trust for all the children of his forthcoming marriage to X. This defines the intended beneficiaries with sufficient certainty, even if the trust is set up before any children are born. The next section describes why this simple trust structure has proved so valuable in so many circumstances.

But not all trusts are created consensually. Equity sometimes imposes trusts in defiance of the parties' intentions. Put another way, there are times where Equity's *remedial orders* will create trusts. It is easy to see how this could happen. Indeed, this idea is what really lies behind the explanation for express trusts. With express trusts, the parties enter into certain arrangements about dividing the management and enjoyment of property. These arrangements have proprietary consequences *only because* Equity insists that the trustee *must* comply with the arrangements, that he must hold the property for the beneficiaries, and that the beneficiaries' rights are so strongly protected that they are transferable and protected from interference by third parties. These express trusts implement to the letter the agreed arrangements between the parties. However, in quite different circumstances Equity might nevertheless consider that the appropriate *remedy* is to insist that a defendant *must* transfer certain property to the claimant, and in the meantime must look after it for her benefit. If Equity, additionally, accords this remedial right the attributes

---

[20] Although the creation of trusts over land must be in writing: Law of Property Act 1925, s. 53(1)(b).

[21] *Hunter v Moss* [1994] 1 WLR 452 (CA); *Associated Alloys Pty Ltd v ACN 001 452 106 Pty Ltd* (2000) 202 CLR 588 (Aust HCt).

[22] The only exception to this is with charitable trusts, where the charitable *purpose* must be clear, although the law takes a restrictive view of what is 'charitable'.

[23] *Re Denley's Trust Deed* [1969] 1 Ch 373 (Goff J); *IRC v Broadway Cottages Trust* [1955] Ch 20 (CA); *McPhail v Doulton* [1971] AC 424 (HL); *Re Baden's Deed Trusts (No 2)* [1973] Ch 9 (CA); *Re Gulbenkian's Settlement Trusts, Whishaw v Stephens* [1970] AC 508 (HL).

of transferability and excludability, then the right is proprietary. It is a right generated by precisely the same sort of thinking that underpins the express trust arrangement. The difference is simply that the trust arises by operation of law (by operation of legal rules on the particular facts), rather than consensually.

At this stage we need do no more than illustrate this mode of Equitable intervention. It comes in two guises, just to add to the complications. Trusts arising by operation of law can be either *constructive trusts* or *resulting trusts*. Take constructive trusts first. We have seen the term 'constructive' already, in 'constructive notice'. In law, 'constructive' usually means 'is not [X], but because of the surrounding circumstances will be treated as if it were [X]'. So constructive notice is not actual notice, but is treated as if it were. Equally, a constructive trust is not an express trust, although presumably it will be treated as if it were. In the interests of justice, the court construes the trust from the circumstances of the case, even though the parties themselves do not intend to create a trust. As we will see in later chapters, constructive trusts can arise in many different circumstances. One simple example will do here.

Recall from the previous chapter that when Common Law damages for breach of contract are inadequate, Equity may sometimes order specific performance of the underlying agreement. A purchaser who has agreed to purchase shares in a private company, for example, can obtain an order that the vendor specifically perform the agreement.[24] The vendor will be ordered to transfer the shares to the claimant and, in the meantime, he will be held responsible for looking after them on the purchaser's behalf. This mirrors the rights under express trusts, although here the trust arises not because the parties intended it, but simply because Equity is prepared to order specific performance of the contract. The similarities do not end there. If the vendor becomes insolvent before he complies with this order to transfer, the shares are protected: the purchaser can withdraw them from the pool of assets to be sold to pay the

---

[24] See Chapter 2, 24–7. A purchaser who has agreed to purchase a Ming vase can also obtain an order that the defendant specifically perform the agreement, but the effect of the order will differ depending upon whether legal title has already passed to the purchaser prior to delivery, as it often does. If the purchaser has already acquired legal title, then there can be no trust: the purchaser is already the legal (and beneficial) owner; she simply does not have possession, and this the court will order the defendant to give her. On the other hand, if property has not passed, and the vendor still has legal title, then the fact that the contract is specifically enforceable will entail that the defendant holds the vase on trust for the purchaser, just as in the case of the shares in the private company.

vendor's creditors. And if the vendor attempts to transfer the shares to a third party, the purchaser can insist that the third party recognize her Equitable rights so long as the third party has actual or constructive notice of those rights. This picture of Equitable protection against interference by strangers confirms that the purchaser has Equitable ownership of the shares, even though the vendor still has the legal title (and will keep this until the shares are formally registered in the purchaser's name). It is therefore appropriate to say that the vendor holds the shares on trust—on constructive trust—for the purchaser.

The legal reasoning that delivers this proprietary result is, by now, quite familiar. Equity first invents a new personal right, the right to specific performance. Equity then protects this right. If the protection is extensive enough, then strangers will not be able to interfere with the right. The right may also be transferable. With these attributes, the right is properly classified as property. Exactly the same two steps were taken by Equity in developing the express trust. Neither step can be regarded as an inevitable legal development, but taken together they effectively generate new interests in property.

There is one potential twist in the story. It has to do with timing. Does the purchaser have a protected property interest in the shares only after the court has formally ordered the defendant to specifically perform the contract, or does she have it much earlier, perhaps as soon as she has entered into the contract with the vendor? It turns out that she has it early. This is critical to her insolvency protection. If she had no property rights until she had been to court, then third parties whose rights arose earlier would almost inevitably defeat her claims to the shares.[25] This means that the timing issue is critical, and potentially controversial.[26] The reasoning on these facts is the same reasoning that operates with express trusts. Think of our express trust beneficiaries. Their Equitable right to sue the trustee does not have to be exercised to give the beneficiaries an interest in the trust property. They have an interest because if they *did* go to court the court would enforce the trust (against strangers as well as against the trustee). The same is true of our purchaser. She has an Equitable right to specific performance. This right is proprietary because *if* she went to court the court would enforce the right (against strangers as well as the vendor). The difference between the two stories is that the beneficiaries of an express trust always have a right to sue their trustee for specific performance of the trust arrangement; it follows that these

---

[25] See Chapter 4, 92–8.   [26] See Chapter 8, 264–7.

beneficiaries always have property rights.[27] The same is not true of purchasers. Not every purchaser can sue for specific performance, so not all purchasers will have property rights. The court may have to decide *whether* the right exists. However, *if* the right exists, it exists from the date of the circumstances that generate it. This same rule applies elsewhere. The court may have to decide whether there has been a breach of contract and what losses are recoverable, for example, but the claimant's *right* to damages, if it exists at all, exists from the date of the breach, not from the date of the court's determination that the right does indeed exist and has a particular value.

The second form of trust which arises by operation of law is a *resulting trust*. The dividing line between resulting trusts and constructive trusts is not clear. What is clear, however, is that with resulting trusts Equitable ownership 'jumps back' ('results back') to the original legal owner. For example, if D transfers shares to C, but C holds them on resulting trust, then C will have legal title to the shares, but D will be their Equitable owner. (Equitable ownership will have 'jumped back' to him.) This feature suggests that resulting trusts are mechanisms for returning property to its rightful owner. Put another way, resulting trusts reverse unjust enrichments. Resulting trusts are considered in more detail later;[28] here, again, a simple example will suffice.

When A transfers property to B without receiving payment from B, Equity will presume that A did *not* intend the transfer to be a gift.[29] This is perhaps surprising, although Equity always seems to treat *volunteers* (meaning, in law, those who have not provided some consideration or counter-performance) rather harshly. Indeed, Equity goes further. It will order B to return the property and, in the meantime, to hold it for the benefit of A unless B can prove that a gift (or some other commercial arrangement) was intended. We know from what has gone before that,

[27] This is not quite true. Beneficiaries of '*discretionary trusts*', where the trustee has a discretion to distribute the trust funds, do not have property rights because even if the trustee's duties are specifically enforced, the beneficiary will not necessarily receive anything from the exercise. See, more generally, *Schmidt v Rosewood Trust Ltd* [2003] 2 AC 709 (PC).

[28] See Chapter 9, 303–7. Constructive trusts, by contrast, appear to be used to remedy breaches of contract and certain other civil wrongs.

[29] There are some twists in this, especially if B is a close relative: see Chapter 8, 257–9. '*Automatic resulting trusts*' provide another illustration: if assets are held on express trusts, but the trust does not provide for the allocation to beneficiaries of the entire interest in all the trust property, then the unallocated property is held by the trustee on resulting trust for the settlor. This is because the settlor, in creating the trust, is automatically presumed to intend to retain an interest in any assets that are not explicitly delivered to others via the trust: *Air Jamaica Ltd v Charlton* [1999] 1 WLR 1399 (PC).

once Equity decides to protect this underlying right, the order is effectively an order that B hold the property on trust for A with all the attendant proprietary protections that involves. This form of resulting trust is known as a *presumed resulting trust*, generated because of Equity's presumptions about the initial transfer.[30]

Here, again, Equity's promotion of a right to proprietary status proceeds by two simple steps. First, an enforceable right defines the extent of the claimant's interest in the underlying property by compelling the property owner to deliver certain benefits derived from the property. Secondly, Equity promotes this right to the status of property by insisting that third parties cannot interfere with it. Once the law has embraced these two steps, the right-holder is regarded as having an Equitable proprietary interest in the underlying property even though the defendant is its legal owner.

Notice that one important difference between express, constructive, and resulting trusts is the different management obligations imposed on the defendant trustee. Each type of trust gives the claimant 'Equitable ownership' of the underlying asset, but this formula merely gives a general flavour of the underlying rights. With express trusts, the trustee is obliged to manage the property according to the terms of the trust deed. This may require the trustee to take an active role in investing and re-investing the funds in the most advantageous way. With constructive trusts, the trustee must invariably take reasonable care of the property, and may even have to do more if the circumstances warrant it. The court will *construe* the appropriate management terms on the basis of what is reasonable given the surrounding circumstances (this is why the trust is a *constructive* trust). Finally, with resulting trusts, the trustee is not generally subjected to any management obligations at all; the only obligation is to re-transfer the property to the claimant.

This abbreviated description of how express, constructive and resulting trusts are created will be revisited in later chapters. Nevertheless, it is already possible to see why these Equitable interests can be so controversial. Every property interest is potentially contentious because its holder is preferred over those who have only personal rights. With constructive and resulting trusts, however, there are added reasons for debate. The parties have not agreed to or paid for insolvency protection. It follows that the various different circumstances in which these trusts arise deserve exacting analysis. Modern courts are becoming more

---

[30] All of this is now becoming increasingly controversial: see Chapter 9, 303–7.

reluctant to decide that the primary right compels the defendant to deliver a benefit related to the underlying property, rather than simply requiring the defendant to make compensation in money. They are also more circumspect in agreeing that the primary right has been accorded proprietary status, so that the right-holder can exclude strangers. And, finally, even when the courts are persuaded that the right is proprietary, they are more sceptical about when the right arises. All of these moves signal a retreat from past practices, where the issues often seemed to be resolved so as to expand the reach of Equitable property.

Past practice was usually to ground the explanation of these trusts in the maxim that 'Equity treats as done that which ought to be done'. *If* Equity insists that the trusted friend must hold the property for the benefit of the family, or that the vendor must transfer the shares to the purchaser, or that the donee must return the 'gift', then the maxim would have it that this is to be treated as already done. Accordingly, the benefits of the estate are treated as already held by the family; the shares are treated as already transferred to the purchaser; and the gift as already returned to the donor. In each case, the implication is that the claimant is the Equitable owner of the underlying property. The use of the maxim in this way has been justifiably criticized as disguising the crucial steps that underpin the conclusion that a proprietary interest has been generated. Equity *may* treat all these things as done, but this statement reflects a conclusion that probably only emerged slowly, as Equity decided what obligations it would enforce, and whether they would be enforced specifically, and how well the resulting rights would be protected against third parties.

THE ADVANTAGES OF TRUSTS

Now that the idea of a trust is clearer, with its ingenious splitting of the ownership 'bundle of rights' into legal and Equitable ownership, it is possible to explore some of the enormous practical advantages of the trust. The most obvious and remarkable feature of express trusts is their complete break with the Common Law doctrines of *privity* and *consideration*. These two doctrines severely limit the enforceability of contractual arrangements. At Common Law, a person cannot enforce a contract unless he is a party to the deal (i.e. unless there is 'privity') and unless the other party has received or been promised something in return (i.e. unless there is 'consideration' or reciprocity in the deal).[31] This means that

---

[31] See Chapter 8, 229–30.

promised gifts are not enforceable. Moreover, the remedy for contractual non-performance is money; only exceptionally will Equity order specific performance of the agreement.[32] The modern trust subverts all of these rules. Beneficiaries are allowed to enforce the arrangement even though they are not parties to the deal and have not provided consideration. Moreover, they can obtain specific performance of the terms of the trust regardless of the unexceptional nature of the underlying property. All of this is very strange to Common Law eyes: promised gifts, when promised by means of a declaration or establishment of a trust, *are* (specifically) enforceable. Interestingly, civil law jurisdictions would see little strange in this; what they do find strange is that the response is mediated through proprietary rights (with all their associated benefits) rather than through personal ones.

Secondly, trusts make it possible for parties to hold interests in property in circumstances where the Common Law would prohibit this. For example, minors can be given property interests in land and other assets that they could not own at law because of their age. Indeed, trusts not only provide the minor with all the benefits of proprietary interests, but they also impose onerous management obligations on the trustee.[33] This combination is far better for the minor than anything that could be achieved by simple contract. Modern trusts are also used, perhaps more questionably, to allow parties to circumvent restrictions on ownership that arise from status rather than from age. For example, Government Ministers cannot have business interests that conflict with their portfolio; foreign nationals cannot own certain domestic assets. Finally, trusts can sometimes be used to avoid the consequences of tax and competition laws. (In the US, competition laws were originally known as 'anti-trust' laws, designed to defeat vast trust-owned monopolies.) Perhaps predictably, the success of the trust device in all these arenas is variable.

Thirdly, trusts enable proprietary interests to be divided along a time line. A trustee can hold a Rembrandt painting on trust 'for A for life, then B for life, remainder to C' (and death need not be the only marker along the time line). This arrangement gives each party (the trustee, A, B and C) some immediate proprietary interest in the painting, with all the protection this entails, even though B and C will have to wait some time before they are entitled to possession of the painting. A contract could achieve a similar result, but again without the important protections that proprietary interests afford. This strategy of dividing interests along a

---

[32] See Chapter 2, 23–7.   [33] See Chapter 5, 129–30.

time line is not peculiar to Equity. The Common Law doctrine of estates makes this type of property split possible with land, although the Common Law refused to extend the practice to personal property.

Fourthly, trusts enable the benefits of ownership to be split from the responsibilities of management. Without the trust, property owners are responsible for the management of their own property. They may employ others to undertake the task, but they remain ultimately responsible for the outcome. With a trust, the Equitable owners obtain the benefits of ownership while the responsibility for management lies with the trustees. Trustees may of course employ others to undertake the task, but the trustees remain responsible for the management of the property. This is as true in small family trusts as in billion pound pension trusts: the family members or the pension beneficiaries reap the benefits of management by trustees. This possibility of specialist management is undoubtedly con- venient, but the trust delivers further advantages that contract cannot fully replicate. In particular, the beneficiaries have the advantage of proprietary protection coupled with the administrative convenience of leaving legal title in the trustees. In addition, trustees are automatically subjected to onerous *fiduciary obligations* of loyalty in carrying out their management functions.[34] Few other management arrangements have *all* these advantages. The split of ownership and control that is evident in modern corporations has obvious parallels, but corporations emerged as legal vehicles only a hundred years ago, several hundred years after the trust. Moreover, there the split is achieved only because the law recog- nizes companies as legal persons; the trust has no need for such fictions.

Fifthly, trusts achieve a unique form of asset partitioning. This is an invaluable and ingenious commercial achievement, and is critically dependent on the peculiar proprietary attributes of the trust. The normal Common Law rule is that each individual holds one undivided patri- mony: *all* of an individual's assets are exposed to the claims of all of the individual's creditors. If an individual runs a business, for example, then his business risks are not isolated from his personal investments: business creditors can look to all the assets, including the family home, for payment of their debts; equally, personal creditors can look to both busi- ness and personal assets for payment of their debts. The law does not recognize any notional divide between business and personal spheres of activity. This inevitably makes both business and personal creditors feel over-exposed to unwarranted risks. The trust vehicle—whether it is a

---

[34] See Chapter 5, 131–4.

business trust or a personal trust—can solve this dilemma. At the simplest level, a businessman can declare that he holds the family home on trust for his partner and children. His business creditors cannot then gain access to this asset when they are seeking payment of their debts. Although the businessman remains the legal owner of the home, his nominated beneficiaries are the Equitable owners. As such, they have the right to exclude strangers (the businessman's general creditors) from interfering. Equally, the strategy could be applied in reverse. The business assets can be isolated in a trust vehicle, protecting them from the claims of the trustees' personal creditors. In this way, particular business risks can be isolated from each other and from non-business risks. Much large-scale commercial activity could not proceed without the protections inherent in this sort of asset partitioning. The trust was one of the earliest vehicles to achieve this goal and to recognize the commercial advantages it could deliver. Similar ends are now achieved by companies and, to a much lesser extent, by modern security law (also invented by Equity).[35] However, the trust mechanism remains unique, and probably the chief reason that civilian jurisdictions did not feel the need to invent their own versions of the trust is that many civil law jurisdictions are familiar with divided patrimony in different contexts, and so the trust's achievement is perhaps not so remarkable to them.

Sixthly, trusts embody the idea of a *fund*. This may seem simple, but it too has significant commercial consequences. It effects a further type of asset partitioning. Suppose the trust property is a bookstore and the trustees have to manage the business so as to maximize the value of the trust assets. The business is regarded as a trust 'fund'. The value of the fund depends on the value of the fixed and circulating assets, less the business debts. The beneficiaries' entitlements are not to particular books or buildings or income, but simply to a share of the 'fund'. This is a net interest, assessed net of the entitlements of the business creditors. Put another way, the business creditors have privileged access to the pool of trust assets; the beneficiaries (and their general creditors, should the beneficiaries become insolvent) are only entitled to a share in the balance remaining in the fund. This means that the 'fund' effects a form of asset partitioning which prioritizes access to the trust fund for the trust's business creditors rather than for the beneficiaries' creditors. This makes trusts attractive to business creditors. These creditors can deal with the business without worrying about the credit standing of all the trust

---

[35] See below, 77–81.

beneficiaries; they can rest confident that they will be paid first, before the beneficiaries can make any claims. This fund-related form of asset partitioning is a still more sophisticated version of the ideas advanced in the previous paragraph. Both forms of asset partitioning are hard to replicate by contract, and are enormously advantageous to business.

Finally, trusts are enormously flexible in slicing up property rights in ways that would be inconceivable without the trust. Consider company shares. A shareholder who wishes to deal with his shares can only transfer full ownership or a security interest in the entire bundle of rights associated with the share. He cannot sell part of a share; he certainly cannot parcel out the different benefits inherent in shareholding to different transferees, giving one the right to dividends, another the right to vote and yet another the right to capital gains. Under the umbrella of a trust, however, all of this is possible. The owner (as settlor) simply has to specify the beneficiaries' rights under the trust in the appropriate way. This idea is used in large-scale 'asset securitization trusts'. Suppose the trust property in the head trust is a bundle of *receivables* of different quality (i.e. debts owed to the trustee by different debtors with different credit standing). A trust beneficiary of this head trust has an Equitable interest in a *pro rata* share of those receivables. He can certainly deal with his interest simply by transferring it (or a part of it), or using it as security. But he can also repackage the receivables into high risk and low risk tranches, and then on-sell those divided tranches to third parties— and he can do all this while he is not the legal owner of any debts, and only has an Equitable part interest in a fund. This astonishing flexibility has real commercial benefit in enabling beneficiaries to deal with their interests in ways that could not be imagined in a non-trust world.

These, in outline, are the principal advantages associated with trusts. The first four would have been obvious from the brief description of trusts given earlier in this chapter. However, it is the last three—the various forms of asset partitioning and the potential for repackaging of proprietary interests—that explain the enormous commercial significance of modern trusts.

CREATING SECURITY INTERESTS—EQUITABLE CHARGES AND EQUITABLE LIENS

The third of Equity's significant contributions to property law, and the final one to be considered in this chapter, is Equity's contribution to security interests. The idea behind security is simple. Security is a proprietary interest granted to back up the performance of a personal obligation. For example, a farmer may promise that if he does not repay a loan then the lender can take the farmer's tractor, sell it, and use the proceeds to recoup the outstanding debt. This reduces the insolvency risk for the lender. Instead of being an unsecured general creditor if the farmer goes bankrupt, he will have a proprietary interest in the tractor, and, at least to the extent that the tractor is a valuable asset, he will be protected from loss. The corresponding advantage to the farmer is that he will find it easier to raise capital if he can offer security. Because security interests are only intended to back up personal obligations (usually loans), three things follow. If the obligation is met, then the security interest lapses. Secondly, if the obligation is breached and the security is enforced, but the proprietary rights realize more for the creditor than the unperformed obligation, then the creditor has to account to the debtor for the excess. Thirdly, if there is a shortfall, the creditor can sue the debtor on his personal obligation to recover the outstanding amount.

The Common Law has its own well-established security arrangements in the form of mortgages, pledges, and Common Law liens. However, all these devices are based on modified rights of Common Law ownership or possession. They do not create new forms of proprietary interest.[36] The ingenuity of Equity's contribution was to create a completely new form of proprietary interest that is quite distinct from ownership or possession. Equity took the debtor's Common Law ownership 'bundle of rights' and hived off from it a smaller bundle of rights for the creditor which it then protected sufficiently so that these rights, too, were classed as property. We can already anticipate how Equity achieved this. It took a personal obligation that related to property, insisted it was specifically enforceable, and then protected the right against interference by strangers.

Take the farmer who promises that his tractor can be appropriated to the discharge of a debt due to his lender. Equity will specifically

[36] For example, a pledge (or pawn) depends upon the debtor giving the creditor possession of the asset; if the debtor defaults, the creditor can then sell the pawned asset and recoup the loan. Common Law liens give creditors the right to retain assets that have come into their possession for other purposes. For example, a garage can keep possession of a car delivered for service or repairs until the owner has paid for the service (the garage has a Common Law lien over the car). Common Law mortgages are based on the debtor transferring legal title to the creditor on the understanding that title will be retransferred if the debt is repaid. Note that modern 'mortgages' of land are *not* Common Law mortgages; they are legal charges created by statute: the debtor remains the legal owner of the house and stays in possession, but the lender can take possession and sell the house if there is a default in repayment.

enforce this contract because Common Law damages would be wholly inadequate: what the parties have agreed to is insolvency-protected repayment; what Common Law damages would deliver is an unsecured personal damages claim ranking equally with other creditors' claims.[37] Specific enforcement of the contract means that the farmer retains ownership and possession of the tractor, but if the farmer defaults the lender is entitled (by the terms of the agreement) to assume possession of the tractor, sell it, and recoup the outstanding debt from the proceeds of sale (with any excess being returned to the debtor). The lender has an interest in the tractor defined by these rights. Equity will not allow strangers to interfere with these rights, as that too would destroy the security.[38] This means the rights are proprietary. These interests are known as *Equitable charges* if they are created by agreement and *Equitable liens* (not to be confused with Common Law liens, with which they have little in common) when they are created by operation of law (i.e. non-consensually, by operation of legal rules in the particular circumstances). Recall the analogous relationship between express trusts (created consensually) and resulting and constructive trusts (created by operation of law). We would say that the farmer has granted the lender a charge over the tractor: the lender has a security interest in the tractor, with the specific rights defined by the security agreement itself. Alternatively, the lender has a lien on the tractor, with the specific rights defined by the particular circumstances.

Equitable charges have two obvious advantages. The principal one is that they provide the creditor with strong protection on the debtor's insolvency. If the debtor becomes insolvent, then the creditor can exercise rights against the secured asset without interference from the debtor or the debtor's general creditors (although sometimes, as noted below, only if the charge is properly registered). In this respect, a charge is an asset-partitioning device like the trust, although the proprietary rights associated with it are far more limited. The second advantage is practical. The debtor retains ownership and possession of the asset. He can continue to use the asset in his business or social life; he is only at risk of losing his

---

[37] Note that Equity will not specifically enforce contracts that are not supported by consideration; it follows that consideration is necessary for the creation of a charge, since without specific performance no property rights would be created: *Re Earl of Lucan* (1890) 45 ChD 470. Trusts, as discussed earlier, really are exceptional.

[38] For the practical difficulties in determining whether charges or some other interest have been created, see *Re Bond Worth Ltd* [1980] Ch 288 (Slade J) and *Clough Mill Ltd v Martin* [1985] 1 WLR 111 (CA).

property if he defaults in his repayments. No Common Law security device delivers this commercial and social benefit to the debtor.

These advantages come at a price, however. There is a risk that strangers may assume that debtors are more wealthy than they really are. Assets that appear to be owned outright may be standing as security for various obligations. To reduce this risk, the law now insists that most charges must be registered on public registers if they are to be effective against strangers. For example, charges over land must be registered in the public land registers; and almost all charges granted by companies over any of their assets must be registered at Companies House. If this is done, then strangers are taken to have constructive notice of the creditor's security interest (by virtue of its registration) and they are then excluded from interfering with it.

Two further features of charges add to their commercial advantages. First, a debtor can promise to charge assets that he does not yet own. This may seem like an odd thing to do, but it allows newly acquired assets to be swept into the security without the need for the parties to enter into a new agreement with each new acquisition. Charges over plant and equipment in a factory, for example, might usefully be structured this way.

The second feature of charges takes a little more explaining, but again it provides strong evidence of the flexibility of Equitable concepts of property, and the commercial motivations which compel this flexibility. All the charges we have considered so far, whether over present or future property, give rise to familiar types of proprietary interests. The security arrangement gives the creditor particular rights over the charged assets that cannot be interfered with by either the debtor or other third parties. This means that the debtor cannot dispose of the charged asset without first obtaining the creditor's consent. If he did he would destroy the creditor's ability to enforce the security because the relevant assets would no longer be in the debtor's possession. This all seems very sensible, until we pause to think about how many businesses operate. A large part of their wealth is tied up in stock ready for sale. Consider the computer factory that has computers rolling off the assembly line by the hour, or the clothing company that duplicates this process with designer jeans. Under the orthodox notion of a charge, this stock cannot be charged because the debtor needs to deal with it to generate the income needed to repay his loan. Nevertheless, from the creditor's perspective, if the debtor *should* default on the loan, then a charge over whatever computers or designer jeans happened to be in the factory or under the manufacturer's control at the time of the default would be better than no charge at all over these assets. The English courts saw the commercial sense in this, and a hundred years ago they sanctioned the creation of a *floating charge*, so named to distinguish it from the orthodox *fixed charge*.

A floating charge over the debtor's computer production, for example, is structured to allow the debtor to deal with his computers in the ordinary course of business, selling them to wholesalers according to his normal practices, all without the need to obtain any consent from the creditor. This state of affairs can continue until the debtor defaults on his loan repayments, or ceases operating his business. At this point the creditor has the right to 'crystallize' the floating charge (according to the terms of the charge agreement). Crystallization of a floating charge is a bit like stopping the music in a game of musical chairs. All the computers that have already left the factory or passed outside the manufacturer's control are free of the security interest; all the computers remaining in the factory or within the manufacturer's control become subject to a fixed charge. These factory computers are then at the *creditor's* disposal as security to back the debtor's outstanding repayment obligations.

This arrangement may not seem troublesome; it may even seem commercially sensible. But courts in the United States, faced with the same problem at the same time as the English courts, declined to adopt this strategy. They regarded the purported 'proprietary' interests of the creditor under an uncrystallized floating charge as too ephemeral to be classed as security. Even today, the United States remains the only common law country without a floating charge, although commercial pressures have ensured that its function is now delivered by a statutory security mechanism made possible by the Uniform Commercial Code.[39] Admittedly, although the floating charge may say much about the inventiveness of Equity, not all the press has been good. Floating charges have come under sustained attack, especially in the past few decades, because they allow powerful debt capital providers (such as banks or major suppliers) to demand security over *all* the assets comprising a business at any given time. If the business then goes under, the secured investor takes all, leaving nothing for the small and unprotected, unsecured creditors.[40]

---

[39] Many other Commonwealth countries are now departing from the Equitable model, and instead adopting this type of statutory security vehicle.

[40] This is often the practical result, although the Insolvency Act 1986 provides some specific relief for unsecured creditors. See *National Westminster Bank Plc v Spectrum Plus Ltd (in creditors' vol liq)* [2005] 2 AC 680, [2005] UKHL 41 (HL) as an illustration of the battles.

THE LIMITS OF EQUITABLE PROPERTY—
PERSONAL RIGHTS AND 'MERE EQUITIES'

So far this chapter has focused exclusively on the enormous power of Equity to create new forms of property and new interests in property. An Equitable right is proprietary, so it seems, if it compels the defendant to hold identified property for the benefit of the claimant, allows the claimant to transfer the right, and excludes strangers from interfering with it. The extent of the benefit determines whether the right is one of ownership or security. But not all Equitable rights can be—or should be—regarded as property. Many Equitable rights are purely personal. They are rights enforceable only against the particular defendant; they are not attached to any particular item of property and do not give the claimant a proprietary interest in any asset. There are numerous examples of such Equitable personal rights. When an injunction is ordered against a newspaper to prevent publication of defamatory material, or against a builder to provide retaining wall support, the injunction is a personal remedy. So too is the remedy of rescission which might be granted to unwind contracts of employment or other contracts for personal services. In none of these cases does the successful claimant acquire an interest in any of the defendant's property, although the remedy may be of enormous value notwithstanding this.

In the middle, in between Equitable proprietary rights and Equitable personal rights, there are interests which have been labelled *mere equities*. Their definition is difficult. However, the class includes at least those interests which, *once pursued*, will entitle their holder to an Equitable proprietary interest in some asset. For example, a claimant with the right to rectify a lease is said to have a mere equity, the assertion of which will lead to the claimant having a revised lease. In the same way, the right to rescind a sale is said to be a mere equity: it will, if exercised, lead to the claimant's acquisition of a proprietary interest in the recovered sale property.[41] A mere equity is not as secure as a full Equitable proprietary right, although it does afford a measure of protection against third parties. If the defendant disposes of the underlying asset before the claimant exercises the mere equity (the right to rescind, for example), then the claimant cannot later claim an overriding proprietary interest unless the third party is a volunteer or has taken an interest

---

[41] Admittedly, this assertion is becoming increasingly controversial: see Chapter 9, 298–303.

in the property with actual or constructive notice of the claimant's conflicting interest. The rule does not simply favour 'Equity's darling' (the bona fide purchaser of a legal interest); it also favours bona fide purchasers of Equitable interests. This means that the attribute of excludability is more limited than with full proprietary interests, but, despite this, these rights are clearly more advantageous than simple personal rights.[42]

REVIEW

The ideas in this chapter are probably the most difficult in the book. They are probably also the most influential and the most engrossing. Certainly they underlie many of the controversies and difficulties exposed in later chapters. Nevertheless, the key concepts are elementary.

The starting point is the concept of property. Property is not a thing, but a relationship with a thing. The elements of a proprietary relationship are not rigidly defined. Quite different 'bundles of rights' can be classed as property. These bundles of rights can be generated by the agreed arrangements between parties or by the form of judicial intervention deemed to be warranted in the circumstances. Agreed arrangements give rise to express trusts and Equitable charges; judicial intervention gives rise to constructive trusts, resulting trusts and Equitable liens. The labels give no more than a flavour of the rights involved. Within this vast range of possibilities, two attributes determine whether a right is proprietary or personal. A right is proprietary if it is transferable and if it entitles the owner to exclude third parties from interfering with the right.

Equity 'created' new proprietary interests by two mechanisms. First, it permitted the transfer of entire 'bundles of rights' that the Common Law had regarded as immobile. These rights (choses in action) were accordingly converted from personal rights which could simply be enjoyed to proprietary rights which could also be traded. Secondly, Equity permitted novel divisions of bundles of rights already regarded as property by the Common Law (and sometimes already regarded as divisible by the Common Law, but not in these novel ways). Equity adopted this 'repackaging of rights' to deliver Equitable ownership (express, resulting and constructive trusts) and Equitable security interests (Equitable charges and Equitable liens).

---

[42] See Chapter 4, 87–9.

Equity

Equitable ownership rights, especially as delivered by express trusts, entitle the right-holder to the benefits of an asset without attracting management responsibilities. The legal owner is the manager, obliged to manage the property in the interests of the Equitable owner. This new division of rights combines strong proprietary protection for the Equitable owner with the advantages of onerous management obligations imposed on the legal owner. This simple vehicle allows for asset partitioning of the trust fund from incursions by either the trustee's or the beneficiaries' general creditors, and also allows for endlessly flexible packaging and repackaging of proprietary interests in ways not possible at Common Law.

Equitable security interests entitle the right-holder to strong proprietary protection to secure the performance of unrelated personal obligations owed by the legal owner of the asset (or any other party). Their advantage is that they do not require the right-holder to take possession of the underlying property: security can be achieved without depriving the legal owner of the commercial and social use of his property. Security interests, too, demonstrate Equity's flexibility in the creation of proprietary interests, as illustrated by the unusual rights and powerful commercial advantages associated with the floating charge.

Explained like this, Equity's decisions about transferability or repackaging of bundles of rights might have been made by any court. The decisive factor is a social, political, and economic perception of what should count as property, and then of course the institutional flexibility that permits 'judicial law-making' to deliver the chosen consequences. When these various changes were mooted, courts of Chancery appeared best able to deliver the coveted ends.

SELECTED BIBLIOGRAPHY

Emery, C., 'The Most Hallowed Principle—Certainty of Beneficiaries of Trusts and Powers of Appointment' (1982) 98 LQR 551.

Grantham, R., 'Doctrinal Bases for the Recognition of Proprietary Rights' (1996) 16 OJLS 561.

Gray, K., 'Property in Thin Air' [1991] CLJ 253.

Gretton, G. L., 'Trusts Without Equity' (2000) International and Comparative Law Quarterly 599.

Goode, R., 'Inalienable Rights?' (1979) 42 MLR 553.

Hansmann, H., and Kraakman, R., 'Property, Contract and Verification: The *Numerus Clausus* Problem and the Divisibility of Rights' (2002) 31 Journal of Legal Studies 373.

—— and Mattei, U., 'The Functions of Trust Law: A Comparative Legal and Economic Analysis' (1998) 73 New York University Law Review 434.

Hayton, D., 'Uncertainty of Subject-Matter of Trusts' (1994) 110 LQR 335.

Honoré, A. M., 'Ownership' in A. Guest (ed.), *Oxford Essays in Jurisprudence* (Oxford: Oxford University Press, 1961), p. 106.

Langbein, J. H., 'The Contractarian Basis of the Law of Trusts' (1995) 105 Yale Law Journal 625.

——, 'The Secret Life of the Trust: The Trust as an Instrument of Commerce' (1997) 107 Yale Law Journal 165.

Penner, J., 'The Bundle of Rights Picture of Property' (1996) 43 University of California at Los Angeles Law Review 711.

Rudden, B., 'Things as Things and Things as Wealth' (1994) 14 OJLS 81.

Scott, A., 'The Nature of the Rights of the Cestui Que Trust' (1917) 17 Columbia Law Review 269.

Waters, D. M. W., 'The Nature of the Trust Beneficiary's Interest' (1967) 45 Canadian Bar Review 219.

Worthington, S., 'An "Unsatisfactory Area of the Law"—Fixed and Floating Charges Yet Again' (2004) 1 International Corporate Rescue 175.

——, 'The Disappearing Divide Between Property and Obligation: The Impact of Aligning Legal Analysis and Commercial Expectation' in S. Degeling and J. Edelman (eds), *Equity in Commercial Law* (Sweet & Maxwell, Thompson, and Carswell, 2006), Ch. 5.

SELECTED CASES

Air Jamaica Ltd v Charlton [1999] 1 WLR 1399 (PC)

Associated Alloys Pty Ltd v ACN 001 452 106 Pty Ltd [2000] 202 CLR 588 (Aust HCt)

Re Baden's Deed Trusts (No 2) [1973] Ch 9 (CA)

Re Bond Worth Ltd [1980] Ch 288 (Slade J)

Clough Mill Ltd v Martin [1985] 1 WLR 111 (CA)

Re Denley's Trust Deed [1969] 1 Ch 373 (Goff J)

Re Goldcorp Exchange Ltd (in rec) [1995] 1 AC 74 (PC)

Re Gulbenkian's Settlement Trusts, Whishaw v Stephens [1970] AC 508 (HL)

Hunter v Moss [1994] 1 WLR 452 (CA)

IRC v Broadway Cottages Trust [1955] Ch 20 (CA)

4

Amplifying Property Rights

The previous chapter considered Equity's capacity to create new forms of property interests. This chapter considers Equity's special techniques for safeguarding those interests. Equity has devised various strategies that not only protect proprietary interests, but also prolong and sometimes even enlarge the proprietary status of an individual's original rights. These Equitable techniques can be highly controversial, especially where their effect is to amplify the claimant's original property rights.[1]

FOLLOWING, TRACING AND CLAIMING— CONCEPTUAL ISSUES

Consider a simple scenario. Suppose X's car is stolen by Y, and Y then sells it to Z for £2,000 and uses the funds to purchase shares. Ignore for the moment X's Common Law damages claims.[2] Focus instead on the potential avenues for proprietary protection or recovery. X could focus on the car: she could '*follow*' the car through Y's hands into Z's, and then attempt to assert ownership of the car notwithstanding Z's competing claim. This dispute will involve a *title conflict* between X and Z in respect of the car. Only one of them can win (although the loser may then have a damages claim against the thief). The controversy in this approach, if there is one, lies in whether the outcome treats X and Z fairly. Both are innocent, yet one will lose the car.

Alternatively, X could focus on the thief: she could '*trace*' the car into its substitutes in Y's hands, first into the £2,000 and then into the shares purchased with those funds. She could then attempt to assert some sort

---

[1] This chapter ignores the possibility of obtaining simple damages (or monetary compensation) to remedy interference with property rights: see Chapter 6, 159–61, 161–2, 174–8, 178–91.

[2] X could sue either Y or Z in tort (the law of civil wrongs) for *conversion* of her car, and recover its value. Interestingly, she could not insist on the return of the car itself, although the court could, in its discretion, order its re-delivery: Torts (Interference with Goods) Act 1977, s. 3. See Chapter 6, 169–74.

of Equitable proprietary interest in the shares (which are legally owned by Y), either by way of Equitable ownership or of Equitable lien. Notice that *if* she is allowed to do this, then she obtains insolvency protection against Y and Y's creditors even though Y no longer has her original property. Notice, too, that *if* the shares increase in value, and *if* X is entitled to assert Equitable ownership rather than a lien, then X will benefit from their increase in value. These two possibilities—continued proprietary protection even though the original asset has passed to others, and the chance of recovering windfall secondary profits from the fortuitous reinvestment by the defendant—are the most controversial aspects of these claims.

These routes illustrate the two approaches to safeguarding property that are the focus of this chapter. The first route is simpler. The original asset must remain identifiable throughout the story (this is the function of the *following* rules). The law must then work out rules for determining whether the original holder of a property right (X, in our story) continues to enjoy her rights notwithstanding that there are others (Z, in our story) who also assert rights in the same asset. These disputes can involve *title conflicts* (where the parties assert identical and therefore inconsistent claims to the same asset) or *priority disputes* (where the parties assert different but competing claims to the same asset and some sort of priority has to be established). The task is to determine whether the original property owner still enjoys an interest in an asset which is now in someone else's hands.

The second route is more novel. It suggests that Equity might see a property owner as *continuing* to enjoy some sort of property right (with all its associated advantages) even though the defendant no longer has the claimant's property. In our example, X's car was exchanged by Y for cash which was then exchanged for shares. The task is to see whether X's property interest in the car[3] is somehow preserved in the cash and then in the shares now that Y no longer has the car. This second mode of protection involves *tracing* property into its substitutes and allowing the tracer to *claim* some sort of proprietary interest in the substitute property. This mechanism for protecting property interests is particularly valuable where the owner can no longer claim the original asset (perhaps because it has been lost or destroyed or, sometimes, transferred to a third party who takes unencumbered title[4]). This mechanism also raises the possibility of

---

[3] X remains the legal owner of the car even though the thief has taken possession of it: see below, 93–4.
[4] See below, 95–7.

recovering windfall secondary profits if the original asset has been re-invested wisely.

The terminology needs reinforcing. Title conflicts and priority disputes involve the claimant and the defendant pointing (metaphorically) to an asset that they both identify as 'theirs' (in the sense that they have some sort of interest in it, although not necessarily an ownership interest). The function of the law is to resolve their dispute. The way that the claimant and the defendant identify an asset as 'theirs' is by a process called *following* (to distinguish it from *tracing*). A claimant follows her *original* asset from one person's hand to another, so that at the end of the process she can point to her asset as being the very property which is the subject of competing claims by different parties. Note that the asset being claimed is precisely the same at the start as at the end of the exercise; it is simply followed from hand to hand to establish its new whereabouts. Having followed her asset, the claimant is not necessarily entitled to lay claim to it. In our story, X could have *sold* her car to Y who might then have re-sold it or given it to Z. X could certainly follow her car into Z's hands, but she would have no legal right to claim it. The exercises of following and claiming are analytically distinct (although, as we shall see later, they are not absolutely independent).

Similar points need to be made about *tracing*. Tracing focuses on a single person (the defendant) and then traces the original asset into its various substitutes as the defendant engages in different deals. The rules of tracing are concerned with whether the law will allow X to say her original asset is still somehow represented in the substituted assets in Y's hands. Again, as with following, it is then a separate issue whether X can lay claim to that substitute asset, and what sort of claim (ownership or lien) she can assert. Tracing and claiming are, again, analytically distinct (but, again, not absolutely independent).

Of course, in practice the facts are rarely so neat. A problem will commonly involve both following and tracing as a claimant who has been deprived of property attempts to recover the very property (by *following*) or its substitutes (by *tracing*) in the hands of a chain of third parties. Even in these more complicated stories, however, proper analysis simply demands serial implementation of the fundamental rules of following and then claiming, or of tracing and then claiming. The rules are strict and quite technical. The reason is obvious: property rights are regarded as too valuable to be reallocated at the whim of some judge; entitlements should be certain.

FOLLOWING AND CLAIMING

The legal rules which govern following and claiming are designed to solve the problems that arise where X is deprived of her property, but knows where it has gone: she can follow it through the hands of various transferees until it arrives with Z. Z will inevitably claim he is entitled to keep the property because he has a legitimate interest in it. Perhaps he bought it, or it was a valid gift, or he took control under a valid security agreement. X will, predictably, claim that the property is still hers, just as it was at the start of the story, because she has not intentionally made any transfers. Each step in the chain has to be examined very carefully to see, at each stage,[5] whether X can follow her property into the hands of the transferee and whether X or the transferee is the 'winner' in the title conflict or priority dispute. At the end of the chain, if X has not lost out at an earlier stage, the dispute will be between X and Z to determine the final allocation of proprietary interests in the disputed asset. The vigour with which these following and claiming exercises are pursued in the courts reflects the value inherent in property rights.

FOLLOWING ASSETS

The first step is to follow the asset: all this requires is dogged tracking of the initial asset (the car, in our earlier example) as it passes from hand to hand. However, there can be complications. The law sometimes insists that the following trail is at an end when common sense suggests otherwise; and it sometimes insists that the rules of following depend upon the behaviour of the defendant rather than the behaviour of the asset.

Take a simple example. If A's eggs are used without authority by B to make a cake then A may see justice in the assertion that her eggs are present in the cake and that she should therefore be entitled to 'follow' them and assert some proprietary claim to the cake. Whatever the scientific realities, the law takes a different view. It insists that the eggs have 'disappeared'; the cake is a completely new, substitute asset. A can no longer point to 'her' eggs. B may have to pay damages to A for converting (or appropriating) her eggs, but A is not entitled to anything more valuable than this personal claim. The new asset belongs entirely to B, its

---

[5] If X does not 'win' against Y (perhaps because he was a bona fide purchaser rather than a thief), then she cannot possibly 'win' against Z.

'manufacturer'.[6] This is despite the fact that shared ownership is possible both at Common Law and in Equity. Indeed, if this is what the parties had expressly agreed, this is what the law would give them.[7] In the face of this it can seem unduly harsh for both the Common Law and Equity to deny A a continuing ('followed') proprietary interest when B is acting in defiance of A's property rights. The point is not trivial. The argument is unlikely to be over a cake, but rather over tonnes of grapes used to manufacture wine, or tonnes of resin used to manufacture chipboard.

The reason for this restrictive stance is pragmatic. There is a recurring tension between the interests of property owners in preserving their proprietary status and the interests of traders in preserving the integrity of transactions. If wrongfully manufactured products resulted in shared ownership between the various contributors, then third party recipients could never be secure in their title to the products. The law has to adopt a practical, if hard-headed, stance in determining how far it will permit proprietary interests to persist. Its position is that where assets are 'followed' the trail necessarily goes cold when the initial asset loses its original identity.[8]

Indeed, pragmatism has persuaded the law to adopt some rather counter-intuitive rules on whether an asset retains its original identity. Bricks used to build a home become *fixtures*, deemed to be part of the land, owned by the landowner; leather used to repair shoes becomes an *accession*, deemed to be part of the shoe, owned by the shoe-owner. The result may disadvantage the owners of the bricks and leather (and the boundaries of the rules on fixtures and accessions are hard-fought), but the benefits to the security of trade and commerce are overwhelming. Later in this chapter we shall see this same pragmatic stance resurface in the context of tracing.

A completely different scenario serves to show that the following rules are also context-specific: following and claiming are not entirely separate.

---

[6] *Borden (UK) Ltd v Scottish Timber Products Ltd* [1981] 1 Ch 25 (CA), 41 (Bridge LJ), 44 (Templeman LJ). The dividing line between 'mixtures' and 'new products' is difficult, and sometimes counter-intuitive: S Worthington, *Proprietary Interests in Commercial Transactions* (1996, Clarendon Press, Oxford), 135–43.

[7] *Coleman v Harvey* [1989] 1 NZLR 723.

[8] The conclusion that the original asset has 'disappeared' renders all of the following's associated *claiming* rules irrelevant: it is irrelevant whether ownership of the eggs is registered (even if it was, there are no longer any eggs to fight over), or whether a third party purchaser from the manufacturer is a bona fide purchaser for value (even if he was, his purchase was not a purchase of eggs): see below, 92–8. On the other hand, the original owner of the eggs might argue, in the alternative, that she can *trace* into the new substitute property (the cake) and preserve her proprietary status in this way: see below, 117–19.

Suppose A's 1,000 barrels of oil are blended, without authority, with B's 1,000 barrels of oil. Neither party has transferred title to the other; neither party can separate their 'own' oil, and yet each knows that 'their' oil is in the mixture.[9] The parties can 'follow' their assets, and the law regards them as owning the entire mass in common in proportion to the value of their initial contributions. Now suppose that 600 barrels of this mixture are lost. Who owns the remaining 1,400 barrels? If A and B are innocent victims of someone else's unauthorized mixing of their goods, then the law presumes that they bear the losses pro rata: A and B will own whatever remains equally. On the other hand, if *B* effected the unauthorized mixing, and so created the problem now facing A and B, then the law will assume that B's share is diminished to the advantage of the innocent party, A: it will assume that B's 600 barrels were lost and A's 1,000 barrels remain. In short, there is one following rule if the defendant is innocent, another if he is 'guilty'.[10] Again, later in this chapter we will see this same approach adopted in relation to tracing rules.

CLAIMING RULES—TITLE CONFLICTS AND PRIORITY DISPUTES

At the end of the following exercise, the claimant points to an asset and says that she has an interest in it (perhaps an ownership interest, perhaps something else). The problem arises because the defendant points to the same asset and insists that he, too, has an interest in it. The next step is to apply the legal rules used to resolve such conflicts. Sometimes these rules operate to preserve the claimant's property interests; sometimes they allow them to perish to the benefit of the defendant. These various rules have their sources in Common Law, Equity, and statute. All need to be considered.

REGISTRATION

Certain property interests are not protected *at all* in title or priority disputes if they are not registered (or '*perfected*') as required by statute.

---

[9] This blend is not regarded as a new, substituted asset, but simply as the owners' original assets confused with each other in the same container. The dividing line between these two conclusions is not scientific. Resin and woodchips combine to give a new product, chipboard; mixed oils or mixed grains (even if they are of different quality) retain their original identity.
[10] *Spence v Union Marine Insurance Co* (1868) LR 2 CP 427, 436–9 (Bovill CJ); *F S Sandeman & Sons v Tyzack & Branfoot Steamship Co Ltd* [1913] AC 680 (HL), 694–9 (Lord Moulton); *Indian Oil Co Ltd v Greenstone Shipping SA (Panama) (The Ypatianna)* [1988] 1 QB 345, 360, 368–71 (Staughton J).

Some statutes apply to specific legal interests (such as interests in land), some to specific Equitable interests. For example, many Equitable charges granted by companies are not protected in disputes between competing claimants to the underlying property unless they are registered in accordance with the Companies Act 1985.[11] These rules reflect policy choices. In the context of company charges, Parliament allows parties to take security to protect their own interests, but only on the condition that other prospective lenders, sellers, or buyers are put on notice of the fact (not necessarily actual notice, but constructive notice from the register, although in practice the register is likely to be searched before third parties engage in large transactions with the company). This is done so that these latter parties are not unwittingly seduced by the debtor's apparent wealth, but can properly assess the risks associated with their proposed dealing. The end result is that a claimant who has an unregistered (but compulsorily registrable) interest may find herself in the same position as if she had no proprietary interest at all when she is in dispute with third parties over the underlying asset.

THE '*NEMO DAT*' RULE

If competing claims *can* be asserted (because the relevant interests are properly registered, should this be necessary) then we need to consider how the law determines priority between the claims. Legal ownership is very carefully protected. Legal owners do not generally lose title to their property unless they deliberately intend to transfer it. If property is stolen, for example, the original owner remains owner. Indeed, if the thief attempts to sell the stolen property, the purported transferee obtains no title, no matter how innocent he is and no matter that he has paid a fair price.[12] Put another way, in any priority dispute between the original owner and any transferees, the original owner will 'win'. This may leave the innocent transferee out of pocket, since the only available remedies are those against the thief, and these will be of little comfort if the thief has disappeared or has no assets.

This rule is encapsulated in the Latin maxim, *nemo dat quod non habet*: 'no one can give what he does not have'. In particular, no one can give a better title than he himself possesses. In applying this maxim, the law is protecting the property rights of owners, but at a cost to the security of

---

[11] Companies Act 1985, ss. 394–5. Note that the provision only avoids the security; it does not invalidate the underlying personal rights embodied in the debt.

[12] *Rowland v Divall* [1923] 2 KB 500 (CA), 506–7 (Atkin LJ).

trade and commerce: a person who takes property, even in good faith and for value, will not necessarily receive good title. This is true of Z, the buyer in our original story, who purchased a car from a thief. Z paid for the car, but did not receive good title because Y (the thief) did not have title to transfer.

This strong property protection principle has its advantages, but it can sometimes work to defeat commercial needs. Accordingly, there are now several exceptions to the rule. The most important Common Law exception to the *nemo dat* rule arises with money (*currency* or *legal tender*). The transfer of coins or bank notes *as currency* to a person taking in good faith and for valuable consideration confers good title on the transferee.[13] It follows that if a thief uses stolen coins to make a purchase, then the innocent vendor will receive good title to the money. Good title is somehow reincarnated in the innocent vendor (and lost by the victim of the theft) even though the thief never has title to the money. The purpose of this rather strange rule is simple; it is to facilitate trade and commerce by allowing everyone to place their trust in the value of currency. Likewise, the most important statutory exceptions to the *nemo dat* rule—contained in the Sale of Goods Act 1979—are also designed to facilitate trade and commerce by favouring security of transactions over the protection of property rights in certain common, but risky, trading situations.

THE 'FIRST IN TIME' RULE

If the *nemo dat* rule permits the transfer of interests to others (because there *is* an interest that can be transferred), then the most basic priority rule is that proprietary rights generally rank according to their order of creation. Put another way, 'the first in time prevails'.

For example, if an owner of property creates two successive charges against the property, then the *prima facie* rule is that the first created charge (provided it is subsequently perfected by registration) has priority, and the second is postponed.[14] This means that if the secured property has to be sold to pay off the debtor's debts, the proceeds will go first to

---

[13] *Miller v Race* (1758) 1 Burr 452.

[14] Where the property is intangible, and the successive interests are both Equitable interests, then the applicable rule is slightly more complicated: the 'first in time' rule gives way to a rule that gives priority to the first assignee to give notice of the assignment to the person required to pay out a fund (the trustee or the debtor, if the successive intangible Equitable interests are interests in a trust fund or Equitable interests in a debt): *Dearle v Hall* (1828) 3 Russ 1, 38 ER 475. E.g., *E Pfeiffer Weinkellerei-Weineinkauf GmbH & Co v Arbuthnot Factors Ltd* [1988] 1 WLR 150, 161–3 (Phillips J).

paying off the first secured creditor's debt in full before any funds are deployed in favour of the second secured creditor.

If the owner is acting appropriately, then the successive interests will not be inconsistent, and the parties will be happy (or at least not too rudely surprised) with the outcome. More often, however, the owner is attempting to deal with his property twice so as to reap double the rewards. In such case, the parties are likely to have conflicting interests. Both are innocent, and the 'first in time' rule simply reflects the most pragmatic way of resolving the impasse.

Since the rule is designed to deliver justice in difficult circumstances, it is predictably subject to certain exceptions. Indeed, the full statement of the rule is qualified: 'where the equities are equal, the first in time prevails'. 'Equities', in this context, is meant in the sense used by Thomas Aquinas, where the justice and fairness of the specific facts are brought into issue. The equities will not be equal where the first party is somehow responsible for the predicament of the second. This is generally seen as the case if the first party somehow represents to the second that the interest *is* available to be taken up. This representation may be something as innocuous as leaving the original owner with all the incidents of title (title deed and so forth), thereby enabling him to represent that he remains fully able to deal with the asset. When this happens, the later interest may prevail.[15]

THE PRIVILEGED POSITION OF BONA FIDE PURCHASERS FOR VALUE—'EQUITY'S DARLING'

To these minor exceptions to the 'first in time' rule must be added one dramatic and far-reaching exception. An illustration helps explain it. Suppose A is a beneficiary of a trust. She has Equitable title and her trustee has legal title to the trust property. Now suppose her trustee wrongfully sells the trust property to B. Both A and B may be innocent victims of the trustee's fraud. In these circumstances the law has to decide who should bear the loss. The 'first in time' rule would favour the beneficiary's earlier Equitable interest. However, the law's utilitarian response is to favour security of *legal* transfers of property. Hidden trust interests are not permitted to defeat the legitimate expectations of genuine purchasers who have bargained for legal title. Once again, the law appears to favour the general security of trade and commerce over the personal property interests of trust beneficiaries (or other holders of

[15] *Rice v Rice* (1853) 2 Drew 73.

Equitable interests). The exceptional priority rule is that 'a bona fide purchaser for value of the legal estate without notice of the prior Equities takes free of them'. Note the critical conditions: B must have *purchased* a *legal* interest *without* having either actual or constructive[16] *notice* of A's earlier *Equitable* interests. When this is the case, B takes the property free of A's interests, and is accordingly sometimes referred to as 'Equity's darling'.[17] The effect of the rule is that property is lost from the trust: the trustee no longer has legal title and the beneficiary is deprived of her Equitable interest. All may not be lost, however. We shall see later that it may be possible for the beneficiary to insist that the sale proceeds received by the trustee be treated as substitute trust property.[18]

Although the bona fide purchaser rule is commonly justified by the need to make (legal) transfers of property secure, this rationalization presupposes that legal ownership is the pre-eminent property right. If *all* interests in property were seen as equally worthy of protection, then the 'first in time' rule ought to have general application. In the face of this, it is sometimes suggested that the rule is not grounded in logic, but in the competitive jurisdictional politics that once existed between the Common Law and Chancery courts, and that Chancery was simply (but perhaps illogically) ceding jurisdiction to the Common Law courts. There is scope for logical justification, however. A trust presupposes that the beneficiary has left the trustee with all the incidents of title and the power (even if not the authority) to deal with the trust property. Given this, it may make sense to reassess the appropriate balance of risk between the beneficiary and an innocent third party, and sometimes (perhaps not always) to favour the third party's security of transaction over the beneficiary's security of property.[19] This forces the beneficiary, not the third party, to bear the risk of the defaulting trustee being unable to meet the claims against him.

This 'bona fide purchaser' rule is often called into play. Consider cases of money laundering. The entitlement to enormous sums of money can

---

[16] This means that *registered* Equitable interests may be privileged. The purchaser will be taken to have constructive knowledge of the claimant's (earlier) registered interests, and he will take his legal interest subject to these.

[17] *Polly Peck International plc v Nadir (No 2)* [1992] 4 All ER 769 (CA); *Macmillan Inc v Bishopsgate Investment Trust plc (No 3)* [1995] 1 WLR 798 (Millett J) (aff'd on different grounds by the CA in [1996] 1 WLR 387).

[18] See below, 98–100.

[19] The power the beneficiary cedes to her trustee is not the only factor. It is also relevant, on the beneficiary's side, that her Equitable interest is registered (and so published to the world), and, on the third party's side, that his rights have been paid for (so increasing his risk).

turn on the outcome of a priority dispute. Typically, A's funds are diverted (stolen) by a fraudster B. The funds may then pass through several hands, C, D, and E—and probably several jurisdictions—before reaching F. When A attempts to recover the funds, the fraudster has often disappeared or is insolvent, C, D and E are innocent recipients who no longer have the money, and A's attention turns to F. *If* A can assert Equitable ownership of the very funds which F received,[20] then the dispute will come down to a priority dispute between A's earlier Equitable interest and F's later legal interest. The bona fide purchaser rule tell us that F's interest will prevail provided he is a bona fide purchaser for value of the legal title to the laundered funds without notice of any earlier Equitable interests; otherwise A's interest will prevail.

THE FRAGILITY OF 'MERE EQUITIES'

There is one further exception to the 'first in time' rule. It concerns *mere equities*.[21] These interests are defeated by *all* subsequent bona fide purchased interests.[22] Again, an illustration helps to explain. Suppose X sells her house to Y under a contract that is voidable for undue influence.[23] In these circumstances we say that X has a mere equity. What we mean is that X could, if she wanted, take action to have the sale contract set aside, and she could then recover her house provided she refunded the purchase money to the purchaser. If Y re-sells the house to Z before X has time to do this, then we have a priority dispute between X, with an earlier mere equity, and Z, with a legal ownership interest. X is first in time, but Z is 'Equity's darling', so Z will win. But mere equities will also be defeated by subsequent bona fide purchasers of *Equitable* interests. For example, if Y had mortgaged the house to the bank, rather than selling it to Z, the bank's subsequent Equitable security interest would prevail over X's mere equity. Although the law agrees that the sale by X to Y is tainted, it will only allow X to recover her house if she recognizes the bank's interest in it.

This means that mere equities are more fragile than Equitable interests. They are defeated by *any* interest subsequently acquired by bona fide

---

[20] To do this, A will need to establish his Equitable title to the funds in the fraudster's hands and then either *follow* or *trace* those funds into F's hands, ensuring that A has an unbroken chain of proprietary interests from start to finish. In this way, the facts often demand application of both the following and the tracing rules discussed in this chapter.

[21] See Chapter 3, 82–3, and Chapter 9, 310–12.

[22] *Phillips v Phillips* (1862) 4 De G F & J 208, 215–18, 45 ER 1164, 1166–7 (Lord Westbury); *Latec Investments Ltd v Hotel Terrigal Pty Ltd* (1965) 113 CLR 265 (Aust HCt), 276–8 (Kitto J), 289–91 (Menzies J).

[23] See Chapter 7, 211–14.

purchasers. The 'first in time' rule governs only in the unlikely circumstance that the subsequent interest is acquired by a purchaser with notice, or by a donee.

The *following* and *claiming* rules that have been the subject of this section are all directed at identifying the claimant's initial asset as it passes from hand to hand, and, at every stage, resolving disputes with other parties who assert inconsistent or competing claims to it. The goal is to determine whether, at the end of the chain of transfers, the claimant still retains any sort of proprietary interest in the asset.

TRACING AND CLAIMING—CORE ISSUES

With Equity's second mechanism for safeguarding proprietary interests, the focus is quite different. The starting assumption is that, at some stage, the claimant had a proprietary interest in an asset held by the defendant. Her problem is that she cannot enjoy this interest because the defendant no longer has the asset. He has exchanged it for something else. In our earlier example, the thief exchanged the claimant's car for money, and then exchanged the money for shares. The law must decide whether the claimant should be allowed to assert some sort of continuing proprietary interest in the substituted asset. To do so, she must first show that *her* property was exchanged and is now represented in the substitute (this is the *tracing* step). Secondly, she must show that in the circumstances she is entitled to assert some sort of claim to the substituted product (this is the *claiming* step). Both steps can be complicated.

Equity's tracing and claiming techniques were developed to deal with problems of defaulting trustees.[24] Take a very simple example. Suppose T (the trustee) holds a painting on trust for B (the beneficiary). T has legal title to the painting, but B is its Equitable owner.[25] If the trust deed *requires* T to sell the painting and invest the proceeds in a particular way, then the proceeds of sale and the new investments (the twice substituted assets) will automatically be held on the original trusts: B will no longer have an interest in a painting, but an interest in different assets in the trust fund. This is a simple case. Suppose, however, that the trust deed requires T to *hold* the painting, not to sell it, but that T nevertheless sells the painting and invests the proceeds in shares, intending to benefit

[24] The Common Law also has a version of tracing, but it never developed to the same extent. In particular, it never overcame the fatal limitation that tracing through mixtures at Common Law was regarded as impossible.

[25] See Chapter 3, 63–7.

personally from the transaction and to disappoint the trust beneficiaries. What is Equity to do to remedy this state of affairs?

Equity has no problem in insisting that even in these circumstances T holds the new investments on the same terms as the original trust. The trustee is not allowed to steal the trust assets and engage in lucrative investments on his own account. His duty requires him to be a loyal manager: Equity says he owes the beneficiary *fiduciary obligations* of loyalty (i.e. special obligations requiring him to promote her interests, not his own, whenever he has a choice).[26] Given this, Equity will simply treat him as having made the investments on his beneficiary's account. The rather immaterial difference is that this trust is a *constructive trust*, construed and imposed by the court even though the investment is unauthorized; it is not an express trust defined by the terms of the trust deed. The tracing and claiming issues are rarely differentiated, but Equity effectively allows a beneficiary to trace the painting into the sale proceeds and then into the shares, and to claim Equitable ownership of the shares. The advantages are twofold. The beneficiary has a property right (with all its associated benefits, including its inherent insolvency protection) even though the original trust property has been lost. Secondly, this property right entitles the beneficiary to enjoy the profits of the unauthorized share investment. The modern tracing and claiming controversies centre on who (other than beneficiaries of express trusts) can take advantage of this type of continuing proprietary protection and the potential for windfall secondary profits.

Before we address the controversies, notice something else about the beneficiary's position. If T's share investment turns out to be a poor substitute for the painting, then B can adopt another strategy. She can forego her claim to have the shares treated as part of the trust estate and can, instead, require T to remedy his breach of trust. This is not a claim to any particular item of property in T's hands, but a personal claim against T requiring him to put the money equivalent of the painting back into the trust fund.[27] However, personal claims carry insolvency risks: if T becomes insolvent, B may not recover her losses. Equity does not force B to resolve this dilemma by accepting ownership of the poor share investment. Instead, it allows her to persist with her compensation claim, and it preserves her insolvency priority by giving her an Equitable lien on the shares.[28] Suppose the painting was worth £5,000, but the shares are

---

[26] See Chapter 5, 131–4.   [27] See Chapter 6, 174–8.
[28] See Chapter 3, 77–9.

only worth £3,000. Because B's personal claim against T for £5,000 is secured against the shares, B can assume control of the shares, sell them, and recoup her losses. This will leave her £2,000 short. She can still claim this amount from T, although the claim may be worth little if T is insolvent. The advantage of the Equitable lien is that B's position is protected at least to the extent that there are traceable substitutes for the painting.

Given that Equity has these strategies for safeguarding property, what are their limits? What is needed to start the tracing trail, to keep it going, and to end it? What determines whether insolvency priority should be preserved in traceable substitutes? Finally, and perhaps most controversially, what determines whether the claimant is entitled to the full benefit of the lucrative investment, not simply the value of the asset lost at the outset? These questions occupy most of the rest of this chapter. As we saw with the rules on following and claiming, the answers appear to be influenced by context. This makes it difficult to keep the tracing technique entirely separate from the claiming exercise, despite modern exhortations to do so.[29] Indeed, although we start with the first question, we cannot finish dealing with all of its issues until much later in the discussion.

STARTING THE TRACING TRAIL

Given that Equity's tracing and claiming techniques were first developed to deal with defaulting trustees, it is perhaps predictable that the trust model came to define their essential prerequisites. Fifty years ago, the orthodox view was that a claimant could 'trace' only if she could show that she was both the Equitable owner of the original asset now in the defendant's hands *and* that the defendant owed her *fiduciary obligations* in dealing with that asset.[30] The need to show both of these trust-like attributes is now roundly doubted, although the courts have not yet fully freed themselves from the strictures.

At the outset, these prerequisites would have seemed well founded. Little if any distinction was drawn between tracing and claiming. Indeed, it was common to refer to the claimant's 'tracing claim'. This 'tracing claim'—or the sum of the claimant's rights against the defendant—was unquestionably dependent on these two prerequisites, especially on

---

[29] *Boscawen v Bajwa* [1996] 1 WLR 328 (CA).
[30] *Diplock, Re* [1948] Ch 465 (CA); aff'd sub nom *Ministry of Health v Simpson* [1951] AC 251 (HL).

whether the defendant owed the claimant fiduciary obligations.[31] No one thought to ask whether other claimants might also have protected rights; no effort was made to uncover the core principles underlying tracing and claiming.

Now, however, the distinction between tracing and claiming is clearly recognized (even if the interaction between the two is still hazy). Tracing is simply the technique for identifying new forms of property that can legitimately be regarded as substitutes for the claimant's initial asset. Even before this insight was clearly articulated, the foundations of the double requirement were crumbling. In cases of complicated following and tracing chains, courts conceded that the *defendant* need not be a fiduciary provided someone, somewhere in the chain, had owed the claimant fiduciary obligations; as against the defendant, the claimant simply had to show that he had her Equitable property.[32] Soon courts ignored even this loose link to a real fiduciary requirement; they simply asserted that if the defendant had the claimant's Equitable property, then *he* owed her fiduciary obligations, although their content might be purely nominal.[33] Moreover, if the defendant *was* a fiduciary, the claimant could trace into unauthorized substitutions even when she had no *Equitable* interest in the initial asset because she had retained legal, not Equitable, title to it (as she might, for example, if she simply passed possession to her agent for specified purposes). In short, the Equitable tracing rules were used to identify substitute assets whether or not the claimant had an Equitable interest in the initial asset, and whether or not the defendant owed her fiduciary obligations. Of course, the results of the *claiming* exercise might be critically dependent on these features, but the crucial point is the general availability of the Equitable *tracing* rules themselves.

This generality is important. Can the tracing rules be used even when there is no hint of either Equitable property or a fiduciary relationship? Can they be used by *anyone*, including a legal owner? If tracing is decoupled from claiming, then this question cannot be answered logically other than in the affirmative. Tracing (like following) concerns *assets*;

---

[31] See below, 102–10.

[32] Now the processes might be more rigorously analysed, and the 'following and claiming' steps distinguished from the 'tracing and claiming' steps. In many of these older cases, the entire process was simply one of identifying the 'tracing claim'.

[33] This strategy led to some justifiably criticized outcomes in different cases: fiduciary status can crucially affect *claiming* issues, so fudging this can lead to unwarranted conclusions.

claiming (in both cases) concerns *interests* in assets. The rules of tracing do not assert that the claimant's Equitable interest in a car can be traced into her Equitable interest in cash and then her Equitable interest in shares. If they did, then the claimant's initial proprietary interest and her fiduciary (or other) relationship with the defendant would undoubtedly be crucial. Instead, the rules of tracing simply say that the *car* can be traced into the *cash* and then into the *shares*. With this focus on the assets and their substitutes, it is impossible to factor in any meaningful requirement for Equitable interests or fiduciary obligations. These can only come into play at the claiming stage. In short, the tracing rules may be 'Equitable', but this can only sensibly reflect their historical provenance, not their necessary link with pre-requisites of Equitable property interests or Equitable fiduciary obligations.[34]

CLAIMING RULES—PRACTICE AND PRINCIPLE

The early failure to distinguish between tracing and claiming affected analysis elsewhere. It encouraged the easy assumption that a 'tracing claim' simply allows the claimant's rights to be transposed to any traceable property. This is what seemed to happen to our defaulting trustee: the claimant's Equitable ownership of the original trust property emerged, after tracing, as Equitable ownership of the substituted assets. Taken further, this assumption seems to suggest that if a defendant steals the claimant's car and exchanges it for cash and then for shares, then the defendant will simply be treated as though he had stolen the claimant's shares (assuming tracing is allowed): he will be liable for the civil wrong of converting 'her' shares, and will have to pay damages accordingly. The claimant's rights as legal owner of the car become rights as legal owner of the substituted shares. This is *not* how the rules work, however. 'Tracing' identifies substitute assets, certainly. But 'claiming' does not simply transpose the claimant's initial rights to substitute assets. It has two quite distinct expressions.

First, it asks whether the claimant's *original* rights (and especially their proprietary status) should be *preserved* in the substitutes. In our example, suppose the claimant could sue the defendant for £2,000 for conversion of her car. *If* the defendant still has the car, then this claim has insolvency

---

[34] See *Foskett v McKeown* [2001] 1 AC 102, 113 (Lord Steyn) and 128–9 (Lord Millett), both *obiter*, both asserting that only one set of tracing rules should be used both at common law and in Equity. This would deliver the same result as argued for here.

priority.[35] Tracing says the car can be traced into the shares; claiming asks whether this *original* right to £2,000 damages should have its insolvency priority preserved against the substitute shares. The claimant will not receive more than £2,000, even if the shares are now worth £4,000.[36] Equally, if the shares are now worth only £1,000, then the claimant's insolvency protection is limited to this. In either case, however, her claim is for £2,000 for conversion of the car, not £4,000 or £1,000 for conversion of the shares. In all of this, it is relatively unimportant that the claimant's asset is a car, or that her interest is legal ownership. The key question is whether the claimant's legal right to damages for conversion is *so* special that, as well as having insolvency priority from the outset, its priority should *also* be preserved in substitute assets. This question allows for rational differentiation: different types of rights can be given different degrees of protection.

Secondly, the claiming rules can subject identified (*i.e* traceable) products and proceeds to a *primary* claim, not a preserved claim. Most reported cases concern defaulting fiduciaries, like our defaulting trustee, and the claimant's access to windfall secondary profits is then justified because the defendant owes fiduciary obligations of loyalty; disloyal behaviour is remedied by stripping the defaulting defendant of all his ill-gotten gains and paying them over to the principal.[37] Tracing identifies these profits; claiming ensures their disgorgement. Certain non-fiduciary types of primary claim are also possible. Indeed, the boundaries of this

---

[35] The preferred insolvency status of legal owners takes a little explaining. Recall the earlier example of X's stolen car. X retains legal title to the car, but it is one of the quirks of the Common Law that this claim does not give X the *right* to have her car back: she only has a *right* to money damages from Y for the civil wrong of conversion of her property. Y can choose whether to pay these damages or hand back the car. (The court has a *discretion* to order specific restitution—Torts (Interference with Goods) Act 1977, s. 3—but it usually only exercises this discretion where the goods are rare or unique: see Chapter 6, 169–72.) Nevertheless, even at Common Law, X's claim has insolvency protection. This is a concession rarely made by the Common Law, but if Y is insolvent and *if* he still has the car, he must either return the car *or* its full value: he cannot keep the car and confine X to a damages claim which abates along with the claims of all of Y's other general creditors. However, if Y no longer has the car, then all that X can claim is damages and her claim will inevitably abate unless the law will allow her preferred proprietary status to be preserved in the substitute assets.

[36] Unless, of course, the claimant can advance a *new* and independent claim to the substitutes; this is the gist of her claim to windfall secondary profits: see below, 106–10.

[37] It may even be possible to adopt this reasoning to explain the lien that secures the trustee's obligation to reinstate the trust fund: see above, 102–3. The trustee cannot profit from his breach, so he cannot claim ownership of the shares (to revert to our initial example) until he has reinstated the trust fund at least to the extent of their value. The Equitable lien achieves this end.

whole area are now fiercely disputed.[38] The remedy in all these cases is assumed to be proprietary, although in some circumstances this view might be criticized.[39] Notice that if the remedy *is* proprietary then it becomes material to ask whether *this* right deserves preserved insolvency priority if the products and proceeds that are its focus are no longer in the defendant's hands.

The principles underpinning these two claiming objectives deserve further attention.

PRESERVING INSOLVENCY PRIORITY

Once the tracing and claiming rules are decoupled, it becomes essential to identify the logic of the claiming rules. Which claims preserve insolvency priority, and why? It is dangerously easy to answer this question by assuming that the effect is the cause: in particular, that because the express trust beneficiary's claim to substitute assets *does* preserve her insolvency priority, then it must be *designed* to achieve that end. The claiming rule then becomes that insolvency priority inherent in the claimant's initial asset is preserved in its substitutes. That leads to the inexorable logic that *if* Equitable ownership interests under an express trust should have insolvency priority preserved in traceable substitutes, then so too should Equitable ownership interests under resulting and constructive trusts; and if these *Equitable* ownership interests should have preserved insolvency priority, then so too should *legal* interests which start out with that preferred status. After all, why should the legal owner of a car that has been stolen have a weaker insolvency protection than an Equitable owner?

In short, legal coherence demands that all these proprietary interests be treated in the same way unless there is some rational justification for distinguishing between them. Any justification must explain why all should *start out* delivering preferred priority on insolvency, but only one (or only some) should also deliver *preserved* insolvency priority when the initial asset is no longer in the defendant's hands but its traceable substitute can be identified. The logic seems compelling. Indeed, the courts appear to be leaning towards this approach, even though, as yet, they decline to articulate the goal. Nevertheless, this explanation is not the only option.

Perhaps the preferred strategy should be to *deny* preserved insolvency priority to *all* these rights. This is an equally coherent response. If this

---

[38] See below, 106–10.   [39] See Chapter 5, 134–40.

were done, then all Common Law and Equitable proprietary rights would deliver insolvency protection at the outset (as befits their proprietary status), but this preferred status would not be prolonged once the original asset disappeared from the picture; it would not be preserved in substitutes. This strategy would recognize that insolvency inevitably involves losers, and if a claimant has proprietary priority then the 'losers' have an even smaller pool of assets from which to recoup their claims. Some rights are important enough to warrant preferred status initially, but it is a separate and crucial question of policy whether they are important enough to warrant its preservation. Civil law jurisdictions have decided that they are not.[40] This provides an alternative and perhaps preferable model.

Interestingly, much of the early case law on 'tracing claims' (both at Common Law and in Equity) appears to apply an intermediate strategy. Unravelling this offers important insights. Both the extreme views just mentioned focus on the claimant's *asset*. Insolvency priority is automatically one of its essential attributes. The key issue then becomes whether some substitute asset should be allowed to give the claimant continuing priority. All assets, it seems, should be treated alike: either all should deliver continuing protection, or none. This focus on assets prevents any sensible attempt to discriminate between different *rights*. By contrast, this is what the early cases appeared to do. Priority only seemed to be preserved in substitute assets when the defendant was a fiduciary. Put another way, proprietary claims against fiduciaries were protected more aggressively than proprietary claims against non-fiduciaries. Even Common Law tracing seemed, empirically, to be restricted to supporting claims in fiduciary contexts: it was applied to agents and partners who had possession of the claimant's legal property for specified ends, but who then acted in defiance of these objectives.[41] Some of these sharp divisions have been lost in more recent cases. Nevertheless, the strategy for discrimination is worth noticing, even if its particular underpinnings now seem to merit reassessment.

The choices presented by these alternatives are important. Equity's old practices hid the crucial issue. So long as courts simply resolved 'tracing

---

[40] Civil law jurisdictions do not preserve insolvency priority in unauthorized substitutions. Authorized investments are protected, as in common law jurisdictions, although this result is achieved by real subrogation rather than by the common law mechanism of Equitable property.

[41] Recall that Common Law tracing remains less well developed than Equitable tracing. It allows tracing into direct substitutes, but not through mixtures.

claims' without decoupling tracing and claiming, they could disguise their goals. Now the reasoning has to be exposed: courts will have to determine whether common law property interests deserve general, radical and far-reaching insolvency protection, or whether the tracing and claiming rules are designed for more limited ends.

CLAIMING WINDFALL SECONDARY PROFITS

The uncertainties do not stop there. It is clear that Equity's claiming rules can (sometimes) be used to access the windfall secondary profits represented by substitute assets. Recall Equity's response in the context of express trusts: there the beneficiary was automatically entitled to Equitable ownership of the substitute shares, even if their value far exceeded the value of the original painting.[42] However, the underlying reasons were never clearly articulated and now the proper rationalization has become highly controversial.

The wider problem is strikingly illustrated by a simple, if unlikely, example: if Y purchases the winning lottery ticket using a £1 coin belonging to X, is X entitled to the lottery millions? If the parties have agreed to the answer, the law will simply support their contract. But if they have not agreed, and Y uses X's money without X's authority, what is the law to do? Should it merely require Y to repay £1 to X in damages, or should it require the lottery millions to be paid over? And should X's entitlement be proprietary (so that X 'owns' the millions and has them preserved for her sole benefit on Y's insolvency), or should the claim be merely personal (so that X's claim abates on Y's insolvency)? More realistic, if less dramatic, examples can easily be contemplated.

Notice that resolution is difficult because the problem concerns *substituted* assets: the claimant's £1 coin is exchanged for a lottery ticket, which is exchanged for the winning millions. The problem is simple if we merely want to know who is entitled to the dividends from the claimant's shares or the fruit from the claimant's apple tree. These are not windfall secondary profits; they are part and parcel of the original asset: they are its 'fruits', and the owner of the 'tree' is entitled to them. The problem of windfall secondary profits only arises if the shares or fruit trees are sold and their proceeds reinvested.

Return to our trust beneficiary. There are at least four reasons for allowing her to claim Equitable ownership of the shares. They represent increasingly liberal approaches to claims to windfall secondary profits.

---

[42] See above, 98–100.

Some, but not all, will justify X's analogous claim to the lottery millions. First, the result may follow because the trustee has a duty to invest the trust funds on behalf of the beneficiary and a discretion to select the investments. In these circumstances, the law may allow the beneficiary to 'ratify' or 'adopt' any unauthorized investment and insist that the trustee has invested the funds for the beneficiary and not for himself. This approach is automatically proprietary, with all the advantages for the beneficiary that flow from that,[43] but it depends on quite specific facts.

Secondly, the result may follow because the defendant trustee is a fiduciary. All fiduciaries must behave loyally; they are not allowed to make secret unauthorized profits out of their position.[44] Defaulting fiduciaries must pay over (or *disgorge*) these disloyal profits to the beneficiary. As the law now stands, this obligation to disgorge is proprietary: the beneficiary is regarded as the Equitable owner of any profits (e.g. the shares) that the trustee must transfer.[45] This privileged status may turn out to be unwarranted, however.[46]

These two rationalizations are unquestionably part of the existing law. If this is as far as the law goes, then claims to windfall secondary profits are conditional on proving wrongdoing, and indeed wrongdoing of a very particular type. (And the reason for distinguishing between these two wrongs, rather than merging them both under the same general head of unauthorized fiduciary profit-making, will become apparent when we return to the detail of the tracing rules.[47])

Thirdly, the law could simply say that all claims to windfall secondary profits follow automatically from the law of property, without the need for any further justification. The logic is simply this: if the claimant owns the original asset, whether at law or in Equity, then she automatically owns all the profits derived from its use. The reason itself compels the conclusion that the right is proprietary. This analysis would justify giving our trust beneficiary and X the Equitable ownership of the shares and the lottery millions, respectively. In the past few years this has been the view increasingly adopted by the judiciary.[48] It has the advantage of simplicity, but its ramifications are profound and, it seems, largely undesirable.

---

[43] *Foskett v McKeown* [2001] 1 AC 102 (HL) *could* be analysed like this.

[44] See above, 98–9, and Chapter 5, 131–40.

[45] *AG for Hong Kong v Reid* [1994] 1 AC 324 (PC). See Chapter 3, 67–73, for the rationale.

[46] See Chapter 5, 134–40.   [47] See below, 110–16.

[48] *F C Jones & Sons (Trustee in Bankruptcy) v Jones* [1997] Ch 159 (CA); *Foskett v McKeown* [2001] 1 AC 102 (HL).

The problems are various. The rule operates fortuitously. Moreover, innocent defendants are treated in the same way as those who are corrupt. A defendant may think he is absolutely entitled to property he receives, and may find out later that he is not. The claimant obviously deserves remedies to protect her original interest.[49] But if, fortuitously, the defendant uses her property to make successful investments, then this version of the windfall profits rule would require him to hand those over too, and to do so even though he owes the claimant no duties to look after her interests, and may not even be aware of her competing claim to the underlying property. Return to our lottery millions: Y will inevitably be caught if he uses X's coin to buy the lottery ticket, but not if he uses his own. Such a conclusion goes well beyond what is required to protect X's property interests, or what is justified by any entitlements necessarily associated with those interests. An owner's rights to use her own property as she wishes and to reap the rewards (and bear the losses) of her own activity, and even to recover her losses when others either interfere with her enjoyment or receive an unjust enrichment at her expense, does not automatically entail that she should reap the rewards of another's use of her property. And if the disgorgement remedy is directed at deterrence,[50] not at protection or entitlement, then it is difficult to see what activities it aims to deter. Defendants who find themselves caught by this rule are often completely ignorant of the circumstances that raise its operation; they are in no position to respond to deterrence. Finally, even if some justification for disgorgement could be found, there seems little merit in according the remedy proprietary status. This might be justified if the claimant were entitled to ownership of the profits,[51] but otherwise the windfall to the claimant comes at an unfair cost to the defendant's creditors in the event of insolvency: the insolvency pool is not simply depleted by the value of the claimant's original asset, but also by the value of any profits the defendant may have made from its use.

The fourth and final justification for permitting claims to windfall secondary profits is based on unjust enrichment. This approach has been

---

[49] If the defendant still has the property, he will have to return it (or its value) to its rightful owner: see the earlier discussion of the 'following and claiming' rules, 90–2. Sometimes the defendant will have to pay the claimant even if he no longer has the property: see Chapter 6, 169–70, 178–89, and Chapter 9, 275–83.

[50] See Chapter 5, 128–9, for a description of this strategy.

[51] This is so only when an express agreement provides for this, or when deviation from such an agreement can be authorized or ratified by the claimant (as in the first justification of the windfall profits rule considered above).

mooted by scholars but not yet adopted by the courts.[52] According to this analysis, profits made from the unauthorized use of another's property are regarded as unjust enrichments that should be returned to the original owner of the property. The assertion has intuitive appeal, yet its underlying rationalization is difficult to pin down. Defendants who receive property that the claimant did not intend them to have are usually required to make restitution.[53] This can sometimes explain why the claimant should recover her original property or its value (subject to defences and special unjust enrichment valuation rules), but it does not explain why the claimant should also recover the windfall secondary profits. Why it is *unjust* to keep the profits derived from the use of another's property? Instinct suggests it is, until it is pointed out that the rule will bite even when the defendant is completely innocent and ignorant of the fact that the property is not his, and even when, had he known, he would simply have returned the claimant's property and used his own for the transaction. If these concerns are brushed aside on the basis that it *is* invariably unjust to retain benefits derived from the use of another's property, then the rationalization seems merely to reiterate the property rationalization currently favoured by the judiciary; it does not directly concern itself with the problems that the law of unjust enrichment is designed to remedy.[54] Without a clear handle on why unjust enrichment law demands that these profits should be disgorged, it is doubly difficult to assess whether the remedy is apt for the task. If the remedy follows the unjust enrichment model, it might be personal, rather than proprietary, although even this is hotly debated; it would, however, be subject to unjust enrichment's special defence of change of position.[55]

It is not clear which of these justifications for claiming windfall secondary profits will eventually find acceptance. Return to the question posed at the outset. Is X entitled to the lottery millions if Y uses her £1 coin to purchase the ticket? Both the 'property' and 'unjust enrichment' analyses suggest that the answer is inevitably yes. The 'wrongs' analysis is much more restrictive; it suggests that disgorgement is only apt if the defendant has breached his management investment agreement or his fiduciary obligations of loyalty. In each case the possible proprietary nature of the response needs further careful assessment.

---

[52] E.g. P Birks, 'Mixing and Tracing' (1992) 45 CLP 69.
[53] See Chapter 9, 275–83.   [54] See Chapter 9, 275–83.
[55] See Chapter 9, 309–10.

Given the discussion in this section and the previous one, it is clear that the principles underpinning the claiming rules require urgent, rigorous analysis. The difficulties have only been fully exposed since the decoupling of tracing and claiming. Surprisingly, and worryingly, all the contemporary analyses in this area go against the general trend in other areas of the law, which is to minimize the proprietary impact of legal claims. Here, by contrast, commentators favour preserving initial insolvency priority in traceable substitutes, and providing generalized (and perhaps even proprietary) access to windfall secondary profits. It is not at all clear what policy objectives justify quite this degree of protection of the claimant's proprietary rights in the initial asset. A more restrictive stance would seem apt to meet the identified objectives;[56] indeed, the old fiduciary prerequisites may have been soundly based.

TRACING AND CLAIMING RULES AT WORK— DIFFICULTIES WITH MIXED SUBSTITUTIONS

So far our illustrations have been unrealistically simple. If A's £1,000 is spent on a painting, then tracing is easy: the substitute for the £1,000 is clearly the painting. The claiming issues are more difficult, of course: can A preserve the insolvency priority of her initial claim to £1,000, or claim the windfall secondary profits inherent in the painting?

The facts are usually far more complicated. A's £1,000 is likely to be deposited in B's bank account, not spent immediately. Suppose this deposit brings B's account balance to £2,000, and B then spends £1,000 on blue chip shares and £1,000 on a skiing holiday. If the aim is to trace through dealings with A's £1,000 in order to identify an asset that represents its substituted value, the difficulty is clear. Will the tracing rules allow A to say that her £1,000 is represented by the shares, or will they compel her to accept that her £1,000 was spent on a skiing holiday, so that there is now no substitute asset? Does the answer depend upon whether B is innocent or a wrongdoer? Does it depend on the type of wrongdoing? Does it depend on why A wants to trace?

Equity initially developed its tracing rules in the context of trustees. If B is a trustee, then his duty is to keep A's trust assets separate from his own so that he can look after them appropriately. B's breach of this duty has made identification of A's funds impossible. In these circumstances

---

[56] This strategy would, therefore, address many of the concerns currently directed at the over-protection of unjust enrichment claimants with proprietary claims to some initial asset: see Chapter 9, 290–4.

all the presumptions run against the wrongdoing trustee. A can maintain that it was *her* £1,000 that was spent on shares, and B cannot prove, definitively, that the contrary is the case. Indeed, B cannot deny A's assertion about the provenance of the expenditure except by compounding his breach of duty as a trustee: he will not be allowed to insist that out of all the possible dealings he might have had with A's trust funds he made the one that was worst for A and best for him. To the extent that it is possible, his breach of duty as a trustee will be construed so as to minimize the disadvantage to his beneficiaries.[57] In reaching this conclusion, the order of payments into and out of the mixed fund is irrelevant: Equity does not analyse the issue on the basis of any mechanical 'first in, first out' principle (which, at least historically, was the Common Law's approach in relation to running accounts[58]). The end result is that A can *elect* to trace into the shares, and B, whose duty it was to ensure that identification was possible, cannot deny her that right. Clearly the justification for this rule depends crucially on the status of the defendant against whom the tracing exercise operates. A rule that so strongly prefers the claimant beneficiary may be defensible in the context of trustees, but perhaps not in other contexts considered later.

Consider what claims this tracing rule will support. Suppose B has an active management role that requires him to reinvest A's funds for her benefit.[59] In these circumstances B cannot deny that a discretion which could have been exercised in the beneficiary's favour was not: he cannot say he simply took A's £1,000, or took it and dissipated it on a skiing holiday, when his actions suggest he *might* have spent it on shares which would have benefited A. A can insist that the trustee invested *her* £1,000 in the shares, and she can ratify or adopt the unauthorized investment. In this way she can claim Equitable ownership of any windfall secondary profits represented by the shares (an attractive option if the shares increase in value to £1,500, for example). This conclusion is quite remarkable. It is one thing to insist that a trustee cannot steal trust funds and invest them for his own benefit. But here it is not certain that the beneficiary's funds were spent on the investment. It is possible they were, but they might not have been: the trustee did have adequate funds of his own to pursue his investment plans. A trustee whose *duty* is to invest

---

[57] *Re Hallett's Estate* (1880) 13 Ch D 696 (CA); *Re Oatway* [1903] 2 Ch 356.

[58] *Clayton's Case* (1817) 1 Mer 572, 605; 35 ER 781.

[59] Perhaps this category should cover all *express trusts*, even where the obligation is simply to *hold* the asset, because the trustee ought to go to court to seek a variation of the trust if simply holding the asset seems unwise.

his beneficiary's funds is not permitted to deny that he did this. The beneficiary can construe the facts as they best suit her, regardless of the trustee's private and less honourable intentions.

On the other hand, the outcome is quite different if B has no discretionary investment role. A can no longer simply ratify or adopt B's investments. She can, however, insist that B disgorge any profits he has made from breach of his fiduciary obligations of loyalty. B clearly profited from the initial £1,000 he took and used for his own benefit. If he still has this profit, then A can recover it.[60] If B made other profits from his breach, then he must disgorge those too. If he used A's £1,000 to purchase shares, then A is entitled to the profits. Indeed, if B's initial breach enabled him to borrow further funds, and he then invested the total sum wisely, A can claim the entire profits of the successful investment, not simply a pro-rata share.[61] The rationale is simple: a fiduciary cannot keep *any* profits generated from his breach of trust. It is immaterial that B could have used his own funds for the same purpose. If *in fact* he has made a profit from his breach, then he must disgorge it. The difficulty lies in identifying the relevant profits.

Our earlier example highlights these difficulties. It also highlights the subtly different uses of the tracing rules. If A can prove that B has made disloyal profits, and that he still has them, then she can insist on their disgorgement. B certainly made a profit of £1,000 when he took A's original assets. Moreover, this profit is still represented in B's assets, preserved in its traceable proceeds, the shares. (Recall that the tracing rules adopt advantageous presumptions against the defaulting trustee.[62]) A is therefore entitled to proprietary disgorgement, at least according to current analyses.[63] She is entitled to an Equitable lien on the shares to secure her claim for £1,000 profits disgorgement. Notice that the tracing rules have been used to confirm that the defendant still has disloyal profits in his hands, and to identify the appropriate assets to stand as security to preserve the proprietary status of this claim. Now consider the share profits. Once B has mixed A's funds with his own in his bank account, A cannot *prove* that B's breach generated the share profits: there

---

[60] Alternatively, A could ignore the fiduciary profit-making, and could, instead, recover her £1,000 by personal claim against the trustee for breach of his duty to comply strictly with the terms of the trust: see Chapter 6, 174–8. Indeed, she would be forced to adopt this strategy if B no longer holds any identifiable profits from his breach.

[61] *Scott v Scott* (1963) 109 CLR 649 (Aust HCt).   [62] See above, 110–11.

[63] But see Chapter 5, 134–40, for an argument that this remedy should be personal, not proprietary.

is no certain factual link. The shares *may* have come from use of her funds; but equally they may have come from use of B's own funds. In these circumstances she cannot insist that the share profits be disgorged because she cannot prove that they were derived from B's breach of trust.[64] The tracing rules (admittedly a subtly different version of them, directed at subtly different ends) do not help her.

As hinted earlier, Equity's tracing rules and their claiming consequences are quite different if the defendant is not a trustee. Duties and presumptions run against trustees in ways that are inappropriate when both the claimant and the defendant are innocent. The problem can arise in a variety of ways. Perhaps A and B are both beneficiaries under different trusts, and their trustee—in breach of *his* duty to each beneficiary—mixes £1,000 from both trust funds in his own (otherwise empty) bank account.[65] In these circumstances both A and B can follow their trust funds into the mixed fund, but neither can identify the provenance of the withdrawn funds with any certainty. Equity's approach to this problem has changed over time. Initially Equity simply applied the Common Law's mechanical 'first in, first out' rule to determine the beneficiaries' fate. This could have entirely fortuitous results. Suppose A's funds are paid into the trustee's account first, then B's, and suppose the trustee then spends £1,000 on blue chip shares and, later, £1,000 on a skiing holiday. The 'first in, first out' rule suggests that A's funds were spent on the shares and B's on the skiing holiday. A can trace into substitute property; B cannot. The more modern approach is to displace this mechanical rule whenever its use seems either unjust or impractical (and it almost always will).[66] The preferred rule is then that the beneficiaries share any proprietary losses and benefits *pro rata*.[67] With this rule, half of each beneficiary's funds will be presumed spent on the skiing holiday and

[64] *Re Tilley's WT* [1967] 1 Ch 1179. And even if A were entitled to windfall secondary profits on the property or unjust enrichment arguments described earlier, 106–10, they would not assist here for the same reason: A cannot prove that *her* property generated the shares; it may have, but it may not.

[65] If the bank account also contains the trustee's personal funds, then the competition between the innocents, A and B, and the guilty, T, is resolved by making presumptions against T as indicated earlier: see above, 110–11.

[66] *Barlow Clowes International Ltd (in liquidation) v Vaughan* [1992] 4 All ER 22 (CA).

[67] If there have been many dealings with the account, then a sophisticated application of this rule requires a rolling calculation of each party's relative interest in the account balance (perhaps including the trustee's interest). This process is common in North America, and is known as the 'rolling charge'. Quite separately from these proprietary consequences, A and B will each have *personal* claims against their common trustee for compensation for breach of trust: see Chapter 6, 174–8.

the other half on the shares. In other words, £500 of both A and B's money will be traceable into the shares; the other half will be untraceable. Notice that once these tracing issues are sorted out, both A and B's claims will be against the trustee, not against each other. Given this, and given that their trustee is not permitted to profit from his breach of trust, the share profits will be divided between A and B, with the remedy regarded as proprietary: A and B will be the Equitable owners of the shares.

The analysis is only slightly different if A's claim *is* against B, another innocent party, rather than against a trustee. We need to alter the facts slightly to see how this possibility could arise. Suppose A's trustee gives £1,000 of A's trust fund to B and B, honestly believing the money to be his, adds it to his bank account which already contains £1,000. A can certainly sue her trustee for breach of trust, but she may also be able to recover from B. Here we are interested in her proprietary rights, not her personal ones.[68] When B first receives the £1,000 from A's trustee, A retains Equitable ownership: A has a prior Equitable interest in the money, and B is a donee, not a purchaser, so he takes subject to this interest even though he has no notice of it.[69] A can trace her initial Equitable interest into substitutions effected by B.

Suppose B, as an innocent party, repeats the transactions mooted in our earlier examples, and spends £1,000 on shares and £1,000 on a skiing holiday. Since B is an innocent party, there is no reason he should be disadvantaged as against A in asserting his own property rights to the mixed fund. It follows that, in the absence of any proven wrongdoing on the part of B, the tracing rules are the same as those used when both parties were trust beneficiaries. In tracing into substitutes, A and B will share both losses and benefits *pro rata*. Here, claiming creates the problems, not tracing. The cases certainly suggest that A is entitled to trace to preserve the insolvency priority of her initial claim. And yet, when the issues are exposed, the merits of this conclusion must be doubted. A has claims against her defaulting trustee, and the insolvency priority of those will be preserved; as against B, there seems to be little justification for such strong protection. Similar doubts surround claims for any secondary profits inherent in the share purchase. A can trace £500 of her trust fund into the share purchase, but should she be entitled to claim half the profits of this investment? This inquiry takes us back to the earlier

---

[68] The restrictions on her personal claim are more extensive than might be expected: see Chapter 6, 178–89.

[69] See above, 94–5.

discussion. If a restrictive view of entitlement to windfall secondary profits is adopted, then A is not entitled to any share of the profits because B is neither a wrongdoing trustee with investment discretions nor a wrongdoing fiduciary with duties of loyalty. On the other hand, if the wider property or unjust enrichment analyses are adopted, then A may be entitled to a share of the profits, but only if she can insist that her property *was* used to purchase the shares (here the facts suggest this is no more than a possibility, so they do not go far enough). These outcomes are all controversial.

One final scenario helps to test the various arguments advanced here. Suppose all the facts remain the same, but the share investment is a disaster rather than a success: the shares purchased for £1,000 are now worth only £500. Where A and B are both innocent trust beneficiaries, the outcome is simple. The original mixed fund contained £1,000 from A and £1,000 from B. Both were assumed to have contributed £500 to the skiing holiday and £500 to the share purchase. The implication is that *both* A and B can assert a lien over the shares to secure repayment of their £500 contribution to the purchase price. Moreover, their liens rank equally—there is no reason to favour A's claim over B's, or vice versa. If the asset is not sufficiently valuable to meet the claims of equally ranking security holders, then the losses are shared pro rata. The result is that A and B are each entitled to £250 from the proceeds of the sale of the shares. The common assumption is that the same response would apply even if the parties were not beneficiaries, but were claiming against each other rather than against their defaulting trustee. As noted earlier, this does depend on the wisdom of continuing to allow A to preserve the insolvency priority of her initial claim against B.

When B is a defaulting trustee, the analysis is more complicated. In some circumstances, A will be entitled to presume that her funds alone purchased the entire share pool and B will not be able to deny her assertion even though the facts suggest that his funds might equally realistically have effected the purchase. This is the case in our original example: A can presume that her funds were spent on the shares and B's on the skiing holiday, even though the opposite is equally plausible. She is then entitled to the entire benefit of the share investment. This is not the case, however, when B's funds *must* have contributed to the purchase of the share parcel. Suppose that £500 of A's trust funds and £500 of the trustee's own funds are used to purchase a parcel of shares which subsequently fall in value to £500. Each party's contribution is absolutely certain, and there seems to be no reason why each cannot claim against the share pool. A cannot insist that the entire share pool was purchased using her funds; B also has an interest which cannot be denied. Defaulting trustees are not necessarily stripped of all their rights; the truth is simply that certain evidential presumptions run against them if their breach has made it impossible to discover the truth.

All of this is difficult, but the essential points can perhaps be summed up quite simply. *If* preserved insolvency priority is deemed appropriate, then the claimant has to identify suitable substitute assets against which her initial claim can continue to be secured. Mixtures make absolute proof of substitution impossible. In 'guessing' the provenance of different substitutions, Equity simply treats innocent parties equally, but allows the claimant to make self-interested assumptions against defaulting trustees. On the other hand, *if* claims to windfall secondary profits are warranted, then the claimant usually has to prove that her assets were *in fact* used to generate the profit. The only assumption then allowed is that a trustee with a *duty* to invest has invested trust assets as advantageously as possible, and this is judged in hindsight (i.e. the beneficiary can elect to treat certain substitutions as made using her assets).

THE END OF THE TRACING TRAIL

A claimant who wants to trace in Equity must be able to say to the defendant, 'At the start of the story you had an asset, P1, which was mine; you used it to acquire P2, so now I am entitled to assert a claim (of some sort) against P2.' The chain can, of course, be much longer than this. Even with this simple example, however, it is clear that the tracing trail will go cold if there is no asset at the end of the chain. This was the case in our earlier example where trust funds were spent on a skiing holiday. It is also clear that the tracing trail will go cold if the claimant cannot prove that P1 *was* used to acquire P2. This is easy to prove if P1 is directly exchanged for P2; perhaps the claimant's £1,000 is used to purchase a parcel of shares, for example. Most cases are more complicated, and rely on certain presumptions, especially against fiduciaries. Nevertheless, it must always be physically *possible* (even if not certain) for the claimant's property to have been used in the dealing to acquire the substitute. The tracing trail goes cold if this is not the case. This has several important consequences.

'LOWEST INTERMEDIATE BALANCE RULE'

If the claimant's funds are paid into the defendant's bank account, then the tracing rules may allow the claimant to presume that the traceable

substitute for her funds remains in the account even though the defendant withdraws money from the account. For example, if the claimant's
£1,000 is paid into an account which already contains £1,000, then it is
possible to maintain the fiction that her traceable funds remains in the
account so long as the balance is something more than £1,000. However,
if withdrawals reduce the balance to £500, that assertion becomes untenable. Even if we presume that the defendant spent all his own money first,
there is clearly only £500 of the claimant's traceable funds left in the
account. This remains true even if later deposits cause the account
balance to rise again to something more than £1,000. Even then, the
claimant can only trace into £500. This is known as the 'lowest intermediate balance' rule.[70] It reflects the physical reality of tracing: whatever
its presumptions, it must at least be *possible* for the claimant's original
asset to be represented in the substitute.

'BACKWARDS TRACING'

Suppose B uses his overdraft facility to purchase a substantial asset and,
some time later, he makes fraudulent (or at least unauthorized) use of A's
trust funds to discharge his overdraft. On the basis of the rules considered so far, A cannot trace her trust funds: they were paid into an
overdrawn bank account, and so they have 'disappeared' in the payment
of the debt to the bank without producing a substitute asset. 'Backwards
tracing', it is suggested, would permit A to prove that the overdraft was
used to purchase an identifiable asset, and that the trust funds were used
to replenish the overdraft, and then to assert that effectively it was the
trust funds which were used to purchase the asset, which can therefore be
regarded as the traceable substitute. So far the courts have rejected this
possibility, although certain comments suggest a potential willingness to
adopt this stance where it appears that the whole operation was part of
a grand scheme devised by B to effect the purchase of the nominated
asset.[71]

MIXED INPUTS

Until now all our examples of mixed substitutions have involved both A
and B making the same *type* of contribution to the substitute asset. They

---

[70] *James Roscoe (Bolton) Ltd v Winder* [1915] 1 Ch 62. Contrast the spurned 'swollen
assets' theory: *Space Investments Ltd v Canadian Imperial Bank of Commerce Trust Co
(Bahamas) Ltd* [1986] 1 WLR 1072, 1074 *per* Lord Templeman.
[71] *Bishopsgate Investment Management Ltd (in liquidation) v Homan* [1995] Ch 211 (CA),
Dillon LJ, but contrast Legatt LJ.

have usually contributed money, so their respective interests in the substitute are easily evaluated. But the facts may not be so fortunate. Recall the example of A's eggs being used without authority by B to make a cake. The law will not allow A to 'follow' her eggs into the cake and make a title conflicts claim.[72] And as the law now stands, nor can she say that her initial proprietary claim to her eggs in B's hands (which she could have asserted had she caught up with B early enough) is 'traceable' into the substitute asset, the cake, enabling her to preserve the insolvency priority of her initial claim (which is to a sum of money for conversion);[73] nor can she advance the even more difficult claim to any windfall secondary profits inherent in the substitute. Yet it is not quite clear why this should be the law. If A's eggs were mixed with B's *eggs*, rather than B's flour, the outcome would favour A's continuing proprietary interest. The theoretical justifications underlying tracing do not seem to be conditional on equivalent types of initial contributions. As noted earlier, the issue is not trivial. The argument is likely to be over tonnes of grapes used to manufacture wine, or tonnes of resin used to manufacture chipboard.

Of course, a change in approach would raise difficult valuation issues. The 'grapes into wine' case is relatively easy. It is more difficult to agree that if a horse eats hay, the hay is 'represented' in the horse, it being the 'substitute asset'. The temptation is to say that the hay cannot be traced into the horse; it simply disappears—it is consumed without producing an end-product. Nevertheless, economic analysis may rationally suggest a different answer, and one that appears to support further liberalization of the rules.

Indeed, the law does seem to be advancing slowly down this route. Older cases where A's funds were used to renovate or improve an asset already owned by B raised this problem of mixed inputs to the substitute asset. A's funds may have been used to build an extension on B's house, or to renovate his kitchen. These cases avoided any analytical difficulties by ruling that tracing was simply impossible in the circumstances.[74] These cases attracted criticism for failing to give legal recognition to the intuitive sense that the claimant's asset (her fund) does not 'disappear'; it *is* represented in the new product.[75] Although it might be difficult to assess the contribution that the expenditure makes to the value of the

---

[72] See above, 90–2.
[73] *Borden (UK) Ltd v Scottish Timber Products Ltd* [1981] Ch 25.
[74] *Re Diplock* [1948] Ch 465; *Borden (UK) Ltd v Scottish Timber Products Ltd* [1981] Ch 25 (CA).
[75] *Boscowen v Bajwa* [1996] 1 WLR 328 (CA).

end-product, that difficulty should not be allowed to deny the claimant's claim. One simple possibility—one that recognizes that idiosyncratic expenditures may even *reduce* the value of the underlying asset—is to quantify the traceable value as *either* the sum expended *or* the resulting increase in the value of the altered asset, whichever is the lower. This at least recognizes the minimum value of the input made by the funds to the end-product.

The point is that the end of the tracing trail must be assessed in a coherent fashion. If proprietary rights are to be protected aggressively, then similar proprietary rights should be treated equally favourably in similar contexts: mixing money and mixing other property should deliver the same protection in the same contexts unless differences can be rationally justified. But this does not automatically suggest that mixed inputs are inevitably traceable into substitutes. The hay may not be traceable into the horse. The real difficulty with mixed inputs is more subtle; it lies not in valuing the relative contributions to the substitute asset, but in determining whether tracing is essentially about *property* substitutions, or merely about *value* contributions.[76]

SUBROGATION

So far, the discussion has been about protecting proprietary interests in two-party situations. Subrogation is concerned with three-party situations. Consider a simple example. If a driver's car is damaged in a road accident then she will be able to claim against her insurer. Perhaps surprisingly, her insurer will then be entitled to sue the other driver. This is so, even though her insurer was not the victim of the accident and had no contractual or other legal relationship with the other driver. The insurer will be able to 'stand in the shoes of the insured' and exercise any rights she may have which could diminish the loss insured against. This idea of 'standing in another's shoes' is subrogation. Subrogation effectively transfers the insured's rights to her insurer, allowing him to sue the wrongdoer.

This strategy could have advantages in the tracing process. Suppose a defendant uses the claimant's funds to pay off his debts. Has the claimant's tracing trail gone cold, or can she be subrogated to the rights of the creditors who were paid off using 'her' money? For example, if the defendant uses the claimant's funds to pay off his mortgage, has the claimant's tracing trail gone cold, or can she insist that she has a right to

---

[76] Akkouh and Worthington (2006) pp. 305–15.

stand in the bank's shoes and revive the bank's mortgage, so that she is now treated as if *she* has a secured claim against the defendant?

Older cases assumed that the tracing trail went cold.[77] They assumed that claimant's money was paid to the bank without producing any substitute product in the defendant's hands. More recent cases differ; they suggest that the claimant *is* entitled to be subrogated to the creditor's rights.[78] The change in thinking is important, especially if the creditor had a secured claim. Note, however, that the claimant's newly acquired proprietary interest may be qualified. Because a subrogated claimant 'stands in the shoes' of the principal creditor, any defects in the principal creditor's rights will affect the subrogated claimant to the same extent.

This idea of subrogation is intelligible in simple tracing terms. If the claimant has a proprietary interest in the funds in the defendant's hands, then the idea of tracing into substitutes suggests that the defendant should be treated as if he had used the claimant's funds to re-purchase the bundle of rights comprising the security interest he had granted to the third-party secured creditor (the bank, perhaps). The claimant's funds will be traceable into that bundle of rights, and she will be entitled to whatever security interest they generate. This rationalization also suggests that the claimant should not be able to trace in this way and obtain proprietary protection if she does not have a proprietary interest in the fund at the outset. The modern subrogation cases confirm this.[79]

REVIEW

Some of the issues discussed in this chapter are controversial. Property needs to be protected, but whether that protection should extend to prolonging and sometimes even enlarging the proprietary status of the underlying right is more doubtful.

Property's primary protection comes from rules that enable disputing parties to resolve title conflicts and priority disputes. Absolute justice is unlikely; the law must simply decide who has the stronger claim. When an asset is stolen and re-sold, for example, the original owner and the new purchaser cannot both own the asset: the law must choose between two innocent victims of the thief's dishonesty. The various legal rules expose the tension between protecting property rights and protecting the

---

[77] *Diplock, Re* [1948] Ch 465 (CA); aff'd sub nom *Ministry of Health v Simpson* [1951] AC 251 (HL).
[78] *Boscowen v Bajwa* [1996] 1 WLR 328 (CA) (Millett LJ).
[79] *Banque Financière de la Cité v Parc (Battersea) Ltd* [1999] AC 221 (HL).

security of transactions in general trade and commerce. The current matrix of Common Law and Equitable rules reflects a consistent and coherent response to these issues. Indeed, the rules themselves are no longer cited with jurisdictional tags to indicate their historical provenance; it is only the underlying property rights that still need historical labels.

Property's secondary protection is more controversial. Equity's tracing and claiming strategies allow claimants to assert new proprietary rights in substitute assets. These rights preserve the insolvency priority of the initial proprietary claim or secure entitlements to windfall secondary profits. Neither of these options follows inevitably from the initial assertion of a proprietary right. Any insolvency priority inherent in the ownership of an asset need not be preserved in substitutes: to do so weights security of property over security of transactions, and dramatically widens the class of third parties affected by the initial property interest. Proprietary claims to windfall secondary profits operate even more aggressively.

Notwithstanding this, the modern trend is to expand the reach of both of these claims. The result is to deliver increased insolvency protection and greater access to windfall secondary profits, and yet there are equally strident claims that the rights of unsecured third parties should be given greater respect. There may be much to be said for the view that these expansive Equitable tracing and claiming rules are appropriate in the trust situation, where they were conceived, but not outside that. In a trust context, these rules effect a necessary division between the trustee's fiduciary and personal patrimony, allocating both primary and substituted assets to one or the other. Outside these limited circumstances, it is arguable that the reach of property should not be unnecessarily enlarged. Certainly, one of the most critical and controversial modern debates concerns the wisdom of preserving insolvency priority in substitutes and requiring the handing over of windfall secondary profits merely because a claimant starts out on the road with a property interest in a completely different asset, and notwithstanding the absence of any wrongdoing on the part of the defendant.

SELECTED BIBLIOGRAPHY

Akkouh, T. and Worthington, S., '*Re Diplock* (1948)' in C. Mitchell and P. Mitchell, (eds), *Landmark Cases in the Law of Restitution* (Oxford: Hart Publishing, 2006), Ch. 11.

Birks, P., 'Mixing and Tracing: Property and Restitution' (1992) 45 CLP 69.

Evans, S., 'Rethinking Tracing and the Law of Restitution' (1999) 115 LQR 469.

Fox, D., 'Common Law Claims to Substituted Assets' [1999] RLR 55.

Goode, R., 'The Right to Trace and its Impact in Commercial Transactions' (1976) 92 LQR 360, 528.

Guest, A. S., 'Accession and Confusion in the Law of Hire-Purchase' (1964) 27 MLR 505.

Kurshid, S. and Matthews, P., 'Tracing Confusion' (1979) 95 LQR 78.

Matthews, P., 'Proprietary Claims at Common Law for Mixed and Improved Goods' (1981) 34 CLP 159.

——, 'The Legal and Moral Limits of Common Law Tracing' in P. Birks (ed.), *Laundering and Tracing* (Oxford: Oxford University Press, 1995), Ch. 2.

Millett, P. J., 'Tracing the Proceeds of Fraud' (1991) 107 LQR 71.

Smith, L., *Tracing* (Oxford: Oxford University Press, 1997).

Williston, S., 'The Right to Follow Trust Property When Confused With Other Property' (1888) 2 Harvard Law Review 28.

Worthington, S., *Proprietary Interests in Commercial Transactions* (Oxford: Clarendon Press, 1996).

——, 'Subrogation Claims on Insolvency' in F. Rose (ed.), *Insolvency and Restitution* (London: LLP, 2000), Ch. 4.

——, 'Justifying Claims to Secondary Profits' in E.J.H. Schrage (ed.), *Unjust Enrichment and the Law of Contract* (London: Kluwer, 2001), p. 451.

——, 'Proprietary Remedies and Insolvency Policy: The Need for a New Approach' in J. Lowry and L. Mistalis (eds), *Commercial Law: Perspectives and Practice* (London: Lexis-Nexis/Butterworths, 2006) Ch. 11.

SELECTED CASES

AG for Hong Kong v Reid [1994] 1 AC 324 (PC)

Bishopsgate Investment Management Ltd (in liquidation) v Homan [1995] Ch 211 (CA)

Borden (UK) Ltd v Scottish Timber Products Ltd [1981] Ch 25 (CA)

Boscowen v Bajwa [1996] 1 WLR 328 (CA)

Re Diplock [1948] Ch 465 (CA); aff'd sub nom Ministry of Health v Simpson [1951] AC 251 (HL)

Foskett v McKeown [2001] 1 AC 102 (HL)

Re Hallett's Estate (1880) 13 Ch D 696 (CA)

Indian Oil Co Ltd v Greenstone Shipping SA (Panama) (The Ypatianna) [1988] 1 QB 345

F C Jones & Sons (Trustee in Bankruptcy) v Jones [1997] Ch 159 (CA)

Latec Investments Ltd v Hotel Terrigal Pty Ltd (1965) 113 CLR 265 (Aust HCt)

Re Oatway [1903] 2 Ch 356 (Joyce J)

F S Sandeman & Sons v Tyzack & Branfoot Steamship Co Ltd [1913] AC 680 (HL)

Scott v Scott (1963) 109 CLR 649 (Aust HCt)

Spence v Union Marine Insurance Co (1868) LR 2 CP 427

Re Tilley's WT [1967] 1 Ch 1179

Part III

Civil Wrongs

5

Restricting Personal Autonomy

Aside from property, Equity's other conspicuous contribution to the common law landscape is its invention of several new and uniquely structured obligations. These obligations all restrict individual autonomy in special and rather aggressive ways. Usually the law restricts autonomy only to the extent that the impugned behaviour harms others. Consider obligations to act with due care or to perform agreements. These obligations are identified and breaches remedied by focusing on the harm caused to the claimant. The Equitable obligations considered in this chapter are unique: they constrain the defendant's autonomy even when his impugned behaviour has caused the claimant no harm.

This may seem odd, but consider the type of problem Equity sought to address. Take trusts: trusts operate by giving trustees management powers that must be exercised for the benefit of others. These powers typically leave trustees with wide administrative discretions, and the wider the discretion the more exposed the beneficiaries are to its abuse. Somehow the law needs to regulate trustees' conduct, yet it is impossible to specify in advance the end-point trustees must reach to carry out their functions properly. Trustees must usually do more than carefully adhere to a settled plan of action. They can often legitimately choose between quite different management approaches. Equity's regulatory strategy in these circumstances is not to prescribe, but to proscribe. It declares certain conduct unacceptable, but outside that prohibited arena it leaves trustees free to choose their own course of action.

Equity developed three distinctive strands of these proscriptive rules. The best known are Equity's *fiduciary obligations*, which demand loyalty and self-denial from trustees and others whose roles entitle them to exercise discretion in managing property belonging to another. More generally, Equity regulates the exercise of *all* powers that are intended to affect the interests of others, regardless of whether the affected interests are proprietary or not. These are Equity's rules on *abuse of power*. Finally, Equity has particular strategies for regulating the use of information.

These are Equity's rules on *breach of confidence*. All three strategies are considered in this chapter.

PRESCRIPTIVE AND PROSCRIPTIVE STRATEGIES

Consider the law's usual strategy in regulating the relationship between individuals. Typically, it imposes an obligation on one party to ensure that the other is put in a particular beneficial end-position (as determined by contract terms) or preserved from particular harm (as defined by civil law obligations). With the claimant's end-position *prescribed* in this way, an efficient legal remedy for breach will simply insist that the defendant put the claimant in the prescribed end-position, at least as far as money can do that.[1] The seller who supplies inferior goods must compensate the buyer for the difference in market value; the careless driver who damages another car must pay to repair the damage.[2]

What distinguishes the situations described in this chapter is the impossibility of defining an end-position.[3] For good commercial and social reasons, people are often given the right to exercise discretions. By definition, the exercise of a discretion cannot be regulated by prescribing an end-position; that would contradict the discretion. Yet somehow the risk of the person abusing his power must be addressed. Equity's strategy (now also used by the Common Law) is clever. It focuses throughout on the defendant, not the claimant. It identifies the type of conduct that is likely to put the claimant most at risk, and bans, or *proscribes*, it. If the defendant acts in breach of these proscriptions, Equity again ignores the claimant (it has no prescribed end-position that might assist in defining remedies). Instead, its strategy is to return the *defendant* to the position he was in before his breach. It strips the defendant of profits disloyally made; it undoes decisions improperly reached; it unwinds irregular deals. This risk of wasted effort is the most effective weapon the law can muster to deter the defendant from engaging in the proscribed conduct.

The impact of this remedial strategy on the claimant deserves special comment. Clearly the remedy does not put the claimant in the same

---

[1] And in some cases it will order an injunction or specific performance to achieve practical delivery, not merely economic equivalence: see Chapter 2, 23–7.

[2] In unjust enrichment cases, too, the end-point is clearly defined: see Chapter 9. Of course, all these cases have their own detailed rules about quantifying the sum to be paid and recognizing relevant defences.

[3] Although see below, 152–4, for doubts on whether this is so for breach of confidence cases.

position (even in money) that she would have been in had the defendant performed properly. That position cannot be defined. Instead, it unwinds improper actions in the hope that they will be taken properly a second time. It also gives the claimant the benefit of any improper gains the defendant has made from his proscribed conduct. Importantly, it does this regardless of whether the claimant has suffered a loss: if the defendant has been especially successful in his wrongdoing, then the claimant may acquire a windfall.

All these differences are often taken as proof that the Equitable rules cannot be integrated within the common law of wrongs. This is doubted. The rules (and their Common Law analogues) are certainly different. They proscribe behaviour rather than prescribing it; their remedies are defendant-focused rather than claimant-focused. But their goal, as with other civil wrongs, is simply to preserve the claimant from unwarranted harm from the defendant's conduct.

FIDUCIARY OBLIGATIONS—DUTIES OF LOYALTY

Fiduciary obligations were first developed in the context of express trusts, although they have now been adapted to remedy similar problems in many other management relationships. The terminology has been generalized accordingly, so that *fiduciaries* (parties in trustee-like roles) owe duties to their *principals* (rather than their beneficiaries). This fiduciary/ principal category includes trustees and their beneficiaries, company directors and their companies, partners and their co-partners, solicitors and their clients, and certain other relationships.[4]

The trust remains the paradigm fiduciary relationship. Consider the problems in the arrangement. A trustee clearly needs flexibility in managing the trust property so that he can respond appropriately to social and market forces. A strategy of maximum empowerment of trustees is therefore advantageous, but risky. The trustee may act completely contrary to instructions, or unacceptably carelessly, or in bad faith, or in a manner that advances his own interests rather than those of his beneficiaries.

The Common Law originally offered no control mechanisms to regulate these problems. It regarded the trustee as the legal owner of the property, and did not consider the beneficiaries to have any contract or

---

[4] See below, 140–2.

property rights. Equity had to provide the necessary regulation. It developed its rules slowly, but by the close of the nineteenth century there were four principal strategies in operation. First, Equity compelled strict compliance with the terms of the trust. If the trust deed provided specific instruction to hold property, or to purchase specific assets, then remedies were available against trustees who ignored these imperatives. Secondly, Equity permitted claims against trustees who executed their management tasks negligently. Thirdly, it controlled the manner in which trustees exercised their management powers. It aimed to ensure that management decisions were based on relevant considerations, not irrelevant ones. And, finally, it imposed fiduciary duties of loyalty to ensure that trustees preferred their beneficiaries' interests to their own in managing the property. The last two strategies are discussed in this chapter; the first two in the next chapter.

The reason for dividing consideration in this way is important. Although all these strategies were developed by Equity to deal with the problems of defaulting trustees, they are not all proscriptive strategies, nor even uniquely 'Equitable'. The duty of strict compliance with the terms of the trust has strong parallels with the Common Law's response to breach of contract. The duty of care in Equity has strong parallels with its Common Law analogue. If the common law landscape is to develop coherently, then these parallels need to be pursued; like cases must be treated alike. Because these first two Equitable strategies prescribe duties that have strong Common Law parallels, their discussion is deferred until the next chapter. The third and fourth strategies are different. They are both proscriptive mechanisms designed to restrict personal autonomy in a unique fashion. Both are considered here.

Before turning to the detail, something more needs to be said about terminology. Because these strategies were first developed in the context of trustees and later extended to all fiduciaries, it was perhaps natural that all four duties were often called 'fiduciary duties'. This terminological amalgamation led to inevitable analytical problems. The different requirements for breach and the different remedial responses became intertwined and confused. Only in the past decade have conscious efforts been made to unravel the different breaches and properly assess the different remedies. Put more pithily, 'Not every breach by a fiduciary is a breach of fiduciary obligation.' The only real 'fiduciary' obligation is the obligation of loyalty; all the other obligations now apply well beyond the confines of fiduciaries.

IDEAS OF LOYALTY AND SELF-DENIAL

Equity insists that beneficiaries are entitled to the single-minded loyalty of their trustees, or, more generally, that principals are entitled to the single-minded loyalty of their fiduciaries.[5] Put starkly, the fiduciary duty of loyalty requires fiduciaries to put their principals' interests *ahead* of their own; it requires fiduciaries to act altruistically.[6] In particular, a fiduciary cannot enter into any transaction that involves a conflict between his personal interests and his management duties unless he has his principal's prior informed consent; in fact, he cannot profit in any secret way from his position.[7] The duty demands a general denial of self-interest: the fiduciary role proscribes certain perfectly legitimate activities unless the principal consents to the fiduciary's involvement. The fiduciary's personal autonomy is correspondingly constrained.

If a fiduciary fails to live up to this standard—and he can fail despite acting within his authority, carefully and in perfect good faith —then Equity demands that the profits resulting from the breach be paid over to, or 'disgorged to', the principal. In English law this *disgorgement remedy* is regarded as proprietary, with all the associated advantages this attracts.[8] The remedy is available whether or not the principal has suffered a loss and whether or not the principal expected to obtain the gain for herself. Notice that the remedy is not designed to repair the principal's harm, but to deter the fiduciary's breach. Because of this, it is often said that the remedy delivers a windfall to the principal.

Consider the impact this duty has. Most obviously, a fiduciary cannot buy from or sell to his principal without the principal's informed consent.[9] And if it seems that these transactions could never happen without such consent, recall that a trustee managing his beneficiaries' estate could readily buy and sell without the beneficiaries' knowledge. It is the trustee,

---

[5] *Bristol & West Building Society v Mothew* [1998] Ch 1 (CA).

[6] This describes the outcome, not (or not necessarily) the motivation. The law does not turn fiduciaries into altruists, intent on self-denial, but it does induce them to behave as altruists, intent on self-denial, would behave. As with all legal rules, it does this by appealing to the fiduciary's self-interest: see above, 128–9, on proscriptive rules and deterrence strategies.

[7] *Bray v Ford* [1896] AC 44, 51–2 (Lord Herschell); *Chan v Zacharia* (1984) 154 CLR 178 (Aust HCt).

[8] *AG for Hong Kong v Reid* [1994] 1 AC 324 (PC); *Boardman v Phipps* [1967] 2 AC 46 (HL) (although perhaps without proper consideration). Also see *Hospital Products Ltd v United States Surgical Corporation* (1984) 156 CLR 41 (Aust HCt).

[9] *Wright v Morgan* [1926] AC 788 (PC); *Holder v Holder* [1968] Ch 353 (CA).

not the beneficiary, who has legal title and management authority to deal with the trust assets. Given this, the trustee could easily act as manager on one side of the transaction and in his personal capacity on the other. He could arrange to buy the trust estate's farm produce at a price that advantages him and disadvantages the trust. The same is true of company directors. They too might find it easy to act for the company on one side of the transaction and in their personal capacity on the other. These transactions are proscribed because of the clear risk that the fiduciary's personal interest in obtaining the best price for himself will override his fiduciary duty to obtain the best price for his principal. There is said to be *a conflict of interest and duty*—meaning a conflict of personal interest and fiduciary duty.

The restrictions inherent in the conflict of duty and interest rule go further than simply constraining dealings *between* a fiduciary and his principal. They also prevent the fiduciary pursuing opportunities for himself that he has a duty to pursue for his principal. For example, company directors cannot pursue lucrative business opportunities for themselves that they ought to be pursuing for their companies.[10] Indeed, so strict is the rule that a remedy is available against the fiduciary even if it can be proved that the opportunity was not one that the principal could have afforded to pursue, or wanted to pursue, or would have succeeded in obtaining whatever his aspirations.[11] The fiduciary is only relieved of his duty if his principal gives prior informed consent to the fiduciary personally pursuing the opportunity. Without this consent, the fiduciary's personal autonomy to act on his own account is constrained by his duty to his principal.

If all of this seems largely academic, then ponder the position of company directors. Modern companies usually have widely defined business objectives; they are legally *able* to pursue a wide range of business opportunities. Should this mean that *any* business opportunity that a director encounters is one that he has a duty to pursue for his company? Clearly not. Directors would find their personal autonomy unacceptably inhibited were this the case. Courts have devoted considerable attention to defining the legitimate reach of 'corporate opportunities'. It is conceded that the director's personal autonomy needs to be constrained beyond the sphere of his company's current operations, but not too far

---

[10] *Cook v Deeks* [1916] 1 AC 554 (PC).
[11] *Keech v Sandford* (1726) 25 ER 223, (1726) Sel Cas Ch 61; *Industrial Development Consultants Ltd v Cooley* [1972] 1 WLR 443.

beyond those boundaries.[12] The restrictions should extend only as far as is necessary to ensure the director's undivided attention to the loyal management of his company.

And if all of this were not enough to ensure loyalty, the fiduciary obligation extends even further. The fiduciary is also barred from taking up opportunities he comes by *because* of his fiduciary role—perhaps he learns of a business opportunity, or is invited to participate in a promising venture. He may have no *duty* to pursue these opportunities on behalf of his principal, but if the opportunity would not have come to him but for his position, then he is forbidden to pursue it on his own account without the prior informed consent of his principal. He is not allowed to make a *secret profit* from his position. When this rule is used to force disgorgement of bribes and corrupt secret commissions, it seems to serve a useful purpose; otherwise, however, its operation can be harsh. The secret profits rule has the potential to catch transactions where there is no whiff of disloyalty or diverted management focus, let alone of bribes and corrupt secret commissions, and to compel the fiduciary to disgorge the benefits.[13] When this happens, the rule seems to have lost its primary footing. It is one thing to require disgorgement of bribes that have been paid to company directors to persuade them to favour a particular bidder in a tendering process. It seems quite another to require disgorgement of the profits from a publishing venture, for example, simply because the opportunity was presented to the director because of the skills he had displayed as director on the board of an art gallery.

As these examples illustrate, loyalty is thus exacted, sometimes in a draconian way. The fiduciary is prevented from pursuing his self-interest when all around him are free to take up the relevant opportunities. This only serves to reinforce the point that the duty of loyalty is not designed to deter fiduciaries from activities which the general law regards as improper, but to deter them from proper activities which the law regards as inimical to the loyal execution of their fiduciary role. The foundation of the rule is a somewhat cynical view of human nature: the assumption is that without such a proscriptive rule the fiduciary would be motivated by

---

[12] *Regal (Hastings) Ltd v Gulliver* [1942] 1 All ER 378, [1967] 2 AC 134n (HL); *Peso-Silver Mines Ltd v Cropper* [1966] SCR 673, 58 DLR (2d) 1 (Can SCt); *Canadian Aero Services Ltd v O'Malley* [1974] SCR 592, (1973) 40 DLR (3d) 371 (Can SCt); *Industrial Development Consultants Ltd v Cooley* [1972] 1 WLR 443.
[13] *Boardman v Phipps* [1967] 2 AC 46 (HL); *Regal (Hastings) Ltd v Gulliver* [1942] 1 All ER 378, [1967] 2 AC 134n (HL). On bribes, see *AG for Hong Kong v Reid* [1994] 1 AC 324 (PC).

self-interest rather than by duty.[14] The remedies are specifically designed to remove the incentive to pursue personal interest.

These fiduciary rules come with one further benefit. They operate as default rules, imposed by law whenever the circumstances warrant it. There is no need for any costly bargaining or contractual formalities to ensure that the fiduciary is bound. This makes fiduciary law 'efficient', as the law and economics scholars would describe it. Indeed, although it is commonly said that no one can be made a fiduciary against his will, the only real escape is to avoid the relationship itself: a party who has consented to be part of a relationship that the law deems fiduciary will have fiduciary obligations imposed upon him.[15]

One final point is necessary. It is crucial to note that loyalty is exacted by these fiduciary duties, but no more than loyalty. A breach of fiduciary duty only occurs when there is disloyalty, not whenever the principal's interests are not, in fact, furthered. If the fiduciary has caused loss to the principal through negligence, or breach of the relationship's settled terms, or abuse of power, then the principal may have a remedy, but it will not be disgorgement for breach of the fiduciary's duty of loyalty. The principal's claim will have to be based on these other causes of action with their own distinctive remedies.[16]

DISGORGEMENT REMEDIES—DIFFICULTIES OF PRINCIPLE AND POLICY

The disgorgement response to fiduciary breaches seems simple, but it is in fact surprisingly troublesome. Its rationale is clear—it is to deter disloyalty by removing any incentive the fiduciary may have to breach the duty—but its implementation is difficult.

Some features are straightforward. Consider the issue of quantification. The motivation for the disgorgement remedy indicates that the disloyal fiduciary is only to be stripped of profits *arising from his*

---

[14] And, as if to emphasize this, *Item Software (UK) Ltd v Fassihi* [2004] EWCA Civ 1244, [2004] BCC 994 (CA) suggests that it is a further breach of the duty of loyalty not to *disclose* these disloyal breaches to the fiduciary's principal. The logic in this is not compelling.

[15] *Hospital Products Ltd v United States Surgical Corporation* (1984) 156 CLR 41 (Aust HCt). And *if* a person is a fiduciary, then contractual exclusion clauses will not be effective to eliminate this irreducible core of fiduciary loyalty: *Armitage v Nurse* [1998] Ch 241 (CA). Of course, such a contractual term would likely defeat the argument that an individual was a fact-based fiduciary, but is material in cases of status-based fiduciaries.

[16] And now there is debate over whether awards of exemplary damages may also be possible: *Re Brogden* (1886) 38 ChD 546 (North J: no); *Harris v Digital Pulse Pty Ltd* (2003) 56 NSWLR 298 (Heydon JA: no; Mason P: yes; Spigelman CJ: undecided).

disloyalty. If these profits are enhanced because of the fiduciary's own input, whether in money or in time, effort and skill, then some discount must be made in his favour.[17] Of course, if these contributions of time, effort, and skill should have been devoted to the beneficiaries' interests in any event, then no allowance is necessary.[18]

The principal difficulties with disgorgement—and there are two—lie elsewhere. First, the disgorgement remedy is commonly regarded as proprietary, rather than personal, and so it is associated with all the special incidents that this status entails. Second, the Equitable response to fiduciary breaches involving contracts *between* the fiduciary and his principal seems inconsistent with the analytical foundations of the fiduciary rule.

First consider the proprietary nature of the disgorgement remedy. The fiduciary holds the profits of his breach on trust for his principal from the moment they are obtained.[19] The principal then has preferred status on the fiduciary's insolvency, and this is inevitably controversial. Nevertheless, the analysis supporting this proprietary status is both simple and historically compelling.[20] Disgorgement requires the fiduciary to pay over the profits of his disloyalty to the principal. From the discussions in earlier chapters,[21] a proprietary reaction in these circumstances is consistent with Equity's treatment of other Equitable obligations that demand payment over to the claimant. If the defendant has the asset in question in his hands, Equity always regards the obligation as specific, and as entitling the claimant to treat the asset as already her own in Equity; it never regards the obligation as merely a personal obligation to pay over the value in money.[22] The maxim, 'Equity treats as done that which ought to be done' is commonly called on as an explanation. It does not explain, although it does describe the importance and the value that Equity accords to the claimant's right to call for the transfer—it is this, not the maxim, which led to the eventual recognition of proprietary status.

However, there is one crucial difference between this obligation to disgorge and all other Equitable obligations to pay over, and that difference

---

[17] *Boardman v Phipps* [1967] 2 AC 46 (HL); *Warman International Ltd v Dwyer* (1995) 182 CLR 544 (Aust HCt).

[18] *Guinness Plc v Saunders* [1990] 2 AC 633 (HL).

[19] *AG for Hong Kong v Reid* [1994] 1 AC 324 (PC).

[20] Although other views have held sway: *Lister v Stubbs* (1890) 45 ChD 1 (CA).

[21] See especially Chapter 3, 63–7.

[22] Although see Chapter 9, 290–4, 298–303, for the modern policy debates surrounding this assertion. *If* the disgorgement response is proprietary (although see the criticisms that follow), then the claimant is entitled to specific redelivery of the asset from her fiduciary: see Chapter 6, 169–72.

arguably undermines the rationale for disgorgement's proprietary status. The aim of the obligation to disgorge is to deter the defendant; the aim of all the other Equitable obligations to pay over is to make the claimant 'whole' again in some particular way. Put another way, the rationale for disgorgement is not that the *claimant* must have the asset; it is that the *defendant* must *not* have it; the rationale in all other cases is quite different. To deliver its deterrence objective, disgorgement does not need to give the claimant preferred proprietary status. A personal remedy will have precisely the same deterrent effect; the disloyal defendant will still be stripped of his profits. If the defendant is solvent, the claimant will receive a windfall. If the defendant is insolvent, then he will be stripped of his disloyal profits in any event, and the rationale for disgorgement does not demand that the claimant be especially favoured in the allocation.

In fact this critical analysis of the rationale for disgorgement's proprietary status can be taken a step further. If the fiduciary is insolvent, then the real debate is whether the fiduciary's principal or the fiduciary's other creditors should reap the benefits of these disloyal gains. A traditional proprietary response favours the principal over the others, allowing her to recover in full even though she has suffered no loss. This forces the other creditors to resort to a correspondingly smaller insolvency pool, thereby increasing the extent of their loss. If the disgorgement remedy were not proprietary, then the principal would also have to share these insolvency losses proportionately. But it seems reasonable to go even further. Given the specific aims of the disgorgement remedy, these claims could legitimately be *deferred* to the compensation claims of other creditors.[23] This would most clearly recognize that the remedial aim of disgorgement is deterrence, not compensation of the principal. Deferred recovery of disgorgement claims would allow the fiduciary's general creditors to be compensated as fully as possible from the estate, but would still ensure that the fiduciary did not benefit from his wrongdoing.

Consider a disloyal fiduciary who owes his principal £5,000 and his general creditors £15,000, but whose assets amount to only £10,000. If the principal has a proprietary claim to the assets in the insolvency pool,[24]

---

[23] Although insolvency analysts fear that altering priorities on insolvency in this way will induce claimants to force defendants into early, and perhaps unwarranted, company liquidation or personal bankruptcy so as to take the benefit of these rules. If the defendant has the funds, however, then all parties will be paid in full; if not, then on this analysis there is no reason to give the principal 'compensation': she is not claiming for any loss.

[24] This depends upon her being able to identify particular assets as traceably representing 'her' profits: see Chapter 4, 98–100.

then she will recover her full £5,000. The other creditors will be forced to share the remaining £5,000: they will get only £0.33 for every £1.00 they are owed. If the principal's disgorgement claim is not proprietary, however, then all the creditors (including the principal) can resort to the full pool, and all will receive £0.50 for every £1.00 they are owed. Going a step further, if the disgorgement claim is deferred, then the entire pool is allocated to the general creditors first. They can recover £0.66 for every £1.00 they are owed. This would exhaust the pool, leaving the principal unpaid, but still leaving the defaulting fiduciary without any of the profits of his fiduciary breach. The deterrence objective would still have been achieved.[25]

This re-analysis is a long way from Equity's current approach, and any change in thinking would have significant ramifications. Part of the incentive to pursue fiduciary breaches is to gain access to proprietary disgorgement remedies. If proprietary status were denied, and especially if personal claims were deferred, then claimants would inevitably examine their alternatives more carefully. Take a simple example. A trustee steals £100 from his trust fund and places a winning bet at the races, realizing £600. This scenario involves a clear breach of the trustee's fiduciary obligations of loyalty: it involves both a conflict of duty and interest and a secret profit. On the revised analysis advocated here, the beneficiary would have a *personal* claim against the trustee for disgorgement of the £600 profit, but not a proprietary claim. Indeed, if the policy arguments are followed, this personal claim would be a deferred insolvency claim. However, if the trust arrangement requires the trustee to invest the trust funds for the beneficiary, then it is open to the claimant to ignore the disloyalty and simply ratify the unauthorized investment (as it will surely be). The £600 will then be swept into the trust fund; the claimant will have a proprietary claim to it. Even if this option is not open, the claimant can certainly sue the trustee for breach of the terms of the trust and require him to reinstate the trust fund by restoring the £100 he has removed. The current orthodoxy is that this claim, too, is proprietary; it can be secured by a lien on the £600 pool of winnings.[26] If the defendant were insolvent, these

---

[25] But if any funds remained in the pool, the principal would be entitled to them. One way or another, all disloyal profits would be stripped from the fiduciary. The issue, on insolvency, is not whether profits should be paid to the principal, but whether the principal's claim to profits should be treated as equally deserving of insolvency priority when compared with other creditors' claims.

[26] For both of these alternatives, see Chapter 4, 102–6.

distinctions would become extremely pertinent. The alternative analysis advocated here would only affect the proprietary status of disgorgement claims founded on breach of the fiduciary's duty of loyalty; other avenues might allow the claimant proprietary access to benefits but on different grounds. A more principled analysis would separate these grounds.

In short, the proprietary status of the disgorgement remedy is controversial. By now it must be clear that proprietary status is inevitably controversial. The dividing line between personal and proprietary rights is widely regarded as one of the most troubling theoretical and practical distinctions currently facing the law, and these problems in the fiduciary area are not unique.

The second difficulty with the disgorgement remedy, mentioned above, can be addressed more concisely. It concerns the approach to contracts *between* the fiduciary and his principal. These contracts invariably involve the fiduciary in a conflict of duty and interest. It follows that Equity will provide the principal with a remedy. However, what Equity does in these circumstances is quite different from its general approach to disgorgement. Equity does not try to calculate the disloyal advantage to the fiduciary. It simply allows the principal to *rescind*—or unwind—the contract.[27] Suppose a company director sells his land to his company without informing the company of his personal interest in the sale. Regardless of the fairness of the deal, or the director's disclosure of all material information (other than his personal interest in the deal), or the company's considered approval of the transaction, the company remains entitled to rescind the contract for breach of fiduciary duty. Each party will then have to restore to the other what was transferred under the deal. This strategy removes any inherent profit from the fiduciary, but the court does not have to calculate what that profit might have been; it does not have to engage in the impossible task of remaking a 'reasonable' bargain between the parties.[28] This strategy is now so embedded that rescission is regarded as the *only* remedy available to a principal who finds

---

[27] Notice that rescission is also the remedy when one party has not properly consented to the contractual engagement (Chapter 7, 204–19), and then the remedy is restitution, directed at reversing any unjust enrichments (Chapter 9, 294–303). These different motivations and correspondingly different doctrinal analyses suggests there ought to be corresponding differences in the remedies, especially in assessing their proprietary nature and any appropriate defences.

[28] *Aberdeen Railway Co v Blaikie Bros* (1854) 1 Macq 661 (HL).

herself in this situation.[29] This limited response can sometimes seem most unfair, either to the principal or to the fiduciary.

At times the unfairness affects the principal. Suppose the director sells land to his company and makes a profit of £40,000 on the sale. If the company resells the land before it discovers the fiduciary breach, then it cannot rescind the contract: it cannot return the land to the director, so it cannot demand that he return the purchase price.[30] This is the rule with rescission.[31] It follows that the company is left without a remedy against its disloyal director even though it can prove his disloyalty. This is inconsistent with the impetus driving fiduciary obligations and fiduciary remedies. Coherence demands a more principled response, which is to calculate the fiduciary's 'profit' from the disloyal sale *in money*, and to strip him of it. Unless this is done, the fiduciary rule lacks practical impact.

At other times, however, the unfairness affects the fiduciary. Again, suppose the director sells land to his company, but this time at a fair market price. Measured in money, the fiduciary has not made *any* profit from his fiduciary breach. Nevertheless, the company is still entitled to rescind the contract. Of course, if the property market is rising, it will not rescind; it will instead affirm the deal and excuse the breach. But if the property market crashes dramatically, then the company is entitled to insist that the director takes back the land and returns the purchase price. In these circumstances the Equitable remedy does not work to force the fiduciary to disgorge disloyal profits; it forces him to carry a market risk that has nothing to do with his duty of loyalty.[32]

---

[29] *Re Cape Breton Co* (1885) 29 ChD 795 (CA); *Ladywell Mining Co v Brookes* (1887) 35 ChD 400 (CA). However, this restrictive stance appears to be disappearing in the face of arguments that courts of Equity can award Equitable compensation for breach of an Equitable duty, and in these circumstances the law can be seen as imposing a duty on directors, not merely placing them under a disability (but contrast *Movitex Ltd v Bulfield* [1988] BCLC 104 (Vinelott J)).

[30] *Alati v Kruger* (1955) 94 CLR 216 (Aust HCt), 223–4, endorsed in *O'Sullivan v Management Agency & Music Ltd* [1985] QB 428 (CA). But see *Smith New Court Securities v Scrimgeour Vickers (Asset Management) Ltd* [1977] AC 254, 262 (Lord Browne-Wilkinson). Furthermore, it seems that rescission is an all-or-nothing process—either the contract is rescinded in its entirety, or it stands with full effect: *TSB Bank plc v Camfield* [1995] 1 WLR 430 (CA); *Maguire v Makaronis* (1998) 188 CLR 449; cp partial rescission in *Vadasz v Pioneer Concrete (SA) Pty Ltd* (1995) 184 CLR 102 (Aust HCt).

[31] See Chapter 9, 293–303, but also see *McKenzie v McDonald* [1927] VLR 134 (although this case is perhaps better interpreted as one delivering Equitable compensation for *loss*).

[32] See the facts in *Re Duckwari Plc* [1999] Ch 253 (CA), although there the remedy was necessarily statutory, since the company no longer owned the sale property and so could not effect rescission in Equity. Recall that Equity's remedy of *laches* is alert to this possibility, and will at least prevent the principal from delaying strategically and then acting in its own self-interest: see Chapter 2, 34–7.

This potential for risk shedding was not anticipated, and certainly not intended, when rescission was adopted as the appropriate response to these breaches. Then it was undoubtedly the fairest remedy: it avoided the need to calculate reasonable and unreasonable profit margins for the 'disloyal' fiduciary, and markets in most assets were sufficiently stable that neither party benefited from external factors. Markets are no longer so stable. Now it is necessary to insulate the fiduciary from external factors. If the problem is disloyalty, then the fiduciary should disgorge disloyal profits, but nothing more.[33] The only way to achieve this alignment of breach and remedy is by money remedies, not proprietary rescission. When the principal complains of a disloyal sale, the courts should calculate the 'profit' from the disloyalty alone, and then strip the fiduciary of it, in money.

This suggestion would solve the difficulties for both principals and fiduciaries. Moreover, if the money remedy were personal, rather than secured by a lien against the sale asset, then the approach would also address the difficulties associated with disgorgement's preferred proprietary status. All of this would require a sea change in Equity's current practices, however. Nevertheless, useful analogies might readily be drawn between these troublesome disgorgement cases, and cases where trustees are personally obliged to reinstate trust assets that they have misappropriated.[34]

THE REACH OF FIDUCIARY REGULATION

Fiduciary law offers some powerful advantages to those who can rely on its reach. Fiduciaries must behave loyally, even in dealings that seem only peripherally related to the fiduciary relationship; disappointed principals can (at least for now) take advantage of proprietary disgorgement remedies to recover windfall profits. These advantages make it essential to know *who* might be subjected to these onerous fiduciary standards.

Recall that fiduciary law evolved from Equity's regulation of the relationship between trustees and beneficiaries. Over time these rules were extended, with minor modifications, to cover other situations that seemed analogous. Now it is accepted that relationships between directors and their companies, agents and their principals, solicitors and their clients, and partners and their co-partners are all fiduciary. These are all 'status-based' fiduciary relationships. The status itself inevitably

---

[33] On the other hand, if the land purchase was also an unwise investment, then the responsible directors may have to compensate the company for losses caused by their negligent mismanagement: see Chapter 6, 165–8.
[34] See Chapter 6, 174–8.

attracts fiduciary impositions: *every* company director is automatically a fiduciary, for example, with all the constraints on personal autonomy associated with that status.

But fiduciary law did not stop there. Claimants argued for fiduciary rules to be applied *whenever* the circumstances suggested that one party ought to be compelled by law to put the other's interests ahead of his own. They argued for 'fact-based' fiduciary status. This is the modern battleground, with advantageous remedies providing the incentive to argue for expansion. Defining this expanded category has proved elusive. Most attempts have focused on earmarking the crucial characteristics of a fiduciary relationship: one party entrusts property to another, or undertakes to act in the interests of another, or relies on another, or is vulnerable to abuse by another, or is able to exercise a discretion affecting the other.[35] But this is not enough. These descriptors often apply when relationships are *not* fiduciary: consider the relationship between garage repairman and vehicle owner, homeowner and housepainter, driver and other road-users. The descriptors remain apt, yet these relationships are all accepted as adequately protected by contract and tort law.

The problem is that the common descriptors miss the essential flavour of the fiduciary imperative. They downgrade it to a requirement to 'act in the interests of the other party'. Every contract requires this; so, too, do most torts. Fiduciary law does more. It requires the fiduciary to *subjugate* his personal autonomy to the interests of the other: his role demands a more general denial of self-interest. But this insight must also address the philosophy that personal freedom should stop only where harm to others starts (this is how contract and tort law rules are worked out). We then get closer to defining fiduciaries. Fiduciary obligations are warranted only if the purpose of one party's role in the relationship *demands* such self-denial; if, without it, the relationship would be unprotected. This purpose-based test is clearly met by status-based fiduciaries; it may be met by others. However, it is not met simply because one party would prefer the other to act selflessly, or has assumed this to be the case; nor is it denied simply because the claimant's interests can still be served not-withstanding some selfish behaviour. The fiduciary imperative is more narrowly, but more carefully, defined.

Claims for an expansion of fiduciary law come from other directions too. Fiduciary law regulates management discretion. For a long time this

---

[35] *Hospital Products v United States Surgical Corporation* (1984) 156 CLR 41 (Aust HCt), 96–7 (Mason J).

was assumed to mean discretion in the management of the principal's property so as to protect his economic interests.[36] Despite this, Canadian jurisdictions have recently sought to use the fiduciary regime to protect non-economic interests, such as bodily integrity, privacy, freedom of information, and family and community values.[37] The real complaint in these cases is invariably that the general law does not offer an appropriate remedy. The doctor who abuses his relationship with his patient by demanding sexual favours in return for drugs does not have 'profits' to disgorge; he is not required to be 'loyal', in the sense intended in fiduciary cases. He *is* required to act in the interests of his patients, however, and if this obligation does not adequately meet the particular facts then direct law reform is needed, not a fiduciary fudge.

A more principled approach to who is a fiduciary and what interests are protected would put an end to the notion that fiduciary law is a modern growth area. General self-denial is rarely *necessary* to achieve the economic purpose of a relationship. Parties' interests are usually adequately protected by public law rules, or by private law rules of contract, tort, unjust enrichment and the non-fiduciary Equitable duties discussed later in this chapter. 'Status-based' and 'fact-based' fiduciaries are the exception, although a crucial exception.

Even if fiduciaries are defined narrowly, the social and economic benefits of fiduciary rules are usually considered self-evident. Given this, it is salutary to realize that civil law jurisdictions manage without them. These jurisdictions allegedly enjoy the benefits of a much more demanding concept of good faith than common law jurisdictions, and they are more comfortable with specific enforcement of contracts; nevertheless, they happily operate without requiring the same degree of self-denial that is demanded of fiduciaries, and without the remedial benefits of proprietary disgorgement.

OBLIGATIONS IMPOSED ON DECISION-MAKERS—RULES REGULATING ABUSE OF POWER

Equity's second category of proscriptive rules is devised to regulate the abuse of power by decision-makers. These rules operate far more widely

---

[36] *White v Jones* [1995] 2 AC 206, 271 (Lord Browne-Wilkinson).
[37] *Norberg v Wynrib* [1992] 2 SCR 226, 92 DLR (4th) 229, 268–9 and 275 (McLachlin J); *Frame v Smith* [1987] 2 SCR 99, 143, 42 DLR (4th) 81 (Wilson J); *M (K) v M (H)* (1992) 96 DLR (4th) 289.

than Equity's fiduciary rules. Their aim is not merely to address fiduciary self-interest or disloyalty; it is to regulate the exercise of *all* powers where the claimant's interests may be compromised by the defendant's decision. Again, these rules do not prescribe decision-making strategies; they proscribe. This rather negative aim is designed to ensure that decisions are not grounded on irrelevant considerations or directed at achieving unacceptable ends.

An example is instructive. Company directors usually have power to issue new company shares. This power can be exercised for various perfectly legitimate reasons, the most obvious being to raise capital for business expansion. What directors cannot do, however, is deliberately use this power to alter the voting majorities within the company, perhaps so that one shareholder becomes better placed to mount a takeover bid than a rival shareholder.[38] This improper purpose would constitute an abuse of the directors' power to issue shares.

As with fiduciary rules, these rules on abuse of power were first worked out in the context of trusts, although their application and impact have now spread well beyond that context. The easiest way to understand this is to consider how they grew out of earlier and less satisfactory alternatives.

LIMITING CAPACITY

The most primitive mechanism for controlling the abuse of power is to limit the power itself. Instead of giving trustees open-ended powers of investment, for example, the settlor might confine the trustee to selection from a short list of options. This dramatically reduces the risk that the power will be misused. Similarly, the powers of company directors can be tightly constrained by provisions in the company's memorandum and articles (these are the two documents comprising the company's management constitution), and agents' powers can be constrained by contract.

Any purported action outside the nominated restriction is without authority, so it (usually) has no legal effect—it is *void*. This is known as the *ultra vires* doctrine: an actor has no capacity to operate beyond the limits of his power, and an act without capacity is said to be *ultra vires*. The doctrine refers to *absence* of power, not abuse of power. The legal consequences are dramatic. The deal made *ultra vires* has to be unwound; in particular, any property transferred under these void contracts can be recovered.[39]

---

[38] *Howard Smith Ltd v Ampol Petroleum Ltd* [1974] AC 821 (PC).
[39] How this is achieved is increasingly controversial: see Chapter 9, 290–4, 294–8.

This basic strategy has its uses, but there are significant drawbacks. The approach is usually unacceptable to trust beneficiaries and principals. The reason is simple. Eliminating discretion is too inhibiting: the whole point of having a trustee (or a company director or an agent) is so that he can take effective delegated decisions in a wide range of circumstances. Indeed, the approach is often equally unacceptable to third parties. Significant risks that contracts might be void make third parties less interested in dealing with the relevant power-holders. The strategy is therefore commercially counter-productive. To reduce these risks to third parties, the law eventually developed a doctrine of 'ostensible authority'. This validates at least some of these unauthorized deals, in particular those where the power-holders are held out by their principals as having more authority than they in fact possess.[40]

GOOD FAITH IN EQUITY AND '*WEDNESBURY*' UNREASONABLENESS AT COMMON LAW

The second advance, developed in response to the shortcomings of the first, concedes that actors need discretions, but recognizes that these discretions need to be regulated somehow. Nevertheless, the regulatory mechanism is relatively crude. An exercise of power is regarded as valid unless the exercise is in bad faith. Bad faith can be proved directly, but it is also assumed to be present if no reasonable person in similar circumstances could ever have come to the same decision. This is the Equitable test of 'bona fides' (good faith),[41] but the Common Law test of '*Wednesbury*' unreasonableness, so named after the Common Law case which set out the classic statement of the grounds for judicial review of administrative actions, is precisely the same.[42]

There is a subtle but important difference between this strategy and the previous one. According to Equity, these acts are within the capacity of the actor. They are not *ultra vires*; they are, at most, an *abuse* of power. They are therefore regarded as valid acts until the disappointed claimant decides to take action. Only then can they be set aside and the improper

---

[40] *Freeman & Lockyer v Buckhurst Park Properties (Mangal) Ltd* [1964] 2 QB 480 (CA). For companies, these Common Law rules are enhanced by statute: Companies Act 1985 ss. 35, 35A.

[41] *Vatcher v Paul* [1915] AC 372 (PC); *Howard Smith Ltd v Ampol Petroleum Ltd* [1974] AC 821 (PC); *Bamford v Bamford* [1970] 1 Ch 212 (CA). All these cases also consider 'proper purposes': see below, 145–7.

[42] *Associated Provincial Picture Houses v Wednesbury Corpn* [1948] 1 KB 223 (CA). See *Edge v Pensions Ombudsman* [1998] Ch 512, 534, 536; aff'd [2000] Ch 602, 628–30, recognizing the analogy.

decision unwound. Equity describes these acts as voidable, not void.[43] As we shall see later, this less aggressive intervention is much kinder to both claimants and third parties.

This strategy makes sense, but in practice it provides little scope for intervention. Bad faith in decision-making is very difficult to prove: the intent and motives of the decision-maker are peculiarly within his own knowledge. And proof of the alternative, that *no* reasonable person could ever have made the same decision, is usually equally difficult.

PROPER PURPOSES

The final and most sophisticated strategy for regulating decision-making came much later. This strategy insists that an exercise of power is only legitimate if the power has been exercised for proper purposes, on relevant considerations. (Equity tends to use the first qualification, the Common Law the second.)[44] Notice that the focus is again on the decision-making process, not on the merits of the decision itself. It is about *how* the decision was reached, not *what* was decided. It follows that even if the court finds that a power has been exercised for improper purposes, it will not substitute its own view of the proper decision; that is not the focus of intervention.[45] It will simply declare the improper exercise voidable and insist that the power-holder re-exercise the power properly.[46]

The potential advantages of this 'proper purposes' approach are obvious, but the strategy makes it necessary to define legitimate and illegitimate purposes and considerations. This is not easy. Powers are commonly granted for a wide variety of purposes. Courts must therefore consider each case on its merits: they consider the individual or body exercising the power, the individuals who are subject to the power, the type of

---

[43] See *Abacus Trust Co (Isle of Man) v Barr* [2003] Ch 409 (Lightman J), and also Chapter 7, 204–6, and Chapter 9, 298–303. The Common Law takes a different, but troublesome, approach. It traditionally analyses these cases as *ultra vires* acts. In the public law context, it does so on the basis that Parliament would not have given the actor the power to act in bad faith or totally unreasonably. Where the power is not derived from Parliament, or where the power is expressly stated to be unlimited, this explanation falters. The Common Law also has difficulty dealing with the practical incidents of void exercises of power and their unwelcome impact on third parties. The illogical, but pragmatic, position often adopted is, it seems, to regard the improper exercise of power as theoretically void but functionally voidable. Some comparisons with Equity might prove fruitful.

[44] *Vatcher v Paul* [1915] AC 372 (PC); *Howard Smith Ltd v Ampol Petroleum Ltd* [1974] AC 821 (PC); *Bamford v Bamford* [1970] 1 Ch 212 (CA).

[45] The court does have a jurisdiction to remove trustees. It can then appoint substitutes or simply order the performance of the trust itself. In these special circumstances it is therefore conceivable that the court could exercise the discretion.

[46] *Re Hastings-Bass* [1975] Ch 25 (CA).

power, and the legitimate expectations of all who are affected by its exercise. No general rules are possible, and yet the strategy works surprisingly well.

These difficulties in assessing proper purposes are not academic. Consider the 'stakeholder' controversy in modern corporate governance debates. Directors must exercise their discretionary powers for proper purposes, but does this mean they should exercise their powers so as to maximize profits for shareholders, or so as to benefit a much wider group of stakeholders, including employees, consumers, local communities and even the environment? The orthodox view is that the shareholders must be the primary focus. Indeed, this view is reinforced by the realization that if proper purposes are too widely defined, then the directors will effectively have an unfettered discretion. *Any* decision they take must be intended to benefit someone from the nominated classes, and so every decision will somehow be for 'proper' purposes. This simple example illustrates both the power and the limitations of the proper purposes rule.

The proper purposes rule has been used to regulate trustees' discretions and to restrict the powers of boards of directors and general meetings of shareholders.[47] The limits of the rule need to be emphasized, however. Legal intervention is directed solely at the question of whether the power has been used for *improper* purposes. Take a simple but important practical illustration. Company shareholders have a statutory right to dismiss directors by simple majority vote at a general meeting.[48] Directors may feel indignant if this power is used to dismiss them when their performance is perfectly satisfactory. Nevertheless, it is unlikely that the shareholders will be found to have acted for improper purposes (except perhaps where there is evidence of bad faith). The option to dismiss without cause is precisely one of the purposes for including the power within the statute. Of course, the director may be able to advance other claims for legal redress; what is significant is that 'improper purposes' is unlikely to be one of them. Context is important, however. Take another example. The trustee of a discretionary trust has a discretion whether to benefit his beneficiaries. If the trustee suddenly and unexpectedly decides to withdraw support from a long-standing recipient of benefits, the court may intervene. This is because the overriding purpose of all trustees' powers is to act in the interests of the beneficiaries.

---

[47] And whether this last example is Equity or the Common Law in action is not clear.
[48] Companies Act 1985, s. 303.

Termination of benefit is possible—it is within the scope of the power —but perhaps its implementation requires reasonable notice to the beneficiary.[49]

Allegations of improper purposes in decision-making can be advanced by anyone potentially affected by the defendant's decision. As with fiduciary law, a claimant does not have to show that she has suffered a loss from the improper decision. For example, a beneficiary under a discretionary trust is entitled to distributions from the trust fund *only if* the trustee decides she should be given the benefit (this is why the trust is 'discretionary'). If she is ignored and can prove that the trustee exercised his discretion improperly, then she is entitled to complain that the decision should be unwound. But when the trustee eventually re-exercises his discretion properly, she may still be ignored. As it turns out, the improper exercise will have caused her no loss, but she is entitled to complain nevertheless. Her 'chance' or expectancy gives her a legitimate interest in the proper exercise of the power.

JURISDICTIONAL COMPARISONS—COMMON LAW AND EQUITY

Many individuals have the right to exercise discretionary powers. Most fiduciaries do, but so too do government agencies, the managers of trade unions and clubs, and even contracting parties, especially where large projects are being undertaken. The strategies used to contain abuses are palpably similar across all these areas, and yet, interestingly, only in the case of fiduciaries is the intervention characterized as Equitable. Otherwise the Common Law intervenes, adopting strategies allegedly invented by Common Law courts with little if any explicit acknowledgement of Equity's parallel developments. These Common Law rules reiterate the Equitable notion that there is no such thing as an unfettered discretion: there is scope for judicial review even if the discretion is specifically wide, and even if the power-granting body seems to exclude the possibility.[50] The parallels even persist on the remedial front. The Common Law departs from its usual approach of confining its remedies to monetary compensation, and in these cases, like Equity, it too compels action. Only recently have courts recognized that these Common Law and Equitable rules are performing

---

[49] *Scott v National Trust* [1998] 2 All ER 705, 718 (deciding whether to alter traditional fund distribution practices, although seemingly on the basis of *Wednesbury* reasonableness).

[50] *Padfield v Minister of Agriculture, Fisheries and Food* [1968] AC 997 (HL); *Anisminic Ltd v Foreign Compensation Commission* [1969] 2 AC 147 (HL); and anticipated in *Associated Provincial Picture Houses v Wednesbury Corpn* [1948] 1 KB 223 (CA).

precisely the same function in almost exactly the same way.[51] Integration across the jurisdictional divide has been effected in all but name.

OBLIGATIONS IMPOSED ON INFORMATION-HOLDERS—REGULATING BREACH OF CONFIDENCE

Equity's final category of proscriptive rules concerns the use of information. The modern perception is that information is power, and indeed some aspects of Equity's regulation of the use of information have strong parallels with its regulation of the use of power, especially a fiduciary's use of his power to deal with the claimant's property. The jurisdiction is vast. For example, if defendants act without permission then these Equitable rules will deliver remedies if an individual's private and personal confidences are sold to a newspaper,[52] or a company's industrial secrets are used to profitable advantage, or government information is used to anticipate market movements. The rules apply without the need for contractual underpinnings, and indeed without the need for any continuing relationship between claimant and defendant. Despite this enormous potential, this area remains the least well-developed of the strategies considered in this chapter. The jurisdiction only emerged in the early nineteenth century, and its rules and their motivations are far more ambiguous than those considered so far.

STRATEGIES FOR PROTECTING INFORMATION

The Common Law's usual strategy for protecting claimants from harm is to make the wrongdoer compensate the claimant. He must pay for any 'minus' he causes to her welfare, whether by harm to her person, her property, or her contractual rights. But when it comes to protecting claimants who have information, this strategy is often worthless. The problem is the peculiar nature of information. When the defendant steals the claimant's information, he does not take it away from her: she still has it, although the defendant has it too.[53] How is her loss to be computed? Until the defendant uses the information, the claimant seems to have lost

---

[51] *Medforth v Blake* [2000] Ch 86 (CA).

[52] Whether this is developing into a 'law of privacy' is hotly contested. The cases still rely predominantly on orthodox breach of confidence rules: *Douglas v Hello! Ltd (No 1)* [2001] QB 967 (CA); *Douglas v Hello! Ltd (No 3)* [2005] EWCA Civ 595, [2005] 3 WLR 881 (CA).

[53] This unusual characteristic is partly what lies behind the law's refusal to characterize information as property, even though information is clearly wealth.

nothing (except, perhaps, the information's secrecy). Even when he does use the information, she may not suffer any financial harm. He may use the information to pursue opportunities quite separate from her business, perhaps to give himself a head-start in developing his own venture, or to allow him to trade against the market, or to sell a story to a publisher. He is not a fiduciary: he is free to pursue his own self-interest without putting the claimant's interests ahead of his own. There seems to be no remedy, and yet this behaviour is clearly unacceptable. The claimant *has* been harmed, even if the harm cannot be measured by a change in her financial or proprietary status. Since control over the use of information is so important to modern societies, the law clearly needs some appropriate regulatory mechanism.

The obvious candidate is Equity's now familiar deterrent remedy, disgorgement. This remedy ignores the claimant's losses and focuses on the defendant's gains. Its objective is to put the defendant in the position he would have been in but for his wrongdoing; it strips him of his ill-gotten profits. Of course, Equity then has to define what will be considered a misuse of information, or a 'breach of confidence', sufficient to attract this remedy. These rules are described in the next section. This deterrent strategy cannot solve all the problems related to misuse of information, but it will operate as an effective disincentive in the many cases where misuse is motivated by financial gain.

There are still remedial gaps, however. Most of these are now regulated by statute; some are regulated by private contract. An example highlights the shortcomings of the Equitable approach and the advantages of alternatives. The employees in a drug company's research laboratory will almost certainly have obligations of secrecy and limitations on personal exploitation of their research results included in their employment contracts. This is not a 'belt and braces' strategy. The Equitable rules do not subject all information to obligations of confidence, and any disgorgement is calculated on the defendant's gains, not on the claimant's losses. This can leave the company unacceptably exposed. Contracts enable the parties to specify which information is to be protected; the remedy for breach is then assessed by reference to the claimant's lost profits or defeated expectations, not the defendant's gains. These differences are often crucial.

BREACH OF CONFIDENCE—BALANCING COMPETING INTERESTS

Equity's rules are directed at misuse of information where this constitutes a 'breach of confidence'. As the terminology suggests, Equity only protects 'confidential' or 'secret' information. It protects it regardless of its physical form or its monetary value, but it protects it only for as long as it remains secret. Information can be secret even if others know of it, so long as it is relatively private or 'not in the public domain'. Once information loses its secrecy, however, it is not protected, even if the reason why it is no longer secret is that someone has published in breach of confidence. This means that newspapers can be made liable for revelations of high-profile private lives, for example, but this disclosure also marks the end of any further protection should other defendants decide to re-publish the information.[54]

If information is secret, then Equity protects it against disclosure or use by anyone who acquires it on the understanding that it is confidential. This might happen because the defendant agrees or knows that the information he receives is confidential, or because circumstances put him on notice that it is confidential. In either case Equity considers it only fair that the defendant should be precluded from using the information in unauthorized ways or disclosing it to others. These rules ensure that the commercial exchange of information, or information discovered by accident or through investigative journalism or industrial espionage, is protected against further disclosure or misuse.

The older cases add another qualification. They suggest that use or disclosure is only precluded if it would cause 'detriment' to the claimant. If the claimant is a private individual, then this requirement is now so watered down that it seems it can be ignored completely: it is enough if the claimant simply prefers that others do not have or use the information.[55] Where the Crown is concerned, however, the rule has teeth. Indeed, the general rule is that disclosure of government secrets is *allowed* unless the disclosure is positively detrimental to the public interest.[56]

In sum, these rules on breach of confidence suggest that information which is disclosed privately and in confidence,[57] or disclosed in commercial negotiations,[58] or discovered in secret investigations[59] is all

[54] *AG v Guardian Newspapers (No 2)* [1990] 1 AC 109 (HL).
[55] *AG v Guardian Newspapers (No 2)* [1990] 1 AC 109 (HL), 256 (Lord Keith), 282 (Lord Goff).
[56] *AG v Jonathan Cape Ltd* [1976] QB 752, 770–1 (Lord Widgery CJ); *Commonwealth v John Fairfax & Sons Ltd* (1980) 147 CLR 39 (Aust HCt), 51 (Mason J).
[57] *Prince Albert v Strange* (1849) 18 LJ Ch 120.
[58] *Coco v A N Clark (Engineers) Ltd* [1969] RPC 41; *Saltman Engineering Co Ltd v Campbell Engineering Co Ltd* (1948) 65 RPC 203; *Lac Minerals Ltd v International Corona Resources Ltd* [1989] 2 SCR 574; [1989] 61 DLR (4th) 14; [1990] FSR 441 (Can SCt).
[59] *AG v Guardian Newspapers (No 2)* [1990] 1 AC 109 (HL).

presumed to be protected, and a defendant who breaches his obligation of confidence is *prima facie* liable to disgorge his unauthorized profits. Protection is not automatic, however. Equity first considers whether this best protects the various competing interests. This balancing exercise is an implicit or explicit part of defining the limits of any civil wrong in the Common Law.

The claimant's interest in confidentiality must be weighed against competing public and private interests in freedom of expression,[60] open government, the pursuit of self-interest, and the maximization of social and economic productivity. The balancing exercise emerges most clearly at the level of defences. The general rule is that the defendant's disclosure of confidential information is permitted if it is in the public interest.[61]

In England, this balancing of competing public interests is overt:[62] there is express recognition of the pressures of social and political opinion. On this basis, defendants have been held to be free to disclose 'confidential' information concerning crimes committed by others, or the accuracy of instruments such as breathalysers used in prosecuting citizens.[63] They have not been free to disclose information concerning the AIDS status of particular doctors, at least where the competing public interest was argued as freedom of the press rather than public health.[64]

Sometimes the public interest argument is turned on its head, and defendants who want to keep information confidential are forced to disclose. For example, journalists may be forced to disclose their sources, or doctors to disclose their records. These cases are primarily concerned with balancing interests in the administration of justice against interests in confidentiality. Interests in the administration of justice will often win out if there is no other way to ensure that a court can make an informed decision in a case where it seems clear that some sort of wrong has been committed. No one is immune from such enforced disclosure, regardless

---

[60] Freedom of expression is a powerful counter-interest, and the tension between this and confidentiality is evident in many cases: *A v B* [2003] QB 195 (CA). The same tension is reiterated in the restrictions to First Amendment in the US and in Art 10 of the European Convention for the Protection of Human Rights and Fundamental Freedoms and now the Human Rights Act 1998.

[61] *AG v Guardian Newspapers (No 2)* [1990] 1 AC 109 (HL), 268–9 (Lord Griffiths), 282–3 (Lord Goff).

[62] Contrast the Australian approach, where the defence is seen to be concerned with what conscionable behaviour demands of the defendant (which, historically, is Equity's general approach).

[63] *Lion Laboratories Ltd v Evans* [1985] QB 526 (CA); but contrast *Schering Chemicals Ltd v Falkman Ltd* [1982] QB 1.

[64] *X Health Authority v Y* [1988] RPC 379.

of any commitments that may have been made about retaining the confidence.[65]

REMEDIES FOR BREACH OF CONFIDENCE

The orthodoxy is certainly that Equity will remedy breaches of confidence by ordering disgorgement of wrongful gains.[66] However, the practice is quite different. The most common remedy is compensation, not disgorgement. This Equitable wrong then begins to look much more like a conventional Common Law tort, not a novel Equitable proscription. When confidences have been breached, claimants are typically given money to remedy the earlier harm and an injunction to prevent future harm. This response parallels the Common Law's response to several important torts. In cases of nuisance, for example, the claimant is often given damages for the harm already caused and an injunction to prevent its continuation. Sometimes the circumstances are such that an injunction would be pointless in these breach of confidence cases, and then the claimants are simply given money.[67] This might be the case where the claimant's invention has already been put into commercial production, or the claimant's idea for a television programme has already been implemented and broadcast. Again, the compensation remedy parallels the Common Law response, although the Common Law needs statutory assistance to enable this sum to be calculated so as to remedy the past harm *and* recognize the future harm from the defendant's continuing use of the information.[68]

These compensation payments must necessarily assess the harm that results when information is misused. Although the law insists that information is not property,[69] these assessments mirror those adopted when property is misused. The claimant's harm is not just her direct loss of the property (or the information); it is also her loss of its 'use value'. 'Use value' is not the value to the defendant of *his* use. That is simple disgorgement. It is the value to the claimant of *her* potential use. It recognizes that she might have bargained with the defendant to allow him to use the property (or the information), and that this chance of bargain has its own commercial value. The calculation of the claimant's 'use value' may make reference to the defendant's profits, but only so as to assess the commercial value of the claimant's bargaining position.

---

[65] *British Steel Corp v Granada Television Ltd* [1981] AC 1096 (HL).
[66] *AG v Guardian Newspapers (No 2)* [1990] 1 AC 109 (HL).
[67] *Seager v Copydex Ltd (No 2)* [1969] 1 WLR 809 (CA).
[68] See Chapter 6, 159–61.   [69] *Boardman v Phipps* [1967] 2 AC 46 (HL).

The final remedy is then compensation, not disgorgement of all the defendant's ill-gotten gains.

All of this makes perfect sense if the Equitable rules are designed to preserve the claimant from harm. Nevertheless, commentators have doubted whether Equity has jurisdiction to do this. The problem is aggravated because the courts themselves simply ignore this doctrinal issue and order 'damages' or 'compensation', with no indication that the terminology is intended to have particular significance. Some academics then insist that the judges must have intended to rely on the Lord Cairns' Act, which allows for damages in addition to or in substitution for an injunction. Others—the doctrinal purists—insist that this Act was only ever intended to apply to *legal* wrongs, so cannot encompass Equitable breaches of confidence; the judges must therefore have intended to rely on Equity's inherent jurisdiction to award Equitable compensation. In fact, if pedantry is to prevail, it seems that Equitable compensation was only ever ordered to remedy damage to property, and since information is not (yet) conceded to be property this cannot afford a justification.[70]

By comparison with all these various compensatory interventions, straightforward disgorgement is rare. Certainly it is ordered if the defendant has not simply breached a confidence, but has misused the information in his fiduciary capacity. Then the remedy is readily justified on traditional fiduciary grounds. Indeed, disgorgement in these cases does not depend upon the information being confidential; the only qualification is that the defendant acquired the information because of his fiduciary role.[71] However, outside these fiduciary cases, disgorgement seems to be a remedy of last resort. It is ordered in cases where any genuine assessment of loss appears to underestimate completely the claimant's real injury. In the most notable modern examples, governments have recovered profits from newspapers that have serialized the life stories of notorious double-agents.[72] In these circumstances the justification may be peculiar and unique: the remedy may reflect an overriding 'public interest' in the administration of the broader institutional framework of government, an interest that can only be advanced if the government is allowed this unusually privileged remedy.[73]

---

[70] See Chapter 6, 174–8. [71] *Boardman v Phipps* [1967] 2 AC 46 (HL).

[72] *AG v Guardian Newspapers (No 2)* [1990] 1 AC 109 (HL).

[73] And, interestingly, quite closely related factual circumstances underpinned the award of a similarly privileged (and, until then, unprecedented) disgorgement remedy for breach of a *contract* of confidentiality between the government and one of its ex-secret service agents: *AG v Blake* [2001] 1 AC 268 (HL). See below, 154–5.

The ambiguities between deterrent (disgorgement) remedies and compensation remedies go beyond quantification. The orthodox view is that the remedy for breach of confidence is a *personal* remedy of account, and that a constructive trust is not appropriate.[74] This is inconsistent with doctrine if the remedy is disgorgement of unauthorized gains. It *would* follow, however, if the remedy were not disgorgement but Equitable compensation for the harm resulting from loss of property. This remedy is explored in the next chapter. This compensation rationale would extend Equity's categories of property still further (or, alternatively, broaden the scope for Equitable compensation to include non-proprietary wrongs), but it would also explicitly ground the remedy in harm for a wrong. Breach of confidence is then simply another civil law wrong with the usual compensation remedy applicable to all such wrongs.

DISGORGEMENT AS A GENERAL REMEDIAL STRATEGY

This is an appropriate point for one further reflection. From what has been said about breach of confidence, it is clear that there is an unresolved tension between the wrong itself and the appropriate legal response. The result is an uncertain remedial framework. Certainty depends upon properly articulating the motivations for legal intervention. These motivations will necessarily define the suitable legal response.

This uncertainly with breach of confidence remedies is reflected in modern Common Law debates. Here, too, there is an important and ongoing legal debate about the place of disgorgement remedies. It is conceded that compensation is the usual remedy for Common Law wrongs. However, there are powerful moves to add disgorgement to the remedial menu. The argument is simple: no defendant should profit from his wrong, and normal legal remedies do not always ensure that this is so. The House of Lords has backed this argument, and held that disgorgement is available in very special and limited cases to remedy breaches of contract.[75] It implicitly recognized that this is also the case for certain property torts.

---

[74] *Lac Minerals Ltd v International Corona Resources Ltd* [1989] 2 SCR 574; [1989] 61 DLR (4th) 14; [1990] FSR 441 (Can SCt) is therefore the subject of much criticism. A majority held that the remedy was a constructive trust; a different majority held that there was a breach of confidence, but only a minority held that the parties were in a fiduciary relationship, which is what orthodox scholarship holds is necessary for such a trust.

[75] *AG v Blake* [2001] 1 AC 268 (HL).

The deterrent effect of a disgorgement remedy is apparent, but it is one thing to order such a remedy against a fiduciary, and quite another to order it against an ordinary wrongdoer. The fiduciary has promised to act altruistically; he ought to be generating profits for his principal. Other wrongdoers usually only concede that they must repair the harm they cause. The law might rationally be otherwise, but this distinction reflects the choice of modern common law. As we saw earlier, changes in remedies automatically effect corresponding changes in legal rights.[76] What this disgorgement debate really illustrates is another stage in the continuing process of refinement and discrimination within the common law. Undifferentiated rights are progressively differentiated, and valued differently, with the different values reflected in distinctive legal remedies. Given that this is the process, if disgorgement is to be used as a tool to differentiate between different types of contracts, or different types of torts, then the rationale for differentiation must be laid bare and the legal advance must proceed rationally and coherently.

REVIEW

It might be said that the function of all law is to regulate personal autonomy. In this chapter, however, the strategies for legal regulation work more aggressively than usual. Here the defendant's autonomy is constrained even if his actions have not caused harm. In most other areas of private law, the defendant's autonomy is constrained only to the extent that his actions actually harm others.

This more aggressive approach is appropriate—indeed, it is the only possible approach—when the law wishes to regulate open-ended situations. In these circumstances the law cannot possibly specify the only acceptable end-point that should be delivered. If civil society demands some form of legal regulation, then the only feasible strategy is to limit the defendant's personal autonomy. Certain activities are proscribed. Outside those bounds, the defendant is left to operate freely. In order to ensure that the defendant complies with these proscriptions, a novel form of *deterrent* remedy is necessary. Instead of compensating the claimant, these remedies focus on the defendant. They aim to render the defendant's unacceptable behaviour a nullity, thereby removing any incentive he might have to pursue the activities that the law regards as unacceptable. He is stripped of his profits; his decisions

---

[76] See Chapter 2, 22–4.

are unwound; if his plans are discovered early enough they are stopped by injunction.

This proscriptive strategy is exceptional, in that it can limit the defendant's freedom of action beyond what is necessary to preserve the claimant from harm. It follows that these strategies need to be carefully confined to situations where they provide the only possible mode of intervention when some sort of intervention is deemed essential. This restrictive test is generally satisfied in the context of fiduciaries and other power-holders, but perhaps not in the context of those who misuse information.

SELECTED BIBLIOGRAPHY

Conaglen, M., 'The Nature and Function of Fiduciary Loyalty' (2005) 121 LQR 452.

Cooter, R. and Freedman, B., 'The Fiduciary Relationship: its Economic Character and Legal Consequences' (1991) 66 NYULR 1045.

Davidson, I. E., 'The Equitable Remedy of Compensation' (1982) 13 Melbourne University Law Review 349.

Duggan, A., 'Is Equity Efficient?' (1997) 113 LQR 601.

Easterbrook, F. H. and Fischel, D. R., 'Contract and Fiduciary Duty' (1993) 36 Journal of Law and Economics 425.

Finn, P. D., 'The Fiduciary Principle' in T.G. Youdan (ed.), *Equity, Fiduciaries and Trusts* (Toronto: Carswell, 1989), Ch. 1.

Goode, R., 'Ownership and Obligation in Commercial Transactions' (1987) 103 LQR 433.

Hayton, D., 'Developing the Obligation Characteristic of the Trust' (2001) 117 LQR 96.

Lowry, J. and Edmonds, R., 'The Corporate Opportunity Doctrine: The Shifting Boundary of the Duties and its Remedies' (1998) 61 MLR 515.

Millett, Sir P., 'Equity's Place in the Law of Commerce' (1998) 114 LQR 214.

Millett, P. J., 'Bribes and Secret Commissions' (1993) 1 RLR 7.

Nolan, R. C., 'The Proper Purpose Doctrine and Company Directors' in B.A.K. Rider (ed.), *The Realm of Company Law* (London: Kluwer, 1998), Ch. 1.

Phillipson, G., 'Transforming Breach of Confidence? Towards a Common Law Right of Privacy under the Human Rights Act' (2003) 66 MLR 726.

Sealy, L.S., 'Fiduciary Relationships' [1962] CLJ 69.

Smith, L., 'The Motive, Not the Deed' in J. Getzler (ed.), *Rationalizing Property, Equity and Trusts* (London: Lexis Nexis: Butterworths, 2003), Ch. 4.

Warren, S. and Brandeis, L. D., 'The Right to Privacy' (1890) 3 Harvard Law Review 289.

Worthington, S., 'Fiduciaries: When is Self-Denial Obligatory?' [1999] CLJ 500.

SELECTED CASES

AG v Guardian Newspapers (No 2) [1990] 1 AC 109 (HL)

AG for Hong Kong v Reid [1994] 1 AC 324 (PC)

Alati v Kruger (1955) 94 CLR 216 (Aust HCt)

Boardman v Phipps [1967] 2 AC 46 (HL)

Canadian Aero Services Ltd v O'Malley [1974] SCR 592, (1973) 40 DLR (3d) 371 (Can SCt)

Chan v Zacharia (1984) 154 CLR 178 (Aust HCt)

Cook v Deeks [1916] 1 AC 554 (PC)

Douglas v Hello! Ltd (No 3) [2005] EWCA Civ 595, [2005] 3 WLR 881 (CA)

Hospital Products Ltd v United States Surgical Corporation (1984) 156 CLR 41 (Aust HCt)

Howard Smith Ltd v Ampol Petroleum Ltd [1974] AC 821 (PC)

Industrial Development Consultants Ltd v Cooley [1972] 1 WLR 443

Lac Minerals Ltd v International Corona Resources Ltd [1989] 2 SCR 574; [1989] 61 DLR (4th) 14; [1990] FSR 441 (Can SCt)

O'Sullivan v Management Agency & Music Ltd [1985] QB 428 (CA)

Regal (Hastings) Ltd v Gulliver [1942] 1 All ER 378, [1967] 2 AC 134n (HL)

Warman International Ltd v Dwyer (1995) 182 CLR 544 (Aust HCt)

6

Supplementing Civil Wrongs

The previous three chapters concerned Equity's distinctive additions to the common law. Equity was seen creating new forms of property, new interests in property, and new civil law obligations. Perhaps surprisingly, none of this generated any serious conflict between Equity and the Common Law. The result was simply increased variety and discrimination within an essentially coherent legal regime. The Equitable rules considered in this chapter are different. Here we see Equity and the Common Law operating alongside each other, but reacting to remarkably similar situations in apparently quite different ways. The potential risk is clear. Like cases may not be treated alike simply because they fall on one or other side of a jurisdictional dividing line. This is cause for concern. Similar rights should generate similar remedies. More than this, rights and remedies should be systematically related: the most highly prized rights should deliver the most highly valued remedies. In short, a logical hierarchy of remedies should be available to protect an acknowledged hierarchy of rights.

The issues covered in this chapter illustrate escalating concerns about the risk of unacceptable disjunctions between Equity and the Common Law. The first section considers the relatively simple matter of Equity supplementing existing Common Law remedies. The next sections consider the more controversial question of Equity and the Common Law embarking on separate paths to deal with the same underlying wrong of negligence. The final sections—the longest and most contentious parts of this chapter—deal with the intractable problem of how Equity protects Equitable property from abuse by the trustee and interference by other third parties. Each section explores the differences between the Equitable rules and their Common Law counterparts. It is crucial that these differences be soundly justified if they are to remain part of the common law.

AUGMENTING COMMON LAW
REMEDIAL STRATEGIES

The Common Law remedies civil wrongs by ordering the defendant to pay compensation to the claimant sufficient to put her in the position she would have been in had the wrong not been committed (so far as money can do that). All Common Law wrongs are remedied this way.[1] The inference is that all these wrongs infringe equally important rights.

A sophisticated legal system must inevitably be more discriminating. Earlier we saw Equity differentiate between wrongs, delivering supplementary injunctive relief in some cases but not in others.[2] Remedial differences acknowledge differences in the value of the underlying rights. This is how a hierarchy of rights develops. Equity also spearheaded yet another strategy that permits further discrimination between different rights: it expanded the availability of damages for certain wrongs.

EXPANDING DAMAGES CLAIMS—'EQUITABLE
DAMAGES'—LORD CAIRNS' ACT

Many Common Law wrongs are isolated events that are easily remedied in money. A negligent driver who damages another's property is simply ordered to pay compensation. The problem is more complicated with ongoing wrongs. Consider the factory owner who creates a nuisance with his noisy production facility. Common Law compensation will only be awarded after the wrong is committed. The victim of ongoing nuisance must therefore take new and repeated court proceedings after the harmful event. This is obviously inconvenient. The problem can be overcome if the court will order an injunction forcing the factory owner to stop the noise. However, a claimant may find that the court decides against an injunction because the balance of competing interests favours the defendant's commercial operation. Before the administration of the Common Law and Chancery courts was fused late in the nineteenth century, the risks associated with Chancery's refusal of an injunction were dramatic: the claimant would then have to start proceedings all over again in the Common Law courts to obtain whatever money remedy might be available for the nuisance already committed.

---

[1] Although recall that there is now statutory provision for ordering injunctions: see below and Chapter 2, 34.

[2] See Chapter 2, 31–4.

To overcome this need to recommence proceedings in the Common Law courts, a statute was enacted: the Chancery Amendment Act 1858 (Lord Cairns' Act).[3] This gave courts the power to award damages 'in addition to or in substitution for' an injunction (and also in addition to or in substitution for an order for specific performance). From the outset, however, it was clear that the Act did more than remedy a simple administrative problem. Chancery could give injunctive relief where there was no course of action at Common Law, so the Act expanded the range of situations for which money damages were allowed. Moreover, damages in substitution for an injunction must, inevitably, relate to the future, not the past. The Act thus allowed damages for anticipated wrongs.[4] Despite these differences, the courts insisted that the *quantification* of damages— what harm could be covered by an award and what could not—was to be assessed in a Common Law fashion.[5] Despite the statutory nature of the remedy and its clear Common Law parallels, these damages are commonly known as *Equitable damages*, a term designed to reinforce jurisdictional divisions in a manner quite contrary to the spirit of the Act itself.

Because the Act clearly expanded the common law's remedial options, the difficulty for the courts was, as always, rational discrimination. Of all the wrongs that had once been seen as important enough to merit injunctive relief, which would now be re-classified as only warranting this new measure of statutory damages? Initially, the rule adopted was that damages should only be awarded in substitution for an injunction where the injuries to the claimant's rights were small, and able to be estimated in money, and adequately compensable by a small sum, and where it would be oppressive to the defendant to grant the injunction requested.[6] This approach attracted two pointed criticisms. First, all the learning on injunctions suggests that if the first three conditions are met, then the court does not have jurisdiction to grant an injunction, so the Act should not apply anyway. Secondly, the last condition is commonly met in cases of trespass and nuisance: the burden of remedying the situation is often out of all proportion to the damage to the claimant. Nevertheless, it is also arguable that courts should be reluctant to allow a defendant to 'buy' his way out of the breach.[7] The dilemma is clear.

---

[3] Now re-enacted in the Supreme Court Act 1981, s. 50.

[4] *Leeds Industrial Co-operative Society Ltd v Slack* [1924] AC 851 (HL); *Wroth v Tyler* [1974] Ch 30.

[5] *Johnson v Agnew* [1980] AC 367 (HL).

[6] *Shelfer v City of London Electric Lighting Co* [1895] 1 Ch 287, 322–3 (A L Smith LJ).

[7] *Jaggard v Sawyer* [1995] 1 WLR 269 (CA), 283–9, 291–2 *per* Millett LJ.

Although the Act is used regularly, these criticisms about how distinctions ought to be drawn have never been adequately answered, and there is still no clear-cut modern rule explaining when the Act should apply. What *is* clear, however, is that the Act provides an additional mechanism for discriminating between superficially similar wrongs. Courts have greater power to construct a rational hierarchy of rights simply by granting better relief for infringement of highly valued rights than for their less valuable counterparts.

PIONEERING NEW CIVIL WRONGS— NEGLIGENCE

Equity does not simply discriminate between existing Common Law rights, privileging some over others. It has also invented new legal rights (and legal wrongs). Here we are concerned with Equity's invention of rights and remedies relating to negligence. Recall that one of the four problems Equity needed to address in regulating the trust was the risk that the trustee would carry out his management functions unduly carelessly.[8] Equity's response was to invent a *duty of care*. This duty now applies to all fiduciaries, and requires them to exercise reasonable care in carrying out their management functions so as to avoid causing harm to their principals. If they breach this duty, then they must compensate their principals for the harm caused by their negligence.

The duty is easy to understand. A trustee administering a family home for trust beneficiaries must look after the house carefully. He must carry out routine maintenance and regular refurbishment, maintain adequate insurance cover, and take steps to reduce the risks of avoidable damage. He must take the same degree of care as would 'an ordinary prudent man in the management of his own affairs'.[9] Similarly, a fiduciary managing an investment portfolio must oversee the balance of investments and make alterations or take up new investments only after due consideration of the existing and predicted market conditions; he must take advice where necessary.[10] Indeed, in selecting new investments, he seems to be under a slightly more onerous duty to take the same degree of care as would 'an ordinary prudent man if he were minded to make an investment for the

---

[8] See Chapter 5, 129–30.

[9] *Speight v Gaunt* (1883) 9 App Cas 1 (HL).

[10] But, absent this duty to manage the investment actively, the trustee is not liable for a loss that results simply from retaining an authorized investment, unless the retention clearly demonstrates want of ordinary prudence: *Re Chapman* [1896] 2 Ch 763 (CA). Contrast *Fry v Fry* (1859) 27 Beav 144.

benefit of others for whom he felt morally obliged to provide'.[11] Even certain non-fiduciaries, such as security holders exercising their power to sell the secured property, are subject to an analogous duty of care.[12]

All of this would be completely unexceptional had the Common Law not then embarked on its own path, 'inventing' and then refining precisely the same type of civil wrong. In a landmark decision in the 1930s, the House of Lords formulated an analogous, but dramatically more wide-ranging, Common Law duty of care.[13] This duty is not simply owed by fiduciaries to principals, but by all individuals to their 'neighbours'. A 'neighbour' is anyone whose welfare might reasonably be seen by the defendant to be at risk because of the defendant's activities. The result is that manufacturers owe a duty of care to consumers, doctors to patients, road users to other road users, and so on. In every case the duty is designed to prevent one party acting without taking reasonable care to prevent foreseeable harm to the other. Prior to this, parties had been forced to rely on contractual agreements to perform activities carefully. Protection was then very limited: road users do not contract with each other; consumers contract with retailers, not with manufacturers. The Common Law duty of care changed all this.

Were it not for the continuing intellectual divide between Common Law and Equity, this development might have been regarded as nothing more than an ongoing trend to have a duty of care apply to a still wider class of defendants. Once the Common Law discovered its own duty of care, however, there were sustained judicial and academic efforts to distinguish the Common Law and Equitable duties. Insurmountable divisions were declared to exist between the respective duties and their remedies and defences. If true, the repercussions might be profound. Put starkly, what differences exist (and should exist) between the Equitable claims of a beneficiary disappointed by her trustee's management of a farm, and the Common Law (non-contractual) claims of a legal owner disappointed by his worker's management of a similar estate?

STANDARDS OF CARE

The common perception is that the Equitable standard of care requires more of defendants than its Common Law counterpart. This seems

---

[11] *Re Whiteley* (1886) 33 ChD 347; *Learoyd v Whiteley* (1887) 12 App Cas 727; *Cowan v Scargill* [1985] Ch 270; *Bartlett v Barclays Bank Trust Co Ltd (No 1)* [1980] Ch 515.
[12] *Cuckmere Brick Co v Mutual Finance Ltd* [1971] Ch 949 (CA); *Medforth v Blake* [2000] Ch 86 (CA).
[13] *Donoghue v Stevenson* [1932] AC 562 (HL).

unlikely. In Equity, defendants have to behave like prudent people managing their own affairs or the affairs of people they feel morally bound to protect. At Common Law, defendants have to behave like reasonable people in the particular circumstances. The qualification is crucial. An ear-piercer does not owe his clients the same standard of care that a surgeon owes his patients. Indeed, the standards expected of a surgeon depend upon whether the operation is an emergency procedure, whether it takes place in a well-equipped hospital or by the roadside, whether the patient has made explicit demands of the surgeon (for example, no blood transfusions), and so on. If the Common Law had to determine how a 'reasonable' fiduciary ought to behave 'in the particular circumstances', it is unlikely it would come up with anything different from the Equitable prescription of the standards expected. Indeed, modern Equity cases now emphasize the importance of context, or 'the particular circumstances', in determining appropriate standards of care for fiduciaries such as company directors and trustees. This practice effectively renounces differences in jurisdictional standards.

PROTECTED INTERESTS

The related assumption is that the Equitable duty of care protects a wider range of interests—especially economic interests—than the Common Law duty. This, too, seems doubtful. First consider the practicalities. If a duty of care is too general, then defendants may be liable to an indeterminate number of claimants for an indeterminate amount. Recall the saying that when a butterfly flaps its wings on one side of the world, a tidal wave erupts on the other. In the same way, a negligent driver whose accident destroys a container-load of goods might be seen as responsible for the losses suffered by the owners of the goods, the factory forced to close down temporarily for lack of supplies, the employees docked wages for the down-time, the local shops faced with reduced turnover, and so on. This is too much. A duty of care cannot cover every conceivable loss to every person harmed by the defendant's activities. Defendants cannot be general insurers.

To avoid this risk, both Equity and the Common Law developed rules restricting the range of potential claimants and the types of damage that would be compensated. In Equity, the rules could be straightforward. Fiduciaries must protect principals against damage to the managed property itself and any economic harm that might result from its mismanagement. The rule is self-limiting both as to claimants and their potential losses. The Common Law task is more difficult. At the outset, a physical link was demanded: claimants could only recover for damage to their own property or person, and any economic losses that were 'directly and foreseeably' related to that. A factory forced to shut down because of a negligent interruption to its electricity supply, for example, could recover for any physical damage to the factory or to the goods being manu-factured, and also any loss of profits that would have been derived from the damaged goods and failed production line. If the interruption caused no physical damage, however, then the factory could not recover for lost production or lost profits. These losses were classed as *pure economic loss* (economic loss not contingent on physical damage), and the Common Law drew its boundary here to exclude recovery.[14] With these limiting rules, the negligent driver in our earlier example would be liable to the owners of the container-load of goods, but not to the factory, its workers, or the local shops.

Another thirty years later, however, the Common Law was persuaded that this limiting rule was not always apt. It extended the notion of duty of care to cover those who gave negligent advice that then caused foresee-able economic loss, but no physical injury.[15] This development freed the parties from the need to establish a contractual obligation to give careful advice, just as the earlier Common Law cases had freed the parties from the need to establish a contractual obligation to deliver safe goods and services.

If fiduciaries were judged according to this expanded Common Law notion of negligence, they would be found to owe the same duty to protect the same physical and economic interests as Equity has long demanded. Indeed, the complaint of some eminent segregationist Equity lawyers is that this important Common Law expansion should never have happened: it was based on an unforgivable fusion of Equity and Common Law (an unforgivable 'fusion fallacy'[16]) involving a mistaken view of an earlier analogous seminal Equity case.[17] Whether or not this is true, the end result is doctrinal integration in all but name.

---

[14] *Spartan Steel and Alloys Ltd v Martin & Co* [1972] 3 All ER 557 (CA). But see the controversial decision in *Junior Books Ltd v The Veitchi Co* [1983] 1 AC 520 (HL).

[15] *Hedley Byrne & Co Ltd v Heller & Partners Ltd* [1964] AC 465 (HL).

[16] The 'fusion fallacy' suggests that it is doctrinally unsound to allow a Common Law defence to an Equitable cause of action (e.g. contributory negligence to a claim for breach of fiduciary duty), or to award a Common Law remedy for an Equitable wrong (e.g. Common Law damages for breach of confidence).

[17] *Nocton v Lord Ashburton* [1914] AC 32.

REMEDIES

The still more important allegation in this area is that remedies and defences differ between jurisdictions, with Equity being considerably more generous to its claimants. When the detail is examined, however, the assertion seems unsustainable. Indeed, it would be rather worrying if there were such differences: it would be difficult to explain why claimants should be better protected against negligence simply because they could argue an historical lineage issuing from Equity.

Some of these allegations are aggravated by loose use of terminology. The money remedy for breach of the Equitable duty of care is called *Equitable compensation*. This term also describes money remedies granted in association with rescission,[18] or when specific restitution of the trust property is unavailable.[19] Specific assertions about Equitable compensation are often assumed, unthinkingly, to apply in all three situations. In particular, there are times when Equitable compensation is not limited by notions of foreseeability, remoteness, and causation. We will see this rule in action later in this chapter, but if it were true in the context of the Equitable duty of care, then the Equitable remedy would indeed be distinguishable from its Common Law counterpart. Common Law damages for negligence are limited: the claimant must be someone reasonably likely to be affected by the defendant's negligent conduct; the damage must be reasonably foreseeable as the sort of damage likely to be suffered as a consequence of the defendant's conduct, and it must in fact result from the defendant's conduct, not from some new intervening cause.[20]

Is the Equitable remedy different? The old view *is* that notions of foreseeability, remoteness, and causation[21] do not limit Equitable liability.[22] But this old view emerges from cases where the fiduciary's negligence also amounts to a deviation from the strict terms of the engagement. This is a wrong which does attract strict liability.[23] When the only wrong is

---

[18] See Chapter 9, 298–303.   [19] See below, 174–8.

[20] *Banque Bruxelles Lambert SA v Eagle Star Insurance Co Ltd* [1997] AC 191 (HL).

[21] There must be some causal link between the fiduciary's breach and claimant's loss, of course, but intervening causes that aggravate the claimant's loss are then ignored: once a fiduciary is implicated, the suggestion is that he is liable to the full extent of the claimant's loss: *Re Dawson (dec'd)* [1966] 2 NSWR 211, 214–16 (Street J), endorsed by Brightman LJ in *Bartlett v Barclays Bank Trust Co Ltd (No 2)* [1980] Ch 515 (CA), 543. See the example in the text, and also below at 166–8.

[22] More recently, see *Target Holdings v Redfern* [1996] AC 421, 434 (Lord Browne-Wilkinson); *Canson Enterprises Ltd v Boughton & Co* [1991] 3 SCR 534, (1991) 85 DLR (4th) 129 (Can SCt), 154 (McLachlin J in the minority).

[23] See Chapter 5, 129–30, and below, 174–8.

negligence, there is now a growing perception that the Common Law limitations are equally apt in assessing the Equitable remedy.[24] It then follows that fiduciaries are only liable for the proximate losses foreseeably caused by their own negligence. This approach is consistent with the earlier discussion of the duty of care and the interests that warrant protection. A solicitor who gives a lender a negligent credit report on a borrower is not necessarily liable for *all* the ensuing losses, including those relating to a dramatic fall in the property market, unless the lender would not have lent *at all* but for the negligent report.[25] Some judges go further still, and acknowledge that these various alignments of Common Law and Equitable practices have resulted in an undifferentiated common law of negligence.[26] This overtly integrationist stance has much to recommend it: it is certainly the most effective strategy to ensure that equivalent rights are given equivalent protection.[27]

Wholesale integration would not eliminate certain distinctive practical differences in remedying fiduciary or trustee negligence, however. Three differences stand out. First, trusts are managed funds. So, too, are many pooled assets managed by fiduciaries. This means that assessment of loss is made by reference to the hypothetical properly managed fund, not by reference to specific assets comprising the fund. Take a slightly fanciful example. Suppose a cleaner negligently sets fire to a house. The legal owner is entitled to recover Common Law damages sufficient to enable her to undertake the necessary repairs. It is irrelevant whether she spends the funds on repairs; she is free to live with the damage and spend the money on an overseas trip.[28] Now suppose a trustee causes similar damage to a house that is trust property. His conduct may be equally 'negligent', but he will *not* necessarily be liable for the costs of repairs. All will depend

---

[24] *Henderson v Merrett Syndicates Ltd* [1995] 2 AC 145 (HL), 204–6 (Lord Browne-Wilkinson); *Bristol & West Building Society v Mothew* [1998] Ch 1 (CA), 16–18 (Millett LJ); *Permanent Building Society (in liq) v Wheeler* (1994) 14 ACSR 109, 155–8 (Ipp J).

[25] *Bristol & West Building Society v Mothew* [1998] Ch 1 (CA), although the result might have been different if the solicitor's dispersal of the funds to the borrower had been seen as a breach of the express terms of the trust: see below.

[26] *Canson Enterprises Ltd v Boughton & Co* [1991] 3 SCR 534, (1991) 85 DLR (4th) 129 (Can SCt), 154 (La Forest J for the majority); *Froese v Montreal Trust Co* [1996] 137 DLR (4th) 725 (BCCA), 730–1; *Day v Mead* [1987] 2 NZLR 443 (NZCA); *Bank of New Zealand v New Zealand Guardian Trust Ltd* [1999] 1 NZLR 664 (NZCA).

[27] See Chapter 10.

[28] Although in some cases the 'cost of cure' is out of all proportion to the loss suffered, and, whether or not the claimant would spend the funds on repairing the faults, the courts may decline to subject the defendant to such costs: *Ruxley Electronics and Construction Ltd v Forsyth* [1996] AC 344 (HL).

upon the damage his actions cause to the 'fund', not the damage they cause to the house. Suppose the trust deed requires the house to be demolished and the land used for other purposes. The fortunate trustee will then escape liability: his negligence will have caused no loss to the 'fund'. Of course, the facts often work to the trustee's disadvantage rather than to his advantage. The point is not that funds are peculiarly Equitable concepts. Quantification of Common Law losses is based on exactly the same idea when the circumstances are apt. The point is that fiduciary and trustee breaches are invariably assessed in this way.

Secondly, the accepted general rule is that Equitable compensation is assessed at the date of the hearing; Common Law damages are assessed at the date of the negligent breach. Depending upon how the market moves, this difference can be material. The date of assessment of damages is becoming increasingly flexible,[29] but this *prima facie* difference between fiduciary negligence and other negligence does have a rational explanation. The fiduciary's duty of care is a continuing duty; he remains liable for the careful management of the principal's assets. The Common Law defendant is responsible for the harm he causes to others, but once the harm is inflicted the *claimant* is under a duty to take steps to mitigate the ensuing losses; she must then manage her own affairs for her own benefit. The remedies for fiduciary and non-fiduciary negligence need to reflect this, and the timing difference achieves the objective.

Finally, different payment mechanisms are used to deliver Equitable compensation and Common Law damages. The reason is simple. In many trust and fiduciary arrangements, the underlying fund is owned by more than one beneficiary. This means that the money remedy cannot simply be paid to one individual (unless there *is* such a person who is fully entitled), but must be paid into the fund to be held according to the terms of the trust or fiduciary arrangement. This is the only way to ensure that each beneficiary is appropriately compensated for the fiduciary's breach of his duty of care. The Equitable terminology is that the fiduciary must 'account' for the losses caused by his breach: he must add the appropriate sum to the account of the managed fund.

All this detail only reinforces the suspicion that any differences between Equity and the Common Law in this area are based on different practicalities or differences 'in the particular circumstances', and not on different

---

[29] The general rule must give way to the overriding principle that the aim of Common Law damages is to adequately compensate the claimant: see *Johnson v Agnew* [1980] AC 367 (HL).

principles. The jurisdictional tags could be dropped without losing these practical refinements.

DEFENCES

The same is true of defences to actions in negligence. The Common Law action is subject to a specific defence of contributory negligence. The defendant can insist that he should not have to bear the entire loss because the claimant's own negligence was a contributing factor. If the claimant was partly (or wholly) responsible for her own predicament, or should reasonably have taken steps to preserve herself from harm, then the defendant's liability will be reduced accordingly. For a long time it was assumed that Equity would never countenance such a defence. The truth, however, is not quite so clear-cut. Certainly a defence which insists that the claimant looks after herself seems incompatible with the fiduciary's duty to fulfil that role. However, where this attitude is not apt— perhaps where no reasonable claimant could have failed to see the need to act to protect her own interests—then certain non-English jurisdictions *have* allowed a fiduciary to rely on the defence.[30]

From all of this it appears that both Equity and the Common Law are either doing, or tending towards doing, the same thing (imposing duties of care) for the same reasons (to protect the vulnerable). The detail only serves to highlight the significant parallels between the two jurisdictional developments. It would seem to do no great violence to principle to amalgamate these two bodies of learning. It would certainly advance the cause of rational and coherent development of the common law.

PROTECTING EQUITABLE PROPERTY AGAINST ABUSE BY THE TRUSTEE

Now it is time to turn to the more controversial aspects of Equity and civil wrongs. It is often said that the most challenging issues confronting those who wish to make sense of the modern common law landscape

---

[30] See *Duke Corporation Ltd (in liq) v Pilmer* (1999) 73 SASR 64, [850]–[888], doubted, *obiter*, on appeal in *Pilmer v Duke Group Ltd (in liq)* (2001) 207 CLR 165, [86] and [170]– [173], although these comments may relate only to the fiduciary's duty of strict compliance (where contributory negligence is, of course, irrelevant); *Day v Mead* [1987] 2 NZLR 443 (NZ CA), 451; *Canson Enterprises Ltd v Boughton & Co* [1991] 3 SCR 534, (1991) 85 DLR (4th) 129 (Can SCt), 1162–3, endorsed in *Corporaçion Naccional del Cobre de Chile v Sogemin Metals Ltd* [1997] 1 WLR 1396, 1403–4. For signs of an English move in the same direction, see *Lipkin Gorman (a firm) v Karpnale Ltd* [1992] 4 All ER 331 (QBD), 361 and *Swindle v Harrison* [1997] 4 All ER 705 (CA).

concern Equitable property and its protection. Chapters 3 and 4 were devoted to Equitable property and its proprietary protection. Here the focus is on its personal protection. How is an Equitable owner of property protected against interference with her rights? We know that her rights may sometimes be preserved in substitute property;[31] we have just seen that she is protected against negligence; but what other protection is available? The issues are complicated. The focus here is on the simplest case of a beneficiary with rights under an express trust. The rights of beneficiaries under resulting and constructive trusts are potentially more troublesome. By contrast, the rights of those with Equitable charges (or liens) are usually adequately protected by the charge document itself (or the circumstances of the case), together with conflict and priority rules; the law of civil wrongs is rarely relevant.

SPECIFIC RESTORATION

The simplest problem concerns assets that can be possessed. If the claimant can point to an asset in the defendant's hands and say 'That's mine', can she insist on being given possession? Common sense suggests that the answer ought to be yes. Matters are not so simple, however.

At Common Law, the rather odd response is 'No': the legal owner cannot demand possession. She may have the better *right* to possession, but she does not have the right to insist on being *given* possession. She can point to her car and insist that it is legally hers, but her only right is to damages for the defendant's refusal to deliver possession. His refusal constitutes the civil wrong of conversion. This rather bizarre result seems to favour certainty of transactions over protection of ownership: security of receipt is favoured over security of ownership.[32] There are few exceptions to this rule. Historically, Equity might order specific restoration if damages at Common Law were inadequate. Such orders often concerned heirlooms or chattels of rare or unique value,[33] although the jurisdiction ranged more widely. It might, for example, be exercised if essential but commonplace business equipment was wrongfully detained:[34] Common Law damages for loss of the equipment might be regarded as wholly

---

[31] See Chapter 4, 98–100.

[32] The 'secure recipient' can be in an unenviable position, however. He may have paid a fraudster for the car, and now he will have to pay damages to the claimant for conversion.

[33] E.g., *Pusey v Pusey* (1684) 1 Vern 273; 23 ER 465 (the Pusey horn); *Fells v Read* (1796) 3 Ves 70; 30 ER 230 (tobacco box of a club).

[34] *North v Great Northern Railway Co* (1860) 2 Giff 64, 69; 66 ER 28, 30 (Sir John Stuart V-C) (54 coal-wagons).

inadequate recompense for the lost business. This inherent Equitable jurisdiction was replicated by statute in the mid-nineteenth century.[35] This means that a legal owner still cannot insist on specific recovery of her property; she has to rely on the discretion of the court to deliver that.[36]

Now consider Equity's response. If the claimant can point to an asset in the defendant's hands and say 'That's mine [in Equity]', can she insist on being given possession? The short answer is 'Often, yes'. Suppose the trust property is a painting. If the claimant is the only person with an Equitable interest in the painting, then she can terminate the trust and call for the trustee to deliver the property to her.[37] This is an important Equitable rule, allowing beneficiaries some measure of control over their trustees. The protection is limited, however. If the beneficiary is not absolutely entitled, then she cannot demand possession. For example, if she has a lifetime interest only, or a quarter interest only, then she cannot demand possession of the underlying asset unless she and all the other beneficiaries with an interest in the asset present a united front to the trustee.

Equity takes this protection further. Consider a fiduciary relationship rather than an express trust. An owner may, for example, transfer property to her agent so that he can sell it for her. Usually she transfers possession, but not title. If the agent reneges on the deal, can the owner recover possession? She can certainly point to the property and say she is the legal owner, but she cannot point to it and say she is the Equitable owner.[38] It might be supposed that she is then confined to Common Law remedies, and cannot recover her property unless damages are inadequate. Equity says otherwise. It focuses on the character of the defendant: he acquired possession of the property only because of his fiduciary status and only for the purposes of that relationship. In these circumstances Equity considers the claimant entitled as of right to an order for specific restoration, whether or not the property is of unique or peculiar value and whether or not money would provide adequate recompense.[39]

What is happening here? It is commonly suggested that these various rules indicate an unacceptable inconsistency between the Common Law

---

[35] Common Law Procedure Act 1854, s. 78, now repeated in the Torts (Interference with Goods) Act 1977, s. 3.

[36] She does have insolvency protection, however: see Chapter 4, 102–4.

[37] *Saunders v Vautier* (1841) 4 Beav 115; aff'd (1841) Cr & Ph 240. The same rule applies if all those with an interest join together to terminate the trust.

[38] See Chapter 3, 66–7.

[39] *Wood v Rowcliffe* (1847) 2 Ph 3, 45 ER 990 (claim against agent for delivery up of furniture and household effects).

and Equity. This is not the case. There *is* discrimination, but the discrimination is coherent and rational. The general Common Law rule protects transactions more than ownership by providing that the only remedy available to dispossessed owners is a money remedy. A more sophisticated response attenuates the general rule when the facts suggest that security of transactions is not the more important value. This is the case when the property is special (rare, unique, exceptional), or when the defendant is special (the fiduciary relationship demands self-denial from the fiduciary, not the privileges of secure receipt). In short, Equity's impact is to create a hierarchy of rights to property protection, but the distinctions are readily and rationally justified.

It is widely supposed that these Equitable rules extend even further than this. If they do, then there may be a serious risk of disjunctions. Consider a simple example: a trustee holds a bicycle on trust for a beneficiary and, in breach of trust, gives the bicycle to an innocent third party. We have already seen that the beneficiary can assert her Equitable title against such a third party: he is not a bona fide purchaser for value, so the conflicts and priorities rules indicate that the beneficiary's property interest persists despite the transfer.[40] This means that the beneficiary can point to her bicycle and say 'That's mine [in Equity]'. The general assumption is that she can then insist that the bicycle be given to her. According to the previous discussion, this is acceptable if the defendant is a fiduciary, but he is not. Although he has to concede the beneficiary's better beneficial title, he does not owe her any fiduciary duties to put her interests ahead of his own. Nor is the bicycle a 'special' asset. Nevertheless, it is commonly assumed that an innocent recipient of the claimant's Equitable property from a defaulting trustee has to give the property back (even though the transfer gave him legal title); but an innocent recipient of the claimant's legal property from a thief does not (although the transfer gave him no title at all). The defendant's interest in security of receipt is devalued in the first case, but not in the second.

These sorts of unexplained (and seemingly inexplicable) disjunctions do the common law no credit. The 'red rules' and 'green rules' are providing different responses in similar circumstances. There may be a rational way out of this dilemma, however. It requires a simple step to be added to the analysis. If the rule were that an absolutely entitled Equitable owner could call for the transfer of the *legal title* (rather than

---

[40] See Chapter 4, 94–5.

the transfer of the *asset*),[41] then unacceptable disjunctions could be elim-
inated. The claimant, as putative holder of the legal title, could compel a
fiduciary defendant to transfer the property *in specie*, regardless of the
type of property, but she could not do the same with a non-fiduciary
defendant. Then she would be confined to damages unless the property
was somehow rare or exceptional. This seems appropriate.[42]

The advantage of this additional analytical step is that it re-enforces
the difference between express trusts and mere title splits that are discovered by application of the conflicts or priorities rules or other remedial
interventions. If the term 'trust' were used *only* to designate a split of
legal and Equitable property interests, it would then be evident that an
express trust is much more than this. Its essential attributes are 'trust'
(used in this proprietary sense) and 'fiduciary obligation' (defining the
personal obligations of the trustee to deal with the trust assets in particular ways). Some remedial consequences follow automatically from the
trust; others from the fiduciary obligation. This makes it obvious that
there is no simple or necessary analogy between the position of beneficiaries under an express trust and other holders of Equitable interests.[43] This
insight assists here and also in the treatment of issues discussed later in
this chapter. Clear language assists clear analysis.

EQUITY, SPECIFIC RESTORATION, AND THIEVES

To take this analysis further, consider an unlikely scenario much loved by
law teachers. Suppose an owner catches up with a thief who has stolen her
(perfectly ordinary) bicycle. Can she insist on being given possession?
The typical response is that she cannot.[44] The statutory discretion to
order specific restoration (replicating Equity's old rules) only operates if
the asset is rare or unique, and the bicycle is not. Otherwise Equity's
jurisdiction only operates against trustee or fiduciary defendants, and the
thief is neither a trustee (he cannot be, because he does not have legal title
to the stolen 'trust' property) nor a fiduciary (he cannot be, most assume,

---

[41] Indeed, this is the sense of the early and seminal cases.

[42] Indeed, there is little if any authority for enforcement of a wider rule, despite the rule's
frequent articulation.

[43] In particular, claimants insisting on specific recovery of assets held under resulting or
constructive trusts could rely on the 'trust' consequences to claim legal title. Specific
recovery would then depend on whether the underlying asset was 'special' or whether the
defendant was a fiduciary. Neither is necessarily the case in these contexts.

[44] Although if she simply takes the bicycle (without committing any other wrong, such as
trespass or assault), then there is nothing the thief can do: the owner's *right* to possession is
better than his.

because he, more than anyone, has never agreed to put the bicycle-owner's interests ahead of his own).[45] The owner must make do with money; she cannot insist on recovery of her bicycle. This seems an unwelcome shortcoming in the law.[46]

One common reaction is to suggest that a thief *should* be classified as a fiduciary because he should be *obliged* to put the claimant's interests ahead of his own, even if his intention is the opposite.[47] But this is snatching at remedies rather than building on principle. A fiduciary regime, with its remedies of specific redelivery and profits disgorgement, would certainly remove the incentive to steal property and reap the rewards from it. However, this regime is not warranted simply because it induces better behaviour and provides better remedies. Much of private law would be subsumed within fiduciary law if this were adequate justification. Fiduciary law is not directed at protecting property, but at protecting its loyal management. With this as its goal, the *only* way the claimant's legitimate interests can be adequately protected is by deterrence regimes that redirect disloyal profits to the intended beneficiary.[48] The law of conversion is quite different. It is directed at protecting property, and the remedies reflect that. If added deterrence is warranted in cases of theft, then it should be provided through criminal law,[49] not fiduciary law.

Fiduciary status is not the only reform strategy, however. Recall the fiduciary logic, especially in relation to specific redelivery. Fiduciaries cannot insist on security of receipt because, as fiduciaries, they acquired the claimant's property subject to obligations of loyalty that require the claimant's interests to be preferred. But fiduciaries are not necessarily the only parties who should be denied security of receipt. The law could justifiably say that thieves cannot insist on security of receipt because of the manner in which they came by the property. Thieves sued in conversion would then have to cede possession of the stolen property to the real owner. The advantage of this approach is that thieves would not then be

---

[45] Although see the contrary suggestions in *Westdeutsche Landesbank Girozentrale v Islington LBC* [1996] AC 669 (HL) (by Lord Browne-Wilkinson); *Black v Freedman* (1910) 12 CLR 105.

[46] But recall that the claimant does at least have insolvency protection, perhaps preserved in traceable proceeds: see Chapter 4, 100–1.

[47] See footnote 44 above. Indeed, this is the approach in some, but not all, cases where constructive trusts are imposed and constructive trustees are deemed to owe fiduciary obligations in dealing with the property. See Chapter 5, 131–4, and below, 179–89.

[48] See Chapter 5, 127–9.

[49] Statutory rules already require certain criminals to disgorge the proceeds of their crimes. This mirrors fiduciary deterrent strategies, although the profits of these crimes are not paid to the victims, but to the State, as befits the interest being protected.

inappropriately subjected to the whole gamut of fiduciary law, including its disgorgement strategies: the expanded conversion remedy would protect the claimant's property, not its loyal management. Moreover, innocent defendants (such as bona fide purchasers from the thief) caught by the law of conversion would not be dealt with in this way; they would be allowed security of receipt, but obliged to pay compensation for their interference with the claimant's ownership interest. To date this possibility of an intermediate protective strategy has been ignored, yet it would provide a rational basis for further discrimination between similar rights. It is an evolution based on the same underlying principles as the fiduciary exception to security of receipt.

BREACH OF THE STRICT TERMS OF THE TRUST

The next problem that might be faced by an Equitable owner is more complicated. Consider the simplest of express trusts. Suppose the trustee holds an asset—a parcel of shares, say—on trust for the beneficiary. The trust deed will tell the trustee what he must do with the shares. Suppose he is simply required to hold them for the benefit of the beneficiary. If the trustee ignores these restrictions and disposes of the shares, what rights does the beneficiary have against him to remedy his wrong? We already know that the beneficiary may be able to ratify the trustee's unauthorised disposition or, alternatively, assert a proprietary claim against the third party who received the shares.[50] But Equity provides a further alternative which is especially useful if these other options do not provide effective recompense. Equity imposes strict personal liability on the trustee to restore the trust fund to the position it would have been in but for the default.[51] He will have to add sufficient funds to the pool of trust assets to achieve this goal, and he will then hold these funds on the same terms as the original trust. The net effect is that an appropriate sum of money will replace the shares as the trust property.

The search for the proper analytical underpinnings of the trustee's duty to account for deviations from the strict terms of the trust has been fraught with problems. If the quantification process is rational it will

---

[50] See Chapter 4, 94–5, 98–100. Also see below, 179–89, for the possibility of making the third party *personally* liable.

[51] *Re Dawson (dec'd)* [1966] 2 NSWR 211, 214–16 (Street J), endorsed by Brightman LJ in *Bartlett v Barclays Bank Trust Co Ltd (No 2)* [1980] Ch 515 (CA), 543; *Target Holdings v Redferns (a firm)* [1996] AC 421 (HL), 433. This is the remedy unless there is court forgiveness under the Trustee Act 1925, s. 61 or forgiveness by the beneficiaries (*Boardman v Phipps* [1967] 2 AC 46 (HL)).

reflect the interest being protected and the motivation for its protection. The instinctive starting point has been to look for parallels with the Common Law property torts. The trustee has 'lost' the beneficiary's asset, so perhaps Equity's response mirrors the Common Law's response to the tort of conversion, or to breach of the duty of care required of those who have custody of another's property (at Common Law, these custodians are called 'bailees' and the various possible custody arrangements are called 'bailments'). Indeed, the idea that the trustee must restore the trust fund to the position it would have been in but for the default seems to reiterate the Common Law compensatory measure of damages.

Unfortunately, however, the similar fact pattern does not follow through into similar remedies. With bailment, for example, liability depends upon the bailee's negligence,[52] and is further limited by principles of causation, remoteness, and foreseeability. By contrast, the trustee is liable regardless of his honesty or carefulness,[53] and his liability is not limited by matters of foreseeability, remoteness, or causation (at least in the sense that Equity does not recognize an intervening cause as breaking the chain of causation linking the trustee to the harm). Liability for Common Law conversion appears to provide a better analogy. Liability is not dependent on negligence or matters of foreseeability, remoteness, or causation. However, the quantification of liability is quite different. At Common Law, if the defendant takes property worth £2,000 belonging to the claimant, then he is strictly liable to pay her £2,000 in damages; the valuation is made at the date of the defendant's breach. By contrast, the trustee is not simply liable to restore the value of the asset he has 'lost'. His duty is to restore the trust *fund* to the position it would have been in but for his default; moreover, the assessment is made at the date of the court hearing, not the date of his breach.

An example illustrates the differences. If the trustee disposes of shares worth £2,000, but evidence shows that the value of these shares would have dropped from £2,000 to £1,000 between the date the trustee 'removed' them and the date of the court hearing, then the trustee is only

---

[52] Although the onus of proof is reversed, so that the loss is assumed to be due to the bailee's negligence unless he can prove that it was not: *Sanderson v Collins* [1904] 1 KB 628 (CA), 630–2 (Collins MR); *Morris v C W Martin & Sons Ltd* [1966] 1 QB 716 (CA), 726, 728–9 (Lord Denning MR). More generally, see *The Pioneer Container* [1994] 2 AC 324 (PC).

[53] *Re Dawson* [1966] 2 NSWR 211, 214–16 (endorsed in *Bartlett v Barclays Bank Trust Co Ltd (No 2)* [1980] Ch 515, 543).

liable to add £1,000 to the trust pool. This would restore the trust fund to the state it would have been in had the proper investments been maintained.[54] On the other hand, and for the same reason, if the evidence shows that the value of the shares would have risen to £4,000 between these dates, then the trustee must add £4,000 to the trust pool. This is quite unlike the remedy for Common Law conversion, where the defendant would simply be liable for £2,000, being the value of the shares on the date they were converted.

Even when close analogies with the Common Law are seen to be wanting, the most common response is to persist with the idea that Equity is remedying a property wrong, but to acknowledge that its mechanism for assessing 'damages' is quite different from the Common Law's. Equity's remedy is simply 'Equitable compensation', not damages. This may be true, but it avoids principled explanation for the intervention.

The real grounds for intervention may have been overlooked in the face of these seductive analogies with property wrongs. The real grounds, it seems, involve an analogy with contract, not with property. Equity insists that the trustee must adhere strictly to the terms of the trust, and it will remedy any breach of this obligation by a money remedy that parallels specific performance of the trust terms themselves. Equity's focus is not on the trust property and the losses experienced; it is, instead, on the associated personal obligations imposed on the trustee and the impact of any unauthorized deviations from these. The analogy with specific performance of contractual obligations explains the remedy's focus on the predicted end-state of the fund; it explains the date on which damages are quantified; and it explains why good faith and carefulness on the trustee's part are irrelevant. The remedy is activated simply by breach of the terms of the trust. The extent of liability is determined by the particular terms of the trustee's management obligations.

This different analysis has three important consequences. First, a trustee is not necessarily liable simply because trust property is 'lost' from the trust fund. Liability is generated by the trustee's intentional (even if honest) deviations from the strict terms of the trust. Take an example. If the trust property is a painting, the trustee will be liable under this head if he takes the painting and either gives or sells it to someone other than the person nominated in the trust deed. It is irrelevant that the disposal

[54] *Target Holdings Ltd v Redferns* [1996] 1 AC 421 (HL), 434. Of course, if the trustee has made a profit from the transaction, then the beneficiaries can sue him for breach of his fiduciary duty of loyalty and recover this: see Chapter 5, 131–4.

might have been motivated by a genuine and reasonable mistake. The trustee will not be liable under this head, however, if the painting is accidentally destroyed by fire. (He may, of course, be liable in negligence, but that is a different wrong, remedied on a different basis.)

The second consequence is related to this, but pursues the underlying ideas a little further. A trustee deviates from the strict terms of the trust whenever he acts without proper authority. Moreover, he acts without proper authority when he has no authority *or* when he abuses his authority. (Recall, however, that as between the trustee and *third parties*, there is an important difference between *absence* of authority and *abuse* of authority.[55] As between trustee and beneficiary, however, both categories are regarded simply as actions without proper authority.) Suppose the trust deed provides that the trust funds must be 'invested in a range of shares listed on the London Stock Exchange'. The trustee will deviate from the strict terms of the trust if he invest the funds in a house in France, but, importantly, he will *also* breach the strict terms of the trust if his selection of listed shares is made without good faith, or is '*Wednesbury*' unreasonable, or is for improper purposes.[56] In every case he will be strictly liable to reinstate the trust fund: he must restore it to the position it would have been in had he invested properly at the outset.

The third consequence of this analysis is by far the most important. An obligations-based analysis makes it clear when an express trustee will be liable to restore the trust fund, but what does it say about the position of resulting and constructive trustees, and fiduciaries in general? Quite a lot, it seems. Take fiduciaries first. A fiduciary need not hold any property on trust. Nevertheless, if the fiduciary deals with his principal's property in defiance of the agreed arrangements, the obligations-based analysis preferred here will deliver precisely the same remedies as if the fiduciary were a trustee holding the assets on express trust. Given the parallels, this seems apt. In both cases the fiduciary or the express trustee is held to the specific performance of his personal (fiduciary) promises in dealing with the property. The property analogies do not work convincingly in these circumstances: the principal has legal title, yet the remedies ordered by the courts do not follow the Common Law models.

Adopting the same arguments, it follows that resulting trustees (this term is not in common use, but its sense is clear) and constructive trustees will only be personally liable to restore the trust fund when their

---

[55] See Chapter 5, 143–6.   [56] See Chapter 5, 144–6.

diminution of it constitutes a breach of the strict terms on which they are holding the property. This will only be the case where the terms 'resulting trust' or 'constructive trust' do not simply indicate a property division between claimant and defendant, but *also* reflect certain personal obligations imposed on the 'trustee' to deal with the property in a particular manner on the claimant's behalf. Resulting trusts and constructive trusts arise in an enormous range of circumstances, some of which encompass this added fiduciary element (personal obligations to deal with the property) and some of which do not. We will see examples of both later in this chapter. The obligations-based analysis advocated here would distinguish between these different classes. The trustee would be personally liable to restore the trust fund only when his dispositions constitute a breach of his personal management obligations in relation to the property. The property analogy cannot discriminate between different resulting and constructive trusts; it would make all resulting and constructive trustees personally liable to restore the trust fund. This is not the law,[57] although some commentators advocate this position.

To summarize, a trustee is personally liable to restore the trust fund to the position it would have been in but for his deviation from the strict terms of his personal obligations to deal with the property in a particular fashion. The analogy with contract, and the notion of a *fund*, are central to evaluating the obligation and quantifying the remedy. If this is the right approach, then it would be more sensible to discuss this form of liability later in the book, in the 'contracts' chapter. However, the obligation and its associated remedy merit extended discussion here because of the prevalent view that this liability is Equity's version of a property wrong.

PROTECTING EQUITABLE PROPERTY AGAINST INTERFERENCE FROM THIRD PARTIES

Strategies for protecting the beneficiary's Equitable property from interference extend beyond claims against trustees for abuse of their management functions. A trustee who transfers trust property to third parties in breach of trust is flouting his duties. For example, a trustee holding a painting on trust for his beneficiary may transfer the painting to a third party in defiance of the terms of the trust deed. The beneficiary may then want to pursue claims against the third party recipient, especially if she

---

[57] See *Westdeutsche Landesbank Girozentrale v Islington LBC* [1996] AC 669 (HL) for the current orthodoxy. Also see below, 164–74, on knowing receipt.

has no worthwhile actions against her trustee.[58] Alternatively, the trustee may need assistance to carry out his disloyal plans. Third parties may help the trustee to dispose of the painting despite the beneficiary's interests. Again, the beneficiary may want to pursue claims against these third-party accessories. This section discusses the potential liability of these types of recipients and accessories. The law is difficult, but important.

RECIPIENT LIABILITY—DEEMED TRUSTEESHIP— 'KNOWING RECEIPT'

Recipient liability is most easily analysed against the background of a simple trust where the trustee transfers a painting, say, to a third party in breach of the terms of the trust. In real life, however, these problems are likely to involve complex commercial frauds where money is laundered from hand to hand, and the victim of the fraud is forced to seek remedies against the intermediaries because the initial fraudster is insolvent or cannot be found.

Before dealing with the detail of recipient liability, two preliminary points need emphasizing. They often cause great confusion. The first has to do with whether the recipient is liable at all; the second with the basis of his liability. If a defaulting trustee makes an unauthorized transfer of trust property to a third party, the third party may still acquire perfectly good title to the property. If this is the case, then the beneficiary cannot make any claim against the recipient, and the analysis can stop immediately. Recall that the priority rules protect subsequent legal owners who are bona fide purchasers for value.[59] In every other case the beneficiary's Equitable interest is preserved: third-party volunteers (i.e. people who have not paid for the property) or third-party purchasers with actual or constructive notice of the beneficiary's interests take the property subject to her interests. They are potentially liable to her.

These third-party recipients are exposed to two sources of liability. The first is a property claim, considered earlier in this chapter. If the third party still has the painting, then the beneficiary can simply rely on her Equitable property rights. The common assumption is that she can insist on recovering possession. This general assumption was criticized, and a narrower analysis suggested. The narrower analysis would allow the beneficiary to insist on recovery of legal title, but would then give her a

---

[58] This will be so if there are no traceable substitute assets and her trustee cannot meet his personal liability: see Chapter 4, 116–20, and above, 174–8.

[59] See Chapter 4, 95–7.

money remedy only unless the painting was 'special' or the third party received it as a fiduciary.

The second type of claim is a personal claim. This is the focus of this section. It is of far greater practical interest, especially in complex money laundering cases, and is what is meant by 'recipient liability'. Can the beneficiary assert a *personal* claim against the third party even if he *no longer has* the property? Is the third party automatically liable to the claimant simply because he once had her property? The law in this area is extraordinarily confused. Some of the confusion arises because the Equitable jurisdiction has not properly worked out its own rules. But further complexity has been added because commentators have suggested that Equity's responses reflect unacceptable disjunctions between Equity and the Common Law, and that efforts at alignment should be pursued.

First consider the current Equitable rules for *'liability in knowing receipt'*, as it is termed.[60] Equity's view is that third-party recipients are *not* automatically liable to the claimant. Personal liability follows only if the third party is a *'knowing'* recipient of the claimant's property.[61] Equity will then say that the third party is 'liable to account as a constructive trustee in knowing receipt'. We have seen the adjective 'constructive' used before.[62] It means that the defendant is liable 'as if he were a trustee although he is not', or, perhaps more accurately, he is liable 'as if he were an express trustee although he is not an express trustee'. The 'imagined' express trust is, at a minimum, one which requires the third party to hold the property for the claimant, but it might be more complicated—it might even precisely mirror the original trust on which the claimant's property was held. The third party's personal liability to the claimant is then quantified by reference to this obligation, with the third party required to restore the trust fund to the position it would have been in had he not taken the particular asset from it. The third party also has to carry out these functions in a fiduciary manner: he is exposed to claims based on disloyalty as well as to claims based on disobeying the terms of the imagined trust. All of these consequences follow from the idea that the third-party recipient should be treated as express trustees are treated, even though he is not an express trustee.

---

[60] *Barnes v Addy* (1874) LR 9 Ch App 244.

[61] More accurately, the rule is probably that the third party must have had the necessary knowledge—whatever that is—when he disposed of the claimant's property, even if he did not have that knowledge when he received her property.

[62] See Chapter 3, 69–70.

Why the third party should be treated in this way, as a 'constructive' trustee, is not very well articulated. At root it is because he took the relevant property *knowing* of the claimant's Equitable interest in it—knowing, therefore, of the special responsibilities attached to holding the property. In these circumstances he is not allowed to deny his own role in that protective trust regime. Older cases, especially, reinforce this idea of third-party complicity in wrongdoing; these older cases treat the liability associated with knowing receipt as having strong links with cases of 'knowing assistance' (now 'dishonest assistance', discussed later in this chapter). The third party's liability is *trustee* liability. Its extent is determined by what the third party knew of the trust arrangements applying to the property. These are the personal property-holding obligations he will be held to; these obligations will define the constructive trust, and his liability as a constructive trustee. The analogies with creating express trusts and fiduciary relationships are patent.

What is clear from all of this is that the third party will not face this personal liability if he is a completely ignorant and innocent player in the story.[63] His personal liability depends on his knowledge of the claimant's rights at the time he receives her asset, or at least at some time before he disposes of it. But what *sort* of knowledge will tip the balance is most unclear. This is where Equity's rules are in complete disarray. There are cases to support every imaginable position. Some suggest that the third party will not be liable unless he had actual knowledge of the claimant's interest. Others impose liability if he would have discovered the facts had he acted honestly. Still others impose liability if he would have discovered the facts had he made reasonable enquiries.[64] There is even one case that

---

[63] This conclusion makes it vital to know how tracing works. If a property right can simply be traced into its substitutes and preserved in that substituted form, then the beneficiary may have a continuing property claim even though the defendant no longer has the original property and even though he is not personally liable to her. On the other hand, if tracing merely secures the insolvency priority of an associated *personal* claim once the original property is gone, then the beneficiary would have no claim here. See Chapter 4, 102–10, where the latter approach is preferred.

[64] For the now rather discredited hierarchy of types of knowledge, see *Baden, Delvaux v Société Générale pour Favouriser le Développement du Commerce et de l'Industie en France SA* [1993] 1 WLR 509 (the case was decided in 1983). For examples of the various stances taken as to what was necessary to attract liability, see: *Re Montagu's ST* [1987] Ch 264 and *Polly Peck International plc v Nadir (No 2)* [1992] 4 All ER 769 (CA), 777; and contrast *Selangor United Rubber Estates Ltd v Cradock (No 3)* [1968] 1 WLR 1555 and *Belmont Finance Corp v Williams Furniture Ltd (No 2)* [1980] 1 All ER 399 (CA), 405. The problem does not seem to be resolved by the Court of Appeal suggestion that these knowledge hierarchies are irrelevant, and that a third party should be personally liable only if it would be unconscionable for him to retain the benefit he has received from the claimant's Equitable property: *BCCI (Overseas) Ltd v Akindele* [2001] Ch 437 (CA), 455 (Nourse LJ).

can be read as imposing strict liability on the third party regardless of any knowledge.[65]

Some attempts to rationalize this unsatisfactory state of affairs have looked to the Common Law for appropriate analogies. Two potential models have been proposed. The first suggests that the Equitable personal claim of a beneficiary against a third-party recipient is analogous to the Common Law of conversion—it is Equity's version of the vindication of property rights. Pursuing the analogy, if the three-party trust fact pattern were replicated at Common Law, so that the third party received the claimant's painting from a thief (rather than from a trustee acting without authority), then the third party would be strictly liable to the claimant in conversion. He would have to pay damages equal to the value of the property converted. It would be irrelevant whether he still had the property, or whether he was aware of the claimant's ownership rights, or whether he was a volunteer or a bona fide purchaser. The inevitable suggestion, given the strong parallels in the story-line, is that Equity should replicate this strict liability rule for its own third-party recipients (with the minor adjustment that bona fide purchasers for value who take the trust property free of the claimant's Equitable interest should escape personal liability). Moreover, liability should require the defendant to compensate the claimant for the value of her property, not to restore the value of the trust fund according to the imposed ('constructive') trust terms.

The other model is the unjust enrichment model. The Equitable 'knowing receipt' claim is seen as analogous to the Common Law claim for restitution of an unjust enrichment. Again, the argument is that if the trust fact pattern were replicated at Common Law, the Common Law claimant would have a personal claim against the third-party recipient, who would have to make restitution to the claimant of the value of the enrichment he had received.[66] There are a number of subtleties associated with this claim, including the valuation of the enrichment, but they are not of prime concern here.[67] What is important is that the defendant's liability is strict: his knowledge of the claimant's interest is irrelevant. However, his liability may be reduced if he can show that he has changed

---

[65] *Diplock, Re* [1948] Ch 465 (CA); aff'd sub nom *Ministry of Health v Simpson* [1951] AC 251 (HL), although this case has also been distinguished on its facts as relating to the special position of executors of wills, not to fiduciaries in general.

[66] Lord Millett, *obiter*, in *Dubai Aluminium Co Ltd v Salaam* [2003] 2 AC 366 (HL), [87], suggested that the Equitable and restitutionary forms of liability might arise concurrently.

[67] See Chapter 9.

his position on the faith of his receipt so that now it would be unjust to require him to repay the value (or the full value) to the claimant.[68] For example, suppose the defendant receives an unjust enrichment of £1,000 and promptly donates £500 to charity because of his new-found wealth. The rule then is that he is only liable to repay £500 to the claimant, not £1,000. This *change of position* defence is unique to claims relating to unjust enrichment. The suggestion is that Equity should replicate this Common Law unjust enrichment analysis: third-party recipients of Equitable property should be strictly liable to make restitution to the claimant, subject to a change of position defence.

Adoption of either of these Common Law analogies would radically alter the existing Equitable rules. As matters stand, Equity insists that liability depends on the defendant's knowledge, although the degree of knowledge remains uncertain. Liability is then trustee liability, requiring the third party to restore the trust fund and effect disgorgement of any disloyal profits. By contrast, both Common Law approaches impose strict liability. Conversion does so without the benefit of defences. Unjust enrichment does so but more generously, with special rules for quantifying the benefit received and a special defence of change of position. In order to ensure coherence across the common law landscape, should Equity now follow either of these strict liability models? Alternatively, should Equity *add* the unjust enrichment strategy to its armoury? This, too, has been suggested as a second-best solution to the problem of coherence, a solution which leaves Equity's distinctive response to be explained as based on wrongdoing by a third party who has assumed the trustee role. Given the acute concerns expressed so far about the need to ensure that similar rights generate similar remedies, it is perhaps surprising that here there seem to be good reasons for Equity to persist with its unique stance.

The conversion model has little to recommend it. The Common Law itself only adopts this strategy with property that can be possessed; intangible assets do not give rise to claims in conversion. It would seem counter-productive, therefore, if the goal is coherence, to adopt the conversion model for Equitable interests, which are invariably intangible.

The unjust enrichment model is another matter. It has attracted powerful academic and judicial support.[69] An educated guess might

---

[68] *Lipkin Gorman (a firm) v Karpnale Ltd* [1991] 2 AC 548 (HL).

[69] See especially Lord Nicholls, 'Knowing Receipt: The Need for a New Landmark', in W R Cornish, R Nolan, J O'Sullivan, and G Virgo (eds), *Restitution: Past, Present and Future* (Oxford: Hart Publishing, 1998), Ch. 15. But contrast L D Smith, 'Unjust Enrichment, Property, and the Structure of Trusts' (2000) 116 LQR 412.

surmise that it will become the new Equitable rule for receipt-based claims against third parties before too long. Those who remain unconvinced base their concerns on diverse grounds. Sometimes the Common Law analogy itself is doubted. There is vigorous modern debate over whether an unjust enrichment claim is ever available when the claimant remains the legal owner of the property alleged to constitute the defendant's enrichment. If the defendant does not obtain ownership of the property, how can he be enriched by its receipt? And if there is no enrichment, then there is no enrichment claim: the claimant must simply pursue whatever claims the law of property allows her. In a further attack on the analogy, there are those who consider that the law of unjust enrichment is not equipped to deal with three-party cases; its concerns are with two-party cases, and more remote parties must be reached by other legal means. This idea is reinforced by the restriction, noted earlier, that claims against third parties are not available unless the claimant can show that the defendant received *her* property (and so is exposed to a property or a wrongs claim). In two-party unjust enrichment cases there is no such limitation; indeed, the essence of the claim is usually that the defendant *has* obtained title to property that was once the claimant's. Still other critics focus on the pragmatic aspects of such a new legal rule, pointing out that the inevitable increase in liability imposed on third-party recipients will seriously harm the conduct of business. The most likely defendants in these third-party claims are banks, solicitors, accountants, and such like. Under a strict liability regime, they will have to prove their own good faith purchase or change of position defence; the onus of proof will not lie on the claimant. They may find it impossible to adopt business strategies that ensure they can prove these issues. But none of this holds the essential key. The most telling argument against adoption of the unjust enrichment analogy relates to the nature of the Equitable rights being protected.

Any difference in the treatment of third-party recipients of legal and Equitable property must be based on differences between the rights being protected. This is the only basis for coherent discrimination. Careful analysis suggests that the three-party trust scenario gives both claimant and defendant radically different rights from the three-party Common Law scenario. If true, then equally radical differences in the remedies may be justified. Return to our painting. In the Equitable scenario, the defaulting trustee gives the painting to a third-party defendant; in the Common Law scenario, the thief gives it to him. In both cases assume that the third party is an ignorant and innocent volunteer. The claimant's position is clear. She remains the owner of the painting in Equity in the first case and at Common Law in the second. To vindicate her rights, assume she wants to pursue a claim in unjust enrichment. (For the purposes of argument, ignore for the moment the earlier doctrinal criticisms of the unjust enrichment analysis as it applies to these Common Law facts.)

First consider the 'unjust factor', or the specific feature that makes it unjust for the defendant to retain the benefit he has received. In the Common Law scenario, the claimant's ignorance or lack of consent to the transfer is said to justify her claim to restitution against the third party (and, presumably, even more so against the thief). The trust beneficiary cannot make quite the same assertion, however. Her trustee has legal title to the property, with all the risks to her that might be associated with that. Her trustee has the capacity to transfer the painting to the third party, even if he does not have the authority to do so. The thief, by contrast, has no capacity to effect the transfer since he does not have title to the underlying property. The third-party recipient from the trustee receives legal title to the painting. This is true even if the defaulting trustee gives the painting away. The beneficiary has consented to the trustee having this capacity, even if she has not consented to his abuse of position. This does not mean that the beneficiary should have *no* rights against third parties who deal with the defaulting trustee, but it is arguable that her rights should be cut back to reflect the agreed arrangement she has with her trustee. This is a risk allocation argument, but this is what underpins all unjust enrichment claims. The issue at stake is whether the law should protect allocation of the claimant's wealth as she properly decides, or security of the defendant's receipt. Her use of a trustee manager affects the allocation of risk. Recall that 'ostensible authority' rules work on the same policy basis.[70]

Next consider the rights of the claimants. At one level any 'rights' argument is potentially circular: the claimant's property rights are measured by the protection the law accords to them, and yet that is the very issue in dispute here. Nevertheless, at a fundamental structural level there is a cardinal difference between Common Law ownership and Equitable ownership. The legal owner of the painting has all the rights in the painting (bar the ability to obtain specific restoration of it from the defendant). The Equitable owner does not. Equitable ownership is derivative. The Equitable owner has an *interest* in the painting, but it is an

---

[70] See Chapter 5, 143–4.

interest measured by the management obligations she is owed by her trustee. Consider what this means for the different roles of the thief and the trustee. If either the thief or the trustee deliberately or negligently damages the painting, then the owner's rights against them have different grounds. The thief is liable to the extent that his actions are inconsistent with the legal owner's full ownership rights; the trustee is liable to the extent that his actions are inconsistent with the management duties he has undertaken. When the painting is given to third parties, the owner's different rights are similarly distinctive. The legal owner can assert precisely the same rights against the third party as she could against the thief—her 'bundle of rights' is unchanged. The Equitable owner is in quite a different position. First, as against the third party she can only assert the third party's invasion of her right to have the property managed by her trustee under the agreed terms[71] and, secondly, the third party's breach of any management powers *he* has agreed to undertake. When we say that the Equitable owner's property rights persist in the hands of the third party, all we mean is that the third party is obliged to concede the Equitable owner's interest in having her property managed by her trustee: the third party has to give way to that right, so far as it is inconsistent with his own claim. *He* does not necessarily have to manage the property in any particular way. If the third party has the property in his possession, this claim will force him to acknowledge the claimant's right to have the property (or its value[72]) restored to the trustee's management. But if he does not have the property in his possession, then this claim has no impact on him. He is only liable if he too has agreed to undertake a management role. This is precisely what the Equitable rules on knowing receipt are directed at ascertaining—whether the third party has assumed a trustee management role of any sort.

This long explanation points out the essential flaw in the arguments for analogous treatment of owners of legal and Equitable property. The assumption which is widely—but erroneously—made is that legal and Equitable property are the same sorts of beasts and behave in the same sorts of ways. It then follows that if X remains the Equitable owner of property despite its transfer from Y to Z, the 'bundle of rights' that X can assert against Y is identical to the 'bundle of rights' which she can assert against Z. This is true for legal property; it is *not* true for Equitable

---

[71] And this only because the property right is protected against volunteers: see Chapter 4, 93–4.

[72] See above, 168–78.

property. Equitable property is defined and circumscribed by the personal obligations owed by the legal owner to the Equitable owner. A transfer of property from Y to Z does not automatically effect a transfer of Y's personal obligations in respect of the property, so that they are now imposed on Z. The 'bundle of rights' that the Equitable owner can assert against Y is *not* the same as the 'bundle of rights' which she can assert against Z.

We can see this played out with force in a non-trust example. Suppose the claimant's Equitable interest is not ownership, but a charge against an item of property legally owned by the borrower. If the borrower, in breach of the security agreement, gives the property to an innocent and ignorant third-party volunteer, what are the Equitable chargee's rights? If the third party still has the property, then the Equitable chargee can assert her interest in the property (this is a result of the Equitable priority rules[73]): she can insist that her interest in having the property available to secure a loan agreement be preserved. But if the third party no longer has the property—perhaps he has sold it—then the Equitable chargee has *no* personal rights against the third party.[74] She cannot insist that he has 'converted' her Equitable property, or that he has been unjustly enriched by it (although if he has sold the property as unencumbered property he will certainly be enriched). The reason is simple. The third-party volunteer undertook no personal management responsibility in respect of the claimant's property, and he is treated accordingly. On the other hand, if he *had* undertaken such obligations—as he might if he took the property expressly subject to the charge—then he *would* be personally liable to the claimant, not for the primary obligation secured by the charge, but for his interference or damage to her proprietary security interest in the asset itself.[75]

All of this only serves to emphasize that Equitable property rights (whether these are ownership or security interests) are quite different from Common Law property rights, and attract quite different consequences. The 'bundle of rights' making up Equitable property is measured by the

---

[73] See Chapter 4, 93–4.

[74] The more difficult question is whether she has any *proprietary* rights to the traceable proceeds of the charged property. As regards traceable proceeds in the chargor's hands, she has rights. As regards traceable proceeds in the third party's hands, however, arguably she does *only* if the third party has personal obligations which can be secured by such a proprietary interest. This is difficult and controversial. See, generally, *Latec Investments Ltd v Hotel Terrigal Pty Ltd* (1965) 113 CLR 265 (Aust HCt) and Chapter 4, 102–4.

[75] This is true not only in relation to charges, but also see the line of cases following *De Mattos v Gibson* (1858) 4 De G & J 276, 45 ER 108.

type of obligations undertaken by legal owners to their beneficiaries. Equity's claim in knowing receipt is directed at discovering whether the third-party recipient has undertaken this sort of obligation. Where the claimant wants to vindicate her Equitable property rights through *personal* claims, then she is restricted to her claims against the *trustee* for breach of his trust management obligations, or against *third parties* for breach of any management obligations *they* can be taken to have assumed.[76] Moreover, both the trustee and the third party have to carry out their respective management functions in a fiduciary manner—they are exposed to claims based on disloyalty as well as claims based on disobeying the particular management terms. On the other hand, when she pursues *proprietary* claims, she is simply asserting a priority as against the legal owner to have the property managed in a particular way and by a particular person for her benefit.

To summarize, Equity has a distinctive jurisdiction which protects the property interests of Equitable owners from interference by third parties. These claims are not analogous to unjust enrichment claims. They are wrongs-based claims, with the wrong being that the third party has acted in breach of the strict terms of the personal obligations he is taken to have assumed when he received the property (or later, perhaps, but before he engaged in the dealing being complained of). These third parties incur the same sort of liabilities as express trustees once it is shown that they have voluntarily and knowingly placed themselves in the same sort of role. The traditional language makes sense, although it is much criticized: these third parties are personally liable as 'constructive' trustees to restore the trust fund to the position it would have been in but for their unauthorized dispositions contrary to the terms of the 'constructive' trust. If the term 'constructive' is so troublesome, it may help to think of these third parties as 'deemed' trustees, personally liable for breaches of the terms of the deemed trust. The presumption is based on what the third party must reasonably be taken to have agreed given his knowledge of the circumstances.

---

[76] 'Knowing receipt' liability is also said to depend upon the third party receiving the property for his own benefit; this requirement exempts from liability any third parties—like banks, solicitors and accountants—who merely receive the property '*ministerially*', for the benefit of another. These parties may, nevertheless, be personally liable to the beneficiary in 'knowing assistance': see below. This qualification impliedly embraces an unjust enrichment analysis of knowing receipt, rather than the analysis advanced here. However, the practical results are the same once both knowing receipt and knowing assistance liabilities are considered.

Similar analyses apply in assessing the personal liabilities of trustees holding property on resulting trusts or constructive trusts. The property-holding element is settled by operation of law in different circumstances, although the 'resulting' and 'constructive' terminology is not necessarily illuminating in determining when these situations have arisen. The associated *personal* liability of these trustees—a liability to restore the trust fund should they dispose of the asset other than in accordance with the terms of the resulting or constructive trust—depends upon the trustee's knowledge. What personal trust management obligations can these trustees be presumed to have agreed to undertake, given their knowledge of the circumstances? This makes it clear that although all resulting and constructive trusts have proprietary consequences, not all are associated with personal 'trustee-type' obligations imposed on the property-holding trustee.

This has been a very long and rather complicated discussion. The issue is controversial, and sensible resolution is sorely needed. On the analysis presented here, the third-party 'knowing recipient' must be just that—knowing—if he is to be made personally liable to restore to the claimant the value of trust property he no longer has. He is not strictly liable in unjust enrichment, even as an alternative claim. He is liable as a 'deemed trustee'. He must know of the claimant's interests, and he must be taken to have agreed to hold the property on that basis, before he can be made personally liable to her as a trustee. The necessary degree of knowledge is difficult, but arguably actual or constructive knowledge of the existence of her Equitable interest would suffice to impose the simplest property-holding trust which would require the third party to account to the claimant for the value of the property disposed of elsewhere. But actual knowledge (including wilful disregard of the possibilities) seems to be necessary if the third party is to be regarded as holding the claimant's property on more complicated trusts, for example trusts mirroring the original trust. Once the requisite degree of knowledge is established, the third party is liable 'as a trustee' for his dealings with the trust property: he must restore the trust fund to the state it would otherwise have been in but for his unauthorized dispositions, and he must disgorge any profits made in breach of his management duties.

ACCESSORY LIABILITY—'KNOWING ASSISTANCE'—'DISHONEST ASSISTANCE'

The final mechanism for protecting Equitable interests offers yet another remedy against third parties. The aim is to safeguard beneficiaries from third parties who deliberately conspire with trustees or assist them in

carrying out breaches of trust.[77] Major frauds against beneficiaries often
need the help of banks, solicitors, or accountants to assist in the surrep-
titious movement of funds. But assistance can also come from more prosaic
sources: auction houses selling paintings without asking too many questions; estate managers delivering produce to questionable sources. If this
form of assistance is regarded as a civil wrong, the risks to beneficiaries
are significantly reduced. The Common Law has a similar tort, which
imposes liability on third parties for inducing a breach of contract by one
the contracting parties. The rationale for both civil wrongs is the same,
and the response in both cases is motivated by the same imperatives.[78] To
deter the third party from acting as an accessory, he is made personally
liable for the damage his assistance causes to the trust beneficiary (or, at
Common Law, to the other contracting party).

Until recently, this wrong was plagued by many of the uncertainties
surrounding 'knowing receipt': what sort of knowledge is necessary to
make someone a '*knowing*' assistant in a breach of trust? Much of this
confusion has been cut away by the convincing explanation that the
wrong concerns accessory liability. What is necessary is that the third
party has *dishonestly* assisted or participated in the trustee's breach of
trust or the fiduciary's breach of fiduciary obligation.[79] To reflect this, the
wrong is now often styled as 'dishonest assistance' or 'accessory liability'.
In assessing dishonesty, context is vitally important. The third party is
not permitted to close his eyes to evidence, or to act in reckless disregard
of the claimant's possible rights, but the degree of investigation he must
undertake to satisfy himself if his suspicions are aroused depends upon
his role and on the nature of the transaction. For example, more may be
expected of solicitors; more may also be expected when the transaction is,
on its face, unusual. Despite this, the concept of dishonesty remains
troublesome. Recent authority indicates that third-party accessories
will only be liable if their conduct is *both* objectively and subjectively
dishonest.[80] To many eyes, a subjective qualification affords unwarranted
protection to the unscrupulous.

If these prerequisites are met, then the third party is liable to the
claimant as if he were an express trustee engaged in committing the
same breach. Again, the older cases describe the third party as 'liable to

[77] *Barnes v Addy* (1874) LR 9 Ch App 244.
[78] *Royal Brunei Airlines Sdn Bhd v Tan* [1995] 2 AC 358 (PC).
[79] *Royal Brunei Airlines Sdn Bhd v Tan* [1995] 2 AC 358 (PC).
[80] *Twinsectra Ltd v Yardley* [2002] UKHL 12, [2002] 2 AC 164 (HL), although note the
powerful dissent by Lord Millett.

account as a *constructive* trustee for knowing assistance'. The language is opaque, but the parallels with the 'deemed trustee' analysis in the previous section are evident. Notice, however, that receipt of the trust property is not part of the wrong. Liability is therefore better described as 'constructive fiduciary' liability rather than 'constructive trustee' liability.

Clearly Equitable accessory liability need not keep its 'Equitable' tag. Both Common Law and Equitable accessory liability are founded on the same bases. The remedial differences do not reflect a different philosophy; depending on the circumstances, the third party is simply liable to compensate for harm resulting from trust breaches or from contract breaches.

PROTECTING INFORMATION

Equity's strategies for protecting information were discussed in the previous chapter. There it was suggested that legal intervention was motivated by a desire to protect the claimant from harm, not by a desire to induce the defendant to use his efforts for the claimant's benefit. The discussion is therefore better placed in this chapter, were it not for Equity's confusing (although perhaps only occasional) use of its deterrent disgorgement strategy.

The idea that breach of confidence is a civil wrong could be developed further to provide the common law with a law of privacy, assuming statute does not intervene sooner.[81] The current rules do not meet this need. For example, breach of confidence does not impugn disclosure unless the information is 'confidential' or 'secret', yet privacy is invaded whenever an individual does not wish to have information revealed in the proposed manner to the proposed audience. Even when the information is confidential, breach of confidence cannot protect all interested parties; it protects only those who 'own' or 'provide' the information at issue. If a patient discloses to her doctor that a third party is the source of some infectious disease, then the patient can restrain disclosure by the doctor (subject to any disclosures compelled in the interests of public health), but it is not clear that the third party, who is the subject of the information, has any such rights.

A law of privacy—a civil wrong dealing with interests in privacy— could deal with these cases. As with all civil wrongs, the reach of legal

[81] See *Douglas v Hello! Ltd (No 3)* [2005] EWCA Civ 595, [2005] 3 WLR 881 (CA).

intervention would be a matter of balancing competing public interests, but protection would undoubtedly be greater than it is now.

NEW CIVIL WRONGS

The path of progress for modern law is one that shows an inexorable willingness to embrace higher standards of conduct. 'Good faith and fair dealing' in relationships with others is increasingly demanded through different sub-rules.[82] The language of the law is changing too. There is increasing use of terms such as 'reasonable expectations', 'reasonable reliance', 'legitimate expectations', 'the fair and reasonable man', 'unjust factors', 'unconscionable conduct'.

Duties to have regard to the legitimate interests or reasonable expectations of others were seen as an increasingly important phenomenon in the previous chapter; and in later chapters it will be clear that the law is increasingly curtailing parties' entitlements to insist on their strict legal rights.[83] What might be on the horizon for civil wrongs, apart from the possibility of a law protecting privacy? There are two candidates that seem to be waiting in the wings.

Duties of disclosure are becoming a prime corrective to prevent unacceptable advantage-taking. The USA leads the way, but the continuing development of business ethics is beginning to curtail the privilege to take advantage of ignorance. Perhaps surprisingly, the justification is often commercial—surprising because the justification for earlier condonation of sharp practices was also commercial. In the same vein, duties to recommend independent advice or to provide adequate explanation have also won new prominence.[84] The old rules surrounding contractual relationships would have required both parties to look after their own interests. In both these areas an expanded law of civil wrongs could play a useful role. Importantly, this strategy would overtly require damages to be assessed on the basis of the claimant's loss, not on some pseudo-contractual basis. This would be fairer to both parties, and would more accurately reflect the interests at stake and the protection they deserve. Interestingly, despite their Equitable overtones, these modern developments do not display any need to claim a particular jurisdictional ancestry; they are simply seen as part of an inevitable evolution in the common law.

---

[82] But see *White and Carter (Councils) Ltd v McGregor* [1962] AC 413, 430.
[83] See Chapters 7, in general, and 8, 230–5.
[84] *Royal Bank of Scotland v Etridge (No 2)* [2002] 2 AC 773 (HL).

REVIEW

This chapter, like the previous one, is concerned with Equity's role in supplementing the law of civil wrongs. Here the focus is not on Equity's unique contributions, but on instances where Equity and the Common Law appear to react to similar circumstances in different ways. However, careful analysis of these differences leads to the rather surprising conclusion that the common law of civil wrongs *is* relatively coherent notwithstanding its divided Common Law and Equitable heritage.

Sometimes persistent assertions of jurisdictional differences lack substance. For example, neither negligence rules nor accessory liability rules need their jurisdictional tags. In both cases the Equitable and Common Law strategies are directed at the same ends for the same reasons, and the common law would be best served by an overt commitment to deliver the same results to disaffected claimants.

Equally, sometimes conscious differentiation is counter-productive, especially in the face of statutes intended to generalize the rules. This is the case with injunctions and 'Equitable damages'. These, when added to Common Law damages, provide remedial variety. They permit the construction of a hierarchy of rights, with more valuable rights protected by more valuable remedies.

Other rules simply need more aggressive analysis to ensure that principled limits to their operation are acknowledged. This is arguably the case with common assumptions about Equity's power to insist on specific restoration of assets. It is suggested here that an absolute Equitable owner should be entitled to call for transfer of the legal title, not transfer of the asset itself. Legal owners should then be entitled to specific restoration only when the property is special (i.e. somehow peculiar or unique) or the defendant is special (i.e. a trustee or fiduciary who has therefore agreed to subjugate his own interests to the claimant's). This would effectively remove one troubling disjunction between the Common Law and Equity's protection of property interests.

Still other rules are in urgent need of clearer and more compelling rationalizations of their underpinnings. Only then can their proper limits be assessed. This is the case with the Equitable wrong of 'knowing receipt'. Various explanations are now commonly advanced, including explanations based on analogies with the Common Law tort of conversion and the Common Law claim in unjust enrichment. The explanation favoured here, however, is one based on analogies with express trusts. On this reasoning, a third-party recipient will be personally liable only if the circumstances suggest that he should be deemed to have accepted the property subject to associated fiduciary obligations to deal with it in a particular fashion. Liability then mirrors the liability of express trustees in similar circumstances, and is perhaps most illuminatingly described as 'deemed trusteeship' liability.

These issues are not insignificant. Nevertheless, it does seem possible to articulate an integrated, rational, and coherent common law of civil wrongs. For the most part, the hierarchy of rights and remedies is reasonably logical and defensible, notwithstanding its jurisdictionally divided development.

SELECTED BIBLIOGRAPHY

Birks, P., 'Receipt' in P. Birks and A. Pretto (eds), *Breach of Trust* (Oxford: Hart Publishing, 2002), p. 213.

Elliott, S. B. and Mitchell, C., 'Remedies for Dishonest Assistance' (2004) 67 MLR 16.

Grantham, R. B. and Rickett, C. F., 'Liability for Interfering in a Breach of Trust' (1998) 114 LQR 357.

Harpum, C., 'The Stranger as Constructive Trustee' (1986) 102 LQR 114, continued at 267.

Hayton, D., 'English Fiduciary Standards and Trust Law' [1999] 32 Vanderbilt Journal of Transnational Law 555.

Langbein, J., 'The Contractarian Basis of the Law of Trusts' (1995) 105 Yale LJ 626.

Mitchell, C., 'Assistance' in P. Birks and A. Pretto (eds), *Breach of Trust* (Oxford: Hart Publishing, 2002), p. 139.

Nicholls, Lord, 'Knowing Receipt: The Need for a New Landmark' in W. R. Cornish, R. Nolan, J. O'Sullivan, and G. Virgo (eds), *Restitution: Past, Present and Future* (Oxford: Hart Publishing, 1998), Ch. 15.

Smith, L., 'W(h)ither Knowing Receipt?' (1998) 114 LQR 394.

——, 'Constructive Trusts and Constructive Trustees' [1999] CLJ 294.

——, 'Unjust Enrichment, Property and the Structure of Trusts' (2000) 116 LQR 412.

SELECTED CASES

Bartlett v Barclays Bank Trust Co Ltd (No 2) [1980] Ch 515 (CA)

BCCI (Overseas) Ltd v Akindele [2001] Ch 437 (CA)

Bristol & West Building Society v Mothew [1998] Ch 1 (CA)

Canson Enterprises Ltd v Boughton & Co [1991] 3 SCR 534, (1991) 85 DLR (4th) 129 (Can SCt)

Re Dawson [1966] 2 NSWR 211 (NSW SCt)

Dubai Aluminium Co Ltd v Salaam [2003] 2 AC 366 (HL)

Henderson v Merrett Syndicates Ltd [1995] 2 AC 145 (HL)

Jaggard v Sawyer [1995] 1 WLR 269 (CA)

Johnson v Agnew [1980] AC 367 (HL)

Medforth v Blake [2000] Ch 86 (CA)

Nocton v Lord Ashburton [1914] AC 32 (HL)

Royal Brunei Airlines Sdn Bhd v Tan [1995] 2 AC 358 (PC)

Shelfer v City of London Electric Lighting Co [1895] 1 Ch 287

Target Holdings v Redferns (a firm) [1996] AC 421 (HL)

Twinsectra Ltd v Yardley [2002] UKHL 12, [2002] 2 AC 164 (HL)

Part IV

Contract

7

Reviewing Promises

Previous chapters concerned Equity's invention of new types of legal rights and remedies. In this chapter the perspective changes. The focus is on Equity's strategies for reviewing promises. Equity will sometimes excuse claimants from performance of the obligations they have purportedly undertaken or promises they have made. In this sense Equity's impact is negative. If performance is still only promised, its delivery will not be compelled; if performance has already been completed, then Equity will unwind the transfers. How Equity unwinds these transfers is a matter for a later chapter.[1] Here the focus is on *why* it does so. Although Equity's review strategies do not create novel types of rights or remedies, their impact on existing rights is dramatic. The defendant loses the right to demand the agreed performance from the claimant or keep the benefits already derived from it; the claimant's rights are correspondingly enhanced.

Equity's review strategies operate in diverse circumstances. A written contract may have inaccurately recorded the agreed sale price; a vendor may have misrepresented the attributes of an asset in his negotiation of a contract of sale; a franchisor may have insisted on an onerous penalty clause if the franchise agreement is breached; a wealthy patient may unexpectedly give a large fortune to her doctor, leaving relatives empty-handed. The examples can be multiplied. In cases like these, Equity may allow the compromised party to escape from her commitments. This is serious intervention. On its face, it contradicts apparently binding contractual agreements and properly intended gifts. It therefore compromises security of transactions and undermines the counter-party's freedom of bargain. Despite this, Equity insists that it is sometimes simply unfair or unconscionable for the defendant to insist on his strict legal rights.

Allegations of unfairness and unconscionability are hardly helpful without a lot more explanation. What really motivates Equity's intervention? The cases are commonly classified under three different heads. The

---

[1] See Chapter 9.

first two are easier to justify than the last. In the first category, the problem is simply that the written documentation, or the *formalities* supporting the arrangement, do not properly reflect the parties' agreed deal. Equity will then sometimes correct matters, although not always; an objective commitment to a formal contract is necessarily accorded a healthy degree of respect.

The second category focuses on the claimant's apparent consent to the arrangement. Contracts and gifts are not legally binding unless the parties properly intend to commit themselves.[2] There is therefore a sound doctrinal basis for intervention if the facts suggest that the claimant did not truly consent to the deal. Perhaps she was mistaken about important details; perhaps she was under intense pressure to act. However, the law usually tests consent objectively: if the claimant appears to have consented, she will be taken to have done so. The real difficulty in these cases is that the claimant does appear to have properly consented to the deal—mistakes and coercion are not necessarily evident to others—but in fact she has not. Equity will intervene, overriding the Common Law's objective view, if the claimant's apparent consent was improperly induced by the defendant. In these circumstances, it seems unfair to allow the defendant to insist on his strict legal rights. The defendant's involvement in some sort of *procedural unfairness* in obtaining the claimant's consent justifies denying him the benefit of his arrangement with the claimant.

The final category is concerned with *substantive unfairness*. Here Equity's intervention is far more paternalistic. It will sometimes intervene if the *terms* of the deal are unfair. This is a most aggressive form of intervention. It means interfering with a bargain even though there is no suggestion that the parties did not truly consent to the arrangement. For reasons now lost to history, this type of intervention is rigidly confined to particular types of arrangements; the law does not oversee all contracts and then intervene whenever there is some type of substantive unfairness.

None of these review options belongs exclusively to Equity. The Common Law also reviews promises and does so on analogous, although generally more limited, grounds. Some of the parallels will emerge in the ensuing discussion. Moreover, although many of the examples concern contractual arrangements, the jurisdiction is not so limited; where the

---

[2] And mere promises of gifts are not binding in any event. The Common Law only enforces *contracts*; this means that promised performance has to be matched by promised counter-performance (i.e. consideration), or the arrangement has to be embodied in a deed.

analogies are apt, purported gifts can be reviewed and then recalled on exactly the same basis.

Working out the appropriate remedies once a promise is reviewed merits a chapter of its own.[3] Nevertheless, one feature deserves mention here. When promises are reviewed on any of the grounds described in this chapter, the concern is whether the claimant is bound by the purported arrangement. It is not with whether the defendant has committed some wrong. The remedies reflect this. If the arrangement has not yet been implemented, then performance is not demanded. If the arrangement has already been implemented, then it must be unwound. This does not mean that the claimant must necessarily be put back in the same economic position she was in before she entered into the arrangement. This is what tort damages would do if the defendant had committed a wrong. Unwinding the deal is less ambitious. It is designed to reverse the enrichment the defendant may have gained from the arrangement once it is clear that the claimant did not effectively consent, or commit, to deliver the benefit to him. The doctrinal difference may seem subtle, but its impact in quantifying the appropriate remedies can be profound.[4]

FORMALITIES WHICH GENERATE UNFAIRNESS

This first category exposes the simplest of problems: that the parties' written deal does not properly reflect their real intentions. Perhaps the writing positively misrepresents what was agreed; perhaps it omits vital terms. In either case, the compromised party will not wish to be bound by a written document that either incorrectly or incompletely represents the deal she intended. Equity has two strategies for dealing with these situations.

RECTIFICATION

The Common Law accords great weight to written documents. It rarely allows parties to escape from their recorded obligations unless there is some sort of serious procedural unfairness.[5] Indeed, the Common Law's

---

[3] See Chapter 9, especially 294–303.

[4] See Chapter 9, 275, 309–10, and contrast Chapter 6, 159–61.

[5] One exception is the Common Law defence of *non est factum* ('it is not my deed'). The defence was initially designed to protect those who could not read. To raise this defence now, notwithstanding the claimant's signature on the document, the claimant must have been incapable in the circumstances of properly understanding the import of the document. The contract is then void, not merely voidable. This consequence can dramatically affect remote third parties; rectification, by contrast, only affects the parties to the agreement.

parol evidence rule forbids oral evidence being admitted to add to, vary or subtract from a written instrument. This can cause problems for parties if their written document misrepresents the real agreement. Equity's less restrictive rules of evidence meant that it was more readily persuaded to rectify the written terms of a document so that they reflected the true accord between the parties. Initially Equity only allowed rectification in cases where the writing did not reflect the true intention of the parties because there had been a mistake in transcribing the document. Slowly it expanded to embrace cases of common (mutual) mistake, where both parties had made the same mistake about some matter.[6] Now it extends to cases where only one party is mistaken, but the other party was aware of the mistake, so that it would be inequitable to allow him to take advantage of it.[7] Equity will also allow rectification of promised gifts where the promise is contained in a deed,[8] and so is regarded by the Common Law as binding even without consideration from the other party to the arrangement. Of course, in every case the claimant has to prove that the written document misrepresents the intended contractual arrangement. This jurisdiction applies only to the rectification of mistakes appearing in documents; it does not allow for the general rectification of oral contracts.

WRITING REQUIREMENTS

Claimants may also be caught out when their intentions are not recorded in an appropriately formal fashion. The Common Law refuses to enforce some agreements unless they are accompanied by particular formalities. For example, contracts for the transfer of an interest in land are of no effect unless they are in writing.[9] These formalities serve a cautionary function: individuals usually think more carefully before they sign than before they speak. Formalities also reduce the likelihood of fraud. As early as the seventeenth century, the Statute of Frauds insisted on writing so as to prevent fraudulent allegations of oral agreements to transfer property. The strategy generally works well, but not always. Sometimes parties set up the statute to fraudulently *deny* a claimant's right to

---

[6] *Joscelyne v Nissen* [1970] 2 QB 86. The mistake must be such that the document does not correctly record the parties' agreement; it is not sufficient that the parties were mistaken about the effect of their transaction: *Frederick Rose (London) Ltd v William Pimm Jr Co Ltd* [1953] 2 QB 450 (CA), 461–2 (Denning LJ).

[7] *Thomas Bates & Son Ltd v Wyndham's (Lingerie) Ltd* [1981] 1 WLR 505 (CA); but see *George Wimpey UK Ltd v V I Construction Ltd* [2005] EWCA Civ 77 (CA).

[8] *Re Butlin's Settlement Trust* [1976] Ch 251. See Chapter 2, 29.

[9] Law of Property (Miscellaneous Provisions) Act 1989, s. 2.

property on the basis that the arrangement is not adequately recorded. Equity refuses to allow the statute to be used in this way: put more poetically, 'Equity will not allow a statute to cloak a fraud'.

This form of Equitable intervention is necessarily limited. Equity cannot simply ignore statutory provisions and arrogate to itself law-making power in defiance of Parliament. Equity intervenes only when it would be fraudulent or dishonest of the defendant to deny the informal arrangement. This is not the case if the defendant simply insists that he is not bound by an oral agreement, perhaps to sell a parcel of land for a nominated price. It is then irrelevant that the purchaser thought the arrangement binding and paid the agreed price; her proper remedy is recovery of the price, not enforcement of the sale.

Equity's intervention usually depends upon more complicated facts. In a typical case, the claimant transfers land to the defendant to be held on trust for nominated beneficiaries. The transfer may be properly formalized, but not the trust (in circumstances where this, too, is necessary[10]). This enables the defendant to insist that he holds the property for himself, even though the (unwritten) facts suggest that the claimant would never have transferred the property to him but for the associated trust arrangement. In these circumstances, Equity will not allow the defendant to set up the statute to deny that others have an interest in the property.[11] Some cases suggest that the claimant must also show that she acted to her detriment in reliance on the defendant's representations that he would fulfil his (unwritten) promises. If this is an additional requirement, then it is usually readily proved. Here, for example, the claimant's detrimental reliance is obvious.

Equity's preferred strategy for remedying these problems is unclear. Equity might simply enforce the unwritten express trust in defiance of the explicit statutory provision requiring writing.[12] Alternatively, it might unwind the entire deal, on the basis that the claimant did not intend her property to benefit the defendant, but to benefit her nominated beneficiaries. The first mechanism is akin to specific performance of the unwritten agreement. The second effectively forces the defendant to make restitution of his unjust enrichment. Notice that the two approaches can sometimes deliver quite different results. Suppose the claimant transfers property to the defendant to hold on (unwritten) trust for X. If

---

[10] This is the case with trusts of land, but not trusts of personal property: Law of Property Act 1925, s. 53(1)(b); Law of Property (Miscellaneous Provisions) Act 1989, s. 2.

[11] *Rochefoucauld v Boustead* [1897] 1 Ch 196 (CA); *Hodgson v Marks* [1971] Ch 892 (CA).

[12] *Rochefoucauld v Boustead* [1897] 1 Ch 196 (CA), 205–6, 208.

Equity enforces the trust even though there is no writing, then X will benefit; if, instead, it unravels the initial transfer to the defendant, then the property will be returned to the claimant. In many of the older cases that came before the courts, the claimant had transferred her property to the defendant intending him to hold it on trust for *her*. Then both approaches fortuitously deliver the same result, and the courts rarely explained exactly how they had decided that the claimant should recover.

On principle, the restitutionary approach seems preferable. It does not countermand explicit statutory provisions indicating that the unwritten deal is void or unenforceable or of no effect,[13] but instead it recognizes that the circumstances make it unjust for the defendant to keep the enrichment that has reached him. Explained like this, Equity will review the claimant's formal promise to the defendant, and may conclude that the written evidence does not fully reflect the deal. Even though the claimant may appear to have transferred her property outright, her intention was that the defendant would hold the property on trust, not that he would take beneficially. Equity's mechanism for unwinding these deals is discussed in detail later.[14] Although this seems the more principled response, Equity does sometimes specifically enforce these promises. This form of intervention is harder to justify.[15]

PROCEDURAL UNFAIRNESS—EXAMINING INTENTION

This next category of cases where Equity reviews promises is by far the largest. Equity (and the Common Law too) will unravel contracts and unilateral promises if the claimant has not properly consented to the arrangement. If objective evidence suggests the claimant has not properly consented to the deal, then no contract ever comes into existence. The purported arrangement is *void*. These cases are relatively rare, but easily dealt with. The problem is usually more subtle. Often the parties *do* appear to have reached this sort of agreement, but somehow the defendant has improperly impaired the claimant's judgement. Perhaps the defendant has misrepresented facts to the claimant, or put the claimant

---

[13] Although the statute specifically retains the role of resulting, implied and constructive trusts: Law of Property (Miscellaneous Provisions) Act 1989, s. 2(5). The intended impact of this is most unclear. Nevertheless, it seems logical to suggest that, however else a constructive trust may arise, it cannot now arise because Equity 'specifically enforces' a contract that the statute says is of no effect. See Chapter 8, 264–6.

[14] See Chapter 9, 298–303.   [15] See Chapter 8, 230–5.

under undue pressure. In these circumstances the law may allow the claimant to withdraw from her contractual obligations.

This is serious intervention. A claimant is given the right to set aside a contract because she has not properly consented to the deal, even though outward appearances suggest otherwise. Both Equity and the Common Law adopt a clever strategy in dealing with these cases. Suppose the defendant misrepresents crucial facts to the claimant. Had the claimant known the truth, she might have declined the deal; on the other hand, she might have proceeded in any event. Viewed objectively, the claimant *has* consented to the deal; viewed subjectively, however, she may or may not truly intend to be bound. In these more ambivalent circumstances, English law persists in its usual objective view, but only up to a point. It presumes that the parties *have* reached a binding agreement but holds to that presumption only until the compromised party takes positive steps to overturn the transaction in reliance on its flawed formation. In these circumstances, the affected party is said to *rescind*, or avoid, the *voidable* contract. This means that the arrangement between the parties operates as a perfectly valid and binding agreement unless and until the compromised party takes effective steps to unwind the deal.

The detail of how these arrangements are unravelled is dealt with later,[16] but notice one crucial difference between void and voidable contracts. Suppose A sells a car to B who then sells it to C. If the contract between A and B is *void*, then B does not get good title to the car, and so nor does C (recall the *nemo dat* rule[17]). This means that C is vulnerable to claims by A to recover the car.[18] On the other hand, if the contract between A and B is merely voidable, then it operates as a perfectly good contract until A takes steps to avoid the deal. This means B gets good title to the car, and can transfer good title to C. If A only discovers the truth after this second sale, she will not be able to advance any claims against C.[19] This distinction is clearly important for third parties. They are better protected if the initial contract is voidable rather than void. This is as it should be, given that the initial contract appears to outsiders to be a perfectly proper contract. This clever strategy is directed to balancing the interests of the claimant in escaping from deals that she did not truly intend against the interests of third parties in security of transactions.

[16] See Chapter 9.   [17] See Chapter 4, 93–4.
[18] See Chapter 6, 169–74, and remember that A does not have a *right* to insist on redelivery of the car.
[19] *Lewis v Averay* [1972] 1 QB 198 (CA); *Car & Universal Finance Co Ltd v Caldwell* [1965] 1 QB 525 (CA).

The next sections describe the various grounds on which Equity permits the claimant to set aside an apparently binding contract or gift. In developing these grounds, Equity invariably built upon grounds already recognized by the Common Law, extending the Common Law rules to allow the claimant greater leeway in arguing that she did not truly consent to the underlying deal.

MISTAKE

The first argument a claimant might advance is that she did not truly intend to be bound by a contract because she was mistaken as to some aspect of the arrangement. The Common Law regards some mistakes as so serious that the purported contract is void. For example, if each party has a completely different perception of what the agreement is about (i.e. *each* is labouring under a *unilateral mistake*), then it is impossible to say that any real agreement has been reached. Typically, the parties may be at odds over the identity of the contracting party or the identity of the subject matter of the contract.[20] Alternatively, the parties may have a shared, but mistaken, perception about their agreement that is sufficient to render the contract void for *common mistake*. For example, the parties may contract to buy and sell a cargo of corn from each other, but unknown to both of them the corn has already been destroyed.[21] In these cases the Common Law must allocate the risk of unforeseen events. The outcome is, of course, quite different if one party has promised the other that something *is* the case—for example, that the subject matter of the contract *does* exist. There is then a valid contract and the injured party can sue for damages.[22] This Common Law jurisdiction to intervene on the ground of mistakes made at the contract-formation stage is exceedingly narrow.[23]

Equity was frequently said to have expanded the jurisdiction in relation to common mistake, although it then regards the affected contract as void-able rather than void.[24] Contracts have been set aside in Equity on the basis of a common mistake as to the value of the underlying sale property,[25] or

---

[20] *Cundy v Lindsay* (1878) 3 App Cas 459 (HL), 463–6 (Lord Cairns LC); *Ingram v Little* [1961] 1 QB 31 (CA).

[21] *Couturier v Hastie* (1856) 5 HLC 673 (HL).

[22] *McRae v Commonwealth Disposals Commission* (1951) 84 CLR 377 (Aust HCt).

[23] *Bell v Lever Bros Ltd* [1932] AC 161 (HL) is the leading case, and, as if to confirm the narrowness of the jurisdiction, the argument failed.

[24] *Solle v Butcher* [1950] 1 KB 671 (CA); *Cooper v Phibbs* (1867) LR 2 HL 149 (HL).

[25] *Grist v Bailey* [1967] Ch 532 (Goff J).

the value of the claim being compromised.[26] These decisions are difficult to justify on any principled basis relating to mistake: Equity simply seems to be mending bad bargains. This is something the law generally abhors, especially where the parties have properly consented to the deal (although some odd exceptions are exposed later in this chapter). No convincing explanation is given of why the defendant, not the claimant, should bear the risk of a deal being a better or worse bargain than anticipated. In other areas, Equity usually allows claimants to escape their commitments only if the defendant has played some role, however innocent, in leading the claimant into her predicament. That is not the case here. These Equitable interventions have attracted trenchant criticism. By contrast, the Common Law's philosophy is one of holding the parties to their bargain unless the facts suggest that there could not possibly have been a bargain. The anomalous Equitable extension of the Common Law rules makes rational integration of the two practices virtually impossible, and modern courts seem justifiably set on eliminating the Equitable outgrowths.[27]

MISREPRESENTATION

The second argument a claimant might advance is that she did not truly consent to the deal because the defendant misrepresented some material aspect of the arrangement to her: but for his misrepresentation, she would not have proceeded with the engagement. A misrepresentation is simply a false statement of fact that induces a party to enter into a contract or otherwise act to her detriment. For example, the vendor may misrepresent the profits of a business he is selling. The purchaser may then complain that, but for his misrepresentation, she would not have gone ahead with the purchase. She may insist that she did not truly consent to the deal she now has; she only consented to the more profitable deal that the vendor misrepresented was on offer.

If the law refuses to review these types of engagements, then consider what alternatives the purchaser is left with. If the vendor's profit forecast is built into the contract, then the vendor must hand over a business that meets this description. If he does not, then he is in breach of his express contractual obligations and must pay damages to the purchaser for her

---

[26] *Magee v Pennine Insurance Co* [1969] 2 QB 507 (CA).

[27] This stance, expressed in the first edition of this book, has now been confirmed: see *Great Peace Shipping Ltd v Tsavliris (International) Ltd* [2003] QB 679 (CA), holding that there is no Equitable jurisdiction to grant rescission of a contract on the grounds of common mistake when the contract is valid at Common Law, disapproving *Solle v Butcher* [1950] 1 KB 671 (CA).

disappointed expectations. The difficulty for the disappointed purchaser is that not all negotiating statements are incorporated as terms of the contract. Even when they are, the purchaser is usually confined to a damages claim; only rarely can she refuse to accept the defendant's inadequate performance.

If the contractual route will not work, then the law of civil wrongs may offer an alternative. If the vendor's misrepresentation is classified as a civil wrong, then the vendor will have to pay damages to compensate for the harm he has caused. The Common Law regards the vendor's misrepresentation as a wrong if it is either fraudulent or negligent. If the vendor is involved in a deliberate scheme to dupe the purchaser into contracting, then he is guilty of the tort of deceit. Because of the defendant's deliberate duplicity, damages are assessed without regard to notions of foreseeability or remoteness. If the vendor's misrepresentation is merely careless, but delivered in circumstances where the vendor is obliged to take care to avoid causing the claimant harm, then he is guilty of the tort of negligent misrepresentation.[28] He is still obliged to compensate the purchaser for the harm caused, but the amount is limited by notions of foreseeability and remoteness. Once again the difficulty is clear. The law of civil wrongs may give the purchaser a money remedy, but it does not allow her to unwind the contract.

Even the Common Law concedes that some of these arrangements do not represent a true accord between the parties, despite objective assessments to the contrary. The jurisprudential difficulty is then to reconcile the competing public interest in security of apparently valid transactions against the claimant's private interest in being held to contracts only when they are properly intended. The Common Law's solution is unforgiving. It favours security of transactions over the claimant's interests unless the defendant is guilty of deceit. Only then can the claimant insist that she has not properly consented to the deal. The engagement is regarded as voidable at Common Law because of the defendant's deceit, and the claimant has the option to unwind the transaction (subject to some quite significant practical limitations).[29]

Equity is far more accommodating. It regards *all* misrepresentations, whether fraudulent, negligent, or innocent, as grounds for denying that there was true consent to the deal.[30] In each case the claimant can choose whether or not to unwind the transaction (again, subject to certain

---

[28] See Chapter 6, 161–2.   [29] See Chapter 9, 298–303.
[30] *Redgrave v Hurd* (1881) 20 Ch D 1; *Senanayake v Cheng* [1966] AC 63 (HL).

significant practical limitations).[31] Intervention is seen as justified because the defendant himself has made it impossible for the claimant to form an unimpaired intention (no matter how innocently he did this). The objective view of intention should therefore give way, at the claimant's option, and the defendant should bear the risk of the engagement falling through. The remedies are then designed to reverse any enrichment the defendant may have gained without the claimant properly intending to deliver it to him.[32] Unlike the Equitable mistake cases discussed in the previous section, this type of Equitable intervention is a readily justifiable extension of the Common Law's protection for contracting parties.

DURESS AND UNDUE INFLUENCE

The third argument that a claimant might advance to persuade the court that a purported arrangement does not represent her real intentions is that her free will was overborne, rather than independent and voluntary, because she was unacceptably pressurized or influenced by the defendant.

Common Law duress—physical and economic duress

The Common Law recognized physical duress as an impairment to consent early in its history. If a claimant is forced at gunpoint to enter into a contract, or to make a gift to someone, then the law must provide for effective recovery once the risk is removed. The Common Law recognizes that the claimant's consent may be impaired by physical violence or threats of violence,[33] by threats of damage to her property,[34] or by economic duress (i.e. illegitimate threats to harm her economic interests).[35] In each case the purported arrangement is voidable; the claimant can rescind the transaction and unwind the underlying transfers.

The idea that these transactions do not reflect the claimant's real intentions seems self-evident. Nevertheless, the proper doctrinal basis for intervention has become the subject of intense scrutiny. The traditional view that the claimant's will has been 'coerced' so as to 'vitiate her consent' is now commonly seen as misrepresenting the facts. The truth, it is argued,

---

[31] Including the statutory provision that permits the court to award damages in lieu of rescission in appropriate circumstances: Misrepresentation Act 1967, s. 2. Quite remarkably, such statutory damages are assessed by analogy with the Common Law rules applying to fraudulent misrepresentation, even when the misrepresentation is innocent: *Royscot Trust Ltd v Rogerson* [1991] 2 QB 297. Also see Chapter 9, 298–303.

[32] See Chapter 9, 294–303.   [33] *Barton v Armstrong* [1976] AC 104 (PC).

[34] *The Evia Luck* [1992] 2 AC 152 (HL).

[35] *Universe Tankships of Monrovia v International Transport Workers Federation* ('The Universe Sentinel') [1983] 1 AC 366 (HL).

is that the claimant does consent to the contract. Indeed, the more real
the pressure, the more real is her consent, even if only to avoid unpalatable alternatives. The real problem, so the argument goes, is not absence
of consent, but the wrongful nature of the threats that have been used to
bring about consent.[36] The distinction matters. Unintended transfers are
remedied by restitution, assessed according to the rules of unjust enrichment law.[37] Wrongdoing is remedied by compensation or, occasionally,
disgorgement, as determined by the law of civil wrongs. Quantification is
different; defences are different. This modern reassessment of the duress
cases suggests that the claimant is entitled to disgorgement for the
wrongdoing, not compensation. Why this is so is not explained: the argument is not easy.[38] If made out, however, then analogies with fiduciary law
suggest that the remedy will capture profits left untouched by unjust
enrichment remedies; moreover, defendants will be unable to rely on
unjust enrichment law's special change of position defence.[39]

This modern re-analysis appears to misconceive the necessary quality
of the consent that is sought in all these areas of intervention. Purported
contracts and gifts are unwound, despite the claimant's objective consent
to the engagement, if her consent was not the product of a free and
informed mind (and if, in addition, the defendant played an unacceptable
part in producing this impaired consent). When the claimant has a gun
held to her head, whatever she might say, her true position is not, 'I *want*
to do this.' It is invariably, 'I *don't* want to do this, but I have no choice.'
Once the pressure ceases, her unimpaired free will is exposed. The focus
is on the reality of her consent. By contrast, the modern re-analysis leads
to the odd conclusion that there is proper consent in cases of physical
duress when the claimant is conscious that her free will is impaired, but
impaired consent when the pressure is more subtle and the claimant is
not conscious of any duress, influence, or misinformation.[40] The more
consistent view, surely, is that consent is impaired in all of these cases, and
all can be remedied in the law of unjust enrichment. Of course, if the
pressure also amounts to a civil wrong, then it will attract additional,
alternative remedies in the law of wrongs.[41]

Impaired consent is just the first step, however. A deal is only unwound
if the claimant did not truly consent *and* the defendant played some

---

[36] See Lord Goff's analysis in *The Evia Luck* [1992] 2 AC 152 (HL).
[37] See Chapter 9, 294–8.   [38] See Chapter 5, 154–5.
[39] See Chapter 9, 312–15 and 309–10.   [40] See below, 211–19.
[41] Although then the usual remedy would be compensation, not disgorgement: see
Chapter 5, 154–5.

unacceptable part in that state of affairs. Both the Common Law and Equity impose this limitation. Otherwise the general rule is that arrangements are binding if, tested objectively, the claimant has properly consented to the deal. A defendant's role may be 'unacceptable' even though it does not amount to a civil wrong. The Common Law and Equity draw the line in different places.

In both jurisdictions, the difficulty is to differentiate between acceptable and unacceptable pressure. Take Common Law economic duress. A large part of commercial life involves hard negotiation for the best deal possible. Everyone acts under pressure, including economic pressure. Some people maintain rigid independence; others succumb to pressure more readily. Those who feel compromised by hard bargaining should not automatically be able to complain that their consent was improperly extracted through economic duress. The boundaries defining unacceptable economic duress are still being worked out.

Equitable undue influence

Exactly the same subtle distinctions face Equity. Equity's concern is with social pressure, not physical or economic pressure, and unacceptable social pressure is referred to as *undue influence*. At the outset Equity's motivation for intervention was a rather paternalistic desire to protect individuals from being victimized by others.[42] For example, Equity might allow a father to rescind a mortgage that had been executed because the banker suggested that he had the means to prosecute the mortgagor's son for forgery.[43] In allowing such deals to be set aside for *actual undue influence*, Equity recognizes that a claimant's consent can be impaired by far more subtle forms of pressure than those acknowledged by the early Common Law.

Equity went further than this. It also recognized *presumed undue influence*. A hundred years ago, the social environment was quite different from today. Religious advisers, doctors, solicitors, fiduciaries, and even parents had far more influential roles than now. Ordinary citizens were easily persuaded that a proposal was advantageous simply because it had been suggested by someone in one of these respected roles; they would suspend their own judgement, or 'defer to their betters'. Of course, this was not true of everyone. However, it was sufficiently true as a generalization to persuade Equity, over time, to develop a presumption that people

---

[42] *Allcard v Skinner* (1887) 36 Ch D 145 (CA), 172 (Cotton LJ), 185 (Lindley LJ).
[43] *Williams v Bayley* (1866) LR 1 HL 200 (HL).

in these roles 'influence' those with whom they deal. Furthermore, their influence is assumed, without further proof, to be 'undue' if (but only if) the deal is to the manifest disadvantage of the claimant.[44] For example, if a client sells a valuable antique to her solicitor, the deal is presumed to be tainted by the solicitor's undue influence if the price is well below the market price, but not if it is at market value.[45] Similarly, large gifts from a child to her parents, or from a postulant to the principal of the nunnery she has joined,[46] are presumed to be motivated by undue influence on the part of the parents or the religious principal. This legal presumption of undue influence is considered justified in the circumstances because gift-giving is not a natural incident of any of these influential relationships. Notice how aggressive this Equitable strategy is, however. Equity *presumes* influence because of the defendant's social or professional status, and it then *presumes* that this influence is undue because of the manifest disadvantage inherent in the deal. These presumptions make it very much easier for the claimant to prove her case and correspondingly more difficult for the defendant to advance his.[47]

By contrast, husbands and wives (and unmarried sexual partners) have never been included within the category of relationships where undue influence might be presumed in this way. This is not because these relationships are not influential. Indeed, when Equity was developing this jurisprudence it was probably widely accepted that wives would generally defer to their husbands. But Equity's target is not simply influence; it is *undue* influence. In these domestic relationships, gift-giving *is* natural. This means that there is no simple test that suggests that any acknowledged influence might have been unduly exercised.

Even when Equity does presume undue influence, the presumption is rebuttable. If the defendant can prove that the claimant exercised her own independent judgement, then the deal will stand. The easiest way to prove this, it seems, is to show that the claimant took independent advice on the matter but still pursued the arrangement. This can, of course,

---

[44] *National Westminster Bank plc v Morgan* [1985] AC 686 (HL), 704. Of course, there is no need to prove manifest disadvantage where there is *actual* undue influence; this necessarily indicates that the claimant's consent is impaired, and grounds for raising some presumption are unnecessary: *CIBC Mortgages plc v Pitt* [1994] 1 AC 200 (HL).

[45] Of course, even a market-value transaction may have been induced by the solicitor's undue influence. In these circumstances, however, the claimant will have to prove *actual* undue influence if she wants to unwind the transaction; she will not be able to rely on a presumption of undue influence.

[46] *Allcard v Skinner* (1887) 36 ChD 145.

[47] *Yerkey v Jones* (1939) 63 CLR 649 (Aust HCt), 675.

raise very difficult questions. What if the advice is ignored (perhaps because the undue influence operated so powerfully), or is manifestly inadequate, or is misunderstood? A reasoned response to these dilemmas depends upon an agreed rationale for Equity's intervention. If Equity embraces the modern Common Law approach to duress, with its emphasis on the wrongfulness of the defendant's conduct, then the defendant's instruction to the claimant to seek independent advice might afford him an excuse, regardless of the impact the advice has. On the other hand, the analysis preferred here is that intervention in all these cases is premised on the claimant's lack of real consent where this is somehow the defendant's responsibility (however innocent his influence might have been). On this analysis, the real issue is whether the independent advice enabled the claimant to reach an independent decision, or at least a decision where the defendant was no longer responsible for any impairment. No blanket answer can be given; sometimes advice (even inadequate advice) will have this impact, but not always. The courts simply have to examine the facts to determine the position.

These presumptions of undue influence continue to operate across the categories of relationships listed earlier—religious advisers and their congregations, doctors and their patients, solicitors and their clients, fiduciaries and their principals, parents and their children—even though social conditions are now so different that the basis of the rule must surely be lost. Moreover, no new categories of 'influential' relationships have been added to the list. This is probably to be expected. An automatic presumption, without regard to the realities of the particular relationship, is no longer justified as a social generalization. Instead, Equity's jurisdiction has expanded in other directions.

The most logical expansion, of course, was for Equity to accept that the same sort of analysis ought to apply even when the claimant is not within a recognized influential relationship, so long as she can prove that her particular relationship with the defendant displays all the same characteristics. If this is the case, *and* the deal in question is manifestly to her disadvantage, then she, too, should be allowed to rely on a presumption that the defendant unduly influenced her. This expanded jurisdiction is, by its own terms, completely open-ended. However, in practice its reach is rather predictable. It often catches husbands and wives, for example. A wife who wants to unwind an arrangement with her husband will offer evidence to prove that her practice is to simply accept her husband's decisions and subject herself to his domination. Once this relationship of influence is accepted, the court will presume that any manifestly disadvantageous transaction between the two was brought about by the husband's undue influence. He can only maintain the arrangement if he can rebut this presumption by showing that in this case at least his wife exercised her own independent will.[48] The same process of reasoning can easily apply to de facto couples, to other family relationships (such as an uncle and his nephew, with the influence operating in either direction), to employer and employee, and so on.

These evolutionary steps mirror those described earlier in the context of the fiduciary jurisdiction.[49] Recall that initially only trustees owed fiduciary obligations. Slowly the jurisdiction expanded to include a defined list of social roles—solicitors, agents, partners, company directors. Finally the jurisdiction expanded still further, with the courts' recognition that a fiduciary relationship might exist outside these defined categories, so long as analogous fiduciary features were manifest in the particular relationship.

Indeed, there is some overlap between the fiduciary role and the undue-influencer role. For example, a solicitor might wear both hats. If the solicitor enters into a contract with his client, the agreement could be unravelled by the client alleging a breach of fiduciary duties or the wielding of undue influence. The two doctrines pursue quite different ends, however. A fiduciary's duty of loyalty is concerned with wrongdoing. The duty is only breached if the transaction is disloyal and undisclosed: the fiduciary cannot make a *secret* profit from his position. Where this is the case, then rescission is designed to effect disgorgement of the disloyal profits. The presumption of undue influence, on the other hand, operates regardless of disclosure and only where the deal is manifestly to the disadvantage of the client. Then rescission is designed to effect restitution of the unjust enrichment that the solicitor has acquired through his dealing. The fact that rescission can be motivated by these two different goals has created several practical difficulties in working out the details of the remedy. One of the most obvious practical differences is that the wrongdoing fiduciary is unlikely to be able to take advantage of the change of position defence, but the undue influencer is; there are also important related differences in quantifying the remedy itself.[50]

---

[48] *Barclays Bank plc v O'Brien* [1994] 1 AC 180 (HL); *Royal Bank of Scotland v Etridge (No 2)* [2002] 2 AC 773 (HL).
[49] See Chapter 5, 140–2.   [50] See Chapters 5, 134–40, and Chapter 9, 298–303.

Three-party cases

One final point is crucial in this area. Many modern cases of undue influence are not simple two-party cases between solicitor and client, or doctor and patient. They are three-party cases involving banks. Typically the problem arises when a husband persuades his wife to mortgage her interest in the family home to secure his expanding business debts. If the bank later repossesses the house because there have been defaults in repaying the loan, can the wife escape from her mortgage agreement with the bank and keep her share of the house? The *bank* has not unduly influenced the wife (or misrepresented aspects of the deal to her), although her husband may have. Can problems between the husband and the wife affect the contract between the bank and the wife? The general rule is that the bank takes the property (the security interest in the family house) subject to the equities of which it has notice.[51] This means that *if* the bank had actual or constructive notice at the time of the deal that the wife's consent was improperly procured, then the wife could set aside her mortgage agreement with the bank.

The problem for banks is that very little evidence now appears to be needed to put them on notice that the wife's consent was improperly procured. In practice, it seems sufficient if the deal is manifestly disadvantageous to the wife (and every security agreement or guarantee automatically falls into this category unless the wife stands to benefit significantly from the underlying loan). The implication is that manifest disadvantage is enough to suggest to the bank that the wife's consent might be affected by undue influence (even though the relationship between husband and wife is not a relationship of presumed influence), or even that it might be affected by misrepresentation. This is odd. Indeed, the suggestion does not hold only for husbands and wives. The modern rule suggests that if the claimant provides security for a deal that is principally designed to benefit another, then the bank is automatically on notice that the claimant's consent might be impaired in some way (and undue influence and misrepresentation are not even distinguished) *unless* the arrangement has some legitimate explanation.[52] The real nature of the relationship between the parties, or the bank's knowledge of it, is seemingly irrelevant.

This rule has forced banks to adopt a self-protective regime to ensure that they do not have such notice. The strategy involves ensuring that the

---

[51] See Chapter 4, 94–5.
[52] *Crédit Lyonnais Bank Nederland NV v Burch* [1997] 1 All ER 144 (CA).

compromised party takes independent advice. Indeed, the House of Lords has effectively legislated for the banks in this area: it has provided a prescriptive set of rules concerning what sort of advice the party must be given, and how, and when, and by whom.[53] These rules are all designed to ensure that the wife cannot allege that the bank knew or ought to have known that her consent was impaired. Note that the role of independent advice in these cases is not quite the same as its role where the 'influencing' party relies on it. The influencing party (the husband, for example, in a deal involving the husband and the wife) has to prove that the advice was such that his wife did *in fact* have unimpaired consent, or at least consent that was no longer impaired by his interference. The bank does not. Inadequate or ignored advice may suffice for the bank's purposes, but not necessarily for the husband's purposes.

These various doctrinal and practical difficulties suggest that there must be a better strategy to deal with these cases. It would perhaps be better to acknowledge outright that the real problem is the relationship between the wife and the *bank*, not her relationship with her husband and the bank's constructive knowledge of it. The advantages of a direct approach are even more apparent when the three-party analysis is contorted to embrace parties whose relationship with each other is far less transparent to outsiders (like banks) than that between husband and wife, including de facto couples and parties whose relationship is merely professional, such as employer and employee. One approach, sometimes adopted in certain jurisdictions other than England, is raised in the next section. Another would be even more straightforward. It would simply recognize banks as owing a duty of care to advise their customers on manifestly risky transactions.[54] In effect, this is what the House of Lords has done in England, although the doctrinal justification remains inappropriately tied to three-party undue influence and misrepresentation analyses.

UNCONSCIONABLE BARGAINS

Finally, Equity has a limited jurisdiction to intervene and unwind *unconscionable bargains*. The real basis for this intervention is not at all clear, and categorization as an aspect of procedural unfairness is provisional only.

---

[53] *Royal Bank of Scotland v Etridge (No 2)* [2002] 2 AC 773 (HL).

[54] See Chapter 6, 161–8. The obvious conflict between the bank's self-interest and the law's imposition of a rather paternalistic duty of care towards its customers is common in this area of the law.

At the outset the jurisdiction was chiefly concerned with contracts between 'expectant heirs' and moneylenders. Young men (usually) would use their anticipated inheritance to finance their current, sometimes profligate, needs. Interest rates of 60 per cent were not unknown.[55] Perhaps because there was a preference for the gentry over usurious moneylenders, Equity began to relieve heirs from these transactions. By the mid-nineteenth century, however, an heir could have a transaction set aside simply because the price was inadequate. In this form the rule became an unwarranted impediment to contractual autonomy and security of transactions. Statutory intervention now ensures that transactions dealing with reversions are not liable to be set aside on the grounds of undervalue in the absence of fraud or unfair dealing.[56] However, these statutory rules expressly retain the jurisdiction of the court to set aside unconscionable bargains.

What remains of this Equitable jurisdiction now appears very restricted, especially in England. It does not apply to gifts, but a contract can be set aside where a stronger party takes unconscionable advantage of a weaker party. This is seen as so only if the weaker party is in a position of special disadvantage arising from poverty or ignorance, has not taken independent advice, and has agreed to contract at considerable undervalue.[57] If the claimant can show all of this, then the transaction will be set aside unless the defendant shows that the terms are 'fair, just and reasonable'. In other common law jurisdictions, by contrast, the need for independent advice and undervalue is not absolute.

The real basis for intervention is never clearly articulated. The cases concern drunken vendors, infatuated lovers, divorcing wives, all entering into unwise contracts that they later regret. Equity strenuously denies that it is motivated simply by unfair terms, especially substantial undervalue in the contract price: it is not remaking bargains. Equally it denies that it intervenes simply because the parties have unequal bargaining power: inequality is not proof of procedural unfairness.[58] Nevertheless, suspicions persist, fuelled by the view that such loose discretions will lead to uncertainty and inconsistency.

---

[55] *Earl of Aylesford v Morris* (1873) 8 Ch App 484.
[56] Law of Property Act 1925, s. 174.   [57] *Fry v Lane* (1888) 40 ChD 312.
[58] But see *A Schroeder Music Publishing Co Ltd v Macaulay* (1974) 1 WLR 1308, 1314–15, 1316; *Lloyds Bank v Bundy* [1975] QB 326 (although 'inequality of bargaining power' disapproved of in *National Westminster Bank plc v Morgan* [1985] AC 686 (HL)); *Creswell v Potter* [1978] 1 WLR 255, 257 (Megarry J) (but doubted, *obiter*, in *Commercial Bank of Australia Ltd v Amadio* (1983) 151 CLR 447 (Aust HCt), 461 (Gibbs CJ)).

Given this, perhaps the best, if unarticulated, rationalization of these
cases *is* procedural unfairness, and the reality of the claimant's consent.
Equity recognizes that there are countless reasons why a claimant may
not be in a position to look after her own interests. As the early
unconscionable bargain cases acknowledged, she may be in financial need,
ignorant, or inexperienced; alternatively, she may be ill or suffering from
impaired faculties. None of this is the defendant's responsibility, and usually the contract between claimant and defendant will be binding if both
parties have, objectively, consented to the deal. However, where the facts
suggest that the defendant knew of the claimant's impaired consent (even
though he was not responsible for it), and snatched the bargain regardless
of this, then the claimant should perhaps be entitled to set the deal aside.[59]

This rationalization demands careful treatment of the factors commonly considered relevant in these cases. The defendant must *know* that
the claimant's consent to the deal is impaired.[60] This knowledge will not
be presumed, even rebuttably; the defendant will not have constructive
notice. This would ignore the rationale for intervention; the defendant is
not responsible, however innocently, for the claimant's impairment.
Nevertheless, given the defendant's knowledge of certain facts, it may
sometimes be reasonable to *infer* that he did actually know that the claimant's consent was impaired.[61] The particular facts and their individual
context will be all-important. Sometimes the coincidence of known personal disadvantage and substantial undervalue in the transaction may be
sufficient to raise this sort of inference. The fragility of this route to
proving actual knowledge is clear, however. If the terms of the deal are
fair and reasonable, or if the claimant took independent advice, then the
inference is not warranted: a reasonable defendant may then have supposed the claimant's consent to be genuine, even though he knew of
the claimant's personally disadvantaged circumstances. Actual proof of
knowledge will be needed. The analysis in the cases is not usually so
careful.[62] When it is not, there is a clear risk that intervention will

[59] *Hart v O'Connor* [1985] AC 1000 (PC).

[60] This would seem to be true even if the justification is to prevent exploitation: *Hart v O'Connor* [1985] AC 1000 (PC).

[61] This is likely to be so only when *no* reasonable person could have supposed, on the given facts, that the claimant's consent was genuine: see Chapter 5, 144 for an analogous use of this test.

[62] This is especially so in modern cases that seek to use this jurisdiction to set aside contracts between banks and third parties who have given guarantees or mortgages. See, for example, *Garcia v National Australia Bank Ltd* (1998) 194 CLR 395 (Aust HCt); *Commercial Bank of Australia Ltd v Amadio* (1983) 151 CLR 447 (Aust HCt).

be motivated by nothing more than a paternalistic desire to refashion seemingly unfair bargains. This crosses the line between acceptable and unacceptable interference with freedom of contract.

Explained like this, there are arguably clear parallels between all the approaches discussed under this broad head of procedural unfairness. All are concerned with claimants whose consent, or actual intent to commit to a deal and its consequential risks and rewards, is impaired by various informational shortcomings or physical, economic, or social circumstances. In misrepresentation, duress, and undue influence cases, the defendant either knows of the impairment or is unwittingly responsible for it. In unconscionable bargain cases, the defendant actually knows of the impairment or his knowledge is inferred because of the way the bargain is 'snatched'. Perhaps this is also true of some of the unsatisfactory Equitable mistake cases: they, too, may be examples of snatching bargains when the defendant knows of the claimant's error. The end result is that, by dint of slow legal evolution in both the Common Law and Equity, the fundamental rule that deals are tested objectively has been modified so that a subjective approach is seen as warranted where the defendant knew of or was responsible for the claimant's impaired consent. In general, this evolution has augmented the protections afforded by the early Common Law in a manner that is both explicable on rational grounds and consistent with the needs of society.

SUBSTANTIVE UNFAIRNESS—APPRAISING TERMS

The third and final major category of Equitable intervention differs from the first two. It is, allegedly, concerned with *substantive unfairness* in deals. The implication is that intervention is based on policy, not doctrine. Promises are vetoed because they offend some important societal interest that overrides the usual priority given to personal autonomy, especially personal autonomy in determining the terms of any deal. However, what that interest might be is not at all clear.

What is clear is that Equity is *not* simply interested in the fairness of the deal. It will not intervene just because a house worth £50,000 has been sold for £150,000. If the parties have properly agreed the price, then the bargain stands. The Common Law's imperative, *caveat emptor*—buyer beware—is equally attractive to Equity. Substantive unfairness has a much narrower compass than that of mending even the most manifestly disadvantageous bargains.

The cases suggest that Equity's concern is exclusively with overly onerous *expressly agreed remedies*. Equity will not enforce a term that specifies what is to happen on breach of contract if the consequences are out of all proportion to the loss suffered by the other party. The reason for this limited focus for substantive unfairness is never articulated. Given Equity's lack of interest in manifest unfairness in the contract price, it cannot simply be its interest in manifest unfairness in the remedy. The remedy, like the price, is a freely negotiated term of the bargain.

It is possible that Equity is simply against the idea of economic compulsion in private bargaining. Equity may insist on specific performance of certain contracts,[63] but it will not allow the parties themselves to bargain for that status. Private bargains will be upheld only if real freedom to exit exists. Exit has its price, of course: the exiting party must pay damages to compensate for the loss of bargain. But Equity will not countenance one party being held to the deal against his will because the economic consequences of exit are so unpalatable that completion is the only realistic course of action. If this is Equity's motivation, then it is blatantly paternalistic. Part of the freedom to bargain is the freedom to bargain away rights. If parties have properly agreed to particular terms, then both social and economic analysis would suggest that the risk of onerous consequences will have been factored into the contract price.

A description of the different circumstances in which Equity interferes only serves to confirm these analytical difficulties. It may, indeed, be preferable to see all these instances as further examples of procedural unfairness. The rationale for this is taken up at the end of this section.

RELIEF AGAINST TIME STIPULATIONS

Up until the nineteenth century, the Common Law regarded all time stipulations in contracts as *conditions*. This meant that if the claimant breached the term, the defendant was entitled to terminate the contract and recover damages for loss of bargain; he was not confined to damages alone. In a contract for the sale of a house, for example, the purchaser may have paid her deposit but found herself unable to complete on the due day. At Common Law, the vendor was entitled to terminate the arrangement, keep the deposit (this is the nature of a deposit), and sue the purchaser for damages for loss of bargain.

Equity's intervention overrode the parties' ability to treat the term as a condition. Equity conceded that the contract had been breached

[63] See Chapter 2, 24–31, and Chapter 8, 264–6.

and that the vendor was entitled to damages, but, subject to that, Equity allowed the purchaser to complete late; it allowed her to sue for specific performance notwithstanding her breach. Since the introduction of the Judicature Acts, the Common Law now operates exactly the same rules in relation to time stipulations.

However, Equity always conceded exceptions to this more lenient stance (and now the Common Law does too). Equity regarded the time stipulation as a condition if the parties had expressly or impliedly made it so in their contract. They could do this by using the expression 'time is of the essence', or by giving appropriate notice (usually after the initial time had passed) stipulating a date for completion and making it clear that time was then to be of the essence. In many commercial contracts, time is made of the essence and the term is upheld even if one party then suffers disproportionate loss as a result. Sometimes this approach can be rationalized. In shipping contracts or securities trading, for example, the interests of certainty and predictability are valued over individual hardship. But the same rules apply even without this justification. Where time *is* of the essence, the clause is stringently enforced. Performance that is only ten minutes late is still too late,[64] and it is completely irrelevant that the counter-party will suffer no loss from the delay. This is the effect of a 'condition' in a contract, both at Common Law and in Equity.

RELIEF WHICH GENERATED THE 'EQUITY OF REDEMPTION'

Equity's leniency in enforcing time stipulations can obviously have profound consequences. Nevertheless, it is perhaps surprising to learn that this leniency eventually led to the creation of a new Equitable property interest—the 'Equity of redemption'. This illustration serves as a timely reminder of the power of persistent interference with contractual rights,[65] whether the justification is substantive unfairness or something else.

In medieval Common Law mortgages, the borrower-mortgagor would convey his land in fee simple (i.e. transfer ownership of his estate) to the lender-mortgagee as security for a loan. The transaction made the lender the legal owner of the estate, but the mortgage would then contain a term that provided for reconveyance if the loan was repaid by a certain date. At Common Law this time stipulation was regarded as a condition. This

---

[64] *Union Eagle Ltd v Golden Achievement Ltd* [1997] 2 WLR 341 (PC). Also see *Steedman v Drinkle* [1916] 1 AC 275 (PC); *Stern v McArthur* (1988) 165 CLR 489 (Aust HCt); *Tanwar Enterprises Pty Ltd v Cauchi* [2003] HCA 57 (Aust HCt).

[65] See Chapter 3, 63–7.

meant that the land was lost forever to the mortgagor if he was even a day late in his repayment. It did not matter that he could pay if given more time, or that his failure was the result of an accident or a misunderstanding, or that the land was worth much more than the outstanding debt.

From the fifteenth century onwards, Equity began to intervene. It did not take the mortgage at face value, as a conveyance of land, but saw it for what it was: a security to guarantee the repayment of a debt. Since the land was only a security, it seemed wrong that it should be lost forever if payment was late. Originally Equity intervened only in very hard cases, but by the seventeenth century Equity would invariably intervene to ensure that the mortgagor could recover his land, no matter how great the delay, and provided only that the mortgagor repaid his debt plus interest and any costs occasioned by the delay. Equity's persistent specific enforcement of the mortgagor's contractual right to recover his property (albeit on terms that compensated for the defendant's financial loss) was eventually recognized as a property right itself; it was the mortgagor's *Equity of redemption*. The mortgagee was given a correlative right to obtain an order for *foreclosure*, or for sale, if there seemed to be no likelihood of the mortgagor being able to repay his debt. An order for foreclosure made the mortgagee the owner of the land free of the mortgagor's interests; an order for sale enabled the land to be sold to pay off the debt (with any excess returned to the mortgagor).

RELIEF AGAINST FORFEITURE OF PROPRIETARY INTERESTS

The Equity of redemption evolved because Equity protected mortgagors against forfeiture of their interests in land. This intervention slowly became more generalized. The position now is that if a contractual term provides for forfeiture of a proprietary interest if the owner does not perform on time, then Equity will intervene and give more time. It will protect the claimant against losing her asset, provided it can do so without harming the defendant. The proviso means that the remedy is conditional on the claimant being able to perform, and on performance (with a money component for lateness) being sufficient to ensure that the defendant does not suffer any detriment.[66] For example, if the claimant has an interest in the defendant's patent provided she pays a monthly fee, then Equity will protect her against a term allowing the defendant to forfeit her rights if the fee is not paid on time. Despite the parties' explicit

[66] *Shiloh Spinners Ltd v Harding* [1973] AC 691 (HL).

agreement, all the claimant is really obliged to do is pay the monthly fee plus damages to compensate for its lateness.

This expanded jurisdiction is rather troublesome in a way that its ancestor, the Equity of redemption, was not. Despite superficial similarities, the move to generality has ignored the original rationale underpinning intervention. It is no longer necessary to show that the forfeited property was only ever intended to provide security. Moreover, the original jurisdiction may also have relied on Equity's power to specifically enforce the reconveyance term in the mortgage, since the underlying property was land; this too is no longer an issue in modern cases. On the other hand, the modern cases confine their relief to forfeitures of possessory or ownership rights.[67] This aspect of the Equity of redemption cases was surely only coincidental: if the security had been over other types of interests, the reasoning would not have altered. All this makes it difficult to identify a coherent rationale. The expanded jurisdiction seems to have retained its factual links with history but discarded its explanatory links.

The proprietary restriction creates some especially uncomfortable divergences between cases. For example, a time charterer of a ship cannot complain if the owner withdraws the ship under a withdrawal clause.[68] The arrangement does not give the charterer a proprietary interest; instead, the charter of a ship operates much like the hire of a taxi cab. Similarly, a contractual licence to use trademarks on sportswear is not protected by Equity's forfeiture rules;[69] this, too, is not a proprietary interest. Yet a part interest in a patent is a proprietary interest, and will be protected.[70] Although the line between interests that are proprietary and those that are not is crucial in many legal contexts, this does not seem to be one of them. There seems to be no rational justification for Equity's protective intervention in one case and not in another.

These cases pose yet another dilemma. The right to an interest in a patent is protected by Equity's forfeiture rules. If the contract granting that right provides for forfeiture of the claimant's interest if she is late with some payment, then Equity will intervene to protect against forfeiture provided the claimant can make the necessary payment, plus damages

---

[67] Contractual forfeiture of payments is remedied, if at all, under the rules relating to penalties (see below, 224–6), or the rules on unjust enrichment (see Chapter 9, 303–7, on unintended gifts).

[68] *Scandinavian Trading Tanker Co AB v Flota Petrolera Ecuatoriana (The Scaptrade)* [1983] 2 AC 694 (HL).

[69] *Sport International Bussum v Inter-Footwear Ltd* [1984] 1 WLR 776 (HL).

[70] *BICC plc v Burndy Corpn* [1985] Ch 232 (CA).

for lateness, and do so without harming the defendant. But the parties could easily deal with late payments quite differently. They could discard the option of a forfeiture clause, and instead insert a clause making time of the essence for payment of the licence charges. Equity regards this as a condition. This means the defendant can terminate the contract if the stipulation is breached. Termination will inevitably abort the claimant's rights to the benefit of the patent; her interest will be forfeited. The inconsistency in result does not persuade Equity to alter its response to 'time is of the essence' clauses. These continue to be treated as conditions in order to ensure that the claimant does not breach her payment obligations with impunity.[71] The net result is that forfeiture for late payment can be secured without a forfeiture clause. All of this seems to make it impossible to articulate any coherent justification for this form of intervention.

RELIEF AGAINST PENALTIES

The doctrine of *penalties* has some parallels with all of this, although it too is a tightly circumscribed jurisdiction. Imagine an employment contract which provides for £100 to be deducted from an employee's pay if she arrives late on any working day. The employer clearly has an interest in his employees being punctual, and will suffer some damage if they are not. If he can simply insert a clause like this in employees' contracts, then it will deter breaches and also relieve him of the need to prove his precise loss whenever there is a breach. However, the stipulated sum is not a genuine pre-estimate of his likely loss; the £100 deduction applies whether the employee is thirty seconds late or three hours late. Such clauses are classified as *penalties*. They are unenforceable except to the extent that they represent the defendant's real loss.[72] The early Equitable jurisdiction to strike down penalty clauses was adopted by the Common Law, and now it is not clear whether there are two parallel jurisdictions, or whether the Common Law has completely taken over the Equitable jurisdiction.[73]

A penalty is any clause which provides that, on breach, the offending party must pay a sum that is extravagant and unconscionable in comparison with the greatest provable loss that could conceivably flow from

[71] *Scandinavian Trading Tanker Co AB v Flota Petrolera Ecuatoriana (The Scaptrade)* [1983] 2 AC 694 (HL); *Sport International Bussum BV v Inter-Footwear Ltd* [1984] 1 WLR 776 (HL).
[72] *Jobson v Johnson* [1989] 1 WLR 1026 (CA).
[73] E V Lanyon, 'Equity and the Doctrine of Penalties' (1996) 9 JCL 234.

the breach.[74] A clause is not a penalty simply because its stipulation sometimes leads to recovery of more than the claimant has lost, even if the amount is penal. Parties can negotiate for agreed damages clauses (or *liquidated damages clauses*). However, the agreed sum must represent a genuine pre-estimate of the likely loss such as might have been calculated at the time the contract was entered into. For example, the employer in our earlier example might provide for pro rata deductions from an employee's salary. Equally, manufacturers might sell to wholesalers on terms that limit sub-sales, and might agree damages of a specific amount per item sold in breach of the restriction.[75] Similarly, an owner might stipulate the liquidated damages payable by a house-builder who fails to complete construction within the nominated time period, and the sum might escalate with each day that completion is delayed.

This jurisdiction appears to provide welcome relief to contracting parties faced with the payment of unreasonably hefty 'liquidated damages'. The rules can be easily evaded, however. A clause is not a penalty if it merely accelerates an existing liability, and contracts can often be drafted in this style.[76] Leasing agreements provide a common example. Nor is the clause a penalty unless the nominated sum is payable on a *breach* of the contract rather than on its performance.[77] The employer in our earlier example could achieve his desired ends simply by providing for radically different rates of pay to apply to employees depending upon their different starting times; no question of a penalty would then arise. Nor does the doctrine of penalties provide a loophole for the recovery of deposits when a contract falls through, on the basis that these are not genuine pre-estimates of damage. If the practice is to require a deposit of a particular percentage of the contract price—and the conventional percentage varies between contract types—then the law will not override the term.[78] However, nor will the law allow real penalties to be disguised as deposits. These disguised penalties *will* be construed as such, and the injured party will be left to recover his real loss at Common Law.[79] All of these features compound the difficulty in identifying a defensible rationale for intervention. Certainly

[74] *Dunlop Pneumatic Tyre Co Ltd v New Garage and Motor Co Ltd* [1915] AC 79 (HL).
[75] *Ibid.*
[76] *O'Dea v Allstates Leasing System (WA) Pty Ltd* (1983) 152 CLR 359 (Aust HCt), although note the comments of Deane J.
[77] *Export Credits Guarantee Department v Universal Oil Products Co* [1983] 1 WLR 399 (HL).
[78] But for purchases of land, see Law of Property Act 1925, s. 49(2).
[79] *Workers Trust and Merchant Bank Ltd v Dojap Investments Ltd* [1993] AC 573 (PC) (concerning a 25 per cent 'deposit' on a transaction for the sale of land).

some of the current doctrinal dividing lines seem to separate situations that appear sufficiently analogous to warrant identical treatment.

SUBSTANTIVE OR PROCEDURAL JUSTIFICATIONS?

All of these instances of Equitable intervention on the grounds of substantive unfairness are problematic. The rationale for interference is not secure. A difficult balance must be struck between the values of security, certainty, and predictability (all promoted by enforcing the contract terms to the letter) and situational justice (promoted by making context-based decisions). Even where Equity might intervene, it might equally be persuaded not to. In the end, it may be better to return to the analysis adopted in the early Equity cases in this area. There the focus was on procedural unfairness, not substantive unfairness. Overly onerous remedies simply raised an inference that the compromised party had not properly agreed to the particular term: there was an inference of impaired consent. This approach has obvious parallels with Equity's interference in unconscionable bargains. Indeed, the same strategy is now routinely adopted by the Common Law to deal with the problem of onerous exclusion clauses. An approach that relies on procedural unfairness, rather than substantive unfairness, is both easier to implement and easier to justify.

REVIEW

This chapter is concerned with instances where Equity allows one party to escape the rigours of an apparently binding promise. The justification for contradicting apparently binding contractual agreements and perfectly properly intended gifts is simply the perception that it is sometimes unfair or unconscionable for the defendant to insist on his strict legal rights. The offending deals are then unwound; the defendant is forced to give up any enrichments that he should not have obtained. The different forms of intervention can be categorized under three heads.

The first category is confined to written contracts, where the writing does not embody the real agreement between the parties. The writing may either misrepresent or omit certain critical features of the deal. Equity may then intervene to ensure that injustice does not ensue.

The second category is devoted to procedural unfairness, and focuses on flaws in the claimant's consent to the underlying deal. The test of consent is not simply objective. Both the Common Law and Equity recognize that different informational, physical, economic, and social pressures may have an impact. Both jurisdictions will intervene if the defendant knew of or was somehow responsible for these factors impairing the claimant's true consent. The two jurisdictions developed different grounds for intervention, but the net effect is that the common law will relieve claimants if their consent is unacceptably impaired by mistake, mis-representation, physical or economic duress, undue influence, or personal disadvantage. Given this, it would require no great leap of faith to say, simply, that the modern law now recognizes certain potential flaws in contract formation and gift-giving. At this level there is no need to ascribe a Common Law or Equity tag. It adds nothing.

The third category, dealing with substantive unfairness, is more dif-ficult. It seems impossible to rationalize the various pockets of Equitable intervention, and there is invariably the possibility of defendants avoiding the operation of the rules by clever drafting. Given this, it would seem better—both more coherent and more rational—to eliminate these excep-tions and insist on the strict autonomy of private arrangements unless there is procedural unfairness in the agreement of their terms. Of course, many of these cases of substantive unfairness would be equally reviewable under this alternative head.

SELECTED BIBLIOGRAPHY

Bigwood, R., 'Undue Influence: "Impaired Consent" or "Wicked Exploitation"?' (1996) 16 OJLS 503.

Birks, P. and Chin, N.Y., 'On the Nature of Undue Influence' in J. Beatson and D. Friedmann (eds), *Good Faith and Fault in Contract Law* (Oxford: Clarendon Press, 1995), Ch. 3.

Capper, D., 'Undue Influence and Unconscionability: A Rationalization' (1998) 114 LQR 479.

Cartwright, J., 'An Unconscionable Bargain' (1993) 109 LQR 530.

Duggan, A., 'Till Debt Us Do Part: A Note on *National Australia Bank Ltd v Garcia*' (1997) 19 Sydney Law Review 220.

Lanyon, E. V., 'Equity and the Doctrine of Penalties' (1996) 9 Journal of Contract Law 234.

Smith, S. A., 'Substantive Fairness' (1996) 112 LQR 138. 56 CLJ 343.

——, 'Contracting Under Pressure: A Theory of Duress' (1997)

Youdan, T., 'Formalities for Trusts of Land, and the Doctrine in *Rochefoucauld v Boustead*' [1984] CLJ 306.

SELECTED CASES

Barclays Bank plc v O'Brien [1994] 1 AC 180 (HL)

Blomley v Ryan (1956) 99 CLR 362 (Aust HCt)

Commercial Bank of Australia Ltd v Amadio (1983) 151 CLR 447 (Aust HCt)

Dunlop Pneumatic Tyre Co Ltd v New Garage and Motor Co Ltd [1915] AC 79 (HL)

Garcia v National Australia Bank Ltd (1998) 194 CLR 395 (Aust HCt)

Great Peace Shipping Ltd v Tsavliris (International) Ltd [2003] QB 679 (CA)

Hart v O'Connor [1985] AC 1000 (PC)

Lloyds Bank v Bundy [1975] QB 326

National Westminster Bank plc v Morgan [1985] AC 686 (HL)

Rochefoucauld v Boustead [1897] 1 Ch 196 (CA)

Royal Bank of Scotland v Etridge (No 2) [2002] 2 AC 773 (HL)

Scandinavian Trading Tanker Co AB v Flota Petrolera Ecuatoriana (The Scaptrade) [1983] 2 AC 694 (HL)

Shiloh Spinners Ltd v Harding [1973] AC 691 (HL)

Tanwar Enterprises Pty Ltd v Cauchi [2003] HCA 57 (Aust HCt)

Union Eagle Ltd v Golden Achievement Ltd [1997] 2 WLR 341 (PC)

8

Enforcing Promises

The previous chapter showed Equity in negative mode, curtailing the impact of promises, reviewing them, and then allowing the unwinding of arrangements that were not deemed properly binding. This chapter shows Equity in positive mode, enhancing promises, enforcing them when the Common Law will not, and crediting them with greater effect than that acknowledged at Common Law. Because of these interventions, the landscape of contract law is broader and more varied than it might otherwise have been.

No legal system enforces all promises. A promise to go to the theatre with a friend does not create legal relations. The friend cannot sue if you change your mind or simply fail to show up. In most civil law jurisdictions this example is contrasted with the many other promises that are seriously intended to create or affect legal relations between the parties. These more serious promises are legally binding, and enforced by the national legal regime.

The Common Law rules are far more prescriptive than their civil law counterparts. The parties must of course intend to create legal relations; their arrangement must also comply with any prescribed formalities; more importantly, however, promises can only be enforced by someone who is a party to the engagement and has provided consideration (i.e. reciprocity in the form of a counter-promise). This means that promised gifts are not enforceable. No matter how seriously the promise is intended, the beneficiary will not have provided the necessary consideration. It also means that many three-party transactions were, until recently, thwarted.[1] If X provides a service to Y on the basis that Y will pay £100 to a third party, T, the Common Law (without the assistance of statute) will not allow T to enforce the deal; he is not a party to the contract and nor has he provided consideration. Indeed, the Common Law even makes it difficult for X to pursue a satisfactory remedy. The Common Law measures contract remedies according to a party's lost expectations, and here X himself

---

[1] Now see Contracts (Rights of Third Parties) Act 1999.

has lost nothing: *he* was never going to benefit in any event. Finally, even when arrangements are regarded as contracts, any intended property transfers may not take effect until long after the deal itself has been agreed. This can expose the parties to unexpected risks if the property is damaged in the interim, or if the transferor becomes insolvent and cannot complete the deal.

All of this means that parties may enter into arrangements thinking that they are acquiring rights against each other, only to find their expectations disappointed. Equity has adopted a number of strategies that modify these Common Law strictures. Indeed, there is now no aspect of contract law that is left untouched by Equitable interventions. What follows describes five quite different Equitable strategies that give the flavour of Equity's various forms of interference.

OVERRIDING THE NEED TO COMPLY WITH FORMALITIES

We saw in the previous chapter that parties can be caught out if their arrangements do not comply with the necessary formalities. The Common Law adopts a strict line: the contract is simply of no effect or is void or is unenforceable (as determined by the specific provisions in the legislation that demand the formalities). For example, contracts for the sale or other disposition of an interest in land are of no effect unless they are in writing;[2] promised gifts are enforceable only if they are contained in a deed (i.e. the document must bear the word 'deed', be signed, witnessed, and delivered); and contracts of guarantee must be evidenced in writing. Equity may sometimes take a more lenient approach, but subject to certain conditions being met. As noted in the previous chapter, however, it is easier to justify unwinding the deal (on the basis that the defendant knew or ought to have known that the claimant's consent was conditional on some critical but unwritten term) than to justify enforcing it despite its failure to comply with the statutory prescriptions.

SPECIFIC PERFORMANCE 'PROPER' AND 'RELIEF ANALOGOUS TO SPECIFIC PERFORMANCE'

One historical distinction is worth airing. Equity used to distinguish between two different forms of specific performance. The first was specific performance 'proper', where the court simply ordered the parties to

[2] Law of Property (Miscellaneous Provisions) Act 1989, s. 2.

sign an executory contract (i.e. a contract where agreement has been reached but neither party has commenced performance).[3] For example, the court might order a party to sign a transfer of land. The parties were then left to pursue whatever legal remedies their signed contract afforded them. Alternatively, the court might order 'relief analogous to specific performance', ordering the parties to specifically perform their executed contract according to its terms. In both cases the remedy was available only if Common Law damages would provide an inadequate remedy.[4]

Modern authorities rarely advert to the distinction. Indeed, the expression 'specific performance' is now invariably assumed to mean 'performance', not 'signing'. However, the distinction is enormously important when it comes to determining the property interests of the parties to a contract. Consider a contract of sale. An order to perform (by transferring specific property to another) has quite different consequences from an order to sign (even an order to sign a document promising to transfer specific property to another). Because Equity 'treats as done that which ought to be done', an order to perform is treated as if the transfer were already effective in Equity.[5] The purchaser is then considered to have Equitable ownership of the promised property. It is immaterial that she will not acquire legal ownership until much later when the transaction is completed. Moreover, her Equitable rights do not depend upon her going to court to obtain the order: she has an Equitable interest in the underlying asset simply because Equity *would* order the transfer if the parties ever went to court over the matter. The potential legal remedy defines the purchaser's legal right.[6] An order to sign does not have this proprietary effect. This means that an order to perform is a more aggressive and more valuable form of intervention.

Some of the doctrinal difficulties evident in the next few sections might be avoided if this historical distinction were revived and the less aggressive form of intervention relied upon more often.

WRITING REQUIREMENTS PRESCRIBED FOR CONTRACTS

In general, when a statute renders a contract unenforceable (or void or of no effect[7]) at Common Law for want of writing, then it is equally unenforceable (or void or of no effect) in Equity. However, there

[3] *Wolverhampton and Walsall Railway Co v London and North-Western Railway Co* (1873) LR 16 Eq 433, 439 (Lord Selbourne LC); *J C Williamson Ltd v Lukey* (1931) 45 CLR 282 (Aust HCt), 297 (Dixon J).
[4] See Chapter 2, 24–31. [5] See Chapter 3, 63–73, especially 72–3, and below, 264–6.
[6] See Chapter 2, 23–4. [7] These words do not all have the same meaning.

were, historically, two categories of case where Equity might sometimes specifically enforce the contract despite the lack of writing.

We have already seen one. Equity would not allow a statute to cloak a fraud. Where the lack of writing was due to fraud or dishonesty on the part of the defendant, and where the claimant had relied to her detriment on the defendant's representations, then Equity might specifically enforce the contract despite the absence of writing.[8] This jurisdiction depends upon more than a vague claim that it would be inequitable to disregard the claimant's expectations.[9] The defendant is usually free to insist that he is not bound by these unwritten contracts. He is only stopped (*estopped*, lawyers would say) from doing this if *he* has induced the claimant to act to her detriment in reliance on his representations that he *will* be bound.[10] Only then is his conduct regarded as unacceptable.

Equity's second mode of interference is similar. Equity would sometimes specifically enforce unwritten contracts for the sale of land if there were sufficient acts of part-performance. Payment of the purchase price was never considered sufficient. However, Equity would enforce the unwritten contract if the claimant had done other things. These acts of part-performance had to be acts that could only be explained by reference to performance of a contract of the type alleged to have been made between the parties, and, moreover, acts that would cause the claimant to suffer unfair detriment if the defendant then relied on the absence of the written contract.[11] For example, the claimant may have gone into possession, made improvements to the property, and granted leases to tenants. In these circumstances it would not be possible, or just, to undo what had been done, and the courts would order specific performance of the unwritten contract. This doctrine of part-performance has now been abolished in the UK.[12]

Both of these doctrines *can* be interpreted widely, conceding to Equity a generous jurisdiction to enforce unwritten contracts even though the Common Law will not. Much narrower interpretations are possible, however, and these seem preferable. Most of the cases concern dealings in land. In the UK, prior to 1989, contracts for the sale of interests in land were merely unenforceable unless they were in writing;[13] writing was needed simply to evidence the (otherwise valid) contract so that it could

---

[8] Also see Chapter 7, 202–4.   [9] Although see *Yaxley v Gotts* [2000] Ch 162 (CA).
[10] E.g. *Hodgson v Marks* [1971] Ch 892 (CA).
[11] *Maddison v Alderson* (1883) 8 App Cas 467 (HL), 475–6 (Lord Selbourne LC).
[12] Law of Property (Miscellaneous Provisions) Act 1989, s. 2(8).
[13] Law of Property Act 1925, s. 40(1), re-enacting part of the Statute of Frauds 1677, s. 4.

be enforced. Now these unwritten contracts are of no effect;[14] writing is necessary for the contract's very existence. This means that in these older cases Equity could enforce the genuine (but, according to the Common Law, unenforceable) contract simply by vetoing the defendant's right to raise the problem that the contract was not in writing: Equity effectively *estopped* the defendant from relying on the procedural point about contract formalities.[15] Of course this estoppel was only warranted if the defendant had somehow induced or encouraged the claimant to rely on the unwritten deal to her detriment. This is the case if the defendant dishonestly induces reliance, or if the defendant allows the claimant into possession and enables her to effect improvements and make commitments to tenants.[16]

Modern contracts dealing in land can no longer be analysed in either of these ways. The doctrine of part-performance has been explicitly abolished by statute. The jurisdiction to prevent a statute being used to cloak a fraud survives. Nevertheless, an unwritten land contract is now of *no* effect, so a mere procedural estoppel will not improve the claimant's position: there simply *is* no underlying contract for Equity to enforce. In these circumstances it seems preferable to adopt the strategy discussed in the previous chapter, and then allow for the *unwinding* of the deal.[17] Restitution, not performance, better reflects the interest that needs to be protected. The defendant has extracted an unwarranted benefit from the claimant. This gives the claimant a right to restitution; it does not automatically give her a right to insist on performance of a contract that Parliament, via statute, insists is non-existent.[18]

Some modern cases have strayed well beyond these two Equitable grounds for overlooking the parties' failure to comply with mandatory writing requirements. They suggest that Equity will order specific

[14] Law of Property (Miscellaneous Provisions) Act 1989, s. 2. Law of Property Act 1925, s. 53(1)(c) imposes a similar rule for dispositions of subsisting Equitable interests: see *Grey v IRC* [1960] AC 1 (HL); *Corin v Patton* (1990) 169 CLR 540 (Aust HCt); but contrast *Neville v Wilson* [1997] Ch 144 (CA), which is difficult to justify on the analysis advanced here.

[15] This looks very much like a form of Equitable estoppel being used as a 'sword': see below, 241–6.

[16] Indeed, the statute expressly permitted reliance on the doctrine of part-performance: Law of Property Act 1925, s. 40(2).

[17] See Chapter 7, 202–4.

[18] The third alternative is compensation for losses. However, unless the defendant has committed a civil wrong (e.g., misrepresentation—see Chapter 6, 161–2), there seems to be no reason to require him to compensate the claimant for losses caused by her reliance on the effectiveness of the unwritten deal.

performance of unwritten contracts, regardless of the defendant's conduct, simply because the underlying property is especially rare or valuable. This suggestion seems completely unsustainable. Indeed, it shows how easy it is to become confused in this area. Equity will, of course, specifically enforce binding contracts where the underlying asset is especially rare or valuable; it will not leave claimants to their remedies at Common Law.[19] Equity does this with written contracts for the transfer of interests in land, and also with contracts for the sale of rare or unique items of personal property, where writing is not required. Moreover, *if* Equity would intervene to order specific performance, then the vendor is regarded as holding the property on constructive trust for the purchaser: the purchaser becomes the Equitable owner well before the legal title is transferred.[20] Statutes that impose writing requirements make it clear that the transfer of these Equitable interests (effected by operation of law as a consequence of the potential order for specific performance) need not satisfy the writing requirements (if any) specified for the consensual and *intentional* transfer of Equitable interests or the *intentional* creation of trusts.[21] However, the first step in generating the purchaser's constructive trust is a specifically enforceable contract. These statutory exceptions offer no relief at all from the usual pre-conditions underpinning an order for specific performance. If these pre-conditions are not met, then there can be no specific performance and no transfer of Equitable interests by operation of law. Specific performance is considered in more detail later in this chapter, but one of the essential preconditions, before Equity will privilege a contract by ordering its specific enforcement, is that there *is*, in fact, a contract to enforce.[22]

Take an example. A trustee may hold a parcel of shares on trust for X. If X wishes to sell his Equitable interest in these shares, then parliament insists that his contract must be in writing.[23] Despite this, courts have, without serious discussion, held unwritten agreements for sale to be specifically enforceable. It then follows that the vendor (X) must hold his Equitable interest in the shares on constructive trust (creating a sub-trust beneath the main trust) for the purchaser.[24] Delivery of a proprietary

---

[19] See Chapter 2, 24–31, and below, 264–6.

[20] See below, 264–6, for additional pre-requisites.

[21] Law of Property (Miscellaneous Provisions) Act 1989, s. 2(5); Law of Property Act 1925, s. 53(2), creating exceptions for constructive, resulting and implied trusts.

[22] See Chapter 2, 24–31, and below, 264–6.

[23] Law of Property Act 1925, s. 53(1)(c).

[24] *Oughtred v IRC* [1960] AC 206 (HL), 227–8 (Lord Radcliffe); *Neville v Wilson* [1997] Ch 144 (CA).

interest to the purchaser via this mechanism (a trust generated by operation of law) is not subject to writing requirements.[25] The difficulty is with the first step; everything afterwards follows perfectly logically. The first step—the assertion that the unwritten contract is specifically enforceable—completely bypasses the essential requirements of specific performance.[26] It ignores altogether Parliament's directive that these contracts are of no effect. Moreover, the same result cannot be reached any more legitimately by suggesting that the vendor can simply assign his Equitable interest in the shares without complying with *any* formalities.[27] It is true that this used to be possible: an Equitable interest could be assigned without formalities so long as the transferor intended to effect an immediate transfer. That possibility cannot survive the statutory enactment, however; it would render it completely otiose.

In summary, if all this is accepted, then claimants can rarely escape the limitations imposed by statutory writing requirements. This is as it should be. Parliament has good reasons for prescribing these formalities, and they should be overridden, if at all, only in exceptional circumstances. It is true that defendants should not be able to retain enrichments unjustly, but that problem is best remedied by restitution,[28] not by specific enforcement of the unwritten contract.

WRITING REQUIREMENTS PRESCRIBED FOR GIFTS— INCOMPLETE GIFTS

If Equity is of so little assistance in overriding statutory writing requirements when the parties intend a contract, then we might predict that it will provide even less assistance where gifts are concerned. Indeed, at first sight Equity's intervention seems unnecessary. If an intended gift is ineffective on the first attempt because there is no writing, then surely the donor can simply make the gift properly a second time. This is certainly true with most gifts; the transfer and its timing are often matters that affect only the donor and the donee. However, the legal niceties become crucial if third parties have potential interests. In applying taxation, succession or insolvency rules, for example, it is crucial to know who owns a particular item of property at a particular moment in time. Is it the donor or the donee?

---

[25] Law of Property Act 1925, s. 53(2).   [26] See below, 264–6.

[27] *Oughtred v IRC* [1960] AC 206 (HL), 230 (Lord Cohen); *Chinn v Collins* [1981] AC 533 (HL), 548 (Lord Wilberforce) (both assuming that the purchaser needed to have paid the price).

[28] See Chapter 9.

The problems typically arise with intangible property. An effective legal transfer invariably demands compliance with some sort of writing requirement.[29] For example, the transfer of legal title to shares is not effective until the transfer is formally registered in the company's register of shares.[30] Imagine that a donor wishes to make a gift of shares to X. He may complete and sign the necessary share transfer form and give it, and the relevant share certificates, to X. At this stage X is not the legal owner of the shares. She cannot become the legal owner until her name is entered in the company's register of shares. Suppose the donor dies before this happens. Moreover, suppose his will indicates that his share portfolio is bequeathed to Y. Who should take the shares, X or Y? The Common Law says they should go to Y: the donor is still the legal owner at the date of his death, and his will therefore determines who should benefit. Equity takes a different view, and Equity's view prevails. According to Equity, an attempted gift will be effective in Equity, even if not at Common Law, if the donor has done all that the donor is *required* to do, notwithstanding that other requirements for an effective legal transfer remain outstanding, so long as those additional matters can be completed by the donee.[31] With this share transfer, they can. The donee has the completed transfer form and the share certificates. *She* can lodge them, and have the company register her interest. She will take the shares, not Y.

Notice what Equity is doing. It is not compelling the donor to complete an incomplete gift. Equity would never do this; it does not enforce promised gifts. It only intervenes where the donor is effectively out of the picture. Provided the donor intends to make the gift and has done all that is required of him to complete the transfer, Equity will presume that all the other necessary steps have already been completed. It treats as done that which ought to be done: it regards the parties as already in their

[29] The general rule for *legal* intangibles is embodied in the Law of Property Act 1925, s. 136: the assignment must be in writing, absolute, and notice must be given to the debtor. The judgment of Windeyer J in *Norman v Federal Commissioner of Taxation* (1963) 109 CLR 9 (Aust HCt) provides a cogent analysis of this provision. Special types of assets (such as shares) have their own special rules. The transfer of subsisting *Equitable* interests also requires writing: Law of Property Act 1925, s. 53(1)(c).

[30] This is still true with transfers of 'uncertificated' or 'dematerialized' shares in companies listed on the Stock Exchange, where settlement is effected by an electronic system known as CREST, rather than by written transfers relating to specific share certificates. In both cases, however, the final step for effective transfer of legal title to shares is registration on the company's share register.

[31] *Re Rose* [1952] Ch 499 (CA); *Corin v Patton* (1990) 169 CLR 540 (Aust HCt). Also see *Milroy v Lord* (1862) 4 De GF & J 264 (CA).

contemplated end-position. Of course, Equity cannot insist that the donee is the *legal* owner (that will have to await completion of the outstanding tasks), but it regards the donee as the owner of the gift in Equity: given the circumstances, the donor holds the asset *for the donee*, not for himself.

The logic of Equity's stance makes it plain that there will be no effective gift in Equity if the donor simply places matters (such as completed transfer forms accompanied by the relevant share certificates) in the hands of *his own* agent, rather than in the hands of the donee. In these circumstances the donor remains at liberty to recall the gift simply by revoking the instructions previously given to his agent.[32] The donor has not done all that is necessary, and the donee is not in a position to control completion of the transfer. Equity's jurisdiction does not extend to compelling donors to deliver contemplated gifts simply because they have raised the donee's expectations, or because it somehow seems unfair for the donor to withdraw.[33] If the donor in our earlier example had merely transferred the papers to his own agent, then Y, not X, would be entitled to receive the shares under the will. This same analysis will also determine whether it is X or Y who is compelled to meet any tax liability on the shares, or forced to relinquish the shares to pay demanding creditors, or entitled to receive dividends payments. The very same problems can also arise with incomplete gifts of land (where there are similar writing and registration requirements).

Notice that all these problems could be avoided if the donor were minded to create a trust rather than make an outright gift. It is true that a trust imposes onerous management obligations on the donor/trustee,[34] but unless the trust property is land the trust can be created without the need to comply with *any* formal writing requirements. Indeed, even trusts of land need only be *evidenced* in writing; they do not need to be *in* writing at the time they are created.[35] However, this radical difference in

---

[32] Of course, this freedom does not exist if the transfer is by contract or by trust rather than by gift.

[33] But contrast the judgment of Arden LJ *Pennington v Waine (No 1)* [2002] 1 WLR 2075, [2002] ECWA Civ 227 (CA). Of course, matters will be analysed quite differently if the deal is a contract rather than a gift (as, arguably, it was in this case): see above, 230–5 (formalities), and below, 241–54 (estoppel).

[34] See Chapter 5, 129–34, and Chapter 6, 161–8, 174–8.

[35] Law of Property Act 1925, s. 53(1)(b). Once the donor declares that he holds the asset on trust for the intended donee, the donor becomes bound by the trust, and the donee can sue to enforce the arrangement even though she is not a party, has not provided any consideration, and has received no documentation. See *Hunter v Moss* [1994] 1 WLR 452 (CA).

formal requirements cannot be used to save ineffective gifts. An arrangement is only construed as a trust if the donor intends to create a *trust*; a simple intention to benefit the donee in some way is not enough.[36]

None of these problems arise with gifts of goods. Goods are transferred by delivery. A gift of a book is effective when the donor delivers possession to the donee, intending to make a present. This is all it takes to transfer legal title from the donor to the donee. There is no need for writing or formal words or witnesses. Sometimes constructive (or symbolic) delivery will suffice in place of physical delivery. For example, handing over the keys to a new car, intending to make a present of it, will amount to an effective gift. Clearly Equity cannot play the same role in these situations as it does with gifts of intangibles. The only essential acts for an effective gift are acts that must be carried out by the donor himself. If the donor does not deliver, intending to make a gift, then Equity will not force him to; the donee will then receive nothing.

From all of this it is clear that Equity has an appropriately limited role in overriding the formal requirements demanded by statute. It intervenes only when it would be fraudulent or dishonest for the defendant to rely on the statute to expand his rights, or where a transaction that is incomplete at law can be properly completed by the claimant/donee without the assistance of the donor.

AVOIDING PRIVITY REQUIREMENTS

The second Common Law limitation on the enforceability of promises is the doctrine of *privity*. This doctrine has two aspects. The first is perfectly understandable. An individual who is not a party to a contract cannot have burdens (or obligations) imposed on her by a contract created by others. For example, A and B cannot agree between themselves that C will be legally obliged to pay one of them £100. This limitation is essential to protect individual autonomy, and Equity does nothing to undermine this protection.

The second aspect of privity is more difficult. It insists that a person who is not a party to a contract cannot sue on the contract, even if the contract is for her benefit. This rule can cause both injustice and inconvenience. Recall the illustration given at the start of the chapter. If X provides a service to Y on the basis that Y will pay £100 to a third party, T, the Common Law will not allow T to enforce the deal: she is not

[36] See *Paul v Constance* [1977] 1 WLR 527 (CA), and Chapter 3, 67–8.

a party to the contract (and nor has she provided consideration).[37] Indeed, as noted earlier, the Common Law even makes it difficult for X to obtain a satisfactory remedy. X has not suffered any loss as a result of the breach; he was never going to benefit in any event, so his damages are nominal.[38]

Notice that the position would be quite different if T could say that this arrangement gave her *property*, rather than some vague personal entitlement.[39] She could then enforce her rights against those holding her property; indeed, she could enforce her rights against most interfering third parties. This insight underpins the stark contrast between three-party contracts and trusts. A trust arrangement delivers a unique type of property right to trust beneficiaries.[40] If Y pays £100 to X on the basis that X will hold it on *trust* for the third party (T), then T becomes the Equitable owner of this trust property. She can sue her trustee (X) to ensure that the terms of the arrangement are enforced. It is irrelevant that she is not a party to the original deal and has provided no consideration. Of course, this insight only further highlights the extraordinary nature of the trust.

Equity has sometimes forced three-party contractual examples into the trust model in order to sidestep the Common Law's privity restrictions. Contracting parties could, of course, explicitly create a trust: X could agree to provide a service to Y on the basis that Y will pay £100 to X to be held by X on trust for T. The trust property is then the £100 when it is received, but in the meantime it is X's contractual right to recover £100 from Y. The parties have created a 'trust of a promise'. T is the beneficiary of this trust, so she has an Equitable interest in the trust property and is allowed to enforce the trust in her own name even though she is not a party to the original agreement. Clearly this is a highly artificial arrangement. Nevertheless, this analysis was sometimes adopted even when the parties had not explicitly structured their arrangements to

---

[37] *Dunlop Pneumatic Tyre Company Ltd v Selfridge* [1915] AC 847 (HL) (Viscount Haldane).

[38] Although recent Common Law cases suggest a growing inclination to allow X to recover for the losses suffered by T: *Linden Gardens Trust Ltd v Lenesta Sludge Disposals Ltd* [1994] 1 AC 85 (CA); *Darlington Borough Council v Wiltshier Northern Ltd* [1995] 1 WLR 68 (CA) (where the contracting party was even deemed to hold the damages on trust for the third party). But contrast *Woodar Investment Development Ltd v Wimpey Construction UK Ltd* [1980] 1 WLR 227 (HL).

[39] An entitlement in *tort*, if it allowed T to sue Y, would also be valuable: *White v Jones* [1995] 2 AC 207 (HL).

[40] See above, 237–8, and Chapter 3, 63–7.

create a trust. The parties' contractual arrangement was simply interpreted as one that *impliedly* required X to hold the benefit of his right to
sue Y on trust for T. T could then sue in her own name.[41] This interpretation invariably fudged the issue of whether the parties had genuinely
intended *to create a trust*. A simple desire to benefit T in some way is not
sufficient for the creation of a valid trust.[42] Arguably the device was
simply a fiction to enable the courts to avoid some of the worst injustices
that arose with contracts for the benefit of third parties. Now, however,
the courts have retreated to orthodoxy, and the trust of a promise device
is practically unheard of.[43] Even so, its brief exposure only serves to reinforce the divide between trust and contract: a trust can achieve what the
doctrines of privity and consideration prevent contract from achieving.

Equity has occasionally made other rather ineffectual incursions into
this area. First, Equity will sometimes order specific performance of the
agreement between X and Y.[44] This delivers the intended benefit to T, but
the pre-requisite for an order for specific performance is that X's contractual damages are inadequate. This suggestion is difficult to justify on
orthodox doctrinal grounds. An orthodox analysis would suggest that X's
damages are not inadequate; they *do* reflect *his* loss from Y's breach. Were
Equity simply to concede that X's remedy is inadequate because it does
not deliver the intended benefits to T, then *all* three-party deals would
become specifically enforceable, while very few two-party deals would be.
Contracts might then deal with similar subject matter, but one class of
claimants could insist on performance, the other on money damages.
This seems unacceptable.

Secondly, Equity makes it possible for the parties to structure their
dealings differently to achieve the same ends. The parties can replace the
one-step agreement with a two-step arrangement. First, X agrees to provide a service to Y on the basis that Y will pay £100 to X. X then assigns
his contractual rights against Y to T. This assignment is effective to
transfer X's intangible contract rights to T (provided this is not prohibited by the agreement between X and Y).[45] T can then sue Y to

---

[41] *Fletcher v Fletcher* (1844) 4 Hare 67; *Les Affréteurs Réunis v Walford* [1919] AC 801
(HL); *Trident General Insurance Co Ltd v McNeice Bros Pty Ltd* (1988) 165 CLR 107
(Aust HCt).

[42] Chapter 3, 67–8.

[43] *Vandepitte v Preferred Accident Corp of New York* [1933] AC 70.

[44] *Beswick v Beswick* [1968] AC 58.

[45] The assignment can be implemented at law according to the rules in the Law of
Property Act 1925, s. 136 (an absolute assignment, in writing, with notice to the obligor, Y),
or in Equity in advance of complying with all these formalities.

enforce payment of the £100. It seems anomalous that the law permits these ends to be achieved by a two-step mechanism, but not by a one-step one: it allows existing rights to be assigned, but it prevents the creation of enforceable rights in T at the outset. What the two-step process does, however, which may be thought to be a valuable protection for Y, is that T takes 'subject to the equities', so any defence that Y could have raised against X will also be available against T.

These Equitable modifications fall well short of meeting the reasonable demands of contracting parties. The overwhelming sentiment is that the law should support three-party agreements according to their intended terms. X and T should not be left without adequate remedies if Y refuses to perform his side of the bargain. In England, the problem has been partly resolved by statute.[46] Subject to certain important conditions, T has a statutory right to sue Y directly to enforce the promised benefit. The Common Law has also made its own moves. Modifications to the rules on damages are slowly expanding the circumstances in which X (not T) can recover substantial damages for Y's failure to provide a benefit to T; T's problem is then to ensure that these damages somehow find their way into her hands.

RE-EXAMINING CONSIDERATION

The third Common Law limitation on the enforceability of promises is the doctrine of consideration. This is commonly regarded as the most significant mechanism employed by English law to identify enforceable agreements. An agreement is not enforceable—it is not a contract—unless it is supported by consideration. This means that both parties must give something of value to create a bargain. The simplest illustration is a contract between vendor and purchaser: the vendor supplies goods; the purchaser supplies counter-performance by paying the price. Although this simple rule provides a ready badge of enforceability, many seriously intended promises are then deemed unenforceable. As already noted, this need for consideration distinguishes the Common Law from many of its civil law counterparts.

Recall that at Common Law promised gifts are unenforceable: the donee has not provided consideration. Equally, contracts for the benefit of third parties are unenforceable by the third party: she has not provided

---

[46] Contracts (Rights of Third Parties) Act 1999.

consideration.[47] In practice, other examples are even more significant. Many negotiations do not generate enforceable contracts because there is no final resolution of promised performance and counter-performance. Nevertheless, the parties often carry out parts of the contemplated agreement. The eldest son may assist with the family business on the understanding that he will inherit the property; a landowner may demolish a building on the understanding that he will be engaged to build a replacement. If these understandings are dashed, what should happen? Equally seriously, many routine variations to the terms of established contracts are unenforceable according to orthodox contract law. Builders may renegotiate agreed schedules or revise materials specifications without any associated price change. Orthodox contract law suggests that the contractor has not paid for these variations—he has not provided consideration—so neither party can enforce their terms.[48]

These examples illustrate why the doctrine of consideration has come under sustained attack. The courts, for their part, have refused to override the need for consideration in enforceable contracts, yet they have sometimes used the rather opaque ground of *estoppel* to enforce deals (or perhaps provide some more limited remedy) where the agreement lacks formal consideration. The relationship between estoppel and consideration is distinctly troublesome. One analysis is advanced here, but first it is necessary to appreciate the key features of the most popular forms of estoppel.[49]

ESTOPPEL BY REPRESENTATION

Most estoppels are best appreciated through examples. Suppose your employer overpays you by £500. He then insists, when you query it, that the sum is rightfully yours. You spend the money. Two months later your employer discovers his mistake and attempts to recover the amount as money paid under a mistake of fact. Both Common Law and Equity will allow you to resist the claim on the narrow ground that your employer is *estopped* by his earlier representation.[50] The basic principle is that people

---

[47] Although now see the Contracts (Rights of Third Parties) Act 1999.

[48] Although see *Williams v Roffey Bros & Nicholls (Contactors) Ltd* [1991] 1 QB 1 (CA), where the builder negotiated a price rise for substantially the same work, and the court accepted that the builder had provided a 'commercial advantage' or 'practical benefit', not measured in money, as adequate consideration to support the variation of contract, which would otherwise have been gratuitous and therefore unenforceable.

[49] And both Common Law and Equitable versions have the same attributes: *West v Jones* (1851) 1 Sim (NS) 205, 207–8, 61 ER 79, 81. For procedural estoppel, see above, 231.

[50] *Avon CC v Howlett* [1983] 1 WLR 603 (CA).

cannot go back on their representations of existing fact if others have been induced to act to their detriment in reliance on the representation.

Notice the limitations. The representation must be one of fact;[51] it cannot be a representation of intention or law. More importantly, the estoppel only acts as a defence (here, to an obligation to repay); it cannot be used to assert a new right (to a higher salary). This procedural limitation allows the court to deny that it is creating a second class of contracts based on *reliance* rather than consideration. Put another way, the estoppel can only be used as a 'shield'; it cannot be used as a 'sword'. Finally, this form of estoppel operates as a complete bar to the defendant's insistence on his legal rights (here, his right to restitution of the mistaken overpayment).[52]

To see the impact of these various limitations, imagine a change to the facts in our example. Suppose your employer mistakenly notifies you that you will shortly receive a performance bonus of £500. You then go on a spending spree in anticipation of your newfound wealth. When your employer discovers his mistake, he informs you that you will not be receiving the bonus. In these circumstances you cannot insist on being paid the additional £500 as bonus. The employer's representation is one of intention, not fact (although the courts have been known to stretch this boundary); more importantly, this estoppel cannot be used as a sword to create a new right.

This very narrow version of estoppel is largely where Common Law development of the doctrine stopped. Indeed, the Common Law's modern practices suggest that even this may be pared back. Take the earlier example of our mistaken employer. He has a legal right to obtain restitution of the overpaid wages. The remedy is not novel, although the distinctive head of liability—unjust enrichment—was formally recognized by the English courts just fifteen years ago.[53] Formal recognition brought with it a new defence of change of position. The employee is allowed to show that she has changed her position in good faith in reliance on the receipt so that it would now be inequitable to insist that she repays the

[51] *Jorden v Money* (1854) 5 HL Cas 185 (HL), for the rule in Equity, but see *Foran v Wright* (1989) 168 CLR 385 (Aust HCt), 435 (Deane J). By contrast, estoppel by convention (which operates where the parties have made *common* assumptions about the basis of their engagement) applies to assumptions of law as well as fact: *Republic of India v India Steamship Co Ltd (The Indian Endurance) (No 2)* [1998] AC 878, 913.

[52] Although see *Scottish Equitable plc v Derby* [2001] EWCA Civ 369, [2001] 3 All ER 818 (CA); *National Westminster Bank plc v Somer International (UK) Ltd* [2001] EWCA Civ 970, [2002] 3 WLR 64 (CA).

[53] *Lipkin Gorman (a firm) v Karpnale Ltd* [1991] 2 AC 548 (HL).

amount in full. This defence is far more discriminating than estoppel. It applies only if the employee acts in good faith, so the employer's insistence that the sum is rightfully hers may be relevant. It only recognizes exceptional reliance expenditure, being expenditure that she would not have incurred but for a belief that the newfound wealth was hers to keep. This means that the employee has changed her position if she spends the funds on a previously unplanned holiday to Australia, but not if she spends them on rent and groceries. It would be unfair to demand full repayment in the first case, but not in the second. Finally, the defence need not operate as a complete bar on the employer's rights: if the employee has a change of position defence for £200 of expenditure, then the employer can still recover the other £300. Contrast this with estoppel, which requires a representation but then only concedes the good faith limitation. The modern dilemma is clear. Is change of position, which emerged so recently, a more highly evolved defence that has superseded its earlier estoppel counterpart, or are the two analyses distinct and distinctive? The issue remains uncertain. Both techniques are directed at the same ends, and arguably change of position should swallow this form of estoppel:[54] the more highly evolved legal form should replace its factual ancestor; it would be counter-productive for the legal system to continue to support the differential evolution of both.

PROMISSORY ESTOPPEL

Although the Common Law did not pursue estoppel doctrines beyond the primitive versions just considered, Equity did. Significantly, it extended estoppel beyond representations of fact to accommodate promises of future intention. This is 'promissory' (or Equitable) estoppel. If the promisor makes a representation of intention, intending it to be relied upon, then he will be prevented from acting inconsistently later on if this would adversely affect the promisee.

The case that generated this modern doctrine of promissory estoppel was a twentieth-century contract re-negotiation case.[55] Lessees entered

---

[54] The point becomes even clearer if the reclassification of unjust enrichment claims proposed in Chapter 9, 281–3, is adopted. This would treat mistaken payments as 'unintended gifts', not 'vitiated intention' payments. Some representations would then stand as objective proof that a gift was intended, and in those circumstances the defendant could keep the entire overpayment. Otherwise, the overpayment would be recoverable subject to change of position defences.

[55] *Central London Property Ltd v High Trees House Ltd* [1947] KB 130. Also see *Ajayi v R T Briscoe (Nigeria) Ltd* [1964] 1 WLR 1326 (PC). These cases make it difficult to continue to justify the older case of *Jorden v Money* (1854) 5 HL Cas 185 (HL), although not impossible.

into a long-term lease of a large block of London flats. War broke out, and much of London was evacuated. The lessees could not sub-let all the flats and they negotiated with the lessor for a substantial reduction in their agreed rent. When the war ended and the flats were fully let again, the lessor sued for back rent, insisting that the variation was unenforceable as it was not supported by consideration: the lessees had given nothing for the lessor's new promise. The court took the bold step of insisting that in these circumstances it would be inequitable for the lessor to go back on such an unequivocal promise, especially one so clearly made with the intention that the lessee would act upon it. The lessor was *estopped* from relying on its strict contractual rights where this would adversely affect the promisee.[56]

Explained this way, promissory estoppel still only operates as a shield.[57] Moreover, the estoppel only suspends the promisor's rights. The lessees could resist the claim for unpaid rent, but they could not insist that they had a binding low-rent agreement for the future. They would suffer detriment if the lessor went back on the past arrangement, but the lessor was entitled to revert to its original rental agreement once it had given reasonable notice to the lessee.

These limitations still hamper promissory estoppel in England. In Australia, by contrast, the High Court has dramatically extended the doctrine by holding that it can operate as a sword, creating new legal rights.[58] The facts that motivated this advance provide a forceful illustration of its ramifications. The parties were negotiating for a major leasing and construction project. The plan was that the landowner would demolish an existing building and construct a new one to the defendant lessee's specifications. The project was extremely urgent and negotiations had reached an advanced stage. The lessees suggested they were about to sign, and the landowner began to demolish the building. Shortly afterwards the lessees began to have second thoughts. They instructed their solicitors to 'go slow' in finalizing the exchange of contracts, even though they knew the landowner was already engaged on the project. More than a month later, after the landowner had completed over 40 per cent of the new building, they informed him that they were withdrawing from the project. The court allowed the landowner to use promissory estoppel as a

---

[56] This form of promissory estoppel appears indistinguishable from *waiver*, a term used to describe a claimant's renouncing of his contractual rights in a manner considered sufficient to allow the defendant to resist an otherwise enforceable contractual claim.

[57] *Combe v Combe* [1951] 2 KB 215 (CA), 224 (Birkett LJ).

[58] *Waltons Stores (Interstate) Ltd v Maher* (1988) 164 CLR 387 (Aust HCt).

cause of action. Moreover, it insisted that the appropriate remedy was to hold the lessees to their implied promise to conclude the contract.

Notwithstanding this aggressive approach, the Australian High Court insisted that this expanded model of estoppel did not create a new class of 'reliance contracts' in defiance of the Common Law doctrine of consideration. Their rationale was that the estoppel remedy did not entitle the promisee to expectation (contractual) damages, but only to the minimum Equity necessary to avoid the detriment that the promisee would otherwise suffer. Although this minimum Equity *may* indeed be performance of the promise (as it was in the case before the Australian High Court), the theoretical difference meant that estoppel cases constituted a completely separate category from contract cases. Usually estoppel and contract remedies would be quite different. A simple example illustrates the difference. Suppose A offers to pay B £1,000, and B acts on that promise to his detriment by spending £200 that he would not otherwise have spent. Enforcing the arrangement as a contract would give B £1,000 in expectation damages. Allowing B to use promissory estoppel to protect his reliance interest will only give him £200.

This expanded Australian doctrine of promissory estoppel leaves one difficult question: if there is no pre-existing legal relationship, *when* will it be unconscionable for a promisor to go back on a promise? Mere failure to perform a non-contractual promise is not unconscionable. When will the promisee's detrimental reliance make it so? The Australian High Court thought it sufficient that the promisor had induced or encouraged the other party to rely on the assumption that the promise would be performed.[59] The estoppel remedy then protects the resulting reliance loss. Despite the court's protestations, this *could* easily be read as acceptance of a 'reliance' (rather than the existing 'consideration') model of contracts. This debate centres on whether estoppel is unique or is part of contract law, and what forms of 'reliance' effectively define the legal category. As explained later, however, neither conclusion satisfactorily addresses the discriminating subtleties in the various remedies awarded. A better analysis needs to accommodate these too.

PROPRIETARY ESTOPPEL

Proprietary estoppel, the final model of estoppel to be considered here, operates when property owners encourage others to act to their detriment

---

[59] *Waltons Stores (Interstate) Ltd v Maher* (1988) 164 CLR 387 (Aust HCt) (see especially the judgments of Mason and Wilson JJ).

in the belief that they will be granted an interest in the owner's property. The owner of a family farm may encourage his eldest son to work on the farm on the understanding that the business will be left to him.[60] If there is a falling out later on and the arrangement does not amount to an enforceable contract, then the son's remedy will depend upon estoppel. He is fortunate that, even in England, proprietary estoppel is routinely used as a cause of action. This is the surprising divide between proprietary and promissory estoppel. For reasons that seem difficult to justify, detrimental reliance on a promise to deliver a property interest is far better protected than detrimental reliance on other types of promises. Perhaps this is yet another example of the privileged enforcement of differently ranking rights, although this is not the rationale explicitly advanced by the courts.

As with other estoppels, the remedy depends on the circumstances. Sometimes the promise is enforced; sometimes the promisee's detrimental reliance is remedied.[61] Notice that if the court enforces the promise, then the son will acquire the land even though his agreement was not in writing, nor supported by consideration, nor sufficient to meet the conditions for an effective gift (whether at Common Law or in Equity). Equity's intervention ensures that the father holds the property on constructive trust for the son. The justification for all of this needs some unravelling.

Not all proprietary estoppel cases concern land transfers. Lesser interests in property can also be promised. A landowner may negotiate with the council for access points from the landowner's property to the council's road. If the owner establishes from the council that he is likely to be granted these rights, then subdivides his property and sells part of it, he may find his position seriously compromised if the council later declines to grant the access point. The landowner's property may be inaccessible and therefore worthless. The landowner has not contracted with the council for a grant of access, but proprietary estoppel may deliver the functional equivalent.[62]

It is still not clear whether the doctrine of proprietary estoppel applies to personal property. Both principle and authority[63] support a wider

---

[60] *Dillwyn v Llewelyn* (1862) 4 De GF & J 517, [1861–73] All ER Rep 384.

[61] Contrast *Pascoe v Turner* [1979] 1 WLR 431 (CA) and *Gillett v Holt* [2001] 1 Ch 210 (CA).

[62] *Crabb v Arun District Council* [1976] Ch 179 (CA); *Plimmer v Mayor of Wellington* (1884) 9 App Cas 699 (PC).

[63] *Crabb v Arun District Council* [1976] Ch 179 (CA), 187; *Olsson v Dyson* (1969) 120 CLR 365 (Aust HCt); but contrast *Western Fish Products v Penwith District Council* [1981] 2 All ER 204, 218.

application, even though the facts may be less likely to arise in practice. However, then the sword–shield disjunction between proprietary and promissory estoppel becomes even less defensible. The Australian model of estoppel eliminates this problem by allowing both forms to be used as a sword to found a cause of action.

RECLASSIFYING ESTOPPEL CASES

This picture of estoppel is complicated, and there are still further forms of estoppel not considered here. The analysis advanced by the Australian High Court is that all these different estoppel doctrines are simply manifestations of the same broader principle.[64] The common element in every case is induced or encouraged detrimental reliance. If this is present, then estoppel will preclude the strict enforcement of the promisor's legal rights. The induced assumptions can be of fact or intention, and estoppel can be used as a sword as well as a shield. The English courts have not yet reached this integrated position, but the advance seems almost inevitable.[65] The difficulty is the remedy. This is seen as 'the minimum Equity to do justice'. It is conceded that this can mean enforcement of the assumed promise or, alternatively, recovery for detrimental reliance. Nevertheless, 'estoppel' and 'contract' are said to be distinguishable because the two have quite different remedial goals. The goal of estoppel is to repair the harm caused by the induced reliance; the goal of contract is to deliver the promised benefit. This approach sees 'estoppel' as a distinctive category of legal intervention, one that can be contrasted with 'contract'. The advantage of the approach is that it groups together different sub-categories of legal intervention that share a common ground for interference (induced detrimental reliance) and a common range of remedial responses (all directed at repairing detrimental reliance).

The disadvantage, however, is that this grouping still fails to provide a mechanism for rational discrimination. A single ground for intervention (induced detrimental reliance) can lead to any one of two, three, or even four, remedies (adding restitution of unwarranted benefits[66] and procedural estoppel[67] to the current list). How is the appropriate remedy to be determined? 'Repairing the harm' clearly means different things in different circumstances. This suggests that 'estoppel' does not define a

---

[64] See *Waltons Stores (Interstate) Ltd v Maher* (1988) 164 CLR 387 (Aust HCt), especially the judgment of Deane J considering the fusion of Common Law and Equitable estoppel.
[65] Although see *Baird Textile Holdings Ltd v Marks and Spencer plc* [2001] EWCA Civ 274, [2002] 1 All ER Comm 737 (CA).
[66] See Chapter 9.　　[67] See above, 231.

distinctive sub-category of obligations; it cannot be contrasted with 'contract', 'tort' and 'unjust enrichment', each having its own distinctive remedial strategy. Instead, it seems to be a horizontal grouping, gathering together particular elements of contract, tort, and unjust enrichment. This is perhaps obvious from the remedies: recall that rights and remedies are intimately linked; rights are classified because of the protections they attract.[68] If estoppel works as a 'horizontal' category, spanning contract, tort, and unjust enrichment, then it is unlikely to provide a useful analytical tool. Instead, its various manifestations need to be properly, and explicitly, re-assigned to their appropriate locations in contract, tort, and unjust enrichment.

Estoppel and contract

Consider first the suggestion that some estoppel cases can (and should) be re-categorized as contract cases. This is controversial. Nevertheless, the parallels between certain estoppel cases and contracts, especially unilateral contracts, are overwhelming. A unilateral contract, or an 'if' contract, is a contract where A promises to perform *if* B first performs some requested act. For example, A may offer a reward *if* B provides certain information, or performs certain feats.[69] The analogous estoppel scenario is plain: A represents that a benefit will be forthcoming; B then acts to his detriment in reliance on the representation. This is not quite enough to make the estoppel case a unilateral contract, however. The difficulty is to distinguish between enforceable unilateral contracts and unenforceable promised (but conditional) gifts. If A promises to pay £1,000 to B when B gets married, this is likely to be construed as an unenforceable conditional gift.

The conceptual distinction between the two is simple but critical. In the contract cases, the 'condition' is construed as a *request* to B to perform the action in return for the promise. B's performance is then regarded both as B's acceptance of A's offer to contract *and* as B's consideration for the binding deal. In the gift cases, by contrast, B provides no consideration because there is no agreed exchange of acceptable performance and counter-performance. The deal is therefore unenforceable. Although the conceptual difference is clear, its practical application is not. This is especially so when the circumstances are domestic rather than commercial: when parents promise benefits to their children, which analysis

---

[68] See Chapter 2, 22–4.
[69] *Carlill v Carbolic Smoke Ball Co* [1893] 1 QB 256 (CA).

better reflects the arrangement? These difficult cases are almost invariably allocated to the estoppel box, yet this simply disguises the real issues underlying them.

This criticism of the estoppel fudge should not be taken too harshly. Modern analysis of unilateral contracts now seems straightforward, but its explicit acceptance marked a late development from the direct exchange model of contracts, where both parties are bound to the deal at the outset. Unilateral contracts are quite different. Only one party makes a promise, which does not become legally binding until the other party performs. More importantly, the other party is under no obligation to perform, although if he chooses to he can then insist on the promised 'reward'. Equitable estoppel cases perhaps recognized this different (unilateral) form of exchange contracts long before they were recognized by the Common Law, although of course the estoppel cases did not label them so informatively.[70]

This early recognition is best seen in the traditional approach to *proprietary* estoppel cases. These cases are all premised on one party expending money or labour in the expectation of receiving some reciprocal benefit by way of an interest in property. If (and only if) it would be unconscionable for the owner to deny the expected benefit to the improver, then proprietary estoppel will give the improver a remedy. However, the remedy depends upon the circumstances. In one class of cases, the expectation of benefit is encouraged by express representations made by the owner; in another class, the owner simply stands by in the knowledge that the improver is mistaken about her legal rights in the property. Earlier authorities suggested that the claimant's Equity in the first class of case was to have the representation made good, much like specific enforcement of a contract; in the second it was to strip the owner of any unjust enrichment (although this terminology was not used).[71] The first class of case is often indistinguishable from the modern unilateral

---

[70] And note that orthodox contract scholarship would then support specific performance of the contract (in limited circumstances), expectation damages (as the norm), and reliance damages (where these amount to less than the expectation damages, but for some reason proof of the latter is either impossible or unwarranted). *Giumelli v Giumelli* (1999) 196 CLR 101, [1999] HCA 10 (Aust HCt), where the farmer's son received the *value* of the promised property, secured by a lien on the property, can be seen as an illustration of the second option where specific performance was denied because of intervening third-party interests.
[71] So much were the two classes considered separate, that *Dillwyn v Llewelyn* (1862) 4 De GF & J 517, [1861–73] All ER Rep 384 (in the first class) was not cited in *Ramsden v Dyson* (1865) LR 1 HL 129 (in the second class), even though Lord Westbury was involved in both cases.

contract or 'reward' cases. Indeed, modern estoppel cases now mirror modern contract cases even better than they used to. They too now recognize that even the most explicit of representations cannot always be read as a 'reward' case; sometimes it is merely a 'conditional gift' case.[72] The difficulty in Equity, as at Common Law, is to distinguish between the two. Re-posting these Equity cases to a 'contract' classification box would unambiguously recognize that precisely the same task is being undertaken in Equity and at Common Law, and that the learning from both can be integrated.

The re-posting matters. Take land contracts. An estoppel classification suggests that specific enforcement of unwritten land contracts is possible if the right estoppel conditions are met. A contract analysis, on the other hand, indicates that this conclusion is no longer apt. A land contract, including an '*if*' land contract, is now of no effect unless it is in writing.[73] Re-posting would make it clear that estoppel cases are not some exceptional category that can be permitted to stand outside these new statutory rules.[74] The promisees would not be left without *any* remedy, as we shall see, but they would not be entitled to a *contract remedy*.

Estoppel and unjust enrichment

The other options for re-posting estoppel cases can be dealt with more briefly. Consider the unjust enrichment category. Although an arrangement between the parties may not amount to a binding contract, the facts may indicate that the promisee did not intend to make a *gift* of his property or services to the promisor. The farmer's son may not be able to demand that the farm be given to him, but equally it may be clear that he did not intend his services to be gratuitous.[75] In these circumstances it is considered unjust for the promisor to retain the benefit; he will be obliged to make restitution of the unjust enrichment. The justice of this

---

[72] See *Combe v Combe* [1951] 2 KB 215 (CA), which simply held that the husband had not issued an express or implied request to his wife not to apply to the court for a maintenance order, so there was no consideration for his promise to pay an annual allowance, so the purported agreement was not enforceable. This illustrates how fine the dividing line can be. Reclassification of the estoppel cases will not change this; it will merely make the decision more transparent.

[73] See above, 232–3.

[74] The earlier statutory rules were different, and many old estoppel cases explicitly adverted to this: they saw specific enforcement of the unwritten land contract as justified because the absence of writing could be overcome because the deal had been part-performed; see above, 231–2.

[75] *Ramsden v Dyson* (1865) LR 1 HL 129 (although the claim was unsuccessful on the facts).

is apparent, yet this head of obligations was not formally recognized by English courts until the 1990s.[76] Little wonder, then, that other vehicles— including estoppel—were found to deliver the appropriate response. The difficulty is to distinguish *unjust* enrichments from other transferred benefits.[77] The farmer's son, the faithful housekeeper, or the diligent gardener cannot demand a remedy merely because they performed their services *expecting* to be rewarded. In developing appropriate dividing lines, the estoppel cases mirror modern unjust enrichment scholarship. They suggest that it is only unjust for the recipient to keep the benefit if he was somehow responsible for the claimant's misconception (because he had misrepresented the position) or if the circumstances make it plain that a gift was not intended.[78] The estoppel cases that impliedly adopt this analysis, by granting a restitutionary remedy, could usefully be posted to the unjust enrichment category so that the analysis could be made explicit. This would immediately clarify the assessment of the remedy in these cases: it would make it clear that the aim is to reverse the promisor's enrichment, not to repair the promisee's detriment or protect her reliance interest.

Estoppel and tort

The final category to which estoppel cases might be re-posted is tort. Intuitively this is the right category for some of these cases. When a government body or a local authority or even a contract negotiator makes erroneous statements or representations that induce reasonable but detrimental reliance by the counter-party, then the law ought to provide a remedy. Contract and unjust enrichment law are clearly not appropriate for the task. The clearest parallels are with the law of negligent misstatement. Once again, the estoppel cases may have been an early acknowledgement of this head of liability. The Common Law of negligence, and especially the law of negligent misstatement, was formally recognized in England less than fifty years ago.[79] Notwithstanding this, some of the old estoppel precedents mirror modern tort law's imposition of liability and its remedial strategies. The remedy in these cases is usually

---

[76] *Lipkin Gorman (a firm) v Karpnale Ltd* [1991] 2 AC 548 (HL).

[77] See *Falcke v Scottish Imperial Insurance Co Ltd* (1886) 34 Ch D 234 (CA), 248 (Bowen LJ).

[78] See Chapter 9, 281–3, classifying these alternatives as 'unintended transfers' and 'unintended gifts'.

[79] *Hedley Byrne & Co Ltd v Heller & Partners Ltd* [1964] AC 465 (HL). Also see Chapter 6, 161–2.

monetary compensation for detrimental reliance, but occasionally a mandatory injunction might require the promisor to do something (perhaps
comply with the representation, perhaps something less) so as to preserve
the promisee from harm.[80] If these estoppel cases are really tort cases,
then there is no advantage in having parallel development of two strands
of negligence liability. The two bodies of law should be integrated so as to
ensure rational and coherent development of this head of liability.[81]

Several of the examples considered earlier might be best placed under
this head of negligence liability. The case of the landowner unsuccessfully
negotiating with his local authority for an access point to his land cannot
be classified as a classical contract case (the landowner has not provided
any consideration) or as an unjust enrichment case (the local authority
has not received any benefit). Rather, it seems to be a case where the
promisee has reasonably relied on the representations made by the promisor in circumstances where, without doing violence to the law, the promisor can be seen as owing a duty to ensure the reliability or accuracy of the
representations made. Moreover, in these particular circumstances, a
mandatory injunction, not monetary compensation, is really the only
adequate remedy.[82] Similarly, the decision of the Australian High Court
in the dispute between the developer and the lessee might also best be
categorized as a case of negligence (if not worse), again necessarily remedied by a mandatory injunction to make good the harm by proceeding
with the represented contract.[83]

These cases may take the law of negligence beyond its current boundaries, both in ascribing responsibility for negligent representations and in
remedying breaches by injunction rather than money damages. If this is
true, then it is crucial that this is recognized for what it is and the head of
liability reformulated accordingly. The reformulation may go as far as
recognizing that liability for negligent misstatement has developed to
encompass a duty to ensure the reliability of induced expectations.

[80] An injunction in these cases may well extend the law, but not in an unprincipled way.
See Chapter 2, 31–4.
[81] See Chapter 6, 161–8.
[82] See *Crabb v Arun District Council* [1976] Ch 179 (CA), and also Chapter 2, 31. The
decision on appropriate remedies is not easy. In *Commonwealth v Verwayen* (1990) 170 CLR
394 (Aust HCt), the majority favoured a mandatory injunction requiring the government to
adhere to its original representation that it would not take the procedural point that the
limitation period for tort claims had expired; the minority (Mason J) favoured monetary
compensation for the wasted legal expenses incurred by the promisee as a result of his
reliance on the representation.
[83] *Waltons Stores (Interstate) Ltd v Maher* (1988) 164 CLR 387 (Aust HCt).

In short, the best strategic approach to these estoppel cases may be to recognize that they often predate the explicit Common Law recognition of more discriminating heads of liability. Unilateral contracts, unjust enrichment, and tort liability for negligence are the obvious candidates. Logically, therefore, these estoppel cases should now be reallocated to their more appropriate homes. This is the only way to ensure coherent development of the legal system.

IMPLYING TERMS

The fourth area to be considered in this chapter involves a change of focus. Here the concern is not with pre-conditions that determine whether promises are enforceable. It is with the precise terms that will be enforced. The Common Law generally leaves these terms to be defined by the parties themselves. Of course, certain terms are necessarily incorporated because a statute makes them mandatory, or because the general law compels their observance within defined relationships (such as employer and employee), or because the parties are presumed to be contracting in accordance with accepted trade or custom. Other than this, however, the Common Law rarely implies additional terms into the parties' private agreement. It does so only where this is absolutely essential in order to give the arrangement the business efficacy the parties must have intended, and this is the case only when a reasonable bystander would have thought the term so obvious that it went without saying.[84]

Equity's approach appears to be analogous, although its strategies are not usually described in quite the same way. We have already seen that terms may be implied because the parties are in a defined relationship, such as a trust or a fiduciary relationship.[85] Terms may also be implied to give the arrangement or transaction the particular content and characteristics that the parties must obviously have intended. This second mode of intervention is the focus here. Its particular significance is that it permits Equity to read proprietary consequences into engagements even though the parties themselves have not explicitly negotiated for these consequences. Recall that this is exactly how the express trust was originally developed: particular (rather onerous) personal obligations were read into

---

[84] *The Moorcock* (1889) LR 14 PD 64, 68; [1886–90] All ER Rep 530 (CA) (Bowen LJ) and *Shirlaw v Southern Foundries (1926) Ltd* [1939] 2 KB 206 (CA), 227 (MacKinnon LJ), respectively. Also see *BP Refinery (Westernport) Pty Ltd v Shire of Hastings* [1977] HCA 40, (1994) 180 CLR 266, (1978) ALJR 20 (PC).

[85] See Chapter 5, 134.

an arrangement; these obligations were protected or enforced in a particular manner; the resulting protection was so extensive and applied so consistently that the right came to be classified as proprietary.[86] Several further examples illustrate the potential impact of this form of 'implied term' intervention.

QUISTCLOSE TRUSTS

The first illustration centres on commercial loan agreements. The usual assumption is that loan funds become part of the borrower's assets; the borrower's obligation to repay is purely personal. This exposes lenders to the risk of the borrower's insolvency and explains why lenders often take security. If borrowers have no unencumbered assets they can offer as security, however, then the *Quistclose* trust (named after one of the earliest cases to recognize the arrangement) affords a limited alternative.[87]

The idea is simple. If money is lent on the mutual understanding that it should *not* be at the free disposal of the borrower, but should be used exclusively for a specific purpose, then a stipulation will be implied that if the purpose fails then the money must be repaid; the borrower cannot simply use the funds for other purposes. Crucially, these obligations will be specifically enforced; they will therefore give rise to a trust of the loan funds in favour of the lender until the funds are used for the specified purpose.[88] This trust recognizes that the loan funds never form part of the borrower's assets, able to be disposed of as he wishes. The borrower obtains legal title to the funds, it is true, but the lender retains the beneficial interest until the funds are used for the nominated purpose.

These arrangements are often used in corporate rescue operations. Loans are made to enable the debtor to repay specific creditors,[89] or to purchase necessary equipment.[90] The lender's position is secured by the trust, although only for the short time between the borrower's receipt of the funds and his use of them for the nominated purpose. If the debtor collapses before the funds have been spent, then the lender can recover

---

[86] See Chapter 3, 63–7.

[87] *Barclays Bank Ltd v Quistclose Investments Ltd* [1970] AC 567 (HL). Also see *Twinsectra Ltd v Yardley* [2002] UKHL 12, [2002] 2 AC 164 (HL).

[88] See below for other analyses.

[89] *Carreras Rothmans Ltd v Freeman Matthews Treasure Ltd* [1985] 1 Ch 207 (Peter Gibson J). Although an insolvent debtor cannot prefer one of his creditors to the others (this would offend the *pari passu* principle), there is nothing to stop a third party doing this. The third party effectively substitutes himself (and his loan debt) for the original creditor whose claim is satisfied. This switch has no practical effect on the other creditors of the insolvent debtor.

[90] *Re EVTR Ltd* [1987] BCLC 647, (1987) 3 BCC 382 (CA).

the funds themselves; his position is secured. After the funds have been properly spent, however, there is then no trust property (and no breach of trust that would support any tracing into substitutes[91]). The lender is then merely an unsecured creditor, although his hope is that the rescue will have been successful and his (unsecured) position will not be too risky.

Two features of the *Quistclose* trust warrant comment. The first is that the existing cases all relate to trusts of money. Suppliers seem unable to use the same strategy to create trusts over goods, not money, delivered to purchasers.[92] This is odd, since every doctrinal analysis suggests that the strategy should have completely general application. Proper doctrinal analysis is problematic, however, and this is the second point to note. Perhaps surprisingly, it is not at all clear what sort of trust the *Quistclose* trust is. It could be an express trust. The parties do not need to use the term 'trust'; the settlor (lender) must simply intend to create a trust, not some other arrangement, and the trustee (the borrower) must accept the trust property on those terms. These prescriptions are effectively encapsulated in the *Quistclose* requirement that there be a mutual understanding that the loan funds are not at the borrower's free disposal, but must be used for nominated purposes.[93] This analysis perhaps represents the preferred approach. However, the trust might also be a resulting trust, generated because the lender has transferred legal title to the borrower but failed to specify who is to have the beneficial interest beyond indicating that the borrower is not. Finally, the trust could be a constructive trust, generated because the court sees fit to specifically enforce the contractual terms of the security arrangement between the parties. There are sound arguments in favour of each analysis, and none, it seems, countermanding any of them. With trusts of money lent to fund rescue operations, each doctrinal approach delivers exactly the same response. This may not always be the case if the trust grows to have wider application: in particular, differences in formal requirements for creating express trusts,[94] doctrinal requirements underlying resulting trusts,[95] and factual requirements for specific performance[96] may all become material.

---

[91] See Chapter 4, 102–6.
[92] Suppliers can retain *legal* title, however, under simple retention of title clauses: Sale of Goods Act 1979, s. 19.
[93] See Chapter 3, 67–8, on the facts necessary to generate express trusts.
[94] See Chapter 3, 67–8.   [95] See Chapter 3, 71–2, and Chapter 9, 303–7.
[96] See below, 264–6.

PRESUMED RESULTING TRUSTS AND PURCHASE MONEY RESULTING TRUSTS

The second example of Equity implying additional terms into an arrangement arises when property is simply given to others, or when property is purchased using funds from different sources. Recall that if B simply gives property to A, then Equity will *presume* that the transfer was not intended as a gift.[97] More than this, it will imply a term to that effect into the arrangement and then enforce the term specifically. As a result, A will receive the legal title, but not the right to enjoy the property beneficially: A will hold the asset on resulting trust for B (a *presumed resulting trust*). A can claim the full beneficial interest only if he can rebut Equity's presumption.

Equity implies similar terms into arrangements where property is purchased using funds from different sources. Suppose parties purchase a house in A's name alone, although both A and B pay the deposit, sign the mortgage, and make equal monthly contributions to repay the loan. As ever, Equity's presumptions run against gift-giving. If B's contributions were made as contributions to the purchase price, then Equity will rebuttably *presume* that they were intended to deliver an interest in the house to B, not to benefit A. Equity will imply a term to this effect into the arrangements, thus ensuring that A does not have an absolute entitlement to the house, but is forced to recognize B's interest. This implied term is enforced specifically, thereby creating a trust. The effect of this is that A will hold the house on trust (a *purchase money resulting trust*) for A and B in proportion to their respective contributions to the purchase price.[98] This trust is especially significant in protecting B's interests, because statutory exceptions suggest it need not comply with any writing requirements for the transfer of interests in land.[99]

Clearly, presumed resulting trusts are distinctly hostile to gift-giving. Perhaps predictably, Equity found it necessary to develop counter-presumptions in circumstances where gift-giving is natural. The *presumption of advancement* is a rebuttable presumption that B *did* intend to make a gift to A. In England, the presumption applies to transfers from husband to wife[100] (but not vice versa, and not to de facto relationships), and also to transfers from a man to anyone to whom he is *in loco*

---

[97] See Chapter 3, 71–2, but also Chapter 9, 303–7.
[98] *The Venture* [1908] P 218 (Farwell J); *Vandervell v IRC* [1967] 2 AC 291 (HL), 312; *Foskett v McKeown* [1998] 2 WLR 298 (CA), 312–3 (Sir Richard Scott V-C).
[99] Se above, 231–4.   [100] *Jones v Maynard* [1951] Ch 572.

parentis[101] (but not to transfers by a woman in the same circumstances[102]). It follows that if a father gives £3,000 to his son, the son will take the money as a gift unless the presumption of advancement is rebutted; if the father gives the same sum to his own brother, however, the brother will hold the sum on resulting trust for the father unless the presumption of resulting trust is rebutted.[103]

The presumption of advancement can dramatically affect purchase money resulting trusts. A husband's contribution to the purchase price of a house is subject to the presumption of advancement; a wife's to the presumption of resulting trust. If A and B are husband and wife and they purchase a house in the husband's name, then he will hold the house on resulting trust for the two of them: the wife's contribution is presumed to be self-interested. If the house is purchased in the wife's name, however, then she takes absolutely: the husband's contribution is presumed to be for his wife's benefit.[104] This particular operation of the presumption of advancement is now seen as anachronistic, and is usually rebutted by very slender evidence.

Notice that the existence of a purchase money resulting trust, and the parties' respective beneficial interests under it, are firmly established at the date the property is acquired.[105] This is when Equity recognizes that the property is (presumptively) not intended to be at the free disposal of the legal owner, and enforces these presumed terms. The fact that A and B's respective interests in the house are assessed at the time of the purchase can sometimes seem unfair. Suppose A and B purchase a house for £200,000, each paying £10,000 by way of deposit and each assuming equal liability for the mortgage repayments. On these facts, A will hold the house on a purchase money resulting trust for the two of them in equal shares. If it turns out that A makes *all* the mortgage repayments, then A's only remedy is to argue that the parties came to some other enforceable arrangement to divide the property more appropriately,[106] or

---

[101] *Shephard v Cartwright* [1955] AC 431 (HL) (father); *Bennet v Bennet* (1879) 10 Ch D 474, 476–7 (Jessel MR) (mother).

[102] In Australia, by contrast, the presumption of advancement applies equally to men and women *in loco parentis: Nelson v Nelson* (1995) 184 CLR 538 (Aust HCt), 547–9.

[103] For instances of effective rebuttal of the presumption, see *Fowkes v Pascoe* (1875) LR 10 Ch App 343 (CA), 352–3 (Mellish LJ); *Re Vinogradoff* [1935] WN 68, 68 (Farwell J).

[104] *Jones v Maynard* [1951] Ch 572, 575 (Vaisey J).

[105] *Pettit v Pettit* [1970] AC 777 (HL), 814; *Huntingford v Hobbs* [1993] 1 FLR 736 (CA) (see Slade LJ).

[106] See above, 246, (proprietary estoppel), and below 261–4, (constructive trust).

to insist that B must repay A for half of the instalments since he would otherwise be unjustly enriched.[107]

Whatever the shortcomings in these presumed arrangements, they demonstrate yet another mechanism by which Equity implies terms into dealings, and so protects the parties involved. Indeed, it protects them in the strongest way possible by recognizing proprietary interests in assets legally owned by others.

DISALLOWING RELIANCE ON THE PRESUMPTION OF RESULTING TRUST

Presumed resulting trusts and purchase money resulting trusts are clearly designed to help claimants keep their property (or its purchased substitute) even when they appear to have given it away. If the transfer is part of some illegal scheme, then this sort of assistance can seem unwarranted. For example, a claimant may transfer certain assets to a trusted third party so that she appears to be less wealthy, and can then avoid tax, or evade her creditors, or make means-tested claims on the state. Later on, if the trusted friend refuses to re-transfer the property, should the claimant be allowed to rely on Equity's presumptions of resulting trust to assist her in recovering her property? Until relatively recently, the courts' response was clearly guided by overtly moralistic public policy: the claimant could only recover her property if her plan had not yet been put into effect (for example, no creditors had yet been defrauded) *and* she had repented of her illegality. 'Repentance' was often a matter of difficult judgement. It was not enough that the planned scheme had simply become unworkable or unnecessary; genuine remorse was required. Because of the difficulties in proving this, modern English rules have now moved away from such imperatives. The new rules remain in a state of flux, but repentance is clearly irrelevant.

Recovery is allowed if the illegal plan has not been implemented. For example, a father who has transferred assets to his son in order to defraud his creditors can provide the court with evidence of his illegal (but unimplemented) purpose so as to rebut the presumption of advancement. With this presumption rebutted, the son is presumed to hold the property on resulting trust for his father, and the father can therefore insist on specific recovery of his property.[108]

---

[107] See Chapter 9, 303–7.
[108] *Tribe v Tribe* [1996] Ch 107 (CA). Although see Chapter 6, 169–74.

More surprisingly, recovery is also allowed if the illegal scheme *has* been implemented, so long as the claimant does not need to rely on her own illegality to make out her case. This rule can generate some odd results. Suppose two unmarried partners, A and B, plot to buy a house together, but in A's name only, so that B appears less wealthy and can claim social security benefits to the economic advantage of both of them. If A and B fall out, the modern rules will allow B to adduce evidence of her contributions to the purchase price of the house in order to establish a purchase money resulting trust. She can make out this case without reference to her part in the fraud, and can then insist on being given an interest in the house notwithstanding the illegal scheme to which she has been party.[109]

This approach is said to be defensible because it treats Equitable property in the same way as legal property. If a claimant can show that she is the legal owner of property in another's hands, the law does not ask how it got to be in the other's possession; it simply gives her a remedy. What this justification ignores, however, is that the claimant's assertion of Equitable title is only possible because Equity implies terms into the arrangement between the parties and then insists on their enforcement. Common Law title, in analogous circumstances, is always proved outright, not presumed. Take this difference a little further. In these resulting trust cases, the claimant's public, objective, intention is to make an outright transfer to the defendant; her private, undisclosed, and illegal intention is to retain an interest in the property herself. It would seem sensible to insist that the objective view effectively rebuts Equity's presumption against gift-giving, not that the subjective view reinforces it. Indeed, in ignoring this, the modern rules can lead to some strange—and perhaps unfair—results. Suppose the two parties in our earlier example had been husband and wife, with the husband defrauding social security. He would not have the benefit of the presumption of a resulting trust; instead, he would be caught by the presumption of advancement. He would therefore be unable to recover his property because he cannot make out his case without raising his illegal purpose to show that his real intention was not to benefit his wife but to defraud the social security. On the other hand, if his wife were to defraud the social security, she could recover her property. Arguably the approach taken in Australia in recent cases is preferable. There the courts look at all the facts and then decide whether, and on what terms, the claimant can have her property back. For

---

[109] *Tinsley v Milligan* [1994] 1 AC 340 (HL).

example, the court may allow the claimant to recover her house on the condition that she make good her obligations to the defrauded social security agency.[110] This strategy is not as overtly moral as the early rules on illegality, but it does pay conscious regard to the particular policy concerns motivating statutory intervention.

FAMILY HOMES AND COMMON INTENTION CONSTRUCTIVE TRUSTS

This last example of Equity's capacity to imply terms is unquestionably the most difficult to explain and to justify. Intervention is directed at a common modern phenomenon. A cohabiting couple may share a house which belongs, at law, to only one of them. Both may make various economic and social contributions to their joint lives. If the relationship breaks down, the non-owner may feel entitled to a share in the property, or at least to some financial recompense from the owner.[111] The parties are unlikely to have committed any agreement to writing, and yet this is what the Common Law demands for the transfer of interests in land.[112] What should happen?

Estoppel to prevent fraud may help; so too may purchase money resulting trusts, or proprietary estoppel. Intervention on these bases is limited, however, and English courts have suggested there is a further alternative, a *common intention constructive trust*. To date the reasoning has only been applied in the context of domestic disputes over family homes, although nothing in the analysis appears to compel such restricted application.[113]

The English approach[114] is to look for direct evidence of discussion and agreement between the parties that the property will be shared. It does not matter how imperfectly the evidence is remembered or how imprecise the terms of the agreement. Alternatively, the courts may infer an agreement from nothing more than the conduct of the parties. This is controversial, however. Indeed, direct mortgage contributions seem to be the only evidence considered sufficient to raise an inference of a common

[110] *Nelson v Nelson* (1995) 184 CLR 538 (Aust HCt).

[111] If the breakdown involves a divorce, then the English courts have an exceedingly liberal discretion to determine property issues, and reliance on this Equitable jurisdiction is unnecessary.

[112] Law of Property (Miscellaneous Provisions) Act 1989, s. 2; Law of Property Act 1925, s. 53.

[113] Also see the approach in *Banner Homes Holdings Ltd v Luff Developments Ltd* [2000] Ch 372 (CA).

[114] *Lloyds Bank v Rosset* [1991] 1 AC 107 (HL), especially the opinion of Lord Bridge. Also see *Gissing v Gissing* [1971] AC 887 (HL).

intention to share the beneficial interest in the house; other contributions are likely to be equivocal, perhaps suggesting no more than a desire to live together amicably. Once the court has established this common intention, it then imposes a constructive trust that compels some sort of property sharing between the parties. The rationale is simply that it would be unjust for the legal owner to deny the other party an interest in the circumstances. This common intention constructive trust needs some unravelling, especially since English courts insist that a constructive trust is not a general remedy for righting injustices.

Early English cases suggest that the trust is designed to enforce the parties' common intention agreement. Ignoring any scepticism about the reality of the discovered agreement, specific enforcement of informal land contracts was certainly possible prior to 1989: the doctrine of part-performance could be relied upon,[115] and certain proprietary estoppel cases adopted parallel analyses.[116] This route is now blocked by statute. Contracts for the disposition of interests in land must be in writing or they are of no effect. An unwritten land contract cannot, without more, be specifically enforced. The only way to overcome the absence of writing, and adopt the fiction that the contract is nevertheless effective, is to show that the owner would be committing a fraud if he relied on the statute to deny the claimant an interest.[117] This is unlikely where the owner is merely denying the claimant an interest in *his* property, not denying her an interest in property that he duped her into parting with.[118] Indeed, no case suggests this fraud exception is material.

What proof of an informal contract *does* do, however, is indicate that the non-owner did not perform her various services gratuitously; she expected to be rewarded according to the terms of the (void) contract. In these circumstances she should be able to demand restitution.[119] This will not necessarily give her an interest in the land, but merely a remedy for the unwarranted benefits she has conferred on the owner. In short, if the choice for the courts is between specifically enforcing the informal contract or unwinding it, the modern statutory position demands the latter. Notwithstanding this, recent cases appear not to have modified their analysis in any way to accommodate these statutory changes. This

---

[115] See above, 232.   [116] See above, 246–8.

[117] See Chapter 7, 202–4, and above, 231–5.

[118] Throughout this book, the claimant has been referred to as 'she' and the defendant as 'he'. Here, as in other cases, however, either party could be male or female (although, statistically, in these family homes cases, the claimant is often a woman).

[119] See Chapter 9, 303–7.

suggests that perhaps their motivation was never specific performance of the informal agreement but something else.

Indeed, more modern cases have explicitly inclined towards proprietary estoppel.[120] They suggest that there is little if anything dividing common intention constructive trusts and proprietary estoppel. But recall the earlier suggestion that proprietary estoppel cases ought to be reclassified and reassigned to more appropriate heads of contract, tort, or unjust enrichment liability. Contract has already been discussed and discarded because of the statutory impediments. That leaves unjust enrichment and tort (liability for induced reliance). The problem is that these non-contractual heads of liability do not match the remedies ordered by the courts in family homes cases. The courts are *not* (or not often) valuing unjust enrichments or detrimental reliance. They are plainly inferring and enforcing agreements in order to do justice between the parties. Doctrinally, this is questionable.

Courts in other common law countries fare little better. The pragmatist would note that the practical results are invariably comparable. In Canada, the result is justified on the secure doctrinal basis of unjust enrichment, although assessment of the owner's unjust enrichment often seems unduly generous to the non-owner.[121] In New Zealand, decisions are based on the 'reasonable expectations' of the claimant,[122] although it is not clear whether this protects her expectation interest or her reliance interest. In Australia, the responses are underpinned by 'unconscionability'[123] and, again, it is not clear whether this marks a contract, tort, or unjust enrichment reaction to the circumstances. None of this affords much credit to the law.

In reality, modern courts are in the impossible position of having to invent doctrinal justifications for the exercise of a discretion that Parliament ought to have given them long ago to enable them to deal adequately with property disputes between married *and* unmarried couples. Thankfully, such legislation is becoming increasingly widespread.

---

[120] *Lloyds Bank v Rosset* [1991] 1 AC 107 (HL) (Lord Bridge); *Grant v Edwards* [1986] Ch 638 (Browne-Wilkinson V-C); *Oxley v Hiscock* [2004] EWCA Civ 546, [2004] 3 WLR 715 (CA).

[121] See, e.g., *Pettkus v Becker* [1980] 2 SCR 834, (1980) 117 DLR (3d) 257 (Can SCt).

[122] *Gillies v Keogh* [1989] 2 NZLR 327 (NZCA).

[123] *Muschinski v Dodds* (1985) 160 CLR 583 (Aust HCt).

ANTICIPATING AND SECURING THE COMMON LAW OUTCOME

The fifth and final Equitable strategy to be considered in this chapter is Equity's ability to anticipate or secure the Common Law outcome. Consider a contract for the sale of a house. The contract will specify when legal title is to pass. This will undoubtedly be some time after the parties have reached agreement. Both vendor and purchaser may be apprehensive about the risk of intervening difficulties. Equity can allay their fears a little. It regards contracts for the sale of land as specifically enforceable.[124] It will therefore compel both parties to perform their agreement according to its terms. This has one crucial consequence for the parties. Since Equity 'regards as done that which ought to be done',[125] it regards the property as *already* transferred to the purchaser: the vendor has legal title, but he holds the property on trust (a constructive trust) for the purchaser.[126] In this way Equity anticipates the Common Law outcome.

This early delivery of an Equitable interest in the property has enormous advantages for the purchaser. Most obviously, she can insist on specific delivery of the property should the vendor renege on his promise.[127] And if the vendor becomes insolvent midway through the deal, she can extract her property from the pool of insolvency assets; she will not rank as a mere unsecured creditor suing for damages for breach of her uncompleted sale contract. This insolvency protection is one of the greatest advantages associated with Equitable proprietary interests.[128] These advantages aside, Equitable ownership may also be material in determining tax liability, succession entitlements, and claims to dividends and other incidental benefits.

ANTICIPATING OWNERSHIP—SPECIFIC PERFORMANCE AND CONSTRUCTIVE TRUSTS

The possibility of obtaining Equitable ownership in advance of the agreed legal transfer is enormously valuable. Who is entitled to it? Equity

[124] See Chapter 2, 25–6.
[125] Recall that the maxim is rather inadequate shorthand for a process of legal development that took hundreds of years, and involved Equity in creating remedies, consistently insisting on their performance, and protecting the remedial rights in privileged ways that ensured they could be characterized as property. All of this history cannot be reiterated each time there is a need to make reference to the strategy, so the maxim bears the burden of conveying the detail.
[126] See Chapter 3, 63–7.   [127] Although see Chapter 6, 169–74.
[128] See Chapter 3, 52–5.

has a very simple rule. The claimant will have an Equitable interest in the property if the defendant's obligation to transfer legal title is *specifically enforceable* and *unconditional* (i.e. there are no pre-conditions to be met before the defendant can be compelled to perform), and relates to *identifiable property*. These three conditions are determinative. They are met in our contract for the sale of a house: the contract is specifically enforceable; it relates to identifiable property; and the vendor's obligation to transfer is unconditional provided the contract is in writing[129] and the purchaser has paid the purchase price. Once all three conditions are met, Equity will say that the sale property ought to be transferred; if the sale property ought to be transferred, then Equity, 'treating as done that which ought to be done', can regard it as already transferred.

The first and last conditions are usually determinative,[130] but something more should be said about the requirement that the vendor's obligations be unconditional. Formalities and payment of the price are not necessarily the only qualifying factors. Some legal transfers cannot take effect without the consent of a nominated third party, such as a board of directors approving a share transfer, or a Government Minister approving a special land transfer. This can introduce an element of chance into Equity's proprietary protection. Consider an unusual illustration. A testator leaves his land to A and his personal property to B. Before his death he enters into a contract to sell a parcel of his land. The contract requires the consent of a particular Government Minister, but consent is not granted before the testator dies. Who stands to benefit under the will? If the land belongs beneficially to the testator at the date of his death, then A will benefit; if it does not, then B will benefit (by receiving the purchase price). Here, A will benefit: the contract is specifically enforceable and the land is precisely identified, but the contract remains conditional; in these circumstances Equity will not anticipate the transfer, and so the vendor remains the beneficial owner.[131]

Not all conditions operate quite so dramatically. If the vendor can be obliged to act to meet the condition, then Equity will 'regard as done' whatever the vendor ought to do, and the purchaser will have her Equitable interest in the underlying property. For example, registration

---

[129] Law of Property (Miscellaneous Provisions) Act 1989, s. 2.

[130] See Chapter 2, 24–31, and below, 264–6. Recall that contracts for the sale of 'unique' assets are not the only contracts that are specifically enforceable: see Chapter 2, 25–7 and *Adderley v Dixon* (1824) 1 Sim & St 607.

[131] *Brown v Heffer* (1967) 116 CLR 344 (Aust HCt). Also see *Re Fry* [1946] Ch 312 (ChD).

in the company's books is often a mere formality when company shares are sold; the vendor must simply submit the necessary transfer forms to the company. In assessing whether the purchaser has an Equitable interest in the shares, Equity will regard this as already done by both the vendor and the company.[132] In another twist, the relevant condition may have been inserted purely for the purchaser's benefit. She is then free to waive it. If she does this, and the vendor's obligation becomes unconditional, she will then acquire an Equitable interest in the underlying property; until her waiver, however, she is not the Equitable owner because the vendor's obligation is not unconditional.

SECURING PAYMENT—VENDORS' LIENS

It might seem that these rules on specifically enforceable contracts unduly favour purchasers over vendors. Even if the vendor's contract is specifically enforceable and unconditional, there is rarely an identified 'purchase fund' that the vendor could own in Equity in advance of the legal transfer of the price. Equity does not leave such vendors without a remedy, however. If the vendor transfers his land to the purchaser before she pays the full price, then the vendor retains a lien on the land to secure the purchaser's outstanding obligations. The transfer gives the purchaser legal ownership of the land, but the vendor has an Equitable security interest in the property to protect his status. This interest arises by operation of law, and not because of any express agreement between the parties.

This protective rule relating to vendor's liens seems to apply only when the underlying contract is specifically enforceable (and recall that if the purchaser can specifically enforce a contract, then so too can the vendor under the principle of mutuality[133]). This limitation makes sense. Usually a purchaser is simply under a personal obligation to pay the price or face a damages claim. Only when the contract is specifically enforceable, so that she *must* pay, is it appropriate to limit her interest in the asset

---

[132] *Re Rose* [1952] Ch 499 (CA). The arguments for this approach are not all one way, but find some support in Companies Act 1985, s. 183(5) and *Re Swaledale Cleaners Ltd* [1968] 1 WLR 1710 (CA).
[133] See Chapter 2, 25.

she has acquired so as to indicate that she is not at liberty to deal with it freely until her side of the bargain is completed.[134]

THEORY AND PRACTICE

The theory behind constructive trusts and vendors' liens appears so general that its impact is expected to be widespread. It is not. The 1980s provided some dramatic illustrations. 'Investment companies' proliferated: wine investment companies, share investment companies, and bullion investment companies were common. Investors were persuaded to purchase a product (wine, shares, bullion, etc.), and leave it with the investment company for safekeeping. 'Certificates of title' were issued, and investors were assured that the company's stocks were audited to ensure investors' security. If the investment company collapsed, however, then the bank's secured claims against its assets invariably meant there was nothing left for unsecured creditors. Investors could not recoup their losses unless they could establish a proprietary claim to 'their' investment. This they could rarely do. Their 'certificates of title' were worthless: legal title had not been transferred by delivery or any other necessary mechanism. Worse, the conditions for establishing Equitable title were never met. The contracts were usually for the sale of ordinary items, not rare or unique assets, so they were not specifically enforceable. Moreover, the sale property was not sufficiently well identified for a purchaser to say, 'that's my bottle of wine'; indeed, the company had not usually nominated any source of supply. As a result, the investors lost.[135] This could be especially galling if the company's stocks *were* adequate to meet their demands, if only they had been able to successfully assert their own proprietary claims in the face of the bank's competing proprietary interests.

Matters are little better for purchasers who have agreed that vendors should supply the sale property from a nominated bulk. Many commodities—wheat, oil, and wine, for example—are sold in this way. A buyer might purchase 50,000 tonnes of a 100,000-tonne cargo of wheat. Until

---

[134] *Hewitt v Court* (1983) 149 CLR 639 (Aust HCt); *Capital Finance Co Ltd v Stokes* [1969] 1 Ch 261 (CA). Purchasers' liens seem to be more widespread. A purchaser's lien over the sale property in the vendor's hands secures the return of the purchase price to the purchaser should the vendor default and the purchaser seek restitution rather than contract damages: see Chapter 9, 304. More generally, see *Lord Napier and Ettrick v Hunter* [1993] AC 713 (HL).

[135] *Re London Wine (Shippers) Ltd* [1986] PCC 121 (Oliver J); *Re Goldcorp Exchange Ltd (in rec)* [1995] 1 AC 74 (PC). Contrast *Re Harvard Securities Ltd (in liq)* [1997] 2 BCLC 369, [1998] BCC 567 (Neuberger J), where the investors succeeded where English law governed, but not where Australian law did.

recent statutory amendments were enacted, the buyer could not obtain legal title until his wheat was 'ascertained' by separating it from the bulk; and he did not acquire Equitable title in advance because his contract was not specifically enforceable.[136] This could be most frustrating if the vendor became insolvent. The purchaser may have paid for the goods, and may have been able to identify the ship carrying them. Nevertheless he would be forced to prove as an unsecured creditor in the vendor's liquidation because he lacked a proprietary interest. This result was conceded to be contrary to all legitimate business expectations. Now the relevant English statute provides that on payment of the price, or part of it, the purchaser of goods acquires property in an undivided share of the bulk, thereby becoming an owner in common of the bulk.[137] When this amendment applies, the purchaser acquires legal title, and so does not require the assistance of Equity.

Potential problems with sales of other assets from a bulk have not been remedied by statute, and yet dealings in shares, bonds, and other financial instruments are commonly carried out in this way. This raises the question of when, if ever, a purchaser will acquire Equitable ownership of the asset in advance of its legal transfer. The short answer seems to be, very rarely. Suppose a vendor agrees to sell 1,000 shares from his holding of 5,000 shares. Legal title will not pass until the purchaser's name is registered in the company's books. Equitable title may pass in advance of this, but only if the contract is specifically enforceable, unconditional, and relates to identified property.

The contract will not be specifically enforceable if the shares are in a listed company; damages would then provide an adequate remedy, enabling the disappointed purchaser to buy elsewhere.[138] A contract for the sale of shares in a private company, on the other hand, is likely to be specifically enforceable. But even so, will a nominated part of a bulk count as sufficient identification? None of the existing English authorities is definitive, so the answer is open to legitimate debate. An order for specific performance would compel the vendor to segregate the sale property from the bulk and transfer it to the purchaser. Given this, will Equity, considering as done that which ought to be done, assume that the vendor

---

[136] *Re Wait* [1927] 1 Ch 606 (CA). This is not only because the goods are not rare or unique, but also because the Sale of Goods Act 1979, s. 52 limits specific performance to those contracts 'to deliver specific or ascertained goods'.

[137] Sale of Goods (Amendment) Act 1995, which adds s. 20A to the Sale of Goods Act 1979.

[138] *Duncuft v Albrecht* (1841) 12 Sim 189, 59 ER 1104.

has segregated as well as assuming that the vendor *has transferred*? Only this will give the purchaser an Equitable interest in the bulk. Since Equity routinely does this in the context of trusts and tracing exercises—where, in both cases, the principal difference is that the Equitable obligation to segregate and to transfer is derived from some source other than a specifically enforceable contract of sale—there would seem to be no practical or theoretical impediment to adopting the same approach with sales. In fact, consistency might be seen as demanding this. If this were so, some of the most common modern investment practices would generate proprietary interests in the underlying assets for parties further down the investment chain; otherwise their claims would be merely personal.

In short, the pre-conditions for this form of Equitable intervention are so limiting, especially the requirements that the contract be specifically enforceable and that the property be well identified, that few purchasers will ever find themselves in this enviable position.

'REMEDIAL' CONSTRUCTIVE TRUSTS?

The ownership interests described in the previous sections are constructive trusts. In English law, constructive trusts are said to be 'institutional', not 'remedial'. Broadly speaking, this means that the trust arises upon the occurrence of certain fact patterns. If the facts fall within the relevant class, then the court's role is simply to declare that a trust exists, and that it did so from the time the relevant facts occurred. The court has no discretion to affirm or deny the trust's genesis.

A 'remedial' constructive trust, on the other hand, is a remedy delivered by the court, and at the court's discretion. The court determines that the facts call for a remedy and, moreover, that the most appropriate remedy is a proprietary one. Their order 'creates' a remedial constructive trust. Such trusts can arise at the time of the court's order or at some earlier date; all depends upon the exercise of the court's discretion. These trusts give courts enormous flexibility in avoiding unwelcome insolvency consequences: courts can refuse to privilege claimants at the expense of unsecured creditors. 'Remedial' constructive trusts are well accepted in the United States and Canada, but seem unlikely to take hold in England; there the idea is seen as re-distributional justice without a political mandate to support it.[139]

[139] *Re Polly Peck International Plc (in admin); Marangos Hotel Ltd v Stone (Re Polly Peck International Plc (No 2))* [1998] 3 All ER 812 (CA) (Mummery LJ); also see *Fortex Group Ltd v MacIntosh* [1998] 3 NZLR 171 (NZCA).

REVIEW

This chapter has explored a range of Equity's incursions into the Common Law of contract. Undoubtedly other Equitable practices could have been included. Little of the Common Law of contract is left untouched. Nevertheless, there is nothing that seems impossible to integrate within a coherent common law map, except perhaps constructive trusts of family homes. Even so, this chapter has exposed Equity at its most difficult and discordant in this regard. The problem is Equity's underanalysis of its own strategies. This has created internal disjunctions that need resolving before integration with the Common Law can hope to proceed.

The courts' analysis of constructive trusts of family homes appears directed at social policy ends in circumstances where the private agreement, if it exists at all, will only coincidentally mirror the just outcome. The same is true of tort and unjust enrichment remedies. It follows that little progress is likely, no matter how much attention is devoted to sophisticated doctrinal analysis. In all these cases, judges need a legislative discretion to divide assets in a way that seems fair and just in all the circumstances of the domestic relationship breakdown: contract, tort, and unjust enrichment baselines are simply not apt.

Equity's other incursions into the law of contract are easier to accommodate. Take Equity's role in enhancing promises by implying additional terms and specifically enforcing deals, especially in ways that deliver proprietary consequences. In each case, what supports proprietary intervention is a perception that a particular asset is not intended to be at the free disposal of its legal owner. This perception can be generated because of specific and restricted terms (express, implied or presumed) governing A's transfer to B. They can also be generated because of the importance conceded to an agreement by A to transfer the asset to B, an importance largely determined by the nature of the underlying asset (rare or unique) or the purpose of the deal (security). In either case, B will hold the asset on trust for A. This proprietary response to A's predicament reflects and reinforces the subtlety of the 'bundle of rights' ideas discussed earlier.[140]

Equity's interference with Common Law rules settling contractual formalities is more troublesome. The various grounds for intervention need to be better articulated, and the remedies aligned appropriately. Only then, when these foundations have been adequately exposed and

---

[140] See Chapter 3, 57–8.

explained, will it be possible to adapt the analyses to deal with new facts and legislative prescriptions.

Finally, Equity's head of 'estoppel' liability is, analytically, in chaos. Its current state illustrates perfectly the danger of calling different things by the same name and then feigning that there is a coherent pattern in their operation. Arguably estoppel must be completely unravelled and repackaged, so that the estoppel cases are reclassified and reassigned to more appropriate heads of liability.

SELECTED BIBLIOGRAPHY

Bright, S. and McFarlane, B., 'Proprietary Estoppel and Property Rights' [2005] CLJ 449.

Fung, E. and Ho, L., 'Change of Position and Estoppel' (2001) 117 LQR 14.

Gardner, S., 'Rethinking Family Property' (1993) 109 LQR 263.

——, 'The Remedial Discretion in Proprietary Estoppel' (1999) 115 LQR 438.

Glister, J., 'The Nature of *Quistclose* Trusts: Classification and Reconciliation' [2004] CLJ 632.

Garton, J., 'The Role of the Trust Mechanism in the Rule in *Re Rose*' [2003] Conveyancer 364.

Green, B., '*Grey, Oughtred and Vandervell*—A Contextual Reappraisal' (1984) 47 MLR 385.

Ho, L. and Smart, P. S. J., 'Reinterpreting the *Quistclose* Trust: A Critique of Chambers' Analysis' (2001) 21 OJLS 267.

Millett, P. J., 'The *Quistclose* Trust: Who Can Enforce It?' (1985) 101 LQR 269.

Phillips, J., 'Equitable Liens—A Search for a Unifying Principle' in N. Palmer and E. McKendrick (eds), *Interests in Goods* (2nd edn, London: Lloyd's of London Press, 1998), Ch. 39.

Worthington, S., 'Sorting Out Ownership Interests in a Bulk: Gifts, Sales and Trusts' [1999] Journal of Business Law 1.

SELECTED CASES

Banner Homes Holdings Ltd v Luff Developments Ltd [2000] Ch 372 (CA)

Barclays Bank Ltd v Quistclose Investments Ltd [1970] AC 567 (HL)

Central London Property Ltd v High Trees House Ltd [1947] KB 130

Corin v Patton (1990) 169 CLR 540 (Aust HCt)

Crabb v Arun District Council [1976] Ch 179 (CA)

Giumelli v Giumelli (1999) 196 CLR 101, [1999] HCA 10 (Aust HCt)

Re Goldcorp Exchange Ltd (in rec) [1995] 1 AC 74 (PC)

Hewitt v Court [1983] 149 CLR 639 (Aust HCt)

Lloyds Bank v Rosset [1991] 1 AC 107 (HL)

Re London Wine (Shippers) Ltd [1986] PCC 121 (Oliver J)

Muschinski v Dodds (1985) 160 CLR 583 (Aust HCt)

Norman v Federal Commissioner of Taxation (1963) 109 CLR 9 (Aust HCt)

Pascoe v Turner [1979] 1 WLR 431 (CA)

Tinsley v Milligan [1994] 1 AC 340 (HL)

Twinsectra Ltd v Yardley [2002] UKHL 12, [2002] 2 AC 164 (HL)

Re Wait [1927] 1 Ch 606 (CA)

Waltons Stores (Interstate) Ltd v Maher (1988) 164 CLR 387 (Aust HCt)

Part v

Unjust Enrichment

9

Correcting Misconceived Transfers

This chapter is about the strategies Equity has developed to ensure the return of property that has fallen into the wrong hands. If a customer mistakenly pays her gas bill twice, for example, what role (if any) does Equity play in assisting her to recover the second payment? Every society needs some sort of mechanism to remedy the errors that will inevitably occur in social and commercial dealings. The customer will undoubtedly expect to recover the sum, yet neither contract law nor tort law can help her: there is no contract governing the second payment, and the gas board itself has done nothing wrong. The solution is delivered by the law of *unjust enrichment*. This third branch of the law of obligations provides remedies whenever defendants receive some benefit, or enrichment, at the claimant's expense in circumstances that make it unjust for them to keep it.[1] This describes the situation between the customer and the gas board. The law of unjust enrichment obliges the gas board to make *restitution* of its enrichment to the claimant. This is how the common law corrects misconceived transfers. There need not be any contract between the parties, nor any wrongdoing by the defendant.[2]

Moreover, unjust enrichment law does not demand that the defendant compensate the claimant for all her loss; it merely requires him to restore, or pay back, any enrichment that it would be unjust for him to keep. The distinction is important. It generates options for various defences, especially the *change of position* defence, that can reduce or even eliminate the defendant's liability to make restitution.[3] Suppose, for example, that A mistakenly transfers £1,000 to B, and because of his newfound wealth B immediately gives £200 to his favourite charity. If B is an innocent

---

[1] *Banque Financière de la Cité v Parc (Battersea) Ltd* [1999] AC 221 (HL), 227 (Lord Steyn).

[2] Although if the facts *also* indicate a breach of contract or a tort, then the claimant can pursue these alternative remedies so long as they do not lead to double recovery for the harm suffered.

[3] *Lipkin Gorman (a firm) v Karpnale Ltd* [1991] 2 AC 548 (HL).

party, it would seem unfair to compel him to return £1,000. In these circumstances, the change of position defence reduces B's apparent obligation to make restitution of £1,000 to an obligation to make restitution of £800 only.

Equity's role in the law of unjust enrichment is highly controversial. Indeed, it has been the subject of some profound and difficult modern revisions. To understand these debates it is first necessary to understand when and why *any* unjust enrichment remedies are warranted. This takes some explaining, but in many ways it is the most crucial part of what follows. How this model is structured determines, in large measure, how easily Common Law and Equitable learning on this issue can be integrated.

MODELS FOR LIMITING CORRECTION

A jurisdiction to correct misconceived transfers is necessary, but potentially troublesome. If the jurisdiction is too wide, then too many transactions will be upset and social and commercial life will suffer: parties will not know which arrangements they can depend upon and which are likely to be unwound. On the other hand, if the jurisdiction is too narrow, individuals will lose their property when the common perception is that they should not. In our earlier example, most people would think it unfair if the gas board could keep the second payment simply because it acquired it innocently.

The common law adopts a relatively restrictive policy. It allows for recovery of misconceived transfers only when the transfer was not intended. The claimant must be able to say, 'I didn't mean you to have the property in the circumstances.' This is what our customer will say about her second payment to the gas board. This test has to be treated carefully, however. Recovery is not allowed simply because a transfer fails to achieve its intended purpose. A claimant will not be allowed to say to her home decorator, 'I didn't mean you to have my payment if you were going to do such a shoddy job.' Somewhere between these two examples is a line that separates situations where recovery is permitted from situations where a commercial risk has been taken and the claimant finds herself on the losing side.

THE ORTHODOX MODEL

The common law currently draws this line between recoverable transfers and binding transfers using two mechanisms. The first mechanism, based on '*vitiated intention*', allows claimants to say, 'I didn't mean you to have the property. My apparent intention to give it to you was vitiated (or flawed).' The implication is that the claimant's intention to transfer the property was so flawed that the law concedes that it is insufficient to support the deal. These flaws in forming intention will allow a claimant to say, 'I didn't mean you to have the property in the circumstances.' The law of unjust enrichment then steps in with its own rules about what the claimant can recover. As noted earlier, the claimant will not necessarily be able to recover everything she has lost; the defendant may have a good defence to the claim.

Perhaps surprisingly, orthodox unjust enrichment analysis deals with our gas board customer under this first mechanism. It says that her intention to give was vitiated by her mistake, so therefore she can recover. This categorization necessarily suggests that 'vitiated intention' in unjust enrichment law does not mean quite the same thing as it does in the law of contract and promised gifts. Recall that intention is vitiated in the law of contract and promises if the claimant's intention is objectively impaired, or if it is subjectively impaired by some mistake, misrepresentation, duress, or undue influence for which the defendant is responsible.[4] In short, the law only departs from its objective approach if the defendant has played a part in impairing the claimant's intention. In unjust enrichment law, by contrast, the claimant's intention is apparently also vitiated if the claimant's own private mistake caused the unintended transfer. This means that perfectly competent individuals can make unilateral mistakes of fact[5] (like that of the customer paying her gas bill twice) or mistakes of law[6] (as when a party pays because he thinks he is legally obliged, but then discovers he is not), and if the mistake causes the misconceived transfer, then restitution is available.

This expanded conception of 'vitiated intention' exposes defendants to much greater risk of having transactions unwound. In order to reduce this risk of too much restitution, the Common Law demands that a difficult distinction be drawn between 'causal mistakes' (where the claimant's intention is vitiated) and 'causal mispredictions' (where the claimant has simply miscalculated the commercial risk). The former will ground a restitutionary claim; the latter will not.[7] This exceptional approach

---

[4] See Chapter 7, 204–19.

[5] *Lady Hood of Avalon v Mackinnon* [1909] 1 Ch 476 (ChD); *Barclays Bank Ltd v W J Simms Son & Cooke (Southern) Ltd* [1980] QB 677.

[6] *Kleinwort Benson Ltd v Lincoln City Council* [1998] 2 AC 349 (HL).

[7] *Dextra Bank & Trust Co Ltd v Bank of Jamaica* [2002] 1 All ER (Comm) 193 (PC).

to vitiated intention in the law of unjust enrichment merits further exploration later in this chapter.

The law could justifiably insist that this first mechanism defined the outer limits of unjust enrichment claims, and that other transfers were binding. Instead, it adopts a second mechanism. In the interests of further protecting the claimant's original ownership, it allows the claimant to say, 'I only intended you to have the property in certain circumstances. My intention to transfer was qualified, and my qualification has not been met; the basis of the deal has fallen through; the promised counter-performance has not been delivered.' For example, a homeowner may pay her decorator in advance, but the decorator may not turn up to do the job. In these circumstances the claimant can insist that the decorator make restitution of her advance payment.[8] The problem here is not one of flawed intention. It is a problem of '*failure of basis*', or '*failure of consideration*'. Note that in this unjust enrichment context 'failure of consideration' means failure of actual performance; it does not mean that there is some flaw in the contractual *promise* to perform. This special meaning of 'failure of consideration' is unique to unjust enrichment law.[9]

This second mechanism needs to be subjected to further constraints, otherwise it could embrace every case where the defendant does not properly perform his side of the bargain, and the claimant could then say there was a failure of basis or failure of consideration. The law currently imposes two restrictions. It will not allow claimants to recover in unjust enrichment while a contract still governs the relationship between the two parties. For example, if the decorator merely does a shoddy job painting the walls, the homeowner must sue him for breach of contract. She cannot recover her advance payment in unjust enrichment on the basis that there has been a failure of basis, or failure of consideration, alleging she did not intend to pay her money unless the job was satisfactory. Put another way, the law considers her to be on the losing side of a commercial deal, not as having made a misconceived transfer of funds. This limitation is considered uncontroversial: contract trumps unjust enrichment.

---

[8] She must first terminate her contract with the decorator: see the discussion below. She can, alternatively (and whether or not she has terminated the contract), sue her decorator for breach of contract; indeed, in these circumstances she could sue for 'reliance damages' (i.e. the amount of her advance payment), rather than expectation damages.
[9] *Fibrosa Spolka Akcyina v Fairbairn Lawson Combe Barbour Ltd* [1943] AC 32 (HL). In contract law, 'failure of consideration' means that there is no promised counter-performance, so there is no binding contract: see Chapter 8, 241–2.

The second limitation on 'failure of consideration' claims is more difficult. Even when a contract no longer governs the relationship between the parties (because the contract has been terminated), unjust enrichment claims are often denied unless there has been a *total* failure of consideration.[10] If the homeowner pays in advance and the decorator simply refuses to turn up, then there is a total failure of consideration: the homeowner has received *nothing* for her payment. Furthermore, the homeowner can terminate the contract: the decorator's breach is considered so serious that the law gives the homeowner the right to end the commercial engagement.[11] In these circumstances, a contract no longer governs the relationship between the parties, and the claimant can recover her advance payment in unjust enrichment. But if the decorator paints two walls and then walks out, the result is quite different. The homeowner can still terminate the contract for serious breach, but she is not allowed to recover her advance payment in unjust enrichment because the failure of consideration is not *total*. She can only sue for breach of contract.[12] Indeed, this can be the result even when the homeowner receives no tangible benefit at all. If the homeowner employs an architect to remodel her house and he starts work on the plans, then the failure of consideration (or performance) is not *total*, even if he delivers nothing before the contract is terminated. In short, if the claimant receives any part of the promised performance, then the 'failure of consideration' analysis is barred.[13] Modern unjust enrichment scholars suggest that this limitation is unprincipled and should be removed. This would allow recovery in unjust enrichment even where the failure of consideration is only partial, provided, of course, that the contract had been terminated.[14]

---

[10] *Goss v Chilcott* [1996] AC 788 (PC).

[11] Termination has a special legal meaning. The contract stands with full force up to the date of termination, but all the obligations after that date are cancelled. This means the homeowner can still sue for breach of contract, but the decorator cannot insist on continuing with the job, and the claimant cannot be forced to pay him for work done after the termination.

[12] *Baltic Shipping Co v Dillon* (1993) 176 CLR 344 (Aust HCt).

[13] *Hyundai Heavy Industries Ltd v Papadopoulos* [1980] 1 WLR 1129 (HL); *Stocznia Gdanska SA v Latvian Shipping Co* [1998] 1 WLR 574 (HL).

[14] Of course, if the homeowner were allowed to recover her advance payment in unjust enrichment, she would have to make some allowances for the work the decorator had done. Either he could claim a change of position that would make it unjust for him to have to return the *full* payment, or he could claim counter-restitution from the homeowner for the value of his services.

This reform would change the boundary between cases where the claimant is on the losing side of a commercial deal, and cases where there has been a misconceived transfer of property. Reformists find support for their claims in the law's current response where contracts are either frustrated or void, rather than terminated by one of the parties. A contract is *frustrated* when reasonable performance is made impossible because of unexpected circumstances, and the law then excuses further performance by either party. In effect, the contract is terminated by operation of law. For example, the claimant may pay her decorator in advance, only to have a fire destroy her house. Both parties' future performance is then excused because the contract has been frustrated. In these circumstances, a statute now ensures that the total failure of consideration limitation does not apply in assessing recovery by each party from the other.[15] Similarly, where the purported contract between the parties is *void* (usually because a statute treats the bargain as ineffective on public policy grounds), so that contract law never governs the relationship between the parties, then the total failure of consideration limitation does not apply in assessing the unjust enrichment recovery by each party from the other.[16] In short, the 'total failure' limitation is decried because it applies only if the contract is terminated by one of the parties, not if it is excluded by law (as it is with frustrated and void contracts).

This proposed expansion of unjust enrichment law to include cases of partial failure of consideration involves a policy choice, however, and there are cogent arguments on both sides. What is at stake is the boundary between recoverable transfers and binding transfers. This boundary must balance security of the claimant's original ownership against security of the defendant's subsequent receipt. As already noted, the law could quite sensibly allow recovery only if the claimant's intention was vitiated. It goes further. It *sometimes* allows recovery if the claimant's transfer was intended, but conditional, or qualified, and there has been a failure of basis or failure of consideration. Not every failure of basis, or failure of consideration, is accepted, otherwise the defendant would have no security of receipt. A coherent legal response might want to distinguish between contracts terminated by the parties and contracts terminated by operation of law: the claimant's transfer could be considered misconceived if there was no contract because *the law* negates the contractual engagement, but not if *the parties* negate it. Equally, the

[15] Law Reform (Frustrated Contracts) Act 1943. See *BP Exploration Co (Lybia) Ltd v Hunt (No 2)* [1979] 1 WLR 783 (QB).
[16] *Westdeutsche Landesbank Girozentrale v Islington LBC* [1996] AC 669 (HL).

line could be drawn elsewhere. However, the line must be drawn so that like cases are treated alike and different cases are treated in defensibly different ways.

This is not as easy as it sounds. The modern debates are testament to this. Indeed, these debates suggest that 'failure of consideration' may not quite capture the essence of unjust enrichment law's second limiting concept. Take a simple example. Suppose the purported contract between the homeowner and her decorator is void (perhaps because some statute insists that it must be in writing and it is not). Despite this, suppose the decorator completes his job perfectly and the homeowner pays in full. When both parties have received precisely what they bargained for, it seems hard to argue that there has been a 'failure of basis', or 'failure of consideration' (in the special unjust enrichment sense). Nevertheless, here the law *will* unwind the deal, insisting that the defendant has been unjustly enriched by receipt of the payment for his job and, equally, that the claimant has been unjustly enriched by the work the decorator has done. Both must make restitution. This seems contrary to the 'failure of consideration' rationale, yet the courts insist that restitution is warranted because there has been a *total* failure of consideration.[17]

From all of this, it is clear that these orthodox mechanisms for differentiating between effective and misconceived transfers come with analytical difficulties. With 'vitiated intention', the problem is defining and defending the wide reach of mistake. With 'failure of consideration', it is explaining the counter-intuitive response to partial failures of consideration in terminated contracts, and to full performance in void contracts. These difficulties might be resolved by adopting a slightly different approach to the two foundation mechanisms themselves.

A PROPOSED REFORMULATED MODEL

Recall that these mechanisms are needed to differentiate between misconceived transfers, where recovery is allowed, and binding transfers, where it is not. If the mechanisms are too restrictive, the original owner's security of ownership will be undervalued; if they are too liberal, the defendant's security of receipt will be undervalued. It certainly seems

---

[17] *Guinness Mahon & Co Ltd v Kensington and Chelsea Royal London Borough Council* [1999] QB 215 (CA). More rigorous academic analysts suggest result is best explained on the basis that both parties have made mistakes (of law) in assuming, wrongly, that their deal was binding; restitution could then be ordered on the basis of 'vitiated intention', not 'failure of consideration'. This analysis might work now, but recovery was routinely allowed in these cases long before the courts recognized that mistake of law could ground recovery.

right that a defendant should make restitution of his enrichment if the claimant did not intend the transfer at all. It also seems right, however, and eminently desirable, to adopt the same test of intention as that used in the law of gifts and promises to determine whether those commitments are legally recognized. To do otherwise puts claimants in the schizophrenic position that, at law, their intention to enter into a contract or make a gift may be legally binding, but their intention to effect the transfer that implements the contract or gift may be vitiated.[18] The reformulated model therefore proposes measuring intention in the same way as it is measured in other areas of the law of obligations. It discards the possibility of a wide conception of 'mistake' and the difficult disjunction between causal mistakes and causal mispredictions. In short, it replaces the liberal concept of 'vitiated intention' with the much narrower concept of *'unintended transfer'*, and measures intention in familiar ways.

Reformulating the second mechanism is trickier. The difficulty is that the orthodox 'failure of basis' or 'failure of consideration' cannot easily draw a defensible distinction between misconceived transfers and binding transfers without overextending the compass of the former. The problem is not the claimant's intention, but the qualification of it. One clear way to distinguish between completely misconceived transfers (where recovery is allowed) and losing commercial deals (where it is not) is to allow recovery only when the claimant did intend the transfer, but objectively intended it as an engagement in some commercial risk, not as the gift that it now turns out to be. An unintended gift is qualitatively, and dramatically, different from a failed commercial risk. Accordingly, the reformulated model proposes replacing 'failure of consideration' with the much tighter test of *'unintended gift'*. Notice that if this model were adopted, our mistaken gas board customer would be dealt with under this second mechanism, not the first. Her transfer is perfectly properly intended, but intended as a commercial engagement, not as the gift it now turns out to be.

---

[18] Note that the focus here is on the law's recognition of binding *intention*. It is not on the quite separate question of whether legal title to the underlying property has been transferred. Legal title can be transferred even though the claimant does not have a legally recognized intention to transfer (see Chapter 7, 204–19, although the law will then provide the claimant with remedies in unjust enrichment), and, equally, legal title may remain with the claimant even though she has a perfectly proper intention to transfer (as when she fails to fulfil the other requirements for an effective transfer of property; see Chapter 7, 202–4).

It is possible to detect the germ of this idea of 'unintended gifts' in an analysis that enjoyed a few months' popularity—and probably even then only minority popularity—in the early 1990s, before being soundly quashed in favour of the 'failure of consideration' approach.[19] The rejected analysis of the 1990s suggested that restitution was available whenever there was an *'absence of consideration'* for the transfer (using consideration in its orthodox contractual sense). Put another way, restitution was available for transfers that turned out to be by way of gift. The approach suffered because the reason behind the suggestion was never articulated: the goal of distinguishing between misconceived transfers and binding commercial deals was never identified. Critics went further, and suggested that the approach was unacceptable because too much restitution would result. To reinforce the point, it was suggested that all valid gifts would have to be returned: they would all meet the 'absence of consideration' test. This deliberately misrepresents the test, which was clearly never meant to catch *intended* gifts; it was intended to catch transfers where there was no legal consideration *and* no gift was intended. Put like this, the test resonates with civilian law unjust enrichment rationales. It was criticized for this, too, even though the common law has many civilian parallels in both legal rules and legal rationales.

This simple reformulation, resorting to the mechanisms of 'unintended transfer' and 'unintended gift', delivers results that are consistent with decided cases. Significantly, it does so using the same concepts of intention and consideration used throughout the rest of the law of obligations. Perhaps most importantly, and surprisingly, however, it also subtly mirrors the precise rationales adopted by Equity to explain its delivery of remedies for unjust enrichment. It therefore makes it possible to effect a sensible and coherent integration of Equity and the Common Law. Before considering these Common Law and Equity issues, it is useful to compare the operation of the reformulated and orthodox rules.

THE ORTHODOX MODEL AND THE REFORMULATED MODEL COMPARED

The first mechanisms are easily compared. 'Unintended transfer' differs from its orthodox counterpart, 'vitiated consent', in that it does not

[19] See the judgments of the trial judge (Hobhouse J) and the Court of Appeal in *Westdeutsche Landesbank Girozentrale v Islington LBC* [1994] 1 WLR 938. But contrast the opinion of the House of Lords on appeal: *Westdeutsche Landesbank Girozentrale v Islington LBC* [1996] AC 669 (HL).

embrace unilateral mistakes of fact or law, no matter how significant they are in causing the claimant to effect the transfer. The claimant's intention is only impaired, and the transfer is only unintended for unjust enrichment purposes, on the same narrow grounds as those adopted when determining whether contracts and gifts are properly intended. The wider cases of mistake must be dealt with, if at all, under the second mechanism.

The second mechanisms, 'unintended gift' and 'failure of consideration', require more unravelling. The first thing to notice is that the reformulated test characterizes the transaction, not the outcome. It allows the claimant to say, 'I did not mean to make a gift to you; that was plain to all, yet, in the circumstances that is what this transfer is.' Our claimant can say this to the gas board; she cannot usually say it to her decorator.[20] The legal distinction is subtle. It depends upon what the defendant is *obliged* to give the claimant in return for her transfer (i.e. the nature of the transaction), not on what he in fact gives her (i.e. the practical outcome). With the gas board, the claimant's payment is not matched by any obligation on the part of the gas board to do anything for her: there is no consideration at all. This means that the payment is a gift when a gift was clearly not intended. The payment is a misconceived transfer, not an intended engagement with a particular commercial risk. Note that the claimant succeeds simply because she did not intend the transfer to be by way of gift; she does not need to show that she did not intend the transfer itself; indeed, this would be contrary to the facts. The situation with the decorator is different. The decorator is obliged to paint the house. The claimant's advance payment to him is not a gift; it is a payment in return for his obligation to paint. Her complaint is not (usually) that she has made an unintended gift; it is that her decorator has inadequately performed his contractual obligations, and this is where her remedies lie, in an action for breach of contract.

This focus on the nature of the transaction, not its practical outcome, allows the 'unintended gift' analysis to draw a sharp dividing line between misconceived transfers and losing commercial deals. This reduces the risk of 'too much restitution', and its associated undermining of the defendant's security of receipt. However, the 'unintended gift' analysis also neatly explains why restitution is allowed for contracts terminated by the parties on a *total* failure of consideration, but not otherwise. Recall our decorator. If the claimant pays him in advance and he refuses to

---

[20] But see the next paragraph.

perform, then she can terminate his contract. The contract stands with full force up to the date of termination, but all the obligations after that date are cancelled. This means that the claimant has paid her money but the decorator is not obliged (or entitled[21]) to provide any counter-performance; she has made a gift where no gift was intended. She can therefore demand restitution. On the other hand, if the decorator performs *any* part of his contract (even if the contract is terminated later on), then the claimant cannot run this argument. She has paid her money, but not by way of gift. Importantly, the claimant is taken to have received part of the promised performance as soon as the defendant begins to undertake the work he has agreed to do; it is irrelevant whether the claimant physically receives some end-product.[22] Recall the earlier example of a claimant who employs an architect to remodel her house. She cannot argue that her pre-payment is a gift if the architect starts work on the plans, even if he does not deliver any work to the claimant before the contract is terminated. In short, if the claimant receives any part of the promised performance, then the 'unintended gift' analysis is inapt; the claimant will be confined to her action for breach of contract.

The 'unintended gift' analysis thus provides a sharp dividing line between unjust enrichment cases (misconceived transfers) and contract cases (commercial risks). It is important to realize that even this more restricted restitutionary response is not a matter of logical necessity. It reflects a positive choice to extend the reach of unjust enrichment claims to allow the unravelling of some transfers even though they are perfectly properly intended. Some will disagree that the law should go so far, although the extension is a long-standing one; others will think that it does not go far enough, although to its credit it marks an easily and objectively identifiable boundary that enhances the protection of title while still prioritizing security of receipt. Notice too that this 'unintended gift' analysis is easily adapted to deal with different and more complicated contract structures. For example, it can accommodate divisible contracts (where the contract can effectively be divided into sub-contracts, each of which is then subjected to this analysis[23]) and

[21] Although see the controversial decision in *White & Carter (Councils) Ltd v McGregor* [1962] AC 413 (HL).
[22] The orthodox 'failure of consideration' test has problems explaining this result: if the claimant herself receives nothing, it sees reasonable to suggest that the basis of her transfer has failed.
[23] Long-term supply contracts provide a ready illustration: each monthly instalment and its corresponding payment can be regarded as an independent element of the contractual engagement.

entire contracts (where performance is only regarded as such if the entire benefit is delivered[24]). These alternative structures are founded on the parties' clear intentions to allocate their commercial risks more specifically. The 'unintended gift' analysis, with its conscious recognition that the agenda is to identify transfers that are fundamentally misconceived, better reflects the issues at stake in these cases.

Finally, the reformulated analysis can also explain the law's response when the parties' contract is void. Recall that contracts may be void because one or both parties, objectively, lacks the necessary intention to contract.[25] In these cases, the law refuses to identify a legally binding intention to contract or, for the same reasons, to effect any related transfer of property. The claimant can then argue that the transfer was an 'unintended transfer'. This same argument must also be possible when a statute denies one or other party the capacity to engage in the relevant dealing. Statutes typically impose such limitations on minors, the mentally incapacitated, and certain corporations.[26] No matter how much these parties wish to engage in the prohibited transactions, the law denies them capacity to do so; their purported contracts are void. These parties can, thereafter, insist that by law they lack the capacity to form the necessary intention to enter the contract or effect the transfer. Their transfer is then an 'unintended transfer', and recovery is allowed according to the rules of the law of unjust enrichment. Notice that only the incapacitated party can raise this argument; the

---

[24] *Appleby v Myers* (1867) LR 2 CP 651; *Sumpter v Hedges* [1898] 1 QB 673 (CA). Some major construction contracts are deliberately structured in this way so that the manufacturer carries the risk of his own non-performance. A contract for the construction of a ship or an aircraft, for example, may make it plain that the manufacturer will not be regarded as having performed *at all* until full performance is delivered. In these cases the 'unintended gift' (and the 'failure of consideration') analyses can be applied even if the breach that permits the purchaser to terminate occurs part way through the manufacturer's performance of his obligations. Strictly, the issue is one of determining 'entire *obligations*', not 'entire *contracts*': an 'entire obligation' may require delivery of the completed ship; it is unlikely to require absolute compliance with standards of due care. It then follows that failure to deliver a completed ship means that no part of the price becomes payable; by contrast, delivery of a completed, but defective, ship means the price *is* payable, but with a set-off for damages for defective performance (although see *Bolton v Mahadeva* [1972] 1 WLR 1009 (CA)).

[25] See Chapter 7, 204–6.

[26] 'The commercial unattractiveness of this is now well recognized in corporate law, and 'lack of capacity' is now largely a matter for the internal management of a company. The company can pursue remedies against unauthorized directors, but outsiders are protected, and their contracts with the company are binding: Companies Act 1985, s. 35. This reform illustrates the competing issues in striking an appropriate balance between effective and misconceived transfers.

other party is likely to have participated with a properly recognizable legal intention.[27]

Not all void contracts are like this, however. Statutes often render contracts void without any suggestion that the capacity of the participants is in any way compromised. Contracts for the transfer of land are void unless they are in writing, for example; the identity or legal capacity of the parties is irrelevant. With these void contracts, as with every void contract, any performance is necessarily given without the other party being legally obliged to render counter-performance. Each party is unintentionally making a gift to the other. Each should therefore be able to recover in unjust enrichment. This response only seems counter-intuitive when both parties have *fully* performed. Technically, it is true, there is an 'unintended gift' in both directions. In reality, however, the intended commercial risk has been realized: both parties have obtained precisely what they 'contracted' for. In these circumstances it seems odd to allow the parties to justify recovery by arguing that they intended to engage with a commercial risk, not to make a gift. Public policy may provide the key. Refusing to allow the parties to unwind their completed deal would amount to passive enforcement of an engagement prohibited by statute. This, too, seems counter-intuitive. Allowing these restitutionary claims best supports the legal policy that rendered the transfers void in the first place. The only exception is when legal policy suggests that inaction *is* the best response, and then, but only then (usually when the parties have embarked on some illegal scheme in defiance of the statutory prohibitions), are the parties *not* allowed to unwind the deal.[28]

This analysis of void contracts suggests that parties may sometimes be able to choose whether to claim restitution on the basis of the 'unintended transfer' test *or* the 'unintended gift' test. If the remedies are the same, the choice is immaterial. The remedies may be different, however, and the choice then has significance.[29]

To summarize, and to put the differences most starkly, the current orthodox approach to restitution for unjust enrichment allows restitution where the claimant's 'intention to transfer' is vitiated, or where the 'basis for the transfer' has failed. Both grounds are assessed subjectively. There

---

[27] See below, 303–9, for the potential impact of this reformulated approach in cases such as *Westdeutsche Landesbank Girozentrale v Islington LBC* [1996] AC 669 (HL), where the Council lacked capacity to contract.

[28] See the discussion in *Pavey and Matthews Pty Ltd v Paul* (1987) 162 CLR 221 (Aust HCt). Recall similar arguments in Chapter 8, 259–61.

[29] See below, 307–9.

are limits, of course, but generally the claimant is allowed to say that her intention was *in fact* flawed, or that she has not received the counter-performance or consideration she *in fact* expected. Intention and consideration are therefore defined more liberally than in the rest of the law of obligations. By contrast, the reformulated analysis suggested here uses the same narrow, objective definitions of intention and consideration that are familiar elsewhere in the law of obligations. It allows a claimant to demand restitution only if the transfer itself was unintended or, alternatively, if the intended transfer was an unintended gift. Both grounds are assessed objectively. A transfer is only unintended if the claimant lacked any legally recognized intention to make the transfer. Alternatively, the transfer is an unintended gift if, objectively, and notwithstanding the claimant's unimpaired intention to transfer, both parties understood that there would be some counter-performance, and instead the circumstances have ensured that the transaction operates as a gift.

It is true that the results will often be the same regardless of which analytical framework is adopted. This is so with our gas board customer: she will recover in any event, although the analysis differs radically depending upon which approach is adopted. At the margins, however, the answers will be different: the wider orthodox approach will allow recovery where the narrower reformulated approach will not. More importantly, the wider orthodox approach aligns less well with Equitable explanations dealt with later in this chapter.

COMMON LAW AND EQUITY DISJUNCTIONS IN CORRECTING MISCONCEIVED TRANSFERS

So far the analysis has not touched on Common Law and Equitable jurisdictional divides, yet some of the most hard-fought debates over the past decade have concerned the disjunctions between the Common Law and Equitable responses to unjust enrichment. Common Law and Equity give different answers to unjust enrichment questions. This is true regardless of the chosen analytical framework. Some of these differences have already been exposed in earlier chapters.

Take 'unintended transfers'.[30] The Common Law and Equity have evolved different rules for determining whether a claimant's intention to

---

[30] Precisely the same differences apply to the orthodox test of 'vitiated intention', ignoring for the moment its expansive view of mistake. In that, too, there are historical Common Law and Equity differences, although modern developments are effectively eliminating these: see Chapter 7, 204–19.

transfer property is legally effective. Despite this, the combined jurisdictional effort presents a generally rational and coherent profile, clearly founded on broadly consistent policy objectives.[31] The overarching rule suggests that the claimant lacks a legally effective intention to transfer if, objectively, intention is lacking, or if, subjectively, it is lacking and the defendant is somehow responsible for its absence. Especially at the subjective level, the Common Law and Equity hold the defendant responsible for the claimant's flawed intention in different circumstances, adopting different tests for misrepresentation and for unacceptable economic or social pressure. Equity sometimes takes these ideas further by *presuming* that the claimant was subjected to unwarranted pressure for which the defendant was responsible. The claimant will then be saved from having to prove the point, although the defendant is free to rebut it. All of these legal developments are incorporated into the test for misconceived transfers: a transfer is unintended if, and only if, it meets one or other of these common law tests of impaired intention.

There are also Common Law and Equity disjunctions in assessing 'unintended gifts'. The Common Law adopts a purely objective approach to determining whether the claimant intended the transfer to operate by way of gift. Equity, by contrast, adopts certain presumptions. In most cases, Equity presumes that the claimant did *not* intend a gift; in rare cases it presumes that she did. It then leaves it to the disappointed party to present evidence to rebut the presumption.[32] In this way, Equity either makes it easier (with presumptions of resulting trust) or harder (with presumptions of advancement) for a claimant to demand restitution. All of this is easily accommodated within an integrated map of the common law: restitution is warranted where the claimant has made an unintended gift, and that fact can be proved with the assistance (or otherwise) of Equitable presumptions.

These disjunctions between Common Law and Equity are trivial in comparison with the disjunctions that exist in *implementing* restitution. So important and controversial are these that, one way or another, they occupy most of the rest of this chapter. As is so often the case, the division lies in the delivery of personal and proprietary remedies. The simplistic (and slightly inaccurate) perception is that restitution operates as a personal remedy at Common Law but a proprietary remedy in Equity. Suppose the claimant transfers her car to the defendant. At Common Law, even if the deal is so badly misconceived that at Common Law title

---

[31] See Chapter 7, 211–14.   [32] See Chapter 8, 258–9.

either remains with the claimant or revests in her later on, she still only has a *right* to a money remedy, not to specific recovery of her property.[33] To date there has been little offered by way of explanation or justification for this state of affairs. In Equity, by contrast, the claimant is regarded as the Equitable owner of any property that was the subject of the mis-conceived transfer. She is then automatically deemed able to demand its specific recovery,[34] and has the benefit of all the protections and privileges commonly associated with proprietary status.[35]

This remedial difference means that when there are serious reasons for unwinding a transaction and ordering restitution (reasons which are so blatant that the Common Law has long recognized them), then the rem-edy is personal. When the reasons for unwinding the transaction are less evident (reasons which Equity has developed over time by adopting a more attenuated view of the circumstances), then the remedy is propri-etary. Proprietary remedies are more advantageous to claimants than per-sonal remedies, so this disjunction means that interests which have a lesser status or are more fragile receive better protection than interests which are more compelling. This seems irrational. It suggests that the common law's dualistic jurisdictional model has led to a sub-optimal end-product. The rules and their rationales need to be more coherently integrated.

The drive for analytical coherence has led to some radical changes already. Very recent cases have turned settled perceptions upside down by suggesting that Equity does not, and should not, deliver proprietary rem-edies in at least some of these unjust enrichment cases. The pressure for change is clear, and the implication is that integration should pursue the Common Law model, not its Equitable counterpart. However, the oppos-ite strategy is also possible, at least in theory. These are difficult, but important, issues.

POLICY ISSUES IN PROPRIETARY RECOVERY

The first concern is policy. If the preferred outcome is not proprietary status for unjust enrichment claimants, then its elimination should be pursued. Contrary historical precedent should not be allowed to stand in the way of beneficial reform. Take our previous example. If the claimant's

---

[33] See Chapter 6, 169–72.
[34] Although see Chapter 6, 172–4, for criticisms of this general assumption.
[35] See Chapter 4, 87–9.

transfer of her car is misconceived, should the defendant hold the car on trust for her or should he simply be obliged to hand over its value? There are three principal arguments against a proprietary response. However, none seems entirely compelling. Indeed, on the contrary, a privileged, preferred proprietary response seems to be perfectly consistent with the law's usual protective stance in guarding ownership interests.[36]

The first argument against proprietary intervention is the most dramatic, but the most easily dismissed. Equitable proprietary remedies are regarded as unacceptable in the unjust enrichment context because, it is suggested, they would automatically and unfairly impose trustee-type liability on the defendant.[37] This concern is only persuasive if the property split in an Equitable proprietary remedy is necessarily associated with personal trustee liability. This is most unlikely. The possibilities were considered in detail in earlier chapters.[38] In most cases, the unjust enrichment defendant will be in the same position as any other innocent third party holding the claimant's property. Unless he has the requisite knowledge, he will not be a fiduciary, with all that entails,[39] and the claimant's proprietary insolvency protection will persist in substitute assets only to the extent that this is consistent with the defendant's own equally valuable proprietary rights.[40]

The second argument against proprietary intervention is broader. Proprietary remedies are seen as unacceptable because they create uncertainty. When the defendant receives the claimant's property, he is rarely aware that her transfer was misconceived. To then insist that the property is not his but the claimant's (at least in Equity), will, it is argued, expose both him and any third parties with whom he deals to unwarranted commercial risks. This reflects the popular view that parties should not be faced with undisclosed or 'off balance sheet' risks: the ownership of assets should be clear to all. However, this ideal state is not possible even with interests created consensually between parties. Security arrangements, leasing agreements, retention of title schemes, and such like are often opaque to strangers. This fuels claims for compulsory registration schemes. But unjust enrichment proprietary remedies, if they are to exist at all, will arise by operation of law. They cannot possibly be subjected to any notification system. The parties themselves are usually ignorant of

---

[36] See Chapter 4, 98–106, especially.
[37] *Westdeutsche Landesbank Girozentrale v Islington LBC* [1996] AC 669 (HL). See Chapter 5.
[38] See Chapter 6, 180–2.   [39] See Chapter 5, 129–34.
[40] See Chapter 4, 113–16.

their existence until well after the events that generate them. Because of this insoluble problem of transparency, the suggestion is that these interests should not exist at all.[41] This may be an overreaction. Proprietary remedies are the law's mechanism for valuing and protecting rights. If unjust enrichment remedies were made exclusively personal, then property ownership rights themselves would be correspondingly downgraded. As for third parties, proprietary rights generated by unjust enrichment claims will only prevail against volunteers or against third-party purchasers who have notice of the claimant's interests. This seems to provide relatively restrained protection of the claimant's interests when they are in competition with third parties' interests.

The third and final argument against proprietary remedies for unjust enrichment claimants tackles head-on the value of the rights at stake. The allegation is that preferential (proprietary) protection of the claimant's unjust enrichment rights is unwarranted, and is indeed commercially unacceptable. The argument is invariably advanced by analogy. Unjust enrichment claimants are compared with contract claimants, especially unsecured creditors. The supplier of goods who did not intend the transfer at all (the unjust enrichment claimant) should be in no better position than the supplier of goods who did not intend the transfer to be unpaid (the contract claimant). In both cases, it is argued, the defendant has acquired increased wealth at the claimant's expense, and there is no reason why the unjust enrichment claimant should be privileged in her recovery; all should have to share in the insolvency losses equally. This argument treats the competing legal rights as equally valuable, and suggests that personal remedies suffice for all.[42]

By contrast, the counter-argument necessarily privileges the unjust enrichment rights. This stance is best justified by basic economic analysis, but it has the added advantage of mapping consistently onto the existing common law landscape. Property law itself is based on the idea that society's wealth is maximized if property is appropriately protected. This strategy suggests that claimants should have control over their own resources, and that transfers should not stand if (in unjust enrichment terms) 'the claimant did not intend the defendant to have the property in the circumstances'. Assets that have been unintentionally transferred should be returned. Strong proprietary protection is warranted in the

---

[41] *Westdeutsche Landesbank Girozentrale v Islington LBC* [1996] AC 669 (HL).

[42] Tort claimants may appear to be sidelined in this analysis, but no matter how highly the tort claimant's rights are valued, privileged protection is impossible (other than by statute) because there is no asset that could sensibly stand as security for the damages claim.

interests of preserving property to ensure greater productivity for all. Assessed from this perspective, unjust enrichment claimants are in an altogether different position from contract claimants. Contract claimants have made an economic decision about the risks and benefits associated with an arrangement that is enforceable by both participants. The law should certainly protect them against procedural unfairness,[43] and it should support performance and provide substitute remedies (i.e. damages), but it need not protect these claimants from the inherent risk that the counter-party might not be *able* to perform. In short, unjust enrichment claimants could, quite rationally, be privileged over contract claimants by giving the former, but not the latter, a preferred right to recover the property that was theirs originally. Indeed, later sections in this chapter suggest that this preferred treatment *is* the primary approach of both the Common Law and Equity to many unjust enrichment claims (although the Common Law does not then deliver specific restitution of the asset itself).

Even if it is conceded that differentiation between unjust enrichment rights and contract rights is apt, the reach of the associated privileges remains controversial.[44] Although hierarchies of rights are a natural feature of any mature legal system, the precise attributes of the privileged class are a matter of hard-fought debate. Suppose the defendant is insolvent. A strict policy of *pari passu* distribution would favour forcing all claimants to shoulder a proportionate share of the losses regardless of the relative ranking of their respective rights. The common law chooses, instead, to discriminate. It favours those with proprietary claims, shifting an increased burden to those with personal claims. This has always been a controversial policy choice, made all the more controversial because the divide between personal and proprietary rights is narrowing and because even those holding preferred rights lose their privileges if the defendant no longer has the relevant asset or its traceable substitutes. The controversies multiply in questions about whether these privileges should persist in substitute assets, and whether they should permit the capture of any windfall gains generated by such substitutions. Some of these issues have already been aired; some will emerge later in this chapter.[45]

For now, what matters is that the policy arguments are not unequivocally against privileged proprietary protection for unjust enrichment

[43] See Chapter 7, 204–6.   [44] See Chapter 6, 179–89, and Chapter 8, 254–64.
[45] See Chapter 4, 98–110 and below, 310–15.

claimants. Indeed, there may be sound economic reasons for privileging these claims over other claims.

'UNINTENDED TRANSFERS'—DOCTRINAL ISSUES IN PROPRIETARY RECOVERY

Now it is time to turn from policy to doctrine, starting with the simplest cases. The reformulated analysis posits a first class of misconceived transfers comprising 'unintended transfers'. Such transfers may be objectively unintended (and therefore void) or subjectively unintended in circumstances where the defendant is somehow responsible for the claimant's misconception (and therefore voidable, not void). The focus here is on the remedial response of unjust enrichment law to these unintended transfers. It turns out that this response is unambiguously proprietary, both at Common Law and in Equity (even though any Common Law revesting of title does not then entitle the claimant to specific recovery of the asset).

An unintended transfer can be made by way of gift or contract. Unintended gifts are simpler to deal with. The only concern then is the claimant's remedy for her misconceived transfer. With contracts, the issues are more complicated. True, the claimant still wants a remedy for her misconceived transfer, but she may have received assets from the defendant as part of his performance of the purported contract. The law will not allow her to unravel her side of the unintended contractual engagement unless she is in a position to look after the defendant's interests in remedying his own transfer. This requirement for proper counter-restitution to the defendant can impose severe practical limitations on the availability of restitutionary remedies.

OBJECTIVELY UNINTENDED TRANSFERS— VOID TRANSFERS

Transfers are objectively unintended if the claimant is mistaken about the identity of the recipient or the identity of the asset being transferred. These transfers are so flawed that even the Common Law regards them as void.[46] The unjust enrichment response is then undeniably proprietary: the starting assumption is that title to the asset never passes from claimant to defendant. However, the particulars are affected by the nature of the property transferred, and this creates some unexpected anomalies, both for claimants and for third parties.

---

[46] See Chapter 7, 206–7.

Consider goods. If the claimant transfers goods to the defendant, then the defendant obtains possession but the void transfer does not pass the legal title.[47] Title to goods only passes if physical delivery is accompanied by the appropriate legal intention to effect the transfer, and that is lacking here. However, even though the claimant retains legal title, she cannot necessarily recover the goods themselves; she is generally restricted to damages for their conversion if the defendant refuses to redeliver them.[48] It follows that what seems to be the strongest possible Common Law proprietary protection in the face of her misconceived transfer affords her little real control over her own property. Matters are quite different if the property is land or shares, however. Then legal title passes when the transfer is formally registered, however unintentionally. Predictably, Equity insists that the defendant does not enjoy beneficial ownership of property transferred like this; he holds the property on trust for the claimant. This makes a difference. A claimant with Equitable title, not legal title, is assumed able to recover her property *in specie*.[49] Finally, if it is money that is unintentionally transferred, then strict doctrine suggests that legal title does not pass to the defendant. If the defendant mixes this money with his own money, however, then the Common Law, which cannot trace into mixtures, regards legal title as then vested in the defendant, although the claimant retains an Equitable lien on the mixture and can demand realization of her security.[50]

This strongly protective proprietary response to objectively unintended transfers is widely conceded to be apt to meet the law's underlying policy objectives. It favours security of the claimant's original ownership over security of the defendant's receipt in engagements that are fundamentally misconceived. The response is not without its theoretical and practical difficulties, however. At the theoretical level, it has been suggested that if legal title does not pass to the defendant (and maybe even if legal title does pass, but Equitable title does not), then the defendant is not enriched by the transfer, and so the problem cannot belong within the law of unjust enrichment. This matters. Liability rules and defences follow categorization. In correcting misconceived transfers, however, a strong

---

[47] *Ingram v Little* [1961] 1 QB 31 (CA).

[48] Although see Chapter 6, 169–74 and Torts (Interference with Goods) Act 1977, s. 3. See the valuation problems in *Greenwood v Bennett* [1973] 1 QB 195. But explicit reference to claims in unjust enrichment and restitutionary remedies are emerging: *Kuwait Airways Corp v Iraqi Airways Co (No 6)* [2002] AC 883 (HL).

[49] Although see Chapter 6, 168–72.

[50] A lien seems correct in these circumstances, although some argue for proportionate Equitable ownership: see below, 310–12.

and pro-active property response (evident both at Common Law and in Equity) is simply one of several weapons in the law's armoury. Indeed, the fact that the law's response *is* pro-active and immediate, rather than reactive and deferred until the parties seek a remedy in court, might be seen as a measure of the significance of the rights at stake. All the responses considered in this chapter reinforce this as the preferred approach of the common law to misconceived transfers.

The practical difficulties touch various parties. For claimants, one critical issue is the availability of alternative money remedies (i.e. substitute personal remedies) if the defendant no longer has the property that was transferred unintentionally.[51] Suppose the property is a car, but the defendant crashes it, or gives it to his daughter, before the claimant can pursue her claim in unjust enrichment for its misconceived transfer. Surprisingly, early courts never countenanced the possibility of money substituting for recovery of the property itself; they would *not* simply order the defendant to make restitution of, say, £8,000[52] if he no longer had the car.[53] The same rule applied to goods, land, shares, and such like. The Common Law allegedly refused to intervene because it only ordered money damages in response to a legal wrong, and this is not the gist of an unjust enrichment claim. Equity would not intervene because it only ordered money remedies on account, and an account will not be ordered except in relation to some underlying property.[54] The result is that the claimant might be left without an unjust enrichment remedy, and without a remedy at all unless she can pursue alternative claims in contract or tort. Given this, the law's long-standing response when the claimant's unintended transfer concerns *money* is exceptional. Then it is irrelevant whether the original fund remains identifiable in the defendant's hands: the claimant is invariably entitled to a substitute personal money remedy in unjust enrichment.

Whatever the advantages of strong proprietary protection of unjust enrichment claims, the historical corollary that equivalent substitute

---

[51] Substitute *property* remedies are discussed below, 310–12.

[52] Quantified to reflect any defences the defendant might be able to advance.

[53] In the very restricted category of cases under consideration here, legal title to the car does not pass to the defendant. The claimant is therefore in the fortunate position of having an action in conversion against the defendant, and this persists regardless of whether the defendant retains the car in his possession. Moreover, this is a strict liability wrong, not subject to the range of defences that apply to unjust enrichment claims, so there is little practical need for a personal remedy in unjust enrichment. The doctrinal disjunction remains, however.

[54] See the same issue in relation to fiduciaries, Chapter 6, 174–8.

money remedies are generally unavailable seems questionable. Equity's restraint no doubt reflects early jurisdictional battles. The analogous Common Law response is harder to justify. It does not seem to be based on any rigorous analysis or principles. The contradictory response when the claimant's asset is money reinforces this. Now that unjust enrichment law is better analysed, and especially since it has a newly discovered rigorous and systematic approach to defences, there should be little impediment to the development of a principled personal money response to reinforce the usual proprietary response to unjust enrichment claims. The need for this legal development becomes even more apparent in the later sections of this chapter.

The claimant is not the only party affected by the common law's strong proprietary response to this type of misconceived transfer. If the defendant transfers the relevant property, anyone in the subsequent chain of dealings from him may be affected. These subsequent transfers are not inevitably and necessarily misconceived, so third parties are not usually subjected to unjust enrichment claims from the claimant.[55] Nevertheless, these third parties may be exposed to various alternative claims. If the defendant did not receive good title from the original owner (because of the unjust enrichment rules applying to the misconceived transfer), then the third party's title may also be flawed. The original owner and the third party may then dispute ownership of the property. This is a property dispute, raising issues of conflicts or priority; it is not a dispute within the law of obligations.[56] Property can also be important on another front. Common Law conversion is a strict liability tort, so third parties receiving property that belongs, legally, to the claimant can be sued in conversion.

When the initial transfer from claimant to defendant is objectively unintended, these property rules affect third parties in different ways depending upon the nature of the property transferred. In the interests of treating like cases alike, these differences do not always seems defensible. Again, the differences between goods, land, shares, and money are illustrative. With goods, the defendant does not receive legal title to the

---

[55] Although some unjust enrichment theorists focus on the question of the third party's 'enrichment at the claimant's expense', and persuade themselves that the third party's gain is, factually, at the original claimant's expense. This seems analytically suspect, given the principles underpinning unjust enrichment law, unless very special facts (such as the defendant's agency) suggest that the transfer to the third party was an unintended transfer or an unintended gift *from the claimant*. The orthodox reliance on 'vitiated consent' or 'failure of basis' does not assist the argument.

[56] See Chapter 4, 92–7.

goods, so nor do subsequent transferees (recall the *nemo dat* rule[57]). As a result, these third parties are strictly liable to the original claimant in the tort of conversion, whether or not they still have the goods in their possession.[58] If the property is land, shares or money, however, then the third party is better protected. He will take completely free of the original claimant's interest if he is a bona fide purchaser for value without notice of the claimant's Equitable interest.[59] If he is a donee, he is exposed to title conflict and priority claims while he still has the property, but once he does not then he is unlikely to be personally liable as a 'knowing recipient' unless his knowledge of the claimant's competing interest warrants this.[60] This latter approach seems to provide a better balance between the claimant's interest in security of ownership and the defendant's and subsequent transferees' interests in security of receipt. The same is clearly not true for goods. The Common Law's strict liability rules for conversion cause a ripple effect that seems to catch too many unwary transferees.

SUBJECTIVELY UNINTENDED TRANSFERS—VOIDABLE TRANSFERS

The second type of 'unintended transfer' occurs when the claimant's transfer is subjectively unintended, and the defendant is somehow responsible for the claimant's errors. The claimant may have transferred her house or shares or goods, but done so only because of the defendant's misrepresentation or duress or undue influence. These engagements are voidable, not void: the transfer is initially effective, and the defendant obtains legal and beneficial title to the property, but only until such time as the claimant elects to unwind (or 'rescind', or 'avoid') the transfer.[61] Only after rescission does the claimant have any chance of recovering legal or Equitable title to her property. This two-stage process, where the position is different before and after the claimant's decision to rescind the transfer, means that the proprietary consequences of subjectively unintended transfers are different from the consequences of objectively unintended transfers (where the transfer is simply void). Indeed, the picture is further complicated because the Common Law and Equity have different rules about whether a transfer is subjectively unintended in this way, and whether rescission should be allowed in any event.

---

[57] See Chapter 4, 93–4.   [58] *Cundy v Lindsay* (1878) 3 App Cas 459 (HL).
[59] See Chapter 4, 95–7.   [60] See Chapter 6, 179–89.
[61] See Chapter 7, 204–6.

Start with the pre-rescission position. Before the claimant elects to rescind the transfer, the Common Law does not regard her as having any proprietary interest in the transferred property; the Common Law looks only to legal title, and the defendant has that. Equity is more discriminating. It recognizes that the claimant is not in quite the same position as someone who has made a perfectly proper transfer. She has the right to rescind the transfer, and when she does she will then recover Equitable ownership of the asset and may also ultimately recover legal ownership. In these circumstances the claimant is considered to have a mere Equity.[62] This is the weakest of Equity's proprietary interests, but nevertheless it is an interest that can be transferred to others and enforced against third parties who are volunteers or who have notice of her claim, although not against others.[63] It gives the claimant an advantage as against the defendant in protecting her inchoate rights in the property that she has unintentionally transferred.

After rescission, the picture is a little more complicated. Consider the Common Law options first. If the claimant has made an unintended gift (so that she is not constrained by the need to make counter-restitution to the defendant), *and* she is in a position to rescind at Common Law (because even the Common Law regards her intention as subjectively impaired by fraudulent misrepresentation or physical or economic duress), *and* the property is either money or an asset where automatic revesting of Common Law title is possible (as it is with goods, but not with land or shares, where re-registration is essential to the re-transfer of Common Law title), *then*, once the claimant elects to rescind the transfer, Common Law title to the property will automatically revest in her (or, with money, she can insist on a personal unjust enrichment claim).[64] The impact of all these restrictions is that the Common Law can only remedy unintended gifts of money or goods. Money is exceptional, in that the Common Law allows the claimant a personal remedy even if the transferred funds are no longer identifiable in the defendant's hands. With goods, the property must be identifiable because the only unjust enrichment remedy is revesting of legal title, not a straightforward money claim.[65] Recall that with goods, revesting of legal title does not give the claimant the right to demand specific reinstatement; her legal title simply

[62] See Chapter 3, 82–3.
[63] *Re Goldcorp Exchange Ltd (in rec)* [1995] 1 AC 74 (PC); *Daly v Sydney Stock Exchange Ltd* (1986) 160 CLR 371 (Aust HCt).
[64] *Re Eastgate ex p Ward* [1905] 1 KB 465 (KB) (a case of contract, not gift).
[65] See below, 300–2.

entitles her to recover the value of the property in conversion if the defendant refuses to transfer the asset voluntarily.[66] With unintended gifts of other property, even where the claimant's intention was impaired because of the defendant's fraud or duress, the claimant will have to seek her unjust enrichment remedies in Equity, or else ignore these claims and sue the defendant in tort for fraud or duress.

As if this were not enough, the Common Law introduces a further complication. If the claimant's subjectively unintended transfer was made by contract rather than by gift, then the claimant is not allowed to rescind the contract unless she is in a position to make perfect counter-restitution to the defendant of the asset he transferred by way of exchange to her under their contract. If the claimant purchases a car, for example, then she cannot rescind the flawed sale and recover the purchase price unless she is in a position to return the car to the defendant in its original condition.[67] This can be a serious impediment. She may not discover the flaw in her contract until several months after her purchase, and then the ensuing wear and tear on the car will prevent her unwinding the deal at Common Law.[68] With her Common Law unjust enrichment claim barred like this, her only alternatives, at Common Law, are to pursue her remedies (if any) in contract or tort.

There is a rational explanation for this restrictive rule, although one that seems unnecessarily limiting from a modern perspective. Recall that the gist of an unjust enrichment claim is not the defendant's wrong, but the claimant's misconceived transfer. In the absence of a legal wrong, the Common Law was considered to have no jurisdiction to order a money remedy, either by way of account of profits or compensation for loss. All it could do was to revest legal title. If the claim was in unjust enrichment, the Common Law could revest title in the car, for example, but it could not make the claimant pay for wear and tear. In the interests of fairness, therefore, the Common Law only allowed the claimant to rescind if no adjustments were necessary; it only allowed rescission when the claimant could effect strict counter-restitution to the defendant. Now

---

[66] See Chapter 6, 169–72.

[67] Although it is irrelevant whether the property retains its original *value: Armstrong v Jackson* [1917] 2 KB 822, 828 (KB).

[68] See *Clarke v Dickson* (1858) EB & E 148, 154–5; 120 ER 463, 466 (Compton J); *Erlanger v New Sombrero Phosphate Co* (1878) 3 App Cas 1218 (HL), 1278 (Lord Blackburn); but contrast *Alati v Kruger* (1955) 94 CLR 216 (Aust HCt), 225 (Dixon CJ, Webb, Kitto Taylor JJ), suggesting that even at common law the claimant purchaser is not responsible for any deterioration of the property due to its inherent nature, or due to the exercise of rights which the contract gives the purchaser (citing *Head v Tattersall* (1871) LR 7 Exch 7, 12.

that the law of unjust enrichment is on firmer foundations, it might seem sensible to revisit this limitation. The Common Law does not simply remedy wrongs; it also remedies unjust enrichments. Our claimant could, for example, make perfect counter-restitution in money, with the sum calculated to represent the real value of the car she received when the deal was done. Her ability to do this would afford a more principled limitation on her entitlement to rescind the flawed transfer: if she wants to recover her unintended transfer of the purchase price, then she must return the real value of the asset she received by way of the flawed transaction. This personal right to recovery in unjust enrichment has always been available to remedy flawed transfers of money; strict *restitutio* of the coins themselves has never been material.

Without reform to permit 'monetized rescission', the effect of all these rules is that claimants are rarely able to pursue Common Law remedies in unjust enrichment for subjectively unintended transfers. Either their intention is not sufficiently impaired, or the property is not of the type where legal title can revest automatically, or the claimant cannot effect perfect counter-restitution of any property she has received. Equity is more lenient on every front. Recall the wider grounds of misrepresentation, undue influence, and unconscionable bargains on which Equity will admit that the defendant was somehow responsible for the claimant's impaired intention.[69] Recall, too, that Equitable title to property owned by the defendant can revest in the claimant regardless of the nature of the underlying property; there are no special rules differentiating between goods, land, and shares.[70] Finally, when the flawed transfer is by way of contract, Equity is far more lenient than the Common Law in insisting that the claimant must be able to provide counter-restitution to the defendant. Equity simply requires that 'practical justice' be done.[71] This liberal Equitable approach again reflects historical jurisdictional boundaries. Equity was considered unable to award damages for wrongs, but well able to effect a revesting of Equitable title accompanied by an order for an account in respect of any dealings with the underlying property.[72] Take our earlier example. Equity would allow the claimant to rescind and return the car after several months of use, provided she accounted to the defendant for any deterioration in the returned property.[73]

---

[69] Chapter 7, 204–19. [70] Chapter 3, 73–7.

[71] *O'Sullivan v Management Agency and Music Ltd* [1985] QB 428 (CA).

[72] *Erlanger v New Sombrero Phosphate Co* (1878) 3 App Cas 1218 (HL), 1278 (Lord Blackburn).

[73] *Alati v Kruger* (1955) 94 CLR 216 (Aust HCt), 223–4 (Dixon CJ); *O'Sullivan v Management Agency and Music Ltd* [1985] QB 428.

Two issues are worth noting. First, Equity's liberal response does not extend to ordering fully monetized rescission. Some form of proprietary restitution or counter-restitution is necessary; Equity can then order an account that reflects the parties' dealings with the underlying property. In our earlier example, Equity can accommodate the parties' unjust enrichment claim if the claimant has simply used the car for several months; it cannot if she is unable to return the car *at all*. Then rescission is barred.[74] This means that the claimant has no remedy in unjust enrichment, although she may be fortunate enough to have alternative claims in contract or tort. Even in Equity, however, this limitation has never applied when the transferred property is money. Then rescission in Equity is possible even if the money is no longer identifiable in the defendant's hands; the claimant is simply entitled to a personal monetary claim.

All of this means that claimants can win or lose in their unjust enrichment claims by accident of circumstances. If the law wishes to remedy misconceived transfers, then its remedies should be subject to principled limitations, not circumstantial eradication. Indeed, the law has gone some way to recognizing this already. Where contractual transfers are induced by misrepresentation, whether fraudulent, negligent, or innocent, a statute now permits money remedies even if the underlying property cannot be restored.[75] There is no obvious reason for refusing to extend principled recognition of fully monetized rescission to all similarly misconceived property transfers.[76]

The second issue concerns the detail of Equity's proprietary response to rescission. Equity's remedy is to revest Equitable title to the transferred asset in the claimant: the defendant holds legal title to the car, for example, but he holds it on trust for the claimant.[77] As the law now

---

[74] *Clarke v Dickson* (1858) EB & E 148, 154–5; 120 ER 463, 466 (Compton J).

[75] Misrepresentation Act 1967, s. 2(1). Whatever the benefits of this Act, it does seem to have miscategorized the underlying claim. The Act was designed to relieve the practical problems caused by the *restitutio in integrum* bars. On this basis, monetized rescission should be assessed as any other unjust enrichment claim might be assessed. Instead, and controversially, the Act has been interpreted as providing money remedies assessed on the basis of tortious wrongdoing, and *fraudulent* wrongdoing at that. Arguably this overcompensates the unjust enrichment claimant in an unprincipled way. See *East v Maurer* [1991] 1 WLR 461 (CA).

[76] Certain cases suggest a move in this direction: *Spence v Crawford* [1939] 3 All ER 271 (HL); *O'Sullivan v Management Agency and Music Ltd* [1985] QB 428 (CA); *Mahoney v Purnell* [1996] 3 All ER 61 (QB).

[77] *Allcard v Skinner* (1887) 36 ChD 145 (CA) (gifts); *Alati v Kruger* (1955) 94 CLR 216 (Aust HCt) (contracts); *O'Sullivan v Management Agency and Music Ltd* [1985] QB 428 (CA) (contracts); *Daly v Sydney Stock Exchange Ltd* (1986) 160 CLR 371 (Aust HCt) (contracts).

stands, this result affords more advantages to the claimant than revesting of title at Common Law. If Equitable title revests, the claimant is considered able to demand specific restoration of the underlying asset; the Common Law usually restricts the right to monetary compensation for conversion. This difference seems unprincipled. Recall earlier criticisms of this Equitable rule.[78] It would seem preferable to modify the Equitable approach so that Equitable revesting merely entitles the claimant to call for transfer of legal title to the property, not transfer of the asset itself. This intermediate analytical step would have pervasive consequences. A claimant in Equity would then usually only be entitled to a money remedy for conversion; she would be unable to demand specific restoration unless the asset had some unique value, or the relationship between claimant and defendant had special (fiduciary) characteristics that compelled the defendant to especially acknowledge the claimant's interests.

If all of this section on unintended transfers were to be summarized, the key points would be that both Equity and the Common Law respond in an unambiguously privileged proprietary fashion to these claims. The difficulties do not arise from this privileged status, but from two peripheral matters. The first is that neither jurisdiction has yet seen fit to award monetized rescission when the underlying property is no longer in the defendant's hands; the second is that the privileges of Equitable title, especially its assumed associated entitlement to specific restoration, seem overly generous to unjust enrichment claimants in Equity when compared with claimants at Common Law.

'UNINTENDED GIFTS'—DOCTRINAL ISSUES IN PROPRIETARY RECOVERY

The second category of misconceived transfer proposed under the reformulated model is 'unintended gifts'. Here the claimant's intention to transfer is perfectly proper, but her transfer effects a gift in circumstances where a gift is clearly not intended. This category includes our mistaken gas board customer who pays her bill twice. It also includes parties who make transfers under contracts rendered void by statute,[79] or contracts

---

[78] See Chapter 6, 169–74.

[79] Excluding statutes that purport to compromise the claimant's capacity to form a proper intention to transfer. These void contracts should be analysed as 'unintended transfers'. Note that the *proprietary* consequences of contracts rendered void by statute is determined by the particular statute. This need not follow the common law rules described earlier. In particular, many statutes assume that legal title to the property *does* pass, despite the contract being void: e.g. *Stocks v Wilson* [1913] 2 KB 235 (KB).

terminated or frustrated on a total failure of consideration. It may include parties who pay in response to ultra vires demands from the State,[80] or make transfers in anticipation of contracts that are never finalized.[81] Finally, it includes claims generated in reaction to claims based on 'unintended transfers'. This last class needs explaining. If a claimant decides to unwind an unintended contractual transfer, her necessary counter-restitution to the defendant can be seen as a pre-condition to her right to restitution, or, alternatively, as the defendant's independent right to restitution because *his* transfer has become an unintended gift once its purported contractual foundation is removed. (It is not, initially, an unintended transfer *by him*, since *his* intention is not flawed, only the claimant's.)

The appropriate legal remedy in all these instances is much less settled than in the category of unintended transfers. The Common Law now recognizes that these misconceived transfers deserve personal money remedies in unjust enrichment, although this recognition has only emerged slowly during the latter part of the twentieth century. By contrast, the longer-standing Equitable response was, until recently, unrelentingly proprietary. Equity typically ordered re-vesting of the underlying property. Given Equity's historical inability to award straightforward money remedies, this approach is not unexpected, and indeed is remarkably widespread. Equity would rebuttably presume that certain transfers were unintended gifts, without the claimant needing to prove the point. We saw this earlier with presumed resulting trusts and purchase money resulting trusts.[82] Equity also gave proprietary restitutionary responses to transfers motivated by unilateral mistake,[83] or transfers under contracts rendered void by statute,[84] or contracts terminated on a total failure of consideration where Equity might order a purchaser's lien over the sale property in the non-performing vendor's hands in order to secure the claimant's recovery of her purchase price.[85] All of these examples can be united analytically under the head of unintended gifts.

This dramatic difference between Common Law and Equitable approaches is important, especially since both jurisdictions often claim to

---

[80] *Woolwich Equitable Building Society v IRC* [1993] 1 AC 70 (HL).
[81] *British Steel Corp v Cleveland Bridge & Engineering Co Ltd* [1984] 1 All ER 504 (QBD); cf *Regalian Properties plc v London Docklands Development Corp* [1995] 1 WLR 212 (ChD).
[82] See Chapter 8, 257–9.
[83] *Chase Manhattan Bank v Israel British Bank* [1981] 1 Ch 105.
[84] *Sinclair v Brougham* [1914] AC 398 (HL), now overruled by *Westdeutsche Landesbank Girozentrale v Islington LBC* [1996] AC 669 (HL).
[85] *Levy v Stogdon* [1898] 1 Ch 478; *Hewett v Court* (1983) 149 CLR 639 (Aust HCt).

be able to deal with the same factual problems.[86] Take mistaken payments. The problems of our overpaying gas board customer are trivial in comparison with the potential problems if one business mistakenly overpays another to the tune of millions of pounds sterling.[87] If the receiving business is insolvent, it then becomes critical to the payer to know whether its claim is proprietary, for only then will it have insolvency protection. Older Equity cases would suggest it was, but the past decade has seen some of the assumptions about Equity's proprietary role in unintended gifts turned on their head, leaving the law in this area very confused. These debates mark a change in common law approach. Comparisons across the jurisdictional divide and between different common law causes of action guided re-evaluation of the very foundations of Equity's jurisdiction in relation to presumed resulting trusts. The strategy is admirable, although the conclusions reached in this instance are questionable.

Recall that if A simply gives property to B, then Equity will presume that the transfer was not intended as a gift, and it will specifically enforce an implied term to that effect, so that B holds the asset on resulting trust for A (a *presumed resulting trust*).[88] This conclusion is not based on any flaw in A's intention to transfer to B, but simply on Equity's antagonism towards gift-giving. The modern re-analysis of these unjust enrichment cases centres on what, precisely, is presumed in a presumed resulting trust. Is the court presuming that A *did intend to create a trust* (and then allowing her to have the benefit of one)? Or is it presuming that she *did not intend to benefit B* (and then allowing her to recover the benefit under a trust to ensure that result)? Or is it presuming that she *did not intend to benefit B by gift* (and then allowing her to have a trust to ensure that result)? The choice is crucial, because each option requires B to present different evidence to rebut the presumption of a resulting trust. The first option makes it easiest for B; the last makes it hardest: it follows that A's interest in her own property is worst protected under the first option and best protected under the last.

In the 1990s, the House of Lords re-analysed resulting trusts, unfortunately without the benefit of full argument on the doctrinal issues, and plumped for the first option:[89] Equity presumes that the claimant *intended*

[86] This is true of contracts rendered void by statute, or contracts terminated on a total failure of consideration, for example.

[87] *Chase Manhattan Bank v Israel British Bank* [1981] 1 Ch 105.

[88] See Chapter 8, 257–9.

[89] *Westdeutsche Landesbank Girozentrale v Islington London Borough Council* [1996] AC 669 (HL).

to create a trust.[90] This presumption is obviously rebutted by evidence that the claimant intended *any* transaction other than a trust. If the claimant intended a gift or a loan, for example, then she could not have intended a trust, and the defendant will take the transferred asset beneficially; he will not hold it on presumed resulting trust for the claimant. This approach leaves little scope for presumed resulting trusts. Indeed, on this analysis presumed resulting trusts would appear to be rebutted in every single case of unintended gift. If the claimant transfers an asset by mistake, as with our gas board customer, then she cannot have intended to transfer by way of trust. Equally, if she transfers under a contract that is rendered void by statute, or is later terminated or frustrated, then clearly she did not intend to transfer by way of trust. Presumed resulting trusts will only survive where it *cannot* be shown that the claimant *did not intend* a trust. This double negative will rarely reflect reality. The only illustration seems to be where the claimant transfers an asset *intending* a trust, but fails to comply with the statutory formalities so the express trust is unenforceable. A presumed resulting trust will then relieve her of her predicament by returning beneficial title to her rather than leaving it with the defendant trustee.

This highly restrictive view of presumed resulting trusts was favoured because it dramatically reduced the incidence of proprietary remedies, and this was perceived to be a good thing. The policy reasons were examined earlier in this chapter. Despite this, very few commentators or judges appear to subscribe wholeheartedly to this new approach. Instead, they prefer the second option, that Equity presumes that the claimant *did not intend to benefit* the defendant. This leaves only marginally more scope for presumed resulting trusts. As before, the presumption is rebutted if the claimant's transfer was made under a contract, even one that was void from the outset or is later terminated or frustrated. In each of these cases the claimant's intention is undoubtedly to benefit the defendant; her mistake is to assume that the defendant will be contractually bound to provide counter-performance. On the other hand, mistaken transfers generate more dissension. At one extreme, some think that the claimant's unilateral mistake in paying her gas bill twice demonstrates that she *does not* intend to benefit the defendant. Such an overtly subjective approach seems untenable given the law's usual practice in insisting on objective standards unless the defendant is responsible for the flaw in the claimant's

---

[90] *Westdeutsche Landesbank Girozentrale v Islington London Borough Council* [1996] AC 669 (HL) (Lord Browne-Wilkinson).

intention. At the other extreme, some think that the claimant *does* intend to benefit the defendant even when her intention is impaired because of the defendant's misrepresentation, duress or undue influence. This, too, seems untenable: if the claimant's intention is not effective to bind her to her dealings, it seems illogical to regard it as effective to support a finding of intention to benefit the defendant.

In any event, this relatively modern focus on intention to benefit the defendant seems to miss the main point of these presumed resulting trust cases. Historically, these cases (and their purchase money resulting trust analogues) were not at all concerned with the claimant's subjective or objective intention to transfer a benefit to the defendant. In the face of perfectly properly intended transfers, Equity simply presumed that the defendant held the asset on resulting trust for the claimant. This reaction appears best explained on the basis that Equity presumes that the claimant *did not intend her transfer to operate by gift*. Why Equity is so set against gift-giving is another matter, but this is the presumption that seems to lie at the heart of the jurisdiction. This is the third option described earlier. On this basis, apparent gifts, perfectly properly intended without any suggestions of flawed or mistaken or coerced intention, give rise to presumed resulting trusts—the defendant cannot take the asset as a gift unless *he* can prove that this was the claimant's intention. The mistaken gas board customer can have the benefit of this rule, not because her intention to make the transfer is flawed, and not because she did not intend the transfer to benefit the defendant, but because her intended benefit was not meant to be a gift. The same is true of a claimant who transfers an asset under a void or terminated or frustrated contract where the circumstances are such that the defendant is not obliged to provide any counter-performance. Again, the claimant intends the transfer, and she intends it to benefit the defendant, but not by way of gift. Equity allows her to recover her misconceived transfer—her unintended gift—using the presumed resulting trust vehicle. These results, based on a presumption that the claimant did not intend to benefit the defendant by way of gift, are consistent with the case law, which adopts this type of proprietary analysis more often than either of the other analytical options would admit.

This divergent history of modern Common Law personal responses and older Equitable proprietary responses to unintended gifts needs resolving. A principled response demands careful analysis. The next section airs some of the issues.

DISCRIMINATING BETWEEN 'UNINTENDED TRANSFERS' AND 'UNINTENDED GIFTS'

The previous sections, taken together, make three points very plainly. First, restitutionary remedies to correct misconceived transfers are, at least historically, overwhelmingly proprietary.[91] This is true of both the Common Law and Equity in their treatment of unintended transfers, and of Equity in its treatment of unintended gifts. This relatively consistent privileging of unjust enrichment claims can be rationalized as the law's only option given historical perceptions of the Common Law and Equitable jurisdictions, but it can also be justified by modern economic analysis. Secondly, and notwithstanding this modern economic analysis, there is a growing but perhaps unjustified fear of the impact of proprietary remedies and a move to limit their incidence, especially in the context of unintended gifts. Finally, there is an increasing preparedness to award personal monetary restitutionary remedies for unintended gifts, although no similar move with unintended transfers (other than the long-accepted practice when the transferred asset is itself money). This modern practice provides further proof that the Common Law can give money remedies even if a wrong has not been committed.

The law in this area is clearly on the move. However, quite where it should be moving is less certain. The Common Law and Equity are seamlessly integrated in their assessment of whether a transfer is misconceived. Each jurisdiction provides different components to the test of whether a transfer is an unintended transfer or an unintended gift, but the resulting profile is eminently coherent. The same now needs to be achieved on the remedial front. The critical issues are whether unjust enrichment claims should be accorded privileged proprietary status, and whether they should be supported by substitute money remedies when these proprietary remedies are not available.

The answers to these questions will not be found in precedent. The law is at a crossroads. It has to make decisions based on policy. If the economic arguments favouring privileging of unjust enrichment claims are persuasive, then legal evolution in this area might do no more than shake free of the exclusivity of this response, and concede that substitute money

---

[91] Backed occasionally by substitute personal money remedies when the misconceived transfer was itself a transfer of money that was no longer identifiable in the defendant's hands.

remedies (personal claims) ought invariably to be available. This would preserve claimants' rights against accidents of circumstance when one or other of the parties disposes of the underlying asset. Otherwise a uniform proprietary response would prevail. But this is the real sticking point. The modern anti-proprietary movement may reflect a desire to discriminate *between* unjust enrichment claims, privileging one class but not the other. In other areas of the law of obligations, legal evolution has invariably proceeded by affording rules for discriminating between different sub-categories of the same type of claim. On this basis, it may now be appropriate to differentiate between remedying unintended transfers and unintended gifts. Indeed, in striking the right balance between security of ownership and security of transfer, this dual categorization seems to mark an apt divide. Claimants making completely unintended transfers (adopting the law's rigorous approach to legally recognized intention) should have security of ownership vigorously protected; claimants finding themselves in an unexpected non-commercial engagement (where they have made an unintended gift) should perhaps be less well protected. Personal remedies, not proprietary ones, may be all that is warranted. Nevertheless, this move should be recognized for what it is. It involves a change to the law. The competing issues have to be carefully weighed and a policy judgement made.

PROPRIETARY REMEDIES AND THE CHANGE OF POSITION DEFENCE

An integrated stance in the delivery of personal and proprietary remedies to unjust enrichment claims demands an integrated stance in the operation of defences. Suppose the claimant makes a unilateral but misconceived transfer of £1,000 to the defendant, and, because of his newfound wealth, the defendant immediately gives £200 to his favourite charity. This is regarded as the paradigm example of a change of position.[92] The defence is a modern advance in the law of unjust enrichment, and operates to reduce the defendant's personal obligation to make restitution of £1,000 to an obligation to make restitution of £800 only.

---

[92] *Lipkin Gorman (a firm) v Karpnale Ltd* [1991] 2 AC 548 (HL), 579–80 (Lord Goff). The change of position defence has far more limited application where *contractual* arrangements have to be unwound. Then the defence does not embrace gifts to charity of the sort just outlined. It seems to be available *only* where the value of the acquired property has been enhanced because of the efforts of the transferee, or where its value has fallen because of the property's inherent attributes or because of the transferor's specific requests to deal with it in a particular manner. This is a stringent limitation, not yet directly or consistently recognized in discussions of the change of position defence.

If the claimant's unjust enrichment remedy is proprietary, however, then the defendant will hold the £1,000 on resulting trust for the claimant. If the defendant gives £200 to charity from *this* fund, then clearly the resulting trust can only embrace the remaining £800; both the personal and proprietary unjust enrichment claims will be reduced to £800. However, this coincidence is merely fortuitous. What will happen if the defendant gives £200 to charity from his own resources, but still motivated by his newfound wealth? In these circumstances the change of position defence will reduce the personal claim, and it would seem disingenuous if it did not similarly reduce the proprietary claim, notwithstanding that the original £1,000 fund from the claimant remains identifiable in its entirety in the defendant's hands.

This illustration demonstrates the care needed in assessing Equitable proprietary responses. The temptation is to say that the £1,000 fund is the claimant's in Equity. This is not quite true. Because of the misconceived transfer, the claimant has a privileged unjust enrichment *claim*, not outright ownership of the erroneously transferred fund come what may. Equity's mechanism for privileging the claim is to secure enforcement against the original asset (and its traceable proceeds[93]), but it is the unjust enrichment claim that is privileged, not the claimant's ownership of £1,000 fund. If the eventual claim *is* for £1,000, then the claimant can demand the entire fund;[94] but if the claim is for something less, then the original asset merely stands as security to ensure that the claim remains privileged.

This analysis highlights the importance of rigorous doctrinal analysis of the precise claim being advanced by the claimant. If transfers are misconceived, then the claimant is entitled to an unjust enrichment remedy; she is not necessarily entitled to recover her original asset. Her rights arise *because* she has an unjust enrichment claim, not because she remains the legal and beneficial owner of the property transferred. Even if the law's initial response is to deem title retained by the claimant, subsequent events may allow the defendant to raise a defence that cuts back the claimant's preferred rights. By contrast, the proper analysis may be quite different if the claimant is advancing some other proprietary claim, such as a claim for the profits of a fiduciary breach,[95] or if she is asserting a conflicting title claim to specific property.[96]

---

[93] See Chapter 4, 102–6.
[94] Although see Chapter 6, 169–74, for the criticisms of this.
[95] See Chapter 5, 134–40.   [96] See Chapter 4, 92–7.

PRESERVING PROPRIETARY ADVANTAGES BY CLAIMING AN INTEREST IN SUBSTITUTE ASSETS

The next issue for claimants, typically, is the extent to which their initial proprietary claims can be preserved in substitute assets. If the claimant unintentionally transfers her car, and the defendant sells it and reinvests the proceeds in a painting, the claimant will want to preserve the privileges of her initial proprietary claim by securing it against the substituted painting. The same is true if the claimant's wheat has been sold and the proceeds paid into a bank account. If the original property is no longer in the defendant's hands, a claimant can preserve the privileged status of her original rights by securing her claim against any traceable substitutes.[97] These tracing rules are limited, however. Orthodoxy suggests that a claimant can only trace property *that belonged to her in Equity at the time the substitutions were made*. With misconceived transfers, this limitation can be problematic.

Even assuming the remedy is proprietary at all (and this is now a matter of increasing debate), a misconceived transfer is often effective to pass legal and beneficial title to the defendant. The claimant then has no interest in the transferred property until she avoids the voidable transfer or terminates the breached contract. If the defendant deals with the property in advance of this event, then any substitutions he effects are not substitutions for the *claimant's* property, but for his. By contrast, if the misconceived transfer is void, the analysis is more likely to work in the claimant's favour.

Despite this analytical difficulty in tracing into substitutes, the practice when the misconceived transfer concerns *money* suggests that there must at least be a partial way forward. With money, monetized rescission is routinely allowed, and the restitutionary remedy is often secured against traceable substitutes derived from the original purchase fund, notwithstanding any timing difficulties.[98] Unfortunately the underlying analysis is never fully explored. By analogy, however, suppose the misconceived transfer concerned a share swap and the defendant sells the shares and purchases a painting before the claimant acts to avoid the transfer. The availability of monetized rescission would ensure that the claimant was

---

[97] See Chapter 4, 102–6.
[98] E.g. Millett J appears to have assumed this in *El Ajou v Dollar Land Holdings Ltd* [1993] 3 All ER 717 (rev'd on other grounds, [1994] 2 All ER 685 (CA)) ((ChD)), and in *dicta* in *Lonrho plc v Fayed (No 2)* [1992] 1 WLR 1, 12 (ChD).

not barred from pursuing her remedy simply because strict *restitutio in integrum* was no longer possible. She would retain the right to rescind.[99] The second step, securing the claimant's money remedy against the painting as the traceable substitute, might then be justified on the narrow ground that the claimant had an interest by way of mere Equity in the shares,[100] and this interest has been traced into its substitutes;[101] or on the significantly wider ground that as between claimant and defendant the claimant's privileged unjust enrichment right merits preservation in any factual physical substitutions. Both routes would extend orthodox tracing rules, but in a relatively principled way. Given the current hostility to the expansion of proprietary remedies, however, neither may find favour. On the other hand, the next section illustrates a contrary impetus, where modern developments are vigorously expanding the potential reach of proprietary remedies.

ENLARGING RESTITUTIONARY CLAIMS BY DEMANDING PROFITS

The final issue in these unjust enrichment cases concerns the claimant's ability to recover ancillary profits. Defendants often use property acquired under a misconceived transfer to profitable effect before the claimant unwinds the engagement and remedies her error. The claimant will be interested to know what part of these profits, if any, accrue to her.[102] These profits can be divided into three types. Each needs separate consideration.

First, the defendant may profit from market increases in the value of the property or from 'fruits' it has generated. For example, the defendant's newly acquired shares may have increased in value or attracted dividend payments. Secondly, the defendant may profit by using the asset. He may

---

[99] This would mark a step-change in the law, but see *O'Sullivan v Management Agency and Music Ltd* [1985] QB 428 (CA); *Mahoney v Purnell* [1996] 3 All ER 61 (QB).

[100] This analysis is not always open, of course. It is with voidable contracts, but not with contracts that are frustrated or terminated on a total failure of consideration.

[101] By contrast, *Bishopsgate Investment Management Ltd (in liq) v Homan* [1995] 1 All ER 347 denied the possibility of tracing into an asset acquired by the defendant *before* receipt of the claimant's property—such an asset could not possibly be a substitute for the claimant's asset. But see L Smith, 'Tracing into the Payment of a Debt' [1995] CLJ 290, arguing that even this rule should not be universal.

[102] The claimant may have to *elect* whether to pursue her unjust enrichment claim or her other claims (in tort or contract); she cannot recover twice for the same harm: *Tang Man Sit v Capacious Investments Ltd* [1996] AC 514 (PC); *Kuwait Airways Corp v Iraqi Airways Co (No 6)* [2002] AC 883 (HL).

use his newly acquired car as a taxi, or mine his mine for gold.[103] Finally, the defendant may profit because he sells the underlying asset and uses the proceeds to purchase an alternative, more lucrative, investment.[104] He may sell his taxi and purchase a painting that turns out to be a Picasso masterpiece. Moreover, each form of profit may have been generated either before or after the claimant takes steps to avoid her misconceived deal, if such steps are necessary.

Where the profits arise from the original asset, and are an inherent attribute of it, then they accrue to the claimant. This is uncontroversial, and is true regardless of the timing of the improvement in value. If the shares increase in value, the claimant can recover them *in specie* without accounting to the defendant for any gain. Similarly, if dividends have been paid, she can recover those too; indeed, she will have a proprietary claim to them if she can identify them in the defendant's hands. This rule applies to the original property and to any 'fruits' that *necessarily* result from its ownership. The claim is not really a 'profits' claim, but simply a claim to the entirety (including natural accretions) of the transferred property.

With other forms of profit, analysis is easier if the different timeframes are considered separately. If the defendant makes a profit *after* the claimant has established her proprietary claim, then recall that there are various arguments suggesting that the claimant should sometimes (or perhaps always) be entitled to this profit.[105] These arguments are based on property, unjust enrichment, and wrongs. The property argument suggests that the owner of property is entitled, as of right and by virtue of her ownership, to any substitutions generated from her property.[106] This suggests that the claimant would recover the Picasso painting, and perhaps the profits from the mine, but probably not the taxi fare profits. The unjust enrichment argument suggests that a defendant is necessarily unjustly enriched if he uses another's property to generate profits for himself; these profits should therefore be paid over to the claimant. On this analysis, the profits in all of our examples would be recoverable by the claimant. Although the results differ, both of these analyses depend upon

---

[103] And the defendant may not be treated in precisely the same way in these two examples.
[104] The only difficulty with this example is that if the defendant does not have the original asset in his possession then he cannot effect *restitutio* and the claimant may not be allowed to rescind the contract. The potential unfairness of this has already been aired; indeed, the previous section considered the possibility of tracing into substitutes to secure the primary claim despite this hurdle.
[105] See Chapter 4, 106–10, for this debate.
[106] *F C Jones & Sons (Trustee in Bankruptcy) v Jones* [1997] Ch 159 (CA); *Foskett v McKeown* [2001] 1 AC 102 (HL).

the claimant being able to assert a proprietary interest in the underlying property used by the defendant to make a profit. The wrongs argument suggests that a claimant can only demand disgorgement of profits if the defendant's acquisition of those profits constitutes a wrong to the claimant for which disgorgement is the remedy. In our examples, if the defendant is a fiduciary, then all the different forms of post-rescission profit in our examples will have to be disgorged; if he is not, then none will. Clearly it is vital to know which of these three models is correct; each produces quite different outcomes. As yet the debate continues, although here the wrongs analysis is preferred.[107]

More usually, of course, the defendant will make his profit *before* the claimant takes any steps to unwind her misconceived transfer. More often than not he is then making profits at a time when he is the legal and beneficial owner of the property. It follows that the property and unjust enrichment disgorgement models would not generate any disgorgement obligations, *unless*, once rescission is effected, the law elects to treat the defendant for all purposes *as if* he had held the property on trust from the outset. As between the claimant and the defendant, this does seem to be the chosen approach.[108] The property and unjust enrichment arguments might then require disgorgement of pre-rescission profits from defendants just as if those profits had been made after rescission. However, the doctrinal argument is by no means straightforward.[109] By contrast, the wrongs argument will readily generate disgorgement remedies *if* the defendant is a defaulting fiduciary. This analysis does not depend upon property ownership, but simply upon the fiduciary making an unauthorized profit from the relationship. The fact that the argument can be run without too much concern for property ownership separates the wrongs approach from the property and unjust enrichment approaches, where property ownership is crucial. Moreover, the more discriminating conclusions predicted by the wrongs approach are supported by the cases:

---

[107] See Chapter 4, 106–10.

[108] Perhaps *F C Jones & Sons (Trustee in Bankruptcy) v Jones* [1997] Ch 159 (CA) provides an analogy; in this case the property interest arose because of relation back, not because of rescission, but pre-relation back investments were caught, using the property argument. But contrast *Halifax Building Society v Thomas* [1996] Ch 217 (CA).

[109] The problem is property ownership. This is critical to the property and unjust enrichment approaches. It is not clear, for example, that the cases supporting tracing into substitutes in a way that secures the preferred status of the primary claim, can be taken as adequate proof of the property underpinnings that are essential to the profits disgorgement analysis.

fiduciaries who make profits prior to rescission are required to disgorge;[110] other parties are not.[111]

Whether successful claims to profits are, or should be, proprietary is hotly contested. The reason for tracing into profits, and the process of tracing, do not provide an answer. The property analysis of profits, on its terms, suggests a proprietary response. The wrongs analysis does too, at least according to current disgorgement orthodoxy,[112] although earlier chapters proposed a potentially preferable alternative approach.[113] The unjust enrichment analysis is harder to pin down; history suggests that the response is proprietary, but the modern trend is more restrictive, preferring personal remedies.

Clearly these different models of profits disgorgement deliver quite different responses to the same fact situations. Which view should be preferred is currently one of the hotly contested issues in the law of unjust enrichment. The answer matters. If the property or unjust enrichment analyses are correct, then defendants who make profits (whether innocent, ignorant, or otherwise) may have to disgorge them; if the wrongs analysis is correct, then they will not unless they owe specific duties to the claimant in relation to the property.

REVIEW

This chapter has covered a lot of difficult ground. It raises issues that are amongst the most controversial in the common law in describing and defending Equity's role. However, its conclusions can, be summarized briefly.

First, the law of unjust enrichment is aimed at correcting misconceived transfers. The basic rule is that recovery is allowed if the transfer was not intended: it is allowed if the claimant can say, 'I didn't mean you to have the property in the circumstances.' Orthodox unjust enrichment law adopts two mechanisms for deciding whether this statement can be applied to a particular set of facts. It looks for 'vitiated intention' on the claimant's part, or for 'failure of basis' or 'failure of consideration' in the

---

[110] *Ryall v Ryall* (1739) 1 Atk 59; *Bulmer, In re; ex p Greaves* [1937] 1 Ch 499 (CA), 511 (Lord Wright MR); *O'Sullivan v Management Agency and Music Ltd* [1985] QB 428; *Mahoney v Purnell* [1996] 3 All ER 61 (QB).

[111] *Cave v Cave* (1880) 15 ChD 639 (ChD), 645, 647–8 citing Lord Eldon in *Lewis v Maddocks* 17 Ves 48, 57; *Bristol & West Building Society v Mothew* [1998] Ch 1 (CA), 16–17; *Colbeam Palmer Ltd v Stock Affiliates Pty Ltd* (1970) 122 CLR 25 (Aust HCt).

[112] *AG for Hong Kong v Reid* [1994] 1 AC 324 (PC).

[113] See Chapter 5, 134–40.

transaction. If either of these conditions is met, then the claimant can unwind the transfer. This orthodox analysis suffers from certain analytical difficulties, and it could be improved by modifying the two core mechanisms for identifying misconceived transfers. The reformulated model suggested here would remedy misconceived transfers if they were either 'unintended transfers' or 'unintended gifts'. In the first category, the issue is whether the claimant's intention is recognized as adequate at law; in the second it is whether the transfer operates as a gift when a commercial engagement was clearly intended.

The next issue is precisely how these misconceived transfers ought to be remedied. Historically, unjust enrichment remedies were almost invariably proprietary. Now, however, there is a growing impetus to deny a proprietary response to unintended gifts, and a more muted move to do the same with unintended transfers. There is also increasing recognition of the availability of substitute personal money remedies, although so far only for unintended gifts. The law in this area is clearly evolving. Important choices have to be made. Of the several possibilities on offer, the most compelling alternatives seem to be retention of privileged proprietary protection for all unjust enrichment claims, or, alternatively, discrimination so that unintended transfers generate proprietary remedies but unintended gifts do not. In addition, all of these claims should, it seems, generate substitute personal money remedies when the proprietary response fails. This is often the only way to accommodate the intervening dealings with the property so that neither claimant nor defendant is disadvantaged.

Any proprietary advantages, whether ameliorated by change of position defences or not, need to be appropriately protected. It remains a moot point whether the preferred proprietary status of unjust enrichment claims can be preserved in traceable substitutes, especially if the substitution takes place before the misconceived transfer is avoided. Some cases assume this possibility, although convincing doctrinal analysis is difficult, but by no means impossible.

Perhaps more importantly, the law needs to deal in a principled way with any profits that might be generated from the defendant's use of the transferred property, especially profits made before the misconceived transfer is avoided. Three competing analyses attempt to explain when a claimant can recover these profits from the defendant. Here the wrongs analysis is preferred. It suggests that profits disgorgement is only warranted if the defendant's profit-making constitutes a legal wrong for which disgorgement is the appropriate remedy. For example, defendant fiduciaries must disgorge: they cannot take unauthorized profits from the relationship, whether or not those profits come from the use of the claimant's property.

Finally, and crucially, the reformulated model of unjust enrichment claims, which classifies misconceived transfers as 'unintended transfers' or 'unintended gifts', permits the ready integration of Common Law and Equitable strategies. The Common Law and Equity are already integrated seamlessly and coherently in defining these two categories. Their respective patterns of remedial response can also be integrated rationally, with few disjunctions. Indeed, these two categories may set the stage for the next evolutionary step in remedial practices. As already noted, closer attention to these two different categories of unjust enrichment claims may suggest that they warrant different degrees of protection if they are to fit coherently and rationally into the overall hierarchy of common law claims.

SELECTED BIBLIOGRAPHY

Birks, P., 'Restitution and Resulting Trusts' in S. Goldstein (ed.), *Equity and Contemporary Legal Problems* (Jerusalem: Hamaccabi Press, 1992), p. 335.

Burrows, 'Swaps and the Friction between Common Law and Equity' [1995] RLR 15.

Maudsley, R. H., 'Proprietary Remedies for the Recovery of Money' (1959) 75 LQR 234.

Millett, Lord, 'Proprietary Restitution' in S. Degeling and J. Edelman (eds), *Equity in Commercial Law* (Sydney: Lawbook Co., 2005), Ch. 12.

Millett, Sir P., 'Restitution and Constructive Trusts' (1998) 114 LQR 399.

Paccioco, D., 'The Remedial Constructive Trust: A Principled Basis for Priority Over Creditors' (1989) 68 Canadian Bar Review 315.

Stevens, R. and McFarlane, B., 'In Defence of *Sumpter v Hedges*' (2002) 118 LQR 569.

Swadling, W., 'A New Role for Resulting Trusts?' (1996) 16 Legal Studies 110.

——, 'Rescission, Property and the Common Law' (2005) 121 LQR 123.

Weinrib, E., 'Restitutionary Damages as Corrective Justice' (2000) 1 Theoretical Inquiries in Law 1.

Worthington, S., 'The Proprietary Consequences of Rescission' [2002] Restitution Law Review 28.

SELECTED CASES

Alati v Kruger [1955] 94 CLR 216 (Aust HCt)

Bishopsgate Investment Management Ltd (in liq) v Homan [1995] 1 All ER 347

Chase Manhattan Bank v Israel British Bank [1981] 1 Ch 105

Daly v Sydney Stock Exchange Ltd (1986) 160 CLR 371 (Aust HCt)

Erlanger v New Sombrero Phosphate Co (1878) 3 App Cas 1218 (HL)

Foskett v McKeown [2001] 1 AC 102 (HL)

Re Goldcorp Exchange Ltd (in rec) [1995] 1 AC 74 (PC)

Goss v Chilcott [1996] AC 788 (PC)

Halifax Building Society v Thomas [1996] Ch 217 (CA)

F C Jones & Sons (Trustee in Bankruptcy) v Jones [1997] Ch 159 (CA)

Lipkin Gorman (a firm) v Karpnale Ltd [1991] 2 AC 548 (HL)

Mahoney v Purnell [1996] 3 All ER 61 (QB)

O'Sullivan v Management Agency and Music Ltd [1985] QB 428 (CA)

Sinclair v Brougham [1914] AC 398 (HL)

Kuwait Airways Corp v Iraqi Airways Co (No 6) [2002] AC 883 (HL)

Westdeutsche Landesbank Girozentrale v Islington LBC [1994] 1 WLR 938 (Hobhouse J)

Westdeutsche Landesbank Girozentrale v Islington LBC [1996] AC 669 (HL)

Part VI

Conclusion

Moving Forward—Integrating Equity

This final chapter looks back to the issues raised at the outset. In between, a lot of detailed analysis has been covered. Now one key question remains. Should the Common Law and Equity jurisdictions be fully integrated or not? Part of the reluctance is simply innate conservatism. Part is simple and honest divergence in analytical approach. A further part is less honourable, however. It is to preserve an area of developed practical expertise, excluding the ignorant and the untutored. Equity has always managed to preserve a mystique that it is 'hard' law, accessible only to the sophisticated and discerning.

The integrationist agenda promoted here seeks to ensure that legal developments are, as far as possible, coherent, principled, rational, and properly directed to meeting the underlying policy objectives. The common law system could continue with red and green rules, and red and green practices, but this is a sub-optimal strategy. The potential difficulties created by the divide between Common Law and Equity are clear. A coherent common law system requires that similar rights be remedied in similar ways and that the most highly prized rights attract the most highly prized remedies. There should be no disjunctions in the scheme, no circumstances where the hierarchy of rights does not correspond with the hierarchy of remedies. Maintaining this profile as a legal system evolves over time, as it inevitably will, and is invariably difficult. It requires careful and comprehensive oversight of the whole scheme, and a commitment to developing and maintaining logical and defensible patterns of differentiation and discrimination. The historical jurisdictional divide militates against this outcome.

Given this, it would seem that the best way forward for the common law is integration. This has already happened at the administrative level. It is now pressingly needed at the doctrinal level. The most productive course of action is to take all the learning, from both Equity and the Common Law, and attempt to map it into a coherent analytical structure. This may require some surgery: some parts will go; some will be relocated; some will be stretched to cover other areas; but the bases for a more sophisticated, differentiated, and attenuated system are already there. This is not revolutionary. It can be achieved by continuance of historical judicial work. When judges model any new law they build on existing principles, looking for appropriate analogies with existing applications in property, unjust enrichment, tort, and contract. In this way the 'leading' cases typically resort to a breadth of explanatory forces as a necessary mechanism for ensuring coherence in the law. The new advance is made, and its limits defined, by looking at all the relevant related principles, so that then the new rule can be seen as being merely a legitimate, sensible, and coherent extension of the old rules.

In pursuing the argument for integration, this chapter focuses on two objectives. The first is to show that the practical task of integration is unlikely to be as difficult as is often supposed. All the learning exposed and explored in the earlier chapters reinforces this. The picture that emerges is one of significant practical integration and cross-fertilization between the two jurisdictions. This picture, reiterated here, challenges the claim of inevitable dualism.

The second objective is more demanding. Whatever the practical and intellectual advantages of integration, there remains a persistent and powerful perception that integration is now impossible. The arguments invariably focus on allegations of profound and unbridgeable philosophical and jurisprudential divides between the two jurisdictions. The core concerns are that Equity is a uniquely conscience-based and discretionary regime whereas the Common Law is a rules- and rights-based regime. This chapter seeks to challenge that view.

If these two objectives can be achieved, then the ground would seem to be laid open for the intellectual, jurisprudential, and doctrinal integration of the Common Law and Equity.

PRACTICAL DOCTRINAL INTEGRATION

The picture painted in the previous nine chapters is one of significant harmony and surprising consistency and coherence across the common law regime. Admittedly, some of this accommodation is only revealed when the underlying issues are analysed according to fundamental general principles rather than lower-level rules. However, this only serves to reinforce the notion that integration is both possible and advantageous.

Some parts of the common law are already seamlessly and unnoticeably integrated. Recall the two jurisdictions' modern attitudes to the transferability of debts and other choses in action, so that both now recognize these forms of wealth as property.[1] Also recall their approach to regulating decision-making, using the doctrine of proper purposes;[2] and their interference with agreed remedies using the doctrine of penalties.[3] In all these areas there is often little resort to jurisdictional tags and little that divides approaches, either in theory or in practice.

Beyond this, there is also much that could be integrated with little difficulty because the two jurisdictions have produced similar rules and remedies to regulate similar fact patterns. Both jurisdictions now use injunctions, complemented by (the confusingly styled) 'Equitable damages'.[4] Both have concepts of accessory liability, although the Common Law is concerned to regulate interference with contracts and Equity to regulate interference with trusts and other fiduciary relationships.[5] Both have similar strategies for reviewing promises, departing from the objective view only when the defendant either knows of or is somehow responsible for the claimant's impaired consent. In developing these latter rules, the Common Law's focus has been on economic pressure, Equity's on social pressure. Nevertheless, the rules themselves and their responses are clearly motivated by the same imperatives.[6]

These are the easy cases. However, the landscape looks no more hostile when we turn to the rules and practices that many see as illustrating the impossibility of practical integration. In this category, the most obvious candidate is the trust. The trust is generally regarded as Equity's principal contribution to the common law, with is existence critically dependent on an independent Equitable jurisdiction. The qualification is doubted. If the concept of property is pared down to its fundamentals, then a property interest is no more than a right to enjoy defined benefits and, additionally, have those benefits accorded special protection against interference by third parties and special advantages associated with transferability. The trust is easily accommodated within this analysis, no matter how exceptional its 'defined benefits' have turned out to be in both social and commercial contexts.[7] Indeed, if an analogy were needed, it seems that Equitable security interests have already been integrated in this way: little thought is given to the jurisdictional tag accompanying 'Equitable' charges; the focus is simply on the various rights and benefits incorporated within the proprietary bundle.

---

[1] See Chapter 3, 58–60.   [2] See Chapter 5, 145–7.
[3] See Chapter 7, 224–6.
[4] See Chapter 2, 31–4, and Chapter 6, 159–61.
[5] See Chapter 6, 189–91.   [6] See Chapter 7, 204–19.
[7] See Chapter 3, 63–7.

This category of hard cases extends beyond the trust, but again there is little evidence of real impediments to rational integration. Sometimes the difficulties simply come down to differential development problems. The various incursions made by Equitable estoppel can best be seen as individual examples of Equity's evolutionary advances that anticipated the Common Law's better-rationalized equivalents.[8] Analysis of these Equitable estoppels also affords a pointed reminder of the obfuscations that can shelter behind misleading terminology. Despite their common name, all estoppels clearly do not fit within the same sub-category of the law of obligations. Similarly, despite its name, 'Equitable compensation' seems to have more in common with expectation damages designed to remedy a breach of contract than with compensatory damages (or compensation) designed to remedy a civil wrong.[9] These terminological divisions can unnecessarily mislead rational analysis. Finally, sometimes even small differences in analysis on both sides of the jurisdictional divide can disproportionately disguise the underlying commonalities and, instead, magnify the distinctions. Arguably this has been the case with unjust enrichment. Traditional Common Law analysis suggests that personal restitutionary remedies are warranted if the claimant's intention to transfer is vitiated or if there is a failure of basis. Alignment of these pre-conditions with the circumstances that allegedly generate proprietary restitutionary claims seemed irritatingly elusive. However, small modifications to the accepted analysis could substantially reduce the disjunctions.[10] In short, even in these 'hard' cases, there is little standing in the way of determined efforts to develop a rational, coherent, integrated map of the common law landscape.

This is not to deny that there are problems. The attempted mapping reveals some significant disjunctions between the Common Law and Equity. Indeed, some of these disjunctions are only fully exposed by comparisons across the jurisdictional divide. One obvious case is the difference between the Common Law and Equitable rules relating to specific restoration of property.[11] Exploring these inconsistencies makes it possible to advance strategies for rational re-alignment. This purposeful reworking of the system's rules can only be beneficial. There are other difficulties, however. Sometimes it seems that orthodox analysis simply does not yield up a coherent and acceptable rationale. The current rules

---

[8] See Chapter 8, 248–54.   [9] See Chapter 6, 174–8.
[10] See Chapter 9, 281–3.   [11] See Chapter 6, 168–74.

on substantive unfairness may fall into this category.[12] At other times the problem is that the wrong tools, from either jurisdiction, are being used for the job. This is likely to be the case with constructive trusts of family homes: this problem requires statutory intervention, not further fiddling with doctrinal rules that were designed to achieve quite different ends.[13] Finally, sometimes the difficulty is simply that the law has reached a cross-roads and choices have to be made. There is then no avoiding the policy imperatives. Of the several options open to the law, any one of them is likely to offer a rational strategy. The best route for contemporary purposes must nevertheless be chosen. Arguably this is the position the law now faces with disgorgement of windfall secondary profits. Several analytical options have been advanced, and the law needs to commit to its preferred option.[14]

All of this simply serves to suggest that practical doctrinal integration lies well within the grasp of the modern common law. Indeed, even if we do nothing, integration will probably creep up on the common law system. It is simply the rational choice, and evolution is therefore likely to deliver it eventually. If an example is needed, then the USA's common law jurisdiction seems well down this route. But if the system could be improved more rapidly simply by thoughtful and determined effort, then that effort seems worthwhile. As noted earlier, however, these practical arguments for integration are not the only concern. The next section deals with the arguments about jurisdictional philosophy.

JURISPRUDENTIAL INTEGRATION

In the past, the opportunity for integration of Equity and the Common Law has, at best, lapsed through institutional inertia and, at worst, been rejected several times. The critical issue is whether continuing dualism is now inevitable. This is not an idle question. The earlier discussion of children's kindergarten games makes it obvious that a system which chooses to operate with 'red' and 'green' umpires and 'red' and 'green' rules and practices will inevitably run into difficulties in maintaining internal coherence. By using two sets of rules, there is a significant risk that like cases will not be treated alike, and that different cases will not be treated in appropriately different ways. Notwithstanding this, the prevailing view is that integration is impossible; dualism is inevitable.

---

[12] See Chapter 7, 219–26.   [13] See Chapter 8, 261–4.
[14] See Chapter 4, 106–10.

The arguments invariably come down to two core concerns. First, Equity's rationale for intervention is said to be conscience-based and moral in a way that the Common Law's is not. Second, Equity's intervention is said to be irredeemably discretionary in a way that the Common Law's is not. Each assertion seems overstated, but each merits careful consideration.[15]

IS EQUITY A PECULIARLY CONSCIENCE-BASED JURISDICTION?

The first argument focuses on Equity's reasoning and its internal rationalization of its interventionist practices: it suggests that Equity's value system, or its motivation for intervention, is conceptually distinct from the Common Law's, so much so that meshing the two to form a sensible, integrated whole is impossible.

This argument cuts deep. Three leads are commonly pursued to prove the case. The first finds evidence of different value systems in the fact that Equity's outcomes are different from those of the Common Law. They are, but not necessarily because of distinctive conceptual reasoning. Every legal change is necessarily implemented through Equity, the Common Law, or legislation. The inescapable consequence is eventual differences between Common Law and statutory rules, or between Common Law and Equitable rules. Moreover, the preferred reform channel is invariably the one offering least resistance and maximum effectiveness. For some time almost all legal change was delivered through Equity because the Common Law was so hidebound by its own rigid writ system.[16] By contrast, the twentieth century was a particularly vibrant period for the Common Law: it devised and elaborated its rules on negligence, negligent misstatement, economic duress, and unjust enrichment. Now the legislative route is usually preferred.

Importantly, none of this history suggests that different reform mechanisms are chosen for their ability to deliver conceptually different results. Conscience-based reforms do not fall naturally to Equity, leaving other reforms to be mediated through Common Law or statutory regimes. Consider Equity's development of undue influence or the Common Law's analogous development of economic duress.[17] Nor is it true, as some anti-integrationists would have it, that allegedly different conceptual

---

[15] The arguments presented here borrow from an earlier essay, [2002] 55 *Current Legal Problems* 232–64.

[16] See Chapter 1, 9–10.   [17] See Chapter 7, 209–16.

motivations make the transfer of reforms across the Common Law—
Equity divide impossible. Take Equity's early distinctive procedural rules.
Far from being relevant only to an Equitable, conscience-based, jurisdiction, these procedural strategies are now adopted quite generally.[18] The
same sort of cross-fertilization is evident elsewhere.[19]

Indeed, this cross-fertilization is an on-going process. Whatever its
history, Equity is now increasingly looking to borrow from the Common
Law. This is especially evident in the controversial areas of money remedies for rescission,[20] and remoteness and foreseeability limitations in
remedying breaches of the 'Equitable' duty of care (if this distinct duty
exists[21]). This tendency is often decried, and, worse still, pejoratively
tarred with the 'fusion fallacy' brush. The 'fusion fallacy' suggests
that the running together of Common Law and Equitable doctrines is
impermissible: it is doctrinally unsound to allow a Common Law defence
to an Equitable cause of action (e.g. contributory negligence to a claim
for breach of fiduciary duty), or to award a Common Law remedy for
an Equitable wrong (e.g. damages for undue influence).[22] But Equity
borrowed from the outset. For example, it adopted the Common Law's
eleventh- and twelfth-century *in personam* remedies and developed them
into its own more sophisticated regimes. Only later, after the Common
Law's long period of stagnation, did the Common Law attempts wither
and die. The modern remedial differences do not mark an unbridgeable
conceptual divide. They simply reflect the competitions and accidents
along the evolutionary path of legal reform.

The second lead in this debate is more subtle. It sees evidence of
different value systems in Equity's focus on the correction of the errant
defendant's conscience, whereas the Common Law's does not, or at least
it is not so limited. The intended inference is that Equity does not create
rights for successful claimants; it simply prevents defendants from
enforcing their existing Common Law rights where to do so would be
unconscionable.[23] Put another way, Equity's function is not to do justice,
but to restrain injustice—it is reactive, not proactive.

---

[18] See Chapter 2, 40.
[19] See, e.g., the Misrepresentation Act 1967, s. 2 (innocent misrepresentation); and Contracts (Rights of Third Parties) Act 1999. The Common Law has also 'borrowed' from
Equity's rules on mistake, penalties, and fraud on the power.
[20] See Chapter 9, 298–303.   [21] See Chapter 6, 165–8.
[22] Although Common Law borrowings from Equity are not subjected to the same taunts.
[23] *Re Diplock* [1948] 1 Ch 465 (CA); *Westdeutsche Landesbank Girozentrale v Islington LBC*
[1996] AC 669 (HL).

This assertion can be interpreted in two ways. At the particular level, the implication is that Equity intervenes only if the defendant's conscience warrants it; the Common Law is perhaps less fastidious. Equity's test of conscience must presumably relate to the defendant's knowledge or intention. Somewhere along a graduated scale it must be possible to say that the defendant's conscience is 'affected' and Equity should intervene. But in practice there is no such divide. *Both* Equity and the Common Law have strict liability wrongs,[24] for example, and both have wrongs where knowledge or intention or carefulness is crucial to liability. The idea that one jurisdiction is defendant-focused and the other is not is simply not supported by the facts.

Sometimes this idea of differential focus is put another way. Equity is said to focus on duties (the defendant's), while the Common Law focuses on rights (the claimant's). The flaw in this description is best seen by analogy. The same duties—rights difference is also said to divide the common law (meaning *both* the Common Law and Equity) and the civil law. The civil law was known—it was codified—so that a civilian claimant could insist as a matter of principle that he had a specific legal right. His common law counterpart, by contrast, had to wait until the relevant common law rule slowly emerged from an established body of precedent before he could assert, and more importantly establish, that he had a legal right. Given time, a general rule might become established which indicated that in certain circumstances a defendant would be obliged— she would have a duty—to act in a particular way. Of course, once the rule became established, it would then be quite accurate to say that the claimant had a right to have the defendant act in the way her established legal duty obliged her to act. If the right/duty distinction is related to this developmental process, then *both* the Common Law and Equity must necessarily focus on the defendant's duties. In a legal system based on precedent, rights are nothing more than the flip-side of established duties, and new rights must necessarily be built on evolving new duties. Only a moribund common law jurisdiction could be described as 'rights-based'.

The third and final lead in this values-related strand of the anti-integrationist argument is more general still. Its focus is not on differences in remedies or differences in claimant—defendant focus, but differences in reasoning. Equity's reasoning is allegedly moral, or conscience-based, in a way that the Common Law's is not. At the most theoretical level, the

[24] The Common Law's rules on conversion, and Equity's rules on fiduciary duties illustrate this.

assertion plays into longstanding debates on the necessary relationship between law and morality. A crude caricature would paint Equity as grounded in natural law, insisting on some fundamental link between conceptions of morality and justice and any legal interventions made in its name. The Common Law, on the other hand, would be seen as irredeemably positivist, imposing a set of mandatory rules backed by the threat of legal sanctions less tightly tied to any prevailing notion of morality. In truth, both are misleading extremes. The law versus morality divide does not map neatly onto the Common Law—Equity divide.

In particular, it is not true that Equity seeks to promote morality, meaning altruism or other-regarding behaviour, while the Common Law promotes self-interest. *All* legal rules constrain self-interested behaviour in order to preserve and promote the rights of others. This is as true of the Common Law rules of contract and tort as it is of the Equitable rules of loyalty and confidence. Moreover, all legal rules adopt the same strategies to ensure compliance. All assume that parties *are* self-interested, and then create incentives to ensure that self-interest is redirected towards socially desirable ends. The best incentive is to ensure that a breach is just as costly, in financial terms, as proper performance. It follows that the remedy for breach of contract should be expectation damages, for torts, compensatory damages, and for fiduciary breaches, disgorgement. These remedies work because they appeal to self-interest, not to altruism. There is no sharp moral divide between Equitable goals and strategies and Common Law ones.

Nor is it true, at a more philosophical level, that there is a moral input in the development of Equity's rules that is absent from the Common Law's. True, the Common Law has often denied its moral roots, justifying this as a necessary part of the struggle to emancipate law from religion. Equity did not. Even when it was trying to establish its rules as part of the legal system and distance itself from the patronage of the king, it always conceded its moral roots and reformist strategies. Acknowledgement of moral input on the one hand, and denial on the other, may have exaggerated the differences between Common Law and Equity, however. The truth suggested by history is that *every* legal advance is founded on some accepted or evolving moral precepts of the society in which the rules are applied.

The same process can be seen in modern legal developments. Moral ideas slowly become incorporated into the legal fabric. This is perhaps most evident in the laws on racial, religious, and age discrimination, the laws on unfair dismissal in employment, and the laws on consumer protection. But it is also evident at a more subtle level in arbitration practices and judicial review rules that start out as extra-legal practices and then slowly become integrated into the formal legal fabric. Nothing in these developments suggests that Equity is the sole repository of moral reasoning in the law, or even that its claim to this is significantly greater.

The assertion of differences in moral reasoning can also be questioned at the practical level. Modern judges must make both Common Law and Equitable determinations in the same court, often in the same case. It is hard to imagine how they might consistently call upon fundamentally different forms of conceptual reasoning in one context from those they employ in another. Indeed, some judges are quite forthright in insisting that there is nothing special about Equity's concept of conscience. The problem is not a modern one. As early as the sixteenth century, if not before, the Chancellor used to call on Common Law judges to assist him in his determinations. These 'Common Law' judges were required to make 'Equitable' determinations. Their language gives the lie to any notion that conceptually different moral reasoning is being relied upon. Indeed, Common Law and Equity judges have often had to grapple with similar problems and concepts, and their goals then appear much the same. Both will sometimes resort explicitly to moral reasoning. In 'inventing' the modern Common Law tort of negligence, for example, the leading judgment began with the Christian—and unquestionably moral—precept, 'Thou shalt love thy neighbour as thyself', and this became, at law, an obligation not to injure your neighbour.[25] Less explicitly, reliance on doctrinal parallels can disguise parallels in the underlying moral reasoning: see, for example, the parallels between the rules on economic duress and undue influence, or the rules on judicial review and Equitable fraud on the power.

In short, whatever perspective is taken, this argument about Equity's peculiar brand of conceptual reasoning seems unsupportable. On the contrary, the limiting conditions for intervention appear remarkably similar in both jurisdictions. One jurisdiction is often chosen over the other simply to bypass unwelcome limitations in jurisdictional range or remedial response at a given time in history. It seems unreal to suppose that the resulting direction is conceptually different if the Equitable route is chosen rather than the Common Law one.

---

[25] *Donoghue v Stevenson* [1932] AC 562 (HL), 580. Interestingly, the decision was carried by Lord Atkin (a common lawyer) and two Scots lawyers (with a Roman-Dutch legal tradition), in the face of protests by two great Chancery lawyers who argued for no change to the law.

This idea that the Common Law, left to its own devices, would have evolved down a similar path (although perhaps not an identical one) is reinforced by comparisons with the civil law. These comparisons suggest that the ends reached by a dualist common law system are very similar to the ends reached in many civil law jurisdictions. The inference, perhaps unsurprisingly, is that the moral motivations across developed nations are not dissimilar; certainly they are not inconsistent. This makes it even harder to conceive that judges within the same common law jurisdiction —Common Law and Equity judges—could choose to adopt a strategy which required them to operate on the basis of different and irreconcilable moral conceptions.

IS EQUITY'S INTERVENTION PECULIARLY DISCRETIONARY?

The second argument against the integration project is more important. It suggests that Equity and the Common Law cannot be integrated because Equity's intervention is discretionary while the Common Law's is as of right. The Common Law strives for predictability and treats each case as belonging to a generalized type; Equity strives for individual justice and treats each case as being unique. Such antithetical approaches, so it is suggested, cannot possibly be blended or harmonized. This is a very seductive idea. Indeed, when lawyers are asked to describe the important differences between the Common Law and Equity, this, and often only this, is inevitably trotted out. A vivid picture emerges. In Equity, a claimant can have specific performance *if* the judge permits it; she can have an injunction, or a disgorgement remedy for breach of fiduciary duty against her, *if* the judge allows it; her Equitable interest will prevail against a third party *if* the judge permits it. A Common Law claimant, on the other hand, has a *right* to damages once his case is proved, whether it be that he has suffered a breach of contract, had a tort committed against him, or made out a claim for recovery of an unjust enrichment. The same allegations are made in relation to defences and, historically, even in relation to procedural practices. If this is true, then the Common Law is about legal rights but Equity is not. Equity is simply concerned with discretionary judicial orders against defendants.

This picture of discretionary Equity is one that resonates with the vision of Equity as the 'conscience' of the law. Equity is seen as able to demand good faith and deliver justice where the Common Law finds it impossible to do so. It can achieve these ends by modifying procedural rules, refashioning obligations, and reshaping remedies—perhaps all at

Equity

the whim of the judge deciding the case. Equity is then seen as a jurisdiction which is context specific, situational, personal—capricious, even. The Common Law, on the other hand, is perceived as rational, analytical, objective, and universal. This is a somewhat anachronistic vision.

The truth or otherwise of this allegation is crucial to the possibility of integration. The law is about legal rights. More than this, there is an intrinsic interrelationship between rights and remedies: a claimant does not have a legal right unless the court will afford a remedy for its invasion. If the court will not routinely intervene, and intervene in a routine manner, then the claimant has, at most, a moral right. An integrated body of law cannot be built on a combination of legal (Common Law) and moral (Equitable) rights. That would be a nonsense.

Is Equity discretionary in this unacceptable, non-legal way? At the outset it probably was. Equity dealt with cases on an individual basis; its remit was to address the shortcomings in the Common Law. Indeed, it was its early propensity for individualistic responses that led to the snub that Equity varied with the length of the Chancellor's foot. This practice might have continued. Equity could have exercised a simple discretionary power to disaffirm or vary settled Common Law rules in deserving cases. Its jurisdiction would then have been analogous to the power to grant a pardon, or make a gift. These types of powers are supported and even regulated by the legal system, but they do not give rise to legal *rights*.

But Equity did not choose to operate like this. Instead, Equity assumed a legal role; it did, eventually, deliver its remedies in a predictable and principled way, giving rise to enforceable rights. The early Chancellors made determined and successful efforts to integrate Equity within the legal system. The result was 'law', not 'bounty'. In fact, the rules of Equity fast became as rigid and technical as the rules of the Common Law they were supposed to moderate.[26]

Notwithstanding these changes, is it true that Equity is still so discretionary that integration is impossible? It seems not. In fact, parts of modern Equity are arguably *less* discretionary than anything the Common Law now has on offer. Equitable proprietary remedies are certainly not awarded at the discretion of the judge. The law of insolvency would turn into a farce were it otherwise. Nor, it seems, is there such a discretion in the award of Equitable compensation to remedy breach of trust, fiduciary obligation, or confidence. If the claimant wants such a remedy, then she must simply establish her case. Of course, as at Common Law, issues of

[26] *Re National Funds Assurance Co* (1878) 10 ChD 118, 128.

quantification may remain difficult; assessment may require the judge to exercise judgement.

In other circumstances, however, it must be conceded that there is a clear discretionary element in Equity's responses. This discretion is seen at its most pronounced when the claimant wants an order from the court to compel the defendant, personally, to act in a particular fashion—perhaps to complete a job, or to repair damaged property. Then the court's practice is to consider the defendant's circumstances as well as the claimant's, and to decide—in its discretion—whether or not to order the remedy that has been requested.[27]

Nevertheless, this form of discretionary remedialism does not mark Equity out as different from, and incompatible with, the Common Law. In fact, the Common Law adopts precisely the same sort of discretionary practices in almost every area of its operation. Consider, for example, the Common Law's approach in criminal law when assessing issues of provocation and self-defence; in consumer contracts when assessing unfair terms; in contract when assessing issues of Common Law estoppel; in tort when assessing whether there is a duty of care, or whether the defendant's negligence has contributed to his own damage; indeed, consider its decisions across the spectrum of the law of obligations when quantifying compensation. All of these examples are instances of an individualized, discretionary practice in the Common Law, a practice not seen in these instances as fundamentally and irredeemably inconsistent with the Common Law edifice.

Indeed, there is undoubtedly a growing Common Law move to adjudicate via discretionary standards rather than bright-line rules. Increased reliance on the notion of reasonableness—in many ways itself the modern formulation of morality—is the most obvious example of this, but the instances cited above add force to the assertion. This trend may reflect an increased sophistication in the law, or it may simply reflect the impact of economic rationalism on morality, used in its broadest sense. Whatever the cause, both Equity and the Common Law now commonly adopt these discretionary practices to determine whether the defendant should be subjected to the obligation alleged, and whether the requested remedy is warranted. For example, the Common Law exercises discretion in deciding whether a contract exists or whether the defendant is subject to a duty of care in tort; and Equity adopts the same practices in deciding whether the defendant owes fiduciary duties or is subject to obligations of

---

[27] See Chapter 2, 31–4.

confidentiality. In determining the appropriate remedies, the Common Law frequently adopts a standard of reasonableness, and exercises an unstated discretion in determining whether the standard has been met; Equity adopts standards of fairness and conscience, and exercises a similar unstated discretion in determining whether those conditions have been met.

These Equitable and Common Law discretionary practices are not incompatible with each other, nor with the concept of 'law'. They provide no fuel for the anti-integrationist argument. To understand this properly it is important to recognize that there are different forms of discretion. A judge may have a discretion as to whether to *apply* a particular rule or not. Alternatively, he may have a discretion as to whether a particular rule *does* apply in the given circumstances. These two sentences need to be read carefully to see the distinction in issue. The first sentence describes a discretion—or a power—to apply or not apply a rule at will. The exercise need not be based on any formal, rational principles. This is perhaps how the earliest Chancellors operated. This form of discretion is clearly incompatible with the concept of law. If Equity had continued to operate in this way, then it would indeed be incompatible with the Common Law because of its unacceptable and individualistic discretionary practices. But not all discretions are of this type. The second sentence describes a discretion to determine whether, on particular facts, a given rule is applicable. This discretion is compatible with the concept of law; indeed, it is hard to conceive of any legal system operating without such a discretion. It is this second acceptable, indeed ubiquitous, form of discretion that is evident in *both* Equitable and Common Law practices. It mirrors the Aristotelian distinction between bright-line rules and fact-sensitive (discretionary) justice, and its fault lines are certainly not defined by the Common Law—Equity divide.

The important point here is that *both* the Common Law and Equity employ discretion in adjudication. *All* law is necessarily general so that it can meet the need for simplicity, certainty, predictability, and even-handedness; but all law is also pressurized by a countervailing need for judicial discretion to counter the unfairness inherent in generality. There is nothing peculiar or unique about Equity's version of these discretionary practices; they do not militate against integration. Indeed, an integrated legal system would continue to refine and develop existing Equitable and Common Law discretionary inputs.

All of these arguments lead to one point. Despite the longstanding views to the contrary, neither Equity's moral foundations nor its discretionary practices afford compelling grounds for the suggestion that Common Law and Equity are now irretrievably set on a dualist path. Integration is possible. Integration is also desirable in the interests of better justice. It facilitates the aim of treating like cases alike. It also facilitates the sort of rational evolution of the law that is only possible if courts can draw distinctions based on meaningful differences rather than accidental jurisdictional divides. The historical time warp in orthodox description of the divisions needs to be discarded in favour of a contemporary evaluation of the current regime.

REVIEW

This closing review can be brief. History may describe how the rather bizarre common law dualist system came into being, with its distinctive Common Law and Equity jurisdictions. However, history cannot go on to convincingly vindicate what is unquestionably a counter-intuitive choice. The inherent characteristics of a dualist system make it difficult to ensure that like cases are treated alike and that different cases are treated in defensibly different ways. There is no formalized way of maintaining supervision across the jurisdictional boundary and then aligning rules and practices accordingly. By comparison, an integrated legal system is far more likely to deliver coherent, principled, and focused legal rules. These advantages are attractive in any event, but they present added benefits in dealing with the burgeoning body of law that now comprises the common law legal system.

Comprehensive, rational integration of Common Law and Equity doctrines appears to be the only defensible modern option in pursuing principled legal development. This chapter suggests that the practical task of integration would not be as daunting as is often supposed. Even Equity's most famous invention, the trust, can be readily accommodated within such a regime. What inhibits progress is not practice, but theory. The core concern is the same as it has been for hundreds of years. It is that integration is conceptually and philosophically impossible because Equity is a uniquely conscience-based and discretionary regime which is fundamentally incompatible with the Common Law's own rules- and rights-based practices. When this assertion is unravelled, however, it turns out to lack compelling foundation. It should not continue to rule the future.

Integration, pursued with determination and a keen eye for detailed and rigorous analysis, could readily deliver a coherent, sophisticated, and discriminating legal system, well-equipped to meet the needs of modern society. Such comprehensive doctrinal integration must surely be the grand plan for Equity and the Common Law; it is certainly the best plan for Equity in the common law.

SELECTED BIBLIOGRAPHY

Ames, J. B., 'Law and Morals' (1908) 22 Harvard Law Review 97.

Beatson, J., 'Unfinished Business: Integrating Equity' in J. Beatson (ed.), *The Use and Abuse of Unjust Enrichment* (Oxford: Oxford University Press, 1991), Ch. 9.

Burrows, A., 'We Do This At Common Law But That In Equity' (2002) OJLS 1.

Coing, H., 'English Equity and the *Denunciatio Evangelica* of the Canon Law' (1955) 71 LQR 223.

Denning, A., 'The Need for a New Equity' [1952] CLP 1.

Duggan, A., 'Is Equity Efficient?' (1997) 113 LQR 601.

Emmerglick, L. J., 'A Century of the New Equity' (1945) 23 Texas Law Review 244.

Erlich, I. and Posner, R. A., 'An Economic Analysis of Legal Rulemaking' (1974) 3 Journal of Legal Studies 257.

Evershed, R., 'Reflections on the Fusion of Law and Equity After 75 Years' (1954) 70 LQR 326.

Getzler, J., 'Patterns of Fusion' in P. Birks (ed.), *The Classification of Obligations* (Oxford: Clarendon Press, 1997), Ch. 7.

Gleeson, The Hon A. M., 'Individualised Justice—The Holy Grail' (1995) 69 Australian Law Journal 421.

Holdsworth, W. S., 'Equity' (1935) 51 LQR 142.

Kaplow, L., 'Rules Versus Standards: An Economic Analysis' (1992) 42 Duke Law Journal 557.

Mason, The Hon. Sir Anthony, 'Equity's Role in the Twentieth Century' (1997/98) 8 King's College Law Journal 1.

Mason, A., 'The Place of Equity and Equitable Remedies in the Contemporary Common Law World' (1994) 110 LQR 238.

Mason, K., 'Fusion: Fallacy, Future or Finished?' in S. Degeling and J. Edelman (eds), *Equity in Commercial Law* (Sydney: Lawbook Co., 2005), Ch. 3.

Millett, P. J., 'Equity—The Road Ahead' (1995) 9 Trust Law International 35.

——, 'Equity's Place in the Law of Commerce' (1998) 114 LQR 214.

Newman, R. A., *Equity and Law: A Comparative Study* (1961, Oceana Publications Inc., New York).

Pound, R., 'Mechanical Jurisprudence' (1908) 8 Columbia Law Review 605.

Smith, L., 'Fusion and Tradition' in S. Degeling and J. Edelman (eds), *Equity in Commercial Law* (Sydney: Lawbook Co., 2005), Ch. 2.

Bibliography

Adams, G. B., 'The Origin of English Equity' (1916) 16 Columbia Law Review 87.

Akkouh, T. and Worthington, S., '*Re Diplock* (1948)' in C. Mitchell and P. Mitchell (eds), *Landmark Cases in the Law of Restitution* (Oxford: Hart Publishing, 2006), Ch. 11.

Ames, J. B., 'Law and Morals' (1908) 22 Harvard Law Review 97.

Atiyah, P. S., 'Consideration: A Restatement' in P. Atiyah, *Essays on Contract* (Oxford: Clarendon Press, 1988, revised 1990).

Austin, R., 'Fiduciary Accountability for Business Opportunities' in P. D. Finn (ed.), *Equity and Commercial Relationships* (Sydney: Law Book Co., 1987, Ch. 6.

Baker, J. H., *An Introduction to English Legal History* (4th edn, London: Butterworths, 2002).

——, 'The Court of Chancery and Equity' in J. H. Baker, *An Introduction to English Legal History* (4th edn, London: Butterworths, 2002).

Beatson, J., 'Unfinished Business: Integrating Equity' in J. Beatson (ed.), *The Use and Abuse of Unjust Enrichment* (Oxford: Oxford University Press, 1991), Ch. 9.

Bigwood, R., 'Undue Influence: "Impaired Consent" or "Wicked Exploitation"?' (1996) 16 OJLS 503.

Birks, P., 'Misdirected Funds: Restitution from the Recipient' [1989] *LMCLQ* 296.

——, 'Mixing and Tracing: Property and Restitution' (1992) 45 *CLP* 69.

——, 'Restitution and Resulting Trusts' in S. Goldstein (ed.), *Equity and Contemporary Legal Problems* (Jerusalem: Hamaccabi Press, 1992), 335.

——, 'Receipt' in P. Birks and A. Pretto (eds), *Breach of Trust* (Oxford: Hart Publishing, 2002), 213.

Birks, P. and Chin, N. Y., 'On the Nature of Undue Influence' in J. Beatson and D. Friedmann (eds), *Good Faith and Fault in Contract Law* (Oxford: Clarendon Press, 1995), Ch. 3.

Bright, S. and McFarlane, B., 'Proprietary Estoppel and Property Rights' [2005] CLJ 449.

Burrows, A., 'Swaps and the Friction between Common Law and Equity' (1995) RLR 15.

Erlich, I. and Posner, R. A., 'An Economic Analysis of Legal Rulemaking' (1974) 3 JLS 257.

Evans, S., 'Rethinking Tracing and the Law of Restitution' (1999) 115 LQR 469.

Evershed, R., 'Reflections on the Fusion of Law and Equity after 75 Years' (1954) 70 LQR 326.

Finch, V. and Worthington, S., 'The Pari Passu Principle and Ranking Restitutionary Rights' in F. Rose (ed.), *Restitution and Insolvency* (London: Mansfield Press, 2000), Ch. 1.

Finn, P. D., *Fiduciary Obligations* (Sydney: Law Book Co., 1977).

——, 'The Fiduciary Principle' in T. G. Youdan (ed.), *Equity, Fiduciaries and Trusts* (Toronto: Carswell, 1989), Ch. 1.

Fox, D., 'Common Law Claims to Substituted Assets' [1999] RLR 55.

Frankel, T., 'Fiduciary Law' (1983) 71 California Law Review 795.

Fung, E. and Ho, L., 'Change of Position and Estoppel' (2001) 117 LQR 14.

Gardner, S., 'Rethinking Family Property' (1993) 109 LQR 263.

——, 'The Remedial Discretion in Proprietary Estoppel' (1999) 115 LQR 438.

Garton, J., 'The Role of the Trust Mechanism in the Rule in *Re Rose*' [2003] Conveyancer 364.

Getzler, J., 'Patterns of Fusion' in P. Birks (ed.), *The Classification of Obligations* (Oxford: Clarendon Press, 1997).

Gleeson, The Hon. A. M., 'Individualised Justice—The Holy Grail' (1995) 69 Australian Law Journal 421.

Glister, J., 'The Nature of *Quistclose* Trusts: Classification and Reconciliation' [2004] CLJ 632.

Goode, R., 'The Right to Trace and its Impact in Commercial Transactions' (1976) 92 LQR 360, 528.

——, 'Inalienable Rights?' (1979) 42 MLR 553.

——, 'Ownership and Obligation in Commercial Transactions' (1987) 103 LQR 433.

——, 'The Recovery of a Director's Improper Gains: Proprietary Remedies for the Infringement of Non-Proprietary Rights' in E. McKendrick (ed.), *Commercial Aspects of Trusts and Fiduciary Obligations* (Oxford: Clarendon Press, 1992), Ch. 7.

——, 'Proprietary Restitutionary Claims' in W. R. Cornish, R. Nolan, J. O'Sullivan and G. Virgo (eds), *Restitution: Past, Present and Future* (Oxford: Hart Publishing, 1998), 63.

Grantham, R., 'Doctrinal Bases for the Recognition of Proprietary Rights' (1996) 16 OJLS 561.

——, 'Liability for Interfering in a Breach of Trust' (1998) 114 LQR 357.

——, *Enrichment and Restitution in New Zealand* (Oxford: Hart Publishing, 2000), Ch. 7, 285–8.

Grantham, R. B. and Rickett, C. F., 'Disgorgement for Unjust Enrichment?' [2003] CLJ 159.

Gray, K., 'Property in Thin Air' [1991] CLJ 253.

Green, B., 'Grey, Oughtred and Vandervell—A Contextual Reappraisal' (1984) 47 MLR 385.

Gretton, G. L., 'Trusts Without Equity' (2000) International and Comparative Law Quarterly 599.

Guest, A. S., 'Accession and Confusion in the Law of Hire-Purchase' (1964) 27 MLR 505.

Hackney, J., 'More than a Trace of the Old Philosophy' in P. Birks (ed.), *The Classification of Obligations* (Oxford: Clarendon Press, 1997), Ch. 6.

Handley, K. R., 'Exploring Election' (2006) 122 LQR 82.

Hansmann, H. and Kraakman, R., 'Property, Contract and Verification: The *Numerus Clausus* Problem and the Divisibility of Rights' (2002) 31 Journal of Legal Studies 373.

—— and Mattei, U., 'The Functions of Trust Law: A Comparative Legal and Economic Analysis' (1998) 73 New York University Law Review 434.

Harpum, C., 'The Stranger as Constructive Trustee' (1986) 102 LQR 114, continued at 267.

Haskett, T., 'The Medieval English Court of Chancery' (1996) 14 Law and History Review 245.

Hayton, D., 'Uncertainty of Subject-Matter of Trusts' (1994) 110 LQR 335.

——, 'The Irreducible Core Content of Trusteeship' in A. J. Oakley (ed.), *Trends in Contemporary Trust Law* (Oxford: Oxford University Press, 1996), 47.

——, 'English Fiduciary Standards and Trust Law' [1999] 32 Vanderbilt Journal of Transnational Law 555.

——, 'Developing the Obligation Characteristic of the Trust' (2001) 117 LQR 96.

Hazeltine, H. D., 'The Early History of English Equity', in P. Vinogradoff (ed.), *Essays in Legal History* (Oxford: Oxford University Press, 1913), Ch. 13.

Ho, L. and Smart, P. S. J., 'Reinterpreting the *Quistclose* Trust: A Critique of Chambers' Analysis' (2001) 21 OJLS 267.

Holdsworth, W. S., 'The Relation of the Equity Administered by the Common Law Judges to the Equity Administered by the Chancellor' (1916) 26 Yale Law Journal 1.

——, 'Equity' (1935) 51 LQR 142.

Honoré, A. M., 'Ownership', in A. Guest (ed.), *Oxford Essays in Jurisprudence* (Oxford: Oxford University Press, 1961), 106.

Jackson, D., 'Estoppel as a Sword' (1965) 81 LQR 84, 223.

Jones, G., 'Unjust Enrichment and the Fiduciary's Duty of Loyalty' (1968) 84 LQR 472.

Kaplow, L., 'Rules Versus Standards: An Economic Analysis' (1992) 42 Duke Law Journal 557.

Kurshid, S. and Matthews, P., 'Tracing Confusion' (1979) 95 LQR 78.

Langbein, J. H., 'The Contractarian Basis of the Law of Trusts' (1995) 105 Yale Law Journal 625.

——, 'The Secret Life of the Trust: The Trust as an Instrument of Commerce' (1997) 107 Yale Law Journal 165.

Lanyon, E. V., 'Equity and the Doctrine of Penalties' (1996) 9 Journal of Contract Law 234.

Lowry, J. and Edmonds, R., 'The Corporate Opportunity Doctrine: The Shifting Boundary of the Duties and its Remedies' (1998) 61 MLR 515.

Maitland, F. W., *Equity: A Course of Lectures*, A. H. Chaytor and W. J. Whittaker (eds), J. Brunyate (rev.) (2nd edn, Cambridge: Cambridge University Press, 1969), Lectures 1 and 2.

Mason, A., 'The Place of Equity and Equitable Remedies in the Contemporary Common Law World' (1994) 110 LQR 238.

——, 'Equity's Role in the Twentieth Century' (1997/98) 8 King's College Law Journal 1.

Mason, K., 'Fusion: Fallacy, Future or Finished?' in S. Degeling and J. Edelman (eds), *Equity in Commercial Law* (Sydney: Lawbook Co., 2005), Ch. 3.

Matthews, P., 'Proprietary Claims at Common Law for Mixed and Improved Goods' (1981) 34 CLP 159.

——, 'The Legal and Moral Limits of Common Law Tracing' in P. Birks (ed.), *Laundering and Tracing* (Oxford: Oxford University Press, 1995), Ch. 2.

Maudsley, R. H., 'Proprietary Remedies for the Recovery of Money' (1959) 75 LQR 234.

Meagher, R. P., Heydon, J. D. and Leeming, M. J., *Meagher, Gummow and Lehane's Equity: Doctrines and Remedies* (4th edn, Australia: Butterworths, 2002).

Millett, P. J., 'The *Quistclose* Trust: Who Can Enforce It?' (1985) 101 LQR 269.

——, 'Tracing the Proceeds of Fraud' (1991) 107 LQR 71.

——, 'Bribes and Secret Commissions' (1993) 1 RLR 7.

——, 'Equity—The Road Ahead' (1995) 9 Trust Law International 35.

Millett, Sir P., 'Equity's Place in the Law of Commerce' (1998) 114 LQR 214.

——, 'Restitution and Constructive Trusts' (1998) 114 LQR 399.

Millett, Lord, 'Proprietary Restitution' in S. Degeling and J. Edelman (eds), *Equity in Commercial Law* (Sydney: Lawbook Co., 2005), Ch. 12.

Mitchell, C., 'Assistance' in P. Birks and A. Pretto (eds), *Breach of Trust* (Oxford: Hart Publishing, 2002), 139.

Newman, R. A., *Equity and Law: A Comparative Study* (New York: Oceana Publications Inc., 1961).

Nicholls, Lord, 'Knowing Receipt: The Need for a New Landmark' in W. R. Cornish, R. Nolan, J. O'Sullivan, and G. Virgo (eds), *Restitution: Past, Present and Future* (Oxford: Hart Publishing, 1998), Ch. 15.

Nolan, D., 'Following in their Footsteps: Equitable Estoppel in Australia and the United States' (2000) 11 King's College Law Journal 202.

Nolan, R. C., 'The Proper Purpose Doctrine and Company Directors' in B. A. K. Rider (ed.), *The Realm of Company Law* (London: Kluwer, 1998), Ch. 1.

Oakley, A. J., 'Has the Constructive Trust Become a General Equitable Remedy?' (1973) 26 CLP 17.

——, 'Proprietary Claims and their Priority in Insolvency' [1995] CLJ 377.

O'Sullivan, J., 'Rescission as a Self-Help Remedy: A Critical Analysis' [2000] CLJ 509.

Paccioco, D., 'The Remedial Constructive Trust: A Principled Basis for Priority Over Creditors' (1989) 68 Canadian Bar Review 315.

Penner, J., 'The Bundle of Rights Picture of Property' (1996) 43 University of California at Los Angeles Law Review 711.

Phillips, J., 'Equitable Liens—A Search for a Unifying Principle' in N. Palmer and E. McKendrick (eds), *Interests in Goods* (2nd edn, London: Lloyd's of London Press, 1998), Ch. 39.

Phillipson, G., 'Transforming Breach of Confidence? Towards a Common Law Right of Privacy under the Human Rights Act' (2003) 66 MLR 726.

Pound, R., 'The Decadence of Equity' (1905) 5 Columbia Law Review 20.

——, 'Mechanical Jurisprudence' (1908) 8 Columbia Law Review 605.

——, *Law and Morals* (2nd edn, London: Oxford University Press, 1926).

Rickett, C. E. F., 'The Classification of Trusts' (1999) 18 New Zealand Universities Law Review 305.

Ridge, P., 'Uncertainties Surrounding Undue Influence' [2003] New Zealand Universities Law Review 329.

Rudden, B., 'Things as Things and Things as Wealth' (1994) 14 OJLS 81.

Schwartz, A., 'The Case for Specific Performance' (1979) 89 Yale Law Journal 271.

Scott, A., 'The Nature of the Rights of the Cestui Que Trust' (1917) 17 Columbia Law Review 269.

——, 'The Fiduciary Principle' (1949) 37 California Law Review 539.

Sealy, L. S., 'Fiduciary Relationships' [1962] CLJ 69.

——, 'Some Principles of Fiduciary Obligation' [1963] CLJ 119.

Shepherd, J. C., 'Towards a Unified Concept of Fiduciary Relationships' (1981) 97 LQR 51.

Sheridan, L. A., 'Equitable Estoppel Today' (1952) 15 MLR 325.

Sherwin, E. L., 'Constructive Trusts in Bankruptcy' (1989) 2 University of Illinois Law Review 297.

Shiner, R., 'Aristotle's Theory of Equity' (1994) 27 Loyola of Los Angeles Law Review 1245.

Smith, L., 'Tracing into the Payment of a Debt' [1995] CLJ 290.

——, *Tracing* (Oxford: Oxford University Press, 1997).

——, 'W(h)ither Knowing Receipt?' (1998) 114 LQR 394.

——, 'Constructive Trusts and Constructive Trustees' [1999] CLJ 294.

——, 'Unjust Enrichment, Property and the Structure of Trusts' (2000) 116 LQR 412.

——, 'The Motive, Not the Deed' in J. Getzler (ed.), *Rationalizing Property, Equity and Trusts* (London: Lexis Nexis: Butterworths, 2003), Ch. 4.

——, 'Fusion and Tradition' in S. Degeling and J. Edelman (eds), *Equity in Commercial Law* (Sydney: Lawbook Co., 2005), Ch. 2.

Smith, S. A., 'Substantive Fairness' (1996) 112 LQR 138.

——, 'Contracting Under Pressure: A Theory of Duress' (1997) 56 CLJ 343.

Stevens, R. and McFarlane, B., 'In Defence of *Sumpter v Hedges*' (2002) 118 LQR 569.

Swadling, W., 'A New Role for Resulting Trusts?' (1996) 16 Legal Studies 110.

—— 'Rescission, Property and the Common Law' (2005) 121 LQR 123.

Treitel, G., 'Consideration: A Critical Analysis of Professor Atiyah's Fundamental Restatement' (1976) 50 Australian Law Journal 439.

Vinogradoff, P., 'Reason and Conscience in Sixteenth-Century Jurisprudence' (1908) 24 LQR 373.

Waddams, S., 'Johanna Wagner and the Rival Opera Houses' (2001) 117 LQR 431.

Walker, Lord, 'Dishonesty and Unconscionable Conduct in Commercial Life—Some Reflections on Accessory Liability and Knowing Receipt' (2005) 27 Sydney Law Review 187.

Warren, S. and Brandeis, L. D., 'The Right to Privacy' (1890) 3 Harvard Law Review 289.

Waters, D. M. W., 'The Nature of the Trust Beneficiary's Interest' (1967) 45 Canadian Bar Review 219.

Watts, P., 'Property and "Unjust Enrichment": Cognate Conservators' (1998) New Zealand Universities Law Review 151.

Weinrib, E., 'The Fiduciary Obligation' (1975) 25 University of Toronto Law Journal 1.

——, 'Restitutionary Damages as Corrective Justice' (2000) 1 Theoretical Inquiries in Law 1.

Williston, S., 'The Right to Follow Trust Property When Confused With Other Property' (1888) 2 Harvard Law Review 28.

Worthington, S., *Proprietary Interests in Commercial Transactions* (Oxford: Clarendon Press, 1996).

——, 'Fiduciaries: When is Self-Denial Obligatory?' [1999] CLJ 500.

——, 'Reconsidering Disgorgement' (1999) 62 MLR 218.

——, 'Sorting Out Ownership Interests in a Bulk: Gifts, Sales and Trusts' [1999] Journal of Business Law 1.

——, 'Subrogation Claims on Insolvency' in F. Rose (ed.), *Insolvency and Restitution* (London: LLP, 2000), Ch. 4.

——, 'Justifying Claims to Secondary Profits' in E. J. H. Schrage (ed.), *Unjust Enrichment and the Law of Contract* (London: Kluwer, 2001), 451.

——, 'Integrating Equity and the Common Law' (2002) 55 Current Legal Problems 223.

——, 'The Proprietary Consequences of Rescission' [2002] Restitution Law Review 28.

——, 'An "Unsatisfactory Area of the Law"—Fixed and Floating Charges Yet Again' (2004) 1 International Corporate Rescue 175.

——, 'The Disappearing Divide Between Property and Obligation: The Impact of Aligning Legal Analysis and Commercial Expectation' in S. Degeling and J. Edelman (eds), *Equity in Commercial Law* (London: Sweet & Maxwell, Thompson, and Carswell, 2006), Ch. 5.

——, 'Proprietary Remedies and Insolvency Policy: The Need for a New Approach' in J. Lowry and L. Mistalis (eds.), *Commercial Law: Perspectives and Practice* (London: Lexis-Nexis: Butterworths, 2006), Ch. 1.

Youdan, T., 'Formalities for Trusts of Land, and the Doctrine in *Rochefoucauld v Bousted*' [1984] CLJ 306.

Index

Lightning Source UK Ltd.
Milton Keynes UK
16 October 2010

161442UK00002BA/3/P